THE HISTORY OF THE KING'S SHROPSHIRE LIGHT INFANTRY IN THE GREAT WAR 1914-1918

CW01335809

THE HISTORY OF THE KING'S SHROPSHIRE LIGHT INFANTRY IN THE GREAT WAR

1914–1918

EDITED BY

MAJOR W DE B. WOOD

LONDON
THE MEDICI SOCIETY LIMITED
MCMXXV

Printed and bound by Antony Rowe Ltd, Eastbourne

They carry back bright to
the Coiner the mintage of man
A Shropshire Lad

PREFACE

THIS book has been two years in the making, and is the work of past and present officers of The King's Shropshire Light Infantry. Those who have contributed these pages are mostly men fully occupied, and the work has been done in leisure hours which have been gladly sacrificed. The responsibility for the many shortcomings of the book rests with the Editor, who can only say that he has done his best in the time available. If it were not advisable, for a number of reasons, to offer the book to the public now, there is no doubt that greater accuracy could be achieved by giving more time to research.

The chief source of information from which this history has been compiled is the War Diary. These War Diaries were written up daily, so far as the conditions of active service allowed, by the Officer Commanding the unit, and despatched each month to the War Office. To state that these War Diaries were frequently inaccurate is no reflection upon the officers whose duty it was to write them. Units were frequently fighting continuously for days on end, and to attempt an accurate account in a few words of events covering several days, when perhaps more than a half of the unit has become casualties, is an impossible task. Official diaries were also kept by Brigades and the general staffs of Divisions and these sometimes throw light upon the confusion of events related in the unit War Diary. Often, however, the three accounts are irreconcilable and the statements of casualties and the positions of troops quite at variance. Other sources of information have been found in private diaries, letters written home and the recollection of survivors. Unfortunately these sources of information have proved very scanty.

It is hoped that the plan of the book will have the advantage of being easy of reference for those interested primarily in the history of one particular battalion of the regiment.

The thanks of the Editor are due to Brevet Lt.-Colonel B. E. Murray, D.S.O., for material relating to the history of the 1st Battalion; to Brevet-Colonel A. H. J. Doyle, who wrote the account of the depot; Brevet Lt.-Colonel R. E. Holmes à Court, D.S.O., and Captain V. Crane, who wrote the history of the 2nd Battalion; to Lt.-Colonel T. D. Dickin, who wrote an account of the 3rd (special reserve) Battalion; to Captain A. C. L. D. Lees, who wrote the history of the 4th (Territorial Army) Battalion; to Major J. G. Forbes, who contributed the chapter on the 5th Battalion and Major G. A. Delmé-Murray, D.S.O., who provided material for the same; Br.-General E. A. Wood, C.M.G., D.S.O., who wrote on the 6th Battalion; Lt.-Colonel Erskine, D.S.O., who wrote the history of the 8th Battalion; to Lt.-Colonel H. H. Heywood-Lonsdale, D.S.O., T.D., and Lt.-Colonel H. J. Howell-Evans, D.S.O., who supplied valuable material for the account of the 10th Battalion (formerly the Shropshire and Cheshire Yeomanry); to Colonel W. J. Mackeson, Sec. Shrops. T.F.A., and Mrs. Luard, M.B.E., who supplied material for the chapter dealing with the activities of the various voluntary societies in Shropshire and Herefordshire, which worked for the welfare of the troops during the war; and to Miss Smith, who compiled the list of honours.

The account of the 1st, 7th and 10th Battalions has been written by myself.

W de B. WOOD, Major,
A.E.C. (late 7th K.S.L.I.)

August, 1924

CONTENTS

LIST OF APPENDICES

LIST OF MAPS

FOREWORD

THE life of a regiment is like a chain stretching from the past into the future and formed of alternate links of War and Peace. This book deals with one of these links in the life of The King's Shropshire Light Infantry, namely, the Great War of 1914–1918.

At the outbreak of war in 1914 the K.S.L.I. consisted of four battalions, viz., *1st (Regular) in Ireland, *2nd (Regular) in India, and the *3rd (Special Reserve) and 4th (Territorial), whose Headquarters were at Shrewsbury.

During the war the establishment of the regiment was raised to thirteen battalions, mainly recruited in Shropshire and Herefordshire, viz., 1st and 2nd Regular ; 3rd Special Reserve ; 1/4th, 2/4th, and 3/4th Territorial Force ; 4th Reserve, T.F. ; 5th, 6th, 7th, and 8th Service ; 9th Service Reserve ; 10th Service (formerly Shropshire and Cheshire Yeomanry). Of these, eight battalions (1st, 2nd, 1/4th, 5th, 6th, 7th, 8th, 10th) served at the front, whilst the remainder furnished drafts and took part in home defence.

This book is not a history of the war, but it follows the doings of the eight battalions who, scattered along the front from the North Sea to Palestine, could see little but what was happening in their immediate vicinity ; and it describes the work of the battalions at home and at the depot, whilst it further gives an account of the way the counties of Shropshire and Hereford supported the County Regiment, forming Red Cross hospitals, raising funds, and organising relief for prisoners of war and assisting their ex-service men.

* On July 1st 1881, the 53rd Shropshire Regiment, the 85th King's Light Infantry, and the Shropshire Militia, became the 1st, 2nd, and 3rd Battalions of the King's Shropshire Light Infantry.

FOREWORD

Besides those mentioned in the Preface, our thanks are due to the following ex-K.S.L.I. officers :—

To Br.-General F. L. Banon, C.B., for his help and advice on the History Committee ; to Major J. G. Forbes, owing to whose initiative and organising ability as secretary and treasurer this book has been produced ; and to Major W de B. Wood who, as Historical Editor, has judiciously selected and woven together the threads of the various accounts.

With the conclusion of peace the establishment was reduced to four battalions, viz., 1st and 2nd Regular, 3rd Militia and 4th Territorial. But the regiment remains ever ready to uphold its traditions and to justify our motto "AUCTO SPLENDORE RESURGO"

RAYMOND READE,
Major-General, and Colonel
King's Shropshire Light Infantry.

Armistice Day
1924

HONOURS

Honours for the Great War gained by the King's Shropshire Light Infantry, with the battalions that were present.
The President of the French Republic awarded the 4/K.S.L.I. the Croix de Guerre with Palms, to be borne on their colours as a memorial of their gallant action at Bligny.

HONOURS	BATTALIONS
France and Flanders, 1914	1st
„ „ 1915	1st, 2nd, 5th, 6th, 7th
„ „ 1916	1st, 5th, 6th, 7th
„ „ 1917	1st, 4th, 5th, 6th, 7th
„ „ 1918	1st. 4th, 6th, 7th, 10th
Macedonia, 1915-1918	2nd, 8th
Palestine, 1917-1918	10th
Aisnes, 1914	1st
*Armentières, 1914	1st
Gravenstafel	2nd
*Ypres, 1915	2nd, 5th
St. Julien	2nd
*Frezenberg	2nd
Bellewaerde	2nd
Hooge, 1915	1st
Mount Sorrel	6th, 7th
*Somme, 1916	1st, 5th, 7th
Albert, 1916	7th
Bazentin	7th
Delville Wood	5th, 7th
Guillemont	6th
Flers-Courcelette	1st, 5th, 6th
Morval	1st
Le Transloy	1st, 6th
Ancre, 1916	7th
*Arras, 1917	5th, 7th
Scarpe, 1917	7th
Arleux	7th
Hill 70	1st
*Ypres, 1917	5th, 7th
Langemarck, 1917	6th
Menin Road	6th

HONOURS	BATTALIONS
Polygon Wood	7th
Passchendaele	4th
*Cambrai, 1917	1st, 4th, 6th
*Somme, 1918	1st, 7th
St. Quentin	6th, 7th
Bapaume, 1918	4th, 7th
Rosieres	6th
*Arras, 1918	7th
Lys	7th
Estaires	7th
Messines, 1918	4th
Hazebrouck	7th
Bailleul	4th
Kemmel	4th
Bethune	7th
*Bligny	4th
Aisne, 1918	4th
Albert, 1918	7th
Bapaume, 1918	7th
Hindenburg Line	1st
*Epehy	1st, 10th
Canal du Nord	7th
*Cambrai, 1918	1st, 4th
Selle	1st, 4th, 7th
Valenciennes	4th
Sambre	4th
*Doiran, 1917	8th
*Doiran, 1918	8th
Gaza	10th
*Jerusalem	10th
Jericho	10th
Tel Asur	10th

NOTE.—Battles marked * are emblazoned on the King's Colour.

CHAPTER I

THE FIRST BATTALION

ON the 4th August, 1914, the 1st Battalion was stationed at Tipperary and formed part of the 16th Infantry Brigade, 6th Division. The 6th Division was commanded by Major-General J. L. Keir, C.B., and the 16th Infantry Brigade by Br.-General E. C. Ingouville-Williams, C.B., D.S.O. Mobilization orders were received at 6 p.m. on the 4th, and on the 14th the battalion left Tipperary for Queenstown. By August 20th the battalion, together with the other units of the 6th Division, was encamped in the neighbourhood of Cambridge. The 16th Brigade, consisting of the 1st K.S.L.I., 1st Buffs, 1st Leicesters and 2nd York and Lancasters, was kept continuously at intensive training until September 6th, by which time, in spite of the hot weather, all ranks had become hardened and were fighting fit. On September 8th the battalion embarked at Southampton, and in the evening of the 10th the 1st K.S.L.I. landed on French soil, after an absence of just over one hundred years. The following officers disembarked with the battalion at the port of St. Nazaire :—

Lt.-Colonel C. P. Higginson, D.S.O.	In command
Major E. B. Luard	Second in command
Captain H. A. R. Hoffmeister	Adjutant
Lieut. R. A. Eakin	Machine Gun Officer
Lieut. T. D. Perkin	Transport Officer
Lieut. J. W. Smith	Quartermaster
Captain R. G. H. Tate, R.A.M.C.	Medical Officer

A Company	*B Company*
Major R. Masefield	Captain E. R. M. English
Captain C. H. Cautley	Captain B. E. Murray
*Lieut. J. A. S. Mitchell	Lieut. W. Grischotti
*2nd Lieut. C. E. Parker	Lieut. A. W. Herdman
†2nd Lieut. A. C. P. Biddle-Cope	2nd Lieut. F. C. Verner

* From 3rd Battalion   † From Special Reserve of Officers

THE KING'S SHROPSHIRE LIGHT INFANTRY

C Company	D Company
Major W. J. Rowan-Robinson	Major W. A. Payn
Captain P. R. C. Groves	Captain P. C. Huth, D.S.O.
Lieut. G. P. C. Jenings	Lieut. F. H. R. Maunsell
2nd Lieut. E. A. Freeman	Lieut. A. P. Williams-Freeman
2nd Lieut. R. Bryans	*2nd Lieut. J. A. M. Charles

Regimental Sergeant-Major G. Moore

The strength of the battalion on landing was 27 officers, 1 warrant officer and 969 other ranks.

The German advance on Paris had just been checked, and the battle of the Marne, which had been raging for a week, was brought to a successful conclusion on September 11th. The newly arrived 6th Division was allotted to the III Corps and put into general reserve.

On disembarkation, the battalion entrained for Mortcerf, a small town about twenty-five miles east of Paris, on the borders of the Forest of Crecy, arriving, after a long and tedious journey of twenty-six hours, on the afternoon of September 12th. The weather, which up to this date had been fine and exceptionally warm, now broke, and the battalion started on its night march to Crecy in pouring rain. The darkness and heavy state of the roads delayed progress, and it was 3 a.m. on the 13th before all the companies reached their destination. The 6th Division had concentrated in billets in the area Coulommiers-Mortcerf-Marles-Chaume between September 9th and 12th, the 16th Brigade being the last to arrive, and on September 13th commenced its march to the Aisne. On that day the 1st K.S.L.I. arrived at Jouarres, and on the 15th, after a march of twenty-four miles in heavy rain, reached Rocourt, a small village nine miles due north of Château Thierry. The battalion was marching as the advanced guard to the Brigade, and it is recorded

* From Special Reserve of Officers

2

that the first sight of German prisoners was obtained at Rocourt. On the 16th the Brigade advanced another fifteen miles, still moving due north to the Aisne, the battalion halting that night at Buzancy, where for the first time enemy shells were observed bursting on a ridge some two miles away. From Buzancy the battalion, still acting as Brigade advanced guard, turned due east towards Mont Notre Dame arriving there on September 19th. The next day the Brigade moved north to Courcelles and crossed the River Aisne at 10 p.m. on the 21st.

BATTLE OF THE AISNE, 1914

Meanwhile, on the night of September 19th/20th, the 18th Infantry Brigade had relieved the 2nd Infantry Brigade on a line running diagonally from north-east to south-west along the high ground just south of the Chemin des Dames, north and north-east of Troyons. On the 21st, the 17th Brigade relieved the 6th Brigade, and on the same night, 21st/22nd, the 16th Brigade relieved the 7th and 9th Brigades north-east of Vailly. The 16th Brigade thus came into the line on the left centre of the British front. Two companies of the 1st K.S.L.I. (C and D) took over the trenches a quarter of a mile east of Vailly from the 1st Wiltshire Regiment on September 22nd, A and B Companies being in reserve. The battalion remained in these trenches until October 1st, when they were relieved by the 3rd Coldstream Guards. On September 24th, Captain B. E. Murray was slightly wounded, and on the 25th, Lieut. J. A. S. Mitchell was hit, and died of wounds three days later at Braisne. Casualties amongst other ranks for the month of September amounted to 2 killed and 7 wounded.

On October 1st the battalion took over the trenches occupied by the Royal Scots Fusiliers, half a mile west of Vailly, and on the following day those occupied by the Lincolns in addition. The battalion remained in the trenches in this sector by Vailly until October 12th, when they were relieved by the 287th Regiment of French

Infantry. Meanwhile the 6th Division, less the 16th Brigade, was on its way north, the 16th Brigade remaining behind and receiving the thanks of the II Corps for their soldierly conduct.

On the night of the relief by the French the battalion re-crossed the Aisne and marched a distance of some fifteen miles to Fismes, arriving about 3 p.m. on October 13th. Here it entrained on a long journey northward to Cassel to join the rest of the Division, and take its part in what is now commonly known as the First Battle of Ypres. On the 13th October, Captain P. F. Fitzgerald, extra-regimentally employed as A.D.C. to the 6th Divisional Commander, was wounded. The 4th and 6th Divisions were now together, forming the III Corps under the command of Lt.-General Pulteney.

BATTLE OF ARMENTIERES, 1914

On October 14th the 16th Brigade detrained at Cassel, and the battalion marched to scattered billets south-west of the town. The day before the 6th Division had encountered the enemy and was beginning an advance on the line La Couronne–Merris-Fontaine-Houck, the 16th Brigade being in Divisional Reserve. The 1st K.S.L.I. advanced through Sailly on the 17th, and on the 19th was at Bois Grenier, a small village three miles south of Armentières. Heavy firing was heard all round on the night of the 19th/20th, and the battalion stood to arms. On the morning of October 20th the Germans attacked heavily along the whole of the III Corps front. The First Battle of Ypres and the struggle for the Channel ports had begun. In the evening the battalion dug themselves in in a position in defence of Le Quesne farm, no easy task, since most of the work had to be done with entrenching tools. On the same day 2nd Lieut. F. R. E. Savory and 61 other ranks joined the battalion from the base. In the meantime the 6th Division, fighting on a five-mile frontage, was being roughly handled. The K.S.L.I. took over the trenches of the 2nd York and

Lancs and one company of the 1st Leicesters on the 21st, in addition to the line already held. Heavy shelling took place throughout the day and Lieut. R. A. Eakin was severely wounded, dying three years later of his wounds. The following day the heavy shelling continued without much reply from our artillery, and at 4.15 a.m. on the 23rd the Germans attacked in force. The brunt of the attack fell upon the K.S.L.I. and the York and Lancs, and was repulsed with heavy loss to the enemy. Further attacks followed in succession throughout the day without any ground being gained by the enemy. Over 200 enemy dead were counted in front of the K.S.L.I. trenches alone. A last attack was launched against the battalion at 5 p.m., but was repulsed as before. The following officers were wounded during the fighting: Lt.-Colonel Higginson, Major Luard (slightly), Major Payn, Lieut. Huth, 2nd Lieut. Charles (died of wounds, 10.2.15), 2nd Lieut. Biddle-Cope and R. Sgt.-Major Moore. Major Luard took over command of the battalion. Another heavy attack was delivered by the enemy at 5 p.m. on the following day, when Major R. Masefield and C.S.M. Redford were killed; the battalion still holding its ground, although the enemy was now no more than 50 yards from our trenches in some sectors. At 4 a.m. on the 25th October the British Head-quarters was shelled out of its position, and at 2 p.m. the enemy broke through on the right of the 1st Leicesters (on the left), leaving B Company's left platoon temporarily in the air. In spite of being heavily enfiladed, B Company held on until nightfall, when orders were received for the battalion to withdraw to Bois Grenier. Lieut. A. W. Herdman and 2nd Lieut. F. C. Verner were killed and Lieut. A. P. Williams-Freeman was wounded. Early in the morning of October 26th the battalion arrived at Bois Grenier having maintained an unbroken line due to the steadiness and indomitable courage of all ranks. The total casualties for the five days' fighting were : Officers, 3 killed, 8 wounded ; other ranks, 52 killed, 71 wounded, 11 missing. The following awards were made as a result of this engagement in the *London Gazette* of February 18th, 1915 :—

Lt.-Colonel Higginson, D.S.O. to be C.M.G.
Major Luard to be D.S.O.
Captain Huth, D.S.O., to be Brevet-Major.
R.S.M. Moore, the Military Cross.
C.S.M. Busby, Military Cross (won subsequently).

The battalion remained at Bois Grenier until October 31st. The total casualties for the month of October were : Officers, 3 killed, 8 wounded ; other ranks, 81 killed, 133 wounded, 11 missing.

On November 1st the German attack on the Channel ports had developed into a furious assault on Ypres, and the German Emperor was at Courtrai prepared for a triumphal entry into that town. As Lord French has written with reference to that day : " No more than one " thin and straggling line of tired-out British soldiers stood " between the Empire and its practical ruin as an inde- " pendent first-class Power." Such, indeed, was the situa- tion, for it appeared as if the whole littoral from Havre to Ostend must fall into the hands of the enemy, attack- ing, as he was, with an enormous numerical superiority of guns and men. But the " thin line " was there, and the thin line was British.

The 1st K.S.L.I. took over the trenches of the 2nd D.L.I. (18th Brigade) at Rue du Bois, south of Armen- tières. Although the line was continuously under heavy shell fire, to which our starved guns were unable to reply effectively, no infantry attack was made in this southern sector, and the battalion remained here, in relief of the 2nd D.L.I. until November 14th. During this period Lieut. G. P. C. Jenings was killed, and Lieut. F. H. R. Maunsell wounded. Major E. B. Luard left to have his wound attended to on November 13th, and Major Rowan-Robinson took over temporary command. On November 2nd Lieut. T. L. Ingram, R.A.M.C., joined the battalion as Medical Officer in place of Captain Tate, who was admitted to hospital on November 1st. Captain Hulton-Harrop, from the 3rd Battalion, and Captain P. Prince, formerly seconded as Adjutant of the Herefordshire Regiment (T.A.), joined the battalion on November 6th and 8th respectively, bringing drafts totalling 151 other ranks.

On November 14th the battalion moved into billets at Les Quatre Chemins, where they remained until the 23rd. Drafts amounting to 86 other ranks were received from the base during the period of rest. On the 24th the battalion returned to trenches near Flamengerie Farm, and on the same day Captain P. R. C. Groves left the battalion to join the R.F.C. A comparatively uneventful period of trench warfare followed. The First Battle of Ypres was over and we had held our ground; the Ypres salient stood as it was now to stand for nearly four years. News of the Russian advance, and the withdrawal of German troops from the Western front to meet the danger, heartened our men. Lord Roberts and the Prince of Wales joined the troops in the field during the month, the former dying, within a few days of his arrival, as he would doubtless have chosen to die, on active service amongst the Indian troops. The weather throughout the month was bad—the latter part more especially so, bitter cold combining with storms and heavy rains to double the hardships of the men in the trenches. Trench feet, at first labelled as " frost bite," began to make ravages amongst the troops ; one Division, at this period, losing 3,000 men in one week from this cause alone. Also in the history of this month may be chronicled the arrival of the first battalion of the Territorial Army, troops that, from the first, showed themselves worthy of a place beside their gallant comrades of the Regular Army in the trenches. On November 30th Major J. A. Strick of the 2nd Battalion joined and took over command. Captain Orpen-Palmer, Royal Irish Fusiliers, and Lieut. F. Young, Rifle Brigade, were attached to the battalion for duty. A draft of 56 other ranks joined on the same day. The total casualties amongst other ranks for the month were : killed 12, wounded 34.

On December 2nd, Captain C. H. Cautley and 8 other ranks represented the battalion at an inspection by H.M. the King at 11th Divisional Head-quarters. The battalion was relieved on December 9th by the 1st Buffs, and went into billets at Rue Delpierre. The weather during the month was atrocious and the trenches were water-logged, necessitating continuous work in repairing and draining. The battalion was back in the trenches on the 17th, relieving the 2nd York and Lancs, and remained in the line until the 23rd. Christmas was spent in billets at Rue des Lettres, a small village about three miles due north of Fleurbaix. Every officer and man received a Christmas card from the King and Queen, and a present of tobacco from Princess Mary.

Shortly before Christmas the following officers joined the battalion : Lieut. R. S. Whitmore, 3rd Battalion, Lieut. H. G. C. Colville, 3rd Battalion, 2nd Lieut. S. H. Starey, 3rd Battalion, and 2nd Lieut. R. B. Pirrie attached for duty from the 3rd Battalion of The Border Regiment. On December 17th Major Luard rejoined the battalion. During the month two companies of the Artists' Rifles were attached to the battalion for instruction.

On Boxing Day the battalion relieved the 1st Buffs in the trenches again, remaining there to see the old year out. Whilst in this sector Ptes. Moore and Clarke were awarded the D.C.M.

On December 31st Major Rowan-Robinson was invalided to England. The total casualties for the month of December amongst other ranks amounted to 5 killed and 9 wounded. The casualties from sickness, in spite of the bad weather and water-logged trenches, were very light.

THE FIRST BATTALION. JANUARY, 1915

On January 2nd, 1915, the battalion moved into billets in Armentières for a week's rest which was much appreciated, although the town was intermittently shelled. On the 9th the battalion relieved the Royal Fusiliers in the trenches at Rue du Bois about a mile and a half due south of the town. The trenches were in a very bad state, and the men were continually at work reclaiming long stretches that had been abandoned and flooded. Fortunately the enemy remained inactive, and the battalion after a strenuous fortnight's work was able to hand over the trenches to the York and Lancs on the 23rd in a much improved state. The battalion returned to their billets in Armentières where they remained till the end of the month. The following officers joined the battalion during January : 2nd Lieuts. E. G. James, C. T. H. Reaveley, R. H. Marriott and R. A. Black. A draft of 30 other ranks joined on the 19th. The total casualties for the month, amongst other ranks, amounted to 5 killed and 3 wounded.

The next three months, during which the battalion remained in the Armentières sector, were comparatively uneventful. The 6th Division, having made an advance of about six miles since October 14th, was now holding nearly five miles of trenches running south from the town, a line which our troops were still holding when the great German offensive started over three years later. During February Lieut. H. S. Collins and 2nd Lieut. F. K. Symonds-Taylor joined the battalion, and Lieut. C. E. Parker rejoined. Drafts amounting to 103 other ranks were received from the base, and the 1st Canadian Division arrived in the area, being attached for instruction to the 6th Division. Total casualties for the month of February amongst other ranks amounted to 12 killed and 22 wounded. 2nd Lieut. R. B. Pirrie, 3rd Border Regiment, attached to the battalion, was wounded. The same routine of trench warfare continued throughout March, broken only by sudden orders for the 16th Brigade to entrain for the Ypres district. The enemy, attacking in the neighbourhood of St. Eloi, had successfully carried a line of trenches in the 27th Divisional area, and the 16th Brigade were sent in support of the counter-attack. The 1st K.S.L.I. detrained at Vlamertinghe on March 15th, but the counter-attack having been successful, the Brigade was sent back, arriving in Armentières again at 5 a.m. on the 16th.

Early in January, 1915, the Commander-in-Chief had decided on the formation of Armies, and the 2nd Army, consisting of the II, III and V Corps, under the command of Sir Horace Smith-Dorrien, came into being. On March 17th the 2nd Army Commander inspected the battalion at Armentières. During the month 2nd Lieuts. R. W. Bruce and A. Johnston joined the battalion, and drafts amounting to 115 other ranks were received. Two territorial battalions, the 5th L.N. Lancs and 5th S. Staffs, were attached for training, the former battalion being added to the strength of the 16th Brigade. The total casualties during the month amongst other ranks amounted to 9 killed and 8 wounded. The succeeding month was even more uneventful ; along the whole of the 6th Divisional front the enemy was very inactive, whilst the acute shortage of shells made any great activity on our part difficult. The month was spent in consolidating the line, improving the trenches and forti-fying the small farms in rear of the position. Life in Armentières during this quiet period was made as pleasant as possible for the troops, and during the month the famous 6th Divisional " Fancies " started their career. 2nd Lieuts. G. C. Maillard (Leicester Regiment), A. C. Soden (Liverpool Regiment), M. Foulger and H. A. Wilson (Artists' Rifles), and A. N. Macphail (3rd R. Berks) joined the battalion. Further drafts amounting to 110 other ranks were received. The total casualties for the month were 2nd Lieut. F. K. Symonds-Taylor slightly wounded ; other ranks, 3 killed, 6 wounded.

On May 5th Armentières was heavily shelled by the Germans, but the K.S.L.I. billets fortunately escaped, only one man being wounded. On May 7th Lieut. E. A. Freeman was severely wounded whilst on patrol in "No Man's Land." During the month 2nd Lieut. G. C. Maillard left to join the first battalion of his regiment, the Leicesters, and 2nd Lieuts. G. H. Davies and V. H. Pocock joined the battalion. On May 27th the 27th Division came up to relieve the 6th, which proceeded north to join the VI Corps. On May 30th the battalion was relieved by the 1st Royal Scots and marched to Bailleul, where it was inspected on the following day by the Prime Minister—Mr. Asquith. On May 31st Captain B. E. Murray left the battalion and was appointed Staff Captain, 16th Brigade. The following were mentioned in despatches dated May 31st, 1915 : Lt.-Colonel J. A. Strick, Captain and Adjutant H. A. Hoffmeister, No. 8232 Pte. W. E. Holmes, No. 9805 L.-Sgt. G. Rogers, and Captain H. S. Rogers, A.P.M., 6th Division. As a result of the use of poison gas by the Germans in their attack on the Ypres salient on April 22nd, 1915, gas training was taken up during the month and all ranks were issued with respirators. Total casualties amongst other ranks for month of May : 7 killed, 22 wounded.

On June 1st the 6th Division took over its new front, from Ypres–Roulers Railway to Wieltje, in the Ypres salient, where it remained for over fourteen months. The 1st K.S.L.I. marched from Bailleul at 5 a.m. on June 1st, reaching a point two miles west of Poperinghe at noon. At 6 p.m. the battalion moved forward through the town, and bivouacked along the road between Poperinghe and Vlamertinghe. At midnight on June 5th/6th two companies moved into dug-outs along the Yser Canal, just north of Ypres, and two companies into hutments near Breilen. Both half battalions were continually shelled by heavy howitzers during the three days they remained in this sector, and 2nd Lieut. A. M. Macphail, 3rd R. Berks, attached, was wounded. Large working parties were employed nightly digging trenches across the Wieltje salient three miles north-east of Ypres. On June 9th the battalion moved into billets between Poperinghe and Vlamertinghe, and on the 17th the battalion took over the trenches of the 2nd Sherwood Foresters near Potijze. During the relief 2nd Lieut. H. A. Wilson was wounded. On the 20th the enemy attempted a small gas attack on the 16th Brigade front. This was the battalion's first experience of gas, and in spite of the stories current of its dreadful effects the men remained very cool and fired steadily. The enemy did not emerge from his trenches. 2nd Lieut. F. K. Symonds-Taylor was wounded. The battalion remained in the trenches until July 3rd, a tour of over a fortnight. It was during this tour that trench mortars (2") were first used in the British trenches. 2nd Lieut. E. Bird was wounded on June 22nd, and Captain E. R. M. English (slightly) on the 23rd. The casualties for the month amongst other ranks amounted to 13 killed, 35 wounded. The following honours were published during the month of June, 1915 :—

Lt.-Colonel J. A. Strick, D.S.O.
Captain H. A. R. Hoffmeister, M.C.
7665 Sgt. W. Badcock, D.C.M.
7793 L.-Corpl. T. Flanagan, D.C.M.
10101 Corpl. J. Johnstone, D.C.M.

and Captain H. S. Rogers, of the Staff, was promoted Brevet-Major.

2nd Lieut. R. Dymock and 50 other ranks joined the battalion on June 25th, and on June 6th Captain H. B. Orpen-Palmer left to join the 2nd battalion of his regiment—the Royal Irish Fusiliers.

On July 3rd the battalion was relieved by the 2nd Leinster Regiment, and marched to billets at Poperinghe. On the 7th Lord Kitchener inspected the battalion in the square at Poperinghe, afterwards sending the following message to the Commanding Officer through the Brigade: "I am directed by Field-Marshal Earl Kitchener to

" express to the battalion under your command his satis-
" faction at being able to inspect the battalion and his
" appreciation of the smartness of the turn out and the
" efficiency and fitness of the battalion after nine months'
" hard campaigning." On July 11th the battalion relieved
the 2nd D.L.I. in the trenches again. On the 19th a
patrol of the K.S.L.I., when acting as covering party to
a detachment digging a new trench, met a German patrol,
which they successfully drove off with the loss of 2 other
ranks killed and 8 wounded. On July 21st Captain C. H.
Cautley was wounded. On the 27th the battalion was
relieved by the 1st R. Fusiliers and moved into billets
at Poperinghe. During the month the following officers
joined the battalion: 2nd Lieuts. H. H. Buckley, T.
Lloyd, H. S. Pilbrow, A. W. Goodale and F. B. Isaac,
and drafts amounting to 53, including 23 machine gunners,
were received. The total casualties amongst other ranks
for the month amounted to 10 killed, 27 wounded and
4 missing. On July 30th the 14th Division, on the right
of the 6th, was heavily attacked at Hooge and driven
back to Sanctuary and Zouave woods. The 16th Brigade
was concentrated behind Ypres in readiness to support
the counter-attack, but on July 31st the Corps Commander decided to withdrew the 6th Division from
the line for the task of restoring the line at Hooge.
On the 31st the battalion moved to camp north-east of
Vlamertinghe, returning to billets at Poperinghe on
August 2nd.

ACTIONS OF HOOGE, 1915

On August 1st Captain E. R. M. English left the
battalion to take up the appointment of Town Major at
Hazebrouck, and on the 5th Lt.-Colonel Strick left on
appointment as A.Q.M.G., Boulogne base, and Major
E. B. Luard took over command. On August 5th the
battalion relieved the 6th Somerset L.I. in the trenches
at Hooge. The line had been badly knocked about and
the trenches were in a very bad state. By the following

13

day the 6th Division was in position for the attack, and the preliminary bombardment was begun. The 16th and 18th Brigades were detailed for the assault, the former on the left, the latter on the right. The 2nd York and Lancs were on the left of the Brigade front, the K.S.L.I. on the right, with the 18th Brigade on their right. Owing to heavy retaliation by enemy artillery the attack was postponed for twenty-four hours, during which time the ground was carefully reconnoitred. During a reconnaissance of the enemy's trenches on August 8th Lieut. F. R. Currie was killed, and Capt. Hoffmeister, Captain Grischotti and Lieut. Dix-Perkin were wounded. Major Luard, the Commanding Officer, who was also with the party, escaped unhurt. The medical officer, Lieut. Ingram, was slightly wounded. Lieut. E. G. James was appointed Adjutant in succession to Captain Hoffmeister.

The attack was launched at 3.15 a.m. on August 9th on a front of about 1,000 yards, and was completely successful. The artillery co-operation was most skilfully carried out, and largely contributed to the success. Flammenwerthers, which had been used by the enemy against the 14th Division when taking the position, were found in the enemy trenches, one being captured by the battalion. Not only was all the lost ground regained and held, in spite of desperate counter-attacks, but, in addition, an important spur, north of the Menin Road, on the extreme left of the attack, was won and consolidated with the final position. The signal success of this action won great praise for the Division, and the attack was for some time afterwards regarded as a model of the effective use of close co-operation between infantry and artillery. The battalion had done their work splendidly, the men behaving with the utmost steadiness, following their officers confidently and amply justifying the confidence reposed in them. The price was heavy. The following officers were killed: Lieut. G. H. Davis, 2nd Lieuts. M. Foulger, F. P. Isaac and R. B. Pirrie (attached from the Border Regiment). The following were wounded: Lieuts. S. H.

Starey, R. S. Whitmore and R. Bryans (slightly), 2nd Lieuts. A. Johnston, T. Lloyd, R. H. Marriott, R. S. Pilbrow, S. H. H. James and H. H. Buckley. 2nd Lieuts. A. W. Goodale and R. W. Woodland, reported missing, were subsequently found to have been killed. Amongst other ranks the battalion lost 41 killed, 169 wounded and 18 missing. Before this action seven steel helmets were received, and served out for experimental purposes, being found most satisfactory. The following awards were made for gallantry displayed in the engagement :—

Lieut. R. Bryans, M.C.
Lieut. R. H. Marriott, M.C.
Lieut. T. L. Ingram, R.A.M.C. (attached), M.C.
No. 6711 C.S.M. W. Hodkinson, D.C.M.
„ 7280 L.-Sgt. T. Turner, D.C.M.
„ 9865 Corpl. I. Groom, D.C.M.
„ 6533 Pte. T. Knight, D.C.M.
„ 7857 Pte. H. Langford, D.C.M.
„ 17446 Pte. W. Cheetham, D.C.M.

After the action the battalion was relieved by the 1st Buffs, who had been in support, and returned to dug-outs in the canal bank. On August 11th the battalion moved into camp between Vlamertinghe and Poperinghe, where they were inspected by the G.O.C. 16th Brigade, who congratulated them on their success. On the 14th, Lord Plumer, the Army Commander, visited the battalion and added his congratulations on the success of the action and on the gallantry shown by all ranks in the attack. On August 15th Captain B. E. Murray relinquished his appointment as Staff-Captain, 16th Brigade, and rejoined. On the 19th the battalion returned to the trenches at La Brique, relieving the 3rd Worcesters. On August 25th 2nd Lieut. J. V. Spearman, who had only joined the battalion three days previously, was killed, and on the following day 2nd Lieut. J. H. Quirke was wounded. On August 29th the battalion was relieved by the 2nd York and Lancs and returned to the dug-outs in the canal bank. During the month the following officers joined the battalion: 2nd Lieuts. W. G. Rusbridge, C. R. Cook, J. V. Spearman, R. E. Vaughan, J. H. Quirke, W. Lyle, R. W. O. J. Bruce, A. H. Lee, O. Underhill, T. C. N. Hall, A. W. Erskine, A. Fox, W. H. M. Roxby, and C. T. H. Reaveley.

During the month the following Russian honours were gazetted for gallantry at the action at Le Quesne:—

8619 Sgt. L. H. Taylor, Cross of the Order of St. George, 4th Class.

7391 L.-Corpl. W. Degnam, Medal of St. George, 3rd class.

9123 Pte. A. W. Evans, Medal of St. George, 3rd class.

10152 Pte. G. Maddox, Medal of St. George, 4th class.

The total casualties amongst other ranks for the month were 58 killed, 229 wounded, 18 missing. Drafts were received amounting to 98 other ranks.

On September 2nd the battalion moved into billets in Poperinghe until the 9th, when they returned to the trenches on the old 6th Division front (Wieltje–Ypres–Roulers Railway) near Potijze. On the 14th Captain C. E. Parker and Lieut. W. Lyle were wounded. On the following day the battalion was relieved by the 1st Sherwood Foresters, and on the 16th took over the trenches of the 2nd London Regiment at La Brique. On September 22nd Captain H. G. C. Colville, employed as Brigade Machine-gun Officer, was killed whilst on patrol near Forward Cottage. On the same day the battalion was relieved. Lieut. A. Johnston re-joined during September, and the following joined: 2nd Lieuts. H. Bamford, H. G. Lowder and 126 other ranks, including 4 buglers. The total casualties amongst other ranks for the month amounted to 9 killed and 63 wounded.

On October 2nd the battalion was relieved by the 1st Leicesters, and moved to billets in Poperinghe. On the

11th they were back in the trenches at La Brique, where they remained till the 21st when they returned to Poperinghe. On October 14th the 71st Brigade, from the 24th Division, joined the 6th Division, and was replaced in the 24th Division by the 17th Brigade, this arrangement being in pursuance of the policy of mixing the troops of the old and new armies. The 1st Leicesters left the 16th Brigade to join the 71st, being replaced by the 8th Bedfords from that Brigade. On October 22nd the battalion was moved in motor buses to the Hooge sector to relieve the 8th Rifle Brigade in support of the 14th Division, and was employed for the next two days, whilst in reserve, in finding large carrying parties for the front line. On the 30th the battalion moved up and relieved the 1st Buffs in the front line where they remained until November 10th. During this tour the weather was very bad with continuous heavy rain, and the trenches were in a water-logged condition. On October 27th H.M. The King inspected detachments from the units of the 16th Brigade at Abeele. Lt.-Colonel Luard commanded the 16th Brigade detachment, which included Captain Bryans and 25 other ranks from the 1st K.S.L.I. The King sent a message through Lord Plumer, the Army Commander, saying that he was very pleased with the soldierly bearing of the men on parade. On the same day in the trenches 2nd Lieut. R. T. V. Dymock and 2nd Lieut. H. J. Kendall were wounded, the former dying of his wounds that night. During the month 2nd Lieut. H. J. Kendall and 61 other ranks joined the battalion. The total casualties amongst other ranks for October amounted to 8 killed, 34 wounded.

On November 10th the battalion was relieved by the 7th Lincolns and moved into billets in Poperinghe, where on the 13th C.S.M. W. Griffiths was presented with the Medaille Militaire by the Brigade Commander. On the 19th B Company moved up to the canal bank, and on the same day the 6th Division was relieved and sent back for a month's rest in the Houtkerque–Poperinghe area. On

c   17

November 14th Major-General C. Ross, D.S.O., assumed command of the Division, on the appointment of Major-General Congreve, V.C., to command the XIII Corps. So far as the K.S.L.I. was concerned there was little leisure during the period of rest. The battalion (less B Company) moved on the 20th into camp on the Proven road nearly three miles north-west of Poperinghe. The camp was very wet and badly situated, and large working parties had to be found nightly for the 49th Division in the line. On the 21st Lieut. H. W. Bamford was severely wounded, dying of his wounds a week later. On the 26th B Company rejoined the battalion. During the month of November Captain H. S. Collins re-joined and 2nd Lieut. G. Hamilton and 10 other ranks joined the battalion. The following were mentioned in dispatches dated November 30th, 1915 (*London Gazette*, 31.12.15):—

Lt.-Colonel E. B. Luard, D.S.O.	2nd Lieut. S. H. H. James.
	R. Sgt.-Major J. S. Kirving.
Major B. E. Murray.	7527 Sgt. J. Blud.
Major H. S. Rogers (Staff).	10106 Pte. J. T. Coton.
Captain R. Bryans, M.C.	8566 Pte. W. Hyson.
Lieut. R. H. Marriott, M.C.	

Total casualties for the month amongst other ranks amounted to 8 killed and 15 wounded.

On December 1st the battalion moved to billets in Poperinghe, and on the 16th relieved the 8th K.R.R.C. at La Brique. The trenches, owing to the continual bad weather, were in a very dilapidated state and required a great deal of work. Heavy shelling took place on the 17th and 18th and at 5.15 a.m. on the 19th the enemy launched a gas attack. Our troops throughout the salient had received several days' warning of the enemy's intention to use gas, and were fully prepared. The attack lasted an hour, and a strong north-east wind carried the gas across the salient, affecting the support and reserve lines as far south as the Ypres–Commines canal by St. Eloi. Phosgene gas, a sweet-smelling variety, was used on this occasion for the first time. Casualties were light amongst the troops in the line, provided and ready, as they were, with gas helmets; a heavier toll resulted from the unexpected range of the gas, casualties occurring as far back as Poperinghe, eight miles away. The attempted enemy advance following the gas was a complete failure, the attack being driven off by rapid rifle fire. The 1st K.S.L.I., on whose front the attack was launched, behaved very gallantly and coolly, the discipline being perfect. Heavy shelling preceded the attack and continued throughout the day and night. Our casualties were 6 killed and 14 wounded, and by gas, 4 killed and 43 suffering from effects. 2nd Lieut. C. G. Ridout was wounded and gassed, dying of his wounds a few days later. At the end of the day the battalion was full of fight, and the men were singing in the trenches. On the 21st the battalion was relieved by the 2nd York and Lancs and moved to billets in Poperinghe. On Christmas Day the battalion, owing to a threatened German attack, which however did not develop, was sent back to take over the trenches in the La Brique sector once more. On the 26th 2nd Lieut. R. C. Vaughan was wounded, and on the 28th Lt.-Colonel Luard went to the Field Ambulance, suffering from the effects of gas. Major B. E. Murray took over command. The battalion was relieved on the 29th, and spent New Year's Day in camp in Wood " A 30." The following joined the battalion during the month: 2nd Lieuts. H. J. Colbourne, C. Pilkington, C. G. Ridout and G. Whitham, all on December 10th. A draft of 36 other ranks arrived on December 20th. The total casualties amongst other ranks during the month (including gas casualties) amounted to 32 killed and 100 wounded.

On January 3rd, 1916, the battalion relieved the 2nd York and Lancs again in the trenches, and on the 6th Captain H. A. Wilson was killed. The battalion was relieved on the 8th and returned to camp in Wood " A 30." On January 13th the battalion moved to Burgomeister Farm, near Brielen, half the battalion being accommodated in the farm and half in the Ypres–Dixmude canal bank. On the 18th the battalion moved up into the front line near Forward Cottage, where they remained till the 23rd. The remainder of the month was spent in camp at Wood " A 30." During January Lieut. A. Johnston rejoined, and 2nd Lieut. C. A. Hitchcock and S. A. Sinner joined, and drafts amounting to 238 were received. The following awards were gazetted during the month (*Gazette* 14.1.16) :—

Major B. E. Murray, D.S.O.
7929 Sgt. C. Roberts, D.C.M.
9269 Sgt. G. Wildig, D.C.M.
8097 Company Sgt.-Major W. Griffiths, D.C.M.
Pte. Hughes, R.A.M.C., attached, D.C.M.

The casualties amongst other ranks during January amounted to 4 killed and 11 wounded.

The battalion moved back to Burgomeister Farm and the canal bank on February 2nd, moving up to the trenches at Forward Cottage on the 7th. On February 3rd 2nd Lieuts. W. G. Rusbridge and A. W. Erskine, with 34 other ranks, left to join the Brigade Machine-gun Company then in process of formation, taking with them the 4 Vickers guns which were replaced in the battalion by 4 Lewis guns. The month passed uneventfully with the usual tours and reliefs until the 24th, when the battalion moved to new trenches about two miles to the south in Railway Wood, just north of Hooge, relieving the 9th R. Sussex Regiment. The trenches in Railway Wood had just been mined, and were in a very bad state, with large gaps in the front line. In addition the weather throughout the month was at its worst, cold and rain every day, followed on the 23rd, 24th and 25th by a succession of heavy snow storms. The effect of the thaw, following hard frost, on the breast-works in the trenches was disastrous.

The Division was in need of identifications, and patrols were at work nightly throughout the tour. On February

26th 2nd Lieut. O. Underhill was wounded, and on the 29th 2nd Lieut. R. W. O. J. Bruce, Machine-gun Officer, was wounded slightly, but was able to remain at duty. On the 29th the battalion was relieved by the 8th Bedfords, and moved into cellars in Ypres and dug-outs along the canal bank. It is doubtful whether trench warfare has ever been undertaken under worse conditions than those prevailing at this period along the 10 or 12 miles of line between Wytschaete and Boesinghe. The whole of the Ypres salient was a sea of mud, the trenches often deep in water, the task of rebuilding parapets, destroyed as soon as rebuilt, never ending. Add to this a pronounced numerical superiority of enemy artillery, and the long marches back to rest camp, and we might suppose that the hardships produced by such conditions would have depressed the troops. In fact, however, at no time during the war, and on no front, was the morale of the British Army better, the troops more cheerful or more steadfast in their determination to win. The following officers joined during the month: Captain F. L. Hulton-Harrop, Lieut. L. P. Bowen, Lieut. C. P. Hazard, 2nd Lieut. C. E. Evans and 2nd Lieut. E. M. Hannah. Drafts amounting to 73 other ranks were received. The total casualties amongst other ranks for the month amounted to 5 killed, 26 wounded.

The first four days of March were spent in billets in Ypres, which was shelled daily causing several casualties. On March 5th the battalion relieved the 8th Bedfords on the right of the Railway Wood sector, the 2nd Leinsters, 72nd Infantry Brigade, being on our right, and the 1st Buffs on our left. The weather was bitterly cold, snow falling throughout the day on the 7th. The enemy guns kept up a lively bombardment, and some of the shells dropping in the K.S.L.I. sector were identified as Russian. The battalion was relieved on the 10th by the 8th Bedfords, and returned to the hutted camp in Wood " A 30." During this time large working parties 200 strong, all volunteers, were employed digging support trenches in the Brigade sector. On the 14th the 6th Division was relieved by the Guards Division, and went out to rest. The 1st K.S.L.I. was allotted accommodation in the Calais area where they arrived on the 16th, spending a night at Poperinghe on the way. At Poperinghe the G.O.C. 16th Brigade took the opportunity of thanking the C.O. and those volunteers who had worked in the trenches on the nights of the 13th and 14th. These men, tired out after a tour in the trenches, had certainly shown remarkable devotion to duty. At rest the battalion occupied No. 6 Camp Beaumarais, being accommodated under canvas. On March 20th Major Luard rejoined and took over command from Lieut.-Colonel B. E. Murray. Training was carried out on the sands at Beaumarais in warm sunny weather, and the men began to pick up wonderfully in health. On March 26th the 16th Brigade moved to Herzeele (9 miles W. of Poperinghe) via Zutkerque and Bollezeele, where on arrival on March 29th the troops were billeted in farms west of the village. During the month 2nd Lieuts. C. E. Evans and V. H. Pocock were sent to the Field Ambulance, and 2nd Lieut. F. L. Platt joined on first appointment. Drafts amounting to 49 other ranks were received. Casualties during March other ranks: 7 killed, 17 wounded. The following received cards from G.O.C. 6th Division in appreciation of services rendered:—

7527 Sgt. J. Blud	6258 L.-Corpl. G. Speake
8889 Sgt. F. Saunders	15931 L.-Corpl. R. Jackson
9518 Sgt. C. Silver	9156 Pte. P. McKenna
10119 Corpl. P. Layton	

The battalion spent the first five days of April at Herzeele, after which the 16th Brigade moved forward to Poperinghe. The battalion marched on the 6th into camp two miles north-west of Poperinghe, where it remained until the 15th. During this period large parties were found for work on the new railway siding two and a half miles north-west of Poperinghe, and for cable laying in the neighbourhood of St. Jean. On the 15th the battalion moved back to its old quarters in Camp " E " (formerly Camp " A ") in Wood " A 30," and on the following day to Chateau des Trois Tours (half a mile west of Brielen) relieving the 1st Buffs. During the relief 2nd Lieut. G. Hamilton and C.S.M. A. Johnson of D Company were wounded. At this time the companies were commanded as follows: A Company, Captain T. C. N. Hall; B Company, 2nd Lieut. R. C. Norton; C Company, Lieut. A. Fox; D Company, Lieut. R. W. Bruce; and Captain H. S. Collins was acting as second in command. Large working parties were found, whilst in reserve at Château des Trois Tours, for work on a communication trench (Threadneedle Street) in the Forward Cottage sector.

On April 19th the enemy attacked and, after an intense bombardment, succeeded in capturing a portion of the trenches at the Morteldje Estaminet. In consequence B and C Companys, less two platoons, moved up to join A and B Companys east of the canal bank. On the 21st the battalion was detailed to recapture the lost trenches. The attack, timed for 10 p.m., was launched with B Company, Captain H. S. Collins, on the right, A Company, Captain T. C. N. Hall, in the centre, and half C Company on the left. D Company and half C Company were in reserve. The heavy state of the ground and the darkness of the night prevented the three attacks being launched simultaneously. B Company, however, struck off about 10.45, and with two platoons, under 2nd Lieuts. Norton and Hannah, assaulting, reached the enemy trench, which proved to be unoccupied. The assaulting party was then subjected to heavy rifle and machine-gun fire, being enfiladed from the left. Communication was established with the 2nd York and Lancaster Regiment on our right at Algerian Cottage. A bombing party under C.S.M. Evans was then sent out to establish communication on the left. This party gallantly cleared its way as far as the southern end of Willow Walk, but was unable to establish

23

touch with A Company, which in fact had not, as yet, been able to advance. After waiting for the assembly of the left attacking party until 2 a.m. A Company, who were knee deep in mud, advanced and in spite of strong opposition captured their objective, establishing touch with the left of B Company in Willow Walk. Meanwhile the two platoons of C Company under Lieut. Fox, forming the left of the attack, which had lost touch in the rain and darkness, had re-assembled and managed to advance simultaneously with the centre, and after great difficulty owing to the state of the ground, reached the enemy trenches, which they cleared without encountering much opposition. A somewhat half-hearted counter-attack at daybreak was easily beaten off, leaving the battalion in possession of all the lost trenches. During the advance in the centre wounded men were found to have been suffocated in the mud, and in some places on the left the mud was so deep that it was only by crawling almost flat, throwing their rifles in front of them, that it was possible for the men to advance. The situation was further complicated by a new trench, recently dug by the Germans, unknown to us, in the path of the centre of the attack. An intense bombardment between 6 and 7 in the morning of the 22nd followed in retaliation for the successful attack, and during this bombardment Lieut.-Colonel Luard was severely wounded, dying at the Casualty Clearing Station in the evening of the 24th.

The story of this minor operation cannot be too simply told. Its estimate depends not upon gains or losses, but upon the fact that courage, devotion to duty and discipline, had enabled men to achieve, in mud, darkness, and pouring rain what was seemingly impossible. The following casualties occurred during the attack: killed, Lieut. A. Johnston and 2nd Lieuts. C.A. Hitchcock and C.P. Hazard; wounded, Captains H. S. Collins and T. C. N. Hall, Lieut. R. W. Bruce and 2nd Lieuts. R. C. Norton and H. T. Colbourn. Other ranks: 22 killed, 135 wounded, 6 missing.

The battalion was relieved on the night of the 22nd/

23rd and returned to Camp " E " in Wood " A 30," under Major Murray, who had taken over command. On April 25th every available officer and man of the battalion attended the funeral of Colonel Luard, all ranks with a feeling of personal loss. On the 25th a telegram was received forwarding the appreciation of the Army Commander of the " excellent work which the battalion "did on the night of 21st/22nd," and on the 27th the Army Commander (General Plumer), addressing the battalion on parade, congratulated them on their success in person. On the following day the Commander-in-Chief (Sir D. Haig) inspected the battalion and addressing the men said : " The success of the operation was entirely due to " the high standard of discipline which abounds in this " battalion." Further appreciation was shown by the Commander-in-Chief when referring to the battalion in his daily *communiqué*—the first instance of a battalion being mentioned by name. The Corps Commander (Lord Cavan) spoke of the attack as " a magnificent feat of " arms." adding " troops who could do this are to be " entrusted with anything," and writing to Mrs. Luard expressed himself as follows : " I do not think any battalion " was ever set a much more difficult and necessary task, yet " in inky darkness, over shell-destroyed ground, in pouring " rain, the K.S.L.I. went straight to their work, and under " your husband's splendid and gallant direction once " more secured the safety of the left of the British line." The following 6th Divisional wire was forwarded through the 16th Brigade : " Please convey to General Nicholson " and all troops engaged my intense admiration of their " success gained in spite of every kind of difficulty of " ground, weather and an obstinate enemy." The G.O.C. 16th Brigade in ordering this telegram to be read out on parade added : " The Brigadier also wishes you to say to " the battalion that in his opinion the action of the night " of April 21st/22nd will rank very high among the many " glorious exploits of the battalion in the past, that its " success is due to the careful arrangements made by

" Lt.-Colonel Luard, to the gallant leading of the officers
" of the battalion, and to the high standard of discipline,
" soldier-like conduct and personal gallantry which pre-
" vails throughout all ranks of the battalion."

On April 28th the battalion moved up to the canal
bank in support, and on the following day relieved the
1st Buffs in the left sector trenches in the Morteldje
Estaminet area.

The following is a list of decorations awarded for services rendered on the night of April 21st/22nd, 1916:—

> Captain T. L. Ingram, R.A.M.C. (attached), D.S.O.
> 2nd Lieut. A. Fox, M.C.
> 2nd Lieut. E. M. Hannah, M.C.
> Pte. A. Hamilton, R.A.M.C. (attached), D.C.M.
> Sgt. J. Foley, M.M.
> A.-Sgt. J. Wellington, M.M.
> L.-Sgt. J. Hordern, M.M.
> L.-Corpl. A. Murray, M.M.
> L.-Corpl. A. Taylor, M.M.
> L.-Corpl. L. Teal, M.M.
> Pte. J. H. Blower, M.M.
> Pte. W. Doody, M.M.
> Pte. J. Marston, M.M.

Cards from 6th Divisional Commander:—

Sgt. J. Foley	A.-Sgt. J. Wellington
L.-Sgt. J. Hordern	L.-Corpl. A. Murray
L.-Corpl. A. Taylor	L.-Corpl. L. Teal
Pte. F. Richards	Pte. E. C. Roberts
Pte. J. H. Blower	Pte. W. Doody
Pte. J. Marston	

During the month the following officers rejoined from
courses: 2nd Lieuts. F. L. Platt, R. C. Norton, C. A.
Hitchcock, L. P. Bowen and G. Hamilton, and Captain
C. T. H. Reaveley and 2nd Lieut. H. T. Colbourn from
leave. The following left the battalion: Captain Hulton-
Harrop and 2nd Lieut. G. Whitham, to Field Ambu-

lance, and Captain R. Bryans for attachment to 16th Brigade for instruction in staff duties. Captain C. F. B. Winterscale joined, and took over second in command, and Captain C. J. Maclaverty joined and was appointed to command D Company. The following joined on first appointment: 2nd Lieuts. R. W. Taylor, J. K. Mylius and J. M. L. Grover. Drafts amounting to 119 other ranks were received.

The trenches at Morteldje were in a very bad state, the front line containing many gaps, some as much as 150 yards in length. Enemy patrols were very active, but all attempts to break through the gaps were frustrated, and considerable losses inflicted on the enemy. The battalion was relieved on the night of May 5th/6th by the 2nd York and Lancaster Regiment and returned to Camp " E." On the 11th the battalion took over the trenches in the left sector of the Brigade area astride the Ypres–Pilkem road, with the 2nd D.L.I. (18th Brigade) on their left. On the 14th the enemy attacked in the Morteldje area, now on our right, and after four determined assaults captured the two bombing posts at the Estaminet. held by the 1st Buffs, not before the whole garrison in both posts had become casualties. The battalion was relieved on the 17th by the 8th Bedfords. C and D Companies proceeded to the canal bank, and the remainder of the battalion returned to Château des Trois Tours (800 yards west of Brielen). On the 23rd the battalion returned to the left sector until the 29th, when they were relieved and returned to Camp " E," half-way between Poperinghe and Vlamertinghe. The first despatch of Field-Marshal Sir Douglas Haig, covering the period December 19th, 1915, to May 19th, 1916, was published during the last week in May, the battalion being specially mentioned " for good work in carrying out or repelling local attacks " and raids." During the month the following officers left the battalion sick: Captain C. F. B. Winterscale, Lieut. L. P. Bowen, and 2nd Lieuts. H. H. Scott and R. W. Taylor. The following officers joined: Captains

C. D. Harris. W. J. Brooke, E. C. L. van Cutsem, Lieuts. R. S. Whitmore, R. H. Marriott and E. T. Spink. The following rejoined: Captain R. Bryans, Lieut. and Qr.-Master J. W. Smith and 2nd Lieut. S. A. Sinner. The following 2nd Lieuts. joined on first appointment: R. E. Mealing, F. W. Moss, M. Cutler, H. H. Scott, R. G. Pugh, C. R. C. Marsh, H. E. B. de Gruchy and R. S. Foster. During May, 1916, the Companies were commanded as follows: A Company, Captain Harris, B Company, Captain Brooke, C Company, Captain van Cutsem, D Company, Captain Maclaverty. Drafts amounting to 126 other ranks were received. Total casualties for May other ranks: 6 killed, 41 wounded.

The first three days of June were spent at Camp " E " and are memorable on account of an informal visit from H.R.H. the Prince of Wales who stayed for about an hour with the battalion. On the night of the 4th/5th the battalion returned to the trenches in the left sector of the Brigade area, where they remained till the 11th. After a brief tour in reserve, during which large working parties were found nightly, the battalion was relieved by the Irish Guards and returned to Camp " E." On the 21st the battalion moved into billets in Poperinghe, and on the following day marched to the rest area at Herzeele, occupying the same billets in farmhouses as during their former stay in March. On June 24th the G.O.C. 16th Infantry Brigade inspected the battalion, and after complimenting them again on the successful operation at Morteldje, thanked them for the work done in the trenches since that date, adding that he was proud to have such a battalion under his command. During the month the following awards appeared in the King's birthday Honours List. The D.S.O. Captain H. S. Collins; Military Medal, Sgts. J. Blud and F. Saunders, Corpl. P. Layton, Ptes. W. Layton and W. Church. The following were mentioned in Sir. D. Haig's despatch of June 15th, 1916, for gallant and distinguished conduct in the field: Major (temp. Lt.-Colonel) E. B. Luard, D.S.O., Major E. R. M.

THE FIRST BATTALION. JULY, 1916

English, Captain H. S. Collins, 2nd Lieut. (temp. Captain) and Adjutant E. G. James, Sgt. C. W. Silver and L.-Corpl. G. Speake. During the month 2nd Lieut. F. L. Platt left the battalion sick, and Major C. F. B. Winterscale rejoined from hospital, and took over the duties of second in command again. 2nd Lieuts. L. R. Spittal, A. B. Rogers and E. S. de V. Thomas joined on first appointment. Drafts amounting to 80 other ranks were received. Total casualties for month of June: other ranks 2 killed, 19 wounded.

On July 1st the battalion left Herzeele, and marched via Arneeke and Noordpeene to Tatinghem, two and a half miles west of St. Omer, where they were detailed as training battalion for the Second Army Central School at Wisques. Frequent demonstrations were given by companies to the students at the school during the stay at Tatinghem. On the 14th the battalion moved to camp two miles north-west of Poperinghe and the following day were inspected by Lt.-General Lord Cavan, commanding the XIV Corps. He again complimented the battalion on their counter-attack of April 21st, saying that this operation had preserved intact the left flank of the Army. After two years of war he declared he found everything in the battalion just as he wished it to be. Next day the battalion moved into billets in Ypres, and on the night of 17th/18th relieved the 7th K.O.Y.L.I. of the 61st Brigade (20th Division) in the trenches about 1,500 yards due east of Potijze. The battalion was on the left of the Brigade front with the 18th Brigade (6th Division) on their left. On the 23rd 2nd Lieut. R. Tate was slightly wounded during an enemy bombardment of our trenches, and on the 25th 2nd Lieut. J. K. Mylius was slightly wounded. The battalion was relieved by the 8th Bedfords on the night of July 25th/26th, and returned to billets in Ypres, moving to billets in the Rue de Boeschepe, Poperinghe, on the 30th.

Towards the end of the month Br.-General Nicholson was appointed to command the 34th Division, being

THE KING'S SHROPSHIRE LIGHT INFANTRY

succeeded in command of the 16th Brigade by Br.-General W. L. Osborn. The following honours were notified during the month. The Military Cross, C.S.M. John Evans, for gallantry on the night of April 21st/22nd, when he was badly wounded, subsequently losing an eye; and 2nd Lieut. F. W. Moss (gained whilst C.S.M. with the 2nd Essex Regiment). Gallantry cards from G.O.C. 6th Division: Sgt. J. Parker, A.-Sgt. J. Buckley, Ptes. H. Probert, E. Holmes, A. Morrell, W. Degnam, J. Watkiss. Whilst at Tatinghem the battalion signallers distinguished themselves by winning the 16th Brigade signalling competition. During the month Captain van Cutsem left the battalion on appointment as Town Major of Poperinghe, and Lieut. R. Bryans as A.D.C. to the G.O.C. 6th Division. The following officers rejoined: Lieuts. E. Bird and L. P. Bowen, 2nd Lieuts. H. H. Scott and R. W. Taylor from hospital. The following joined on first appointment: 2nd Lieuts. A. F. Tavener, J. F. Addy, R. Tate, E. H. Lee, D. M. B. Williams, F. W. A. Carter, H. J. Beesley and N. V. Webber. Drafts amounting to 97 other ranks were received. Total casualties for the month of July: other ranks 1 killed, 8 wounded.

BATTLES OF THE SOMME, 1916

On the first of August the battalion was notified that the 16th Brigade would proceed south to join General Gough's Reserve Army; accordingly it entrained at Hopoutre, 40 officers and 873 other ranks strong, for the Somme, arriving at Doullens early in the morning of the 3rd. From Doullens the battalion marched to hutments at Authicule, and later via Puchevillers and Acheux to camp in a wood about a mile and a half north-west of Englebelmer, which was reached on August 10th. On the 15th the battalion took over the trenches opposite Beaumont-Hamel from the 2nd Irish Guards. 2nd Lieut. M. Cutler was wounded on the 13th, whilst reconnoitring the sector previous to taking over. The trenches here were deep cut in chalk, and were the best the battalion had seen since leaving Armentières. The 8th Bedfords were on the right of the battalion and the 4th Grenadier Guards on the left. A heavy enemy bombardment with 5·9 howitzers on the 19th caused considerable damage and 2nd Lieut. R. G. Pugh was killed. The battalion was relieved on the 20th, battalion headquarters A and B Companies returned to billets in Mailly-Maillet, C and D Companies to dug-outs in Auchonvillers. On the 25th Auchonvillers was heavily shelled, and one dug-out, occupied by the stretcher-bearers of C Company, received a direct hit. 2nd Lieut. J. K. Mylius with Corpl. E. Glennon, and Ptes. H. Jones and J. Lowe, worked gallantly under heavy shell fire, removing the wounded, and digging out those imprisoned. On the 27th the 16th Brigade was relieved in the trenches by the 144th Brigade and the battalion marched, via Bertrancourt and Amplier, to billets in Naours, half-way between Doullens and Amiens, arriving on the 29th. Gallantry cards were awarded by the G.O.C. 6th Division to Corpl. Glennon and Ptes. H. Jones and J. Lowe for their conduct on the 25th. During August the following officers left the battalion. To the Field Ambulance: Lieuts. L. P. Bowen and J. M. L. Grover, 2nd Lieuts. R. W. Taylor, J. F. Addy, H. J. Beesley and R. Attoe. 2nd Lieut. M. E. Mealing left to join the R.F.C. and 2nd Lieut. R. Tate to join the 16th Trench Mortar Battery. 2nd Lieuts. J. K. Mylius and R. Tate rejoined from hospital and 2nd Lieut. J. H. Busby joined on first appointment. Total casualties for the month: other ranks 3 killed, 23 wounded.

The battalion remained in billets at Naours until September 6th when they proceeded by march route south-east via Villers-Bocage and Corbie to Bois des Tailles, two miles east of Bray-sur-Somme, arriving in camp on the evening of the 8th. On the 11th the 16th Brigade relieved the 167th Brigade, and the battalion took over the trenches one mile north-north-east of Maricourt.

THE KING'S SHROPSHIRE LIGHT INFANTRY

BATTLE OF FLERS-COURCELETTE

On the 14th the battalion moved to trenches about 1,000 yards south-west of Guillemont, preparatory to taking part in the general advance of the Fourth Army. The XIV Corps were to take Bouleaux Wood with the 56th Division, Morval with the 6th Division, and Les Bœufs with the Guards Division. The 6th Division, allotted the centre of the attack, advanced on a two-Brigade front, the 16th Brigade being on the right. The attack was to be made in three waves, the 8th Bedfords were to take the first objective, the 1st Buffs to pass through to the second objective and the 2nd York and Lancasters, supported by 1st K.S.L.I., were to pass through Morval village and establish a line north-east of the village as the final objective. Previous to this attack orders were received to leave a certain number of officers behind to form the nucleus of a fresh battalion if necessary. The attack was launched at 6.20 a.m. on the 15th. The 8th Bedfords were at once held up by a strong point about 1,000 yards north-east of the junction of Leuze and Bouleaux Woods, known as the Quadrilateral. The 1st Buffs were sent to assist the 8th Bedfords, but the second assault was no more successful. A third assault by the 2nd York and Lancs also failed. Shortly after midday orders were received by the 1st K.S.L.I. to make a fourth assault on this formidable strong point from the south-east, but these orders were cancelled during the preparations for the attack, the 16th Infantry Brigade having suffered very heavily. The 18th Brigade made an unsuccessful attempt on the Quadrilateral during the night of the 15th/16th, but by midday on the 16th the strong point remained in the hands of the enemy. A heavy artillery bombardment by our guns followed throughout the day, the Quadrilateral being shelled by 12-inch guns. The enemy replied vigorously and the artillery duel lasted throughout the 17th. The casualties up to now had been comparatively light in numbers, but heavy in the sense of personal loss to the battalion. The Adjutant,

Captain E. G. James, was seriously wounded in the evening of the 17th, dying of wounds a month later, and Captain T. L. Ingram, D.S.O., M.C., the Medical Officer, when out searching for wounded on the night of the 16th/17th, failed to return, his body being recovered some days later. The Chaplain, the Rev. R. E. Inglis, a man loved by all ranks, was killed whilst with a party searching for Captain Ingram. 2nd Lieut. H. H. Scott was buried by a shell and evacuated from concussion. Amongst other ranks 5 were killed, 26 wounded and 4 missing. At one in the morning of the 18th the 1st K.S.L.I. received orders to attack the Quadrilateral. The attack commenced at 5.50 a.m. and by 6.15 the Quadrilateral was taken by C and D Companies, the garrison being killed or taken prisoners. A and B Companies pushed on to the second objective, whilst C and D consolidated the ground gained. That night the battalion was relieved and marched back to bivouac on the Briqueterie road, arriving in pouring rain at about four in the morning of the 19th. Casualties during the 18th were as follows: Officers killed: Captain C. J. Maclaverty, Lieut. R. H. Marriott, and 2nd Lieut. E. H. Lee. Wounded: Lieut. C. K. E. Marsh, 2nd Lieuts. S. A. Sinner, A. E. B. de Gruchy, D. M. B. Williams and F. W. Moss. Other ranks, 20 killed and about 130 wounded. The loss of the Adjutant, Captain E. G. James, was a severe blow to the battalion. He had behaved with great gallantry during the 15th/16th, and received the D.S.O. shortly before he died. The battalion also felt greatly the loss of their gallant chaplain and medical officer. During this engagement the battalion captured about 180 prisoners and 3 machine guns.

BATTLE OF MORVAL

At midday on the 19th the battalion marched to billets in Morlancourt, and on the 21st returned to the trenches south-east of Bernafay Wood in Brigade Reserve. On the 25th the Fourth Army renewed its attack, the objective of the XIV Corps being the villages of Morval and Les Bœufs. The 1st K.S.L.I., advancing in support of the 2nd York and Lancs, were in the centre of the attack, and were to pass through as soon as the first objective was gained and establish themselves on the Morval–Les Bœufs ridge, consolidating and standing ready to assist troops of the 5th Division (right) and Guards Division (left) which were clearing the villages of Morval and Les Bœufs. The assembly point for the attack in the trenches north-east of Ginchy was reached by 11 p.m. on the 24th. The attack commenced at 12.35 p.m. on the 25th, and at 2.10 p.m. the K.S.L.I. advanced with the second wave of the assault and reached their objective, the Morval ridge, by 3 p.m. The attack over the whole of the Corps front was a complete success, the enemy offering but a half-hearted resistance. During the advance, which was executed with great steadiness, 2nd Lieuts. R. S. Foster and L. R. Spittal were wounded. The battalion was relieved on the 26th by the 9th Suffolk Regiment (71st Brigade), and marched back to the trenches at Bernafay Wood in the Briqueterie area. On the 30th the battalion marched back into billets at Meaulte. During September the following officers rejoined the battalion: Captain F. R. H. Maunsell from base and Lieut. J. M. L. Grover and 2nd Lieut. J. F. Addy from hospital; Lieut. R. Bryans rejoined from Head-quarters 6th Division, and took over the duties of Adjutant. The following officers left for the Field Ambulance: Captain C. D. Harris, 2nd Lieuts. F. W. A. Carter and N. V. Webber. Drafts amounting to 86 other ranks were received. Total casualties for the month, other ranks: 39 killed, 282 wounded, 22 missing.

The G.O.C. 6th Division inspected the battalion at Meaulte on October 2nd and congratulated them on their splendid work on September 18th and 25th. The following were awarded the Military Medal: Sgts. Hockenhull, Pugh, Saunderson, Hudson and Parker. Corpl. Jackson,

THE FIRST BATTALION. OCTOBER, 1916

L.-Corpl. Peate. Ptes. H. Carr, G. Bryant, F. Charles, B. Harper, W. Sheffield, C. E. Bradbury, R. Greenhough, J. Bromley and Bandsman J. Lowe.

BATTLE OF THE TRANSLOY RIDGES

On October 7th the battalion moved to Citadel and the following day, via Trones Wood, to the trenches south-east of Gueudecourt, preparatory to an attack to improve our position in front of Le Transloy. The battalion was heavily shelled in the trenches in this sector. 2nd Lieut. A. F. Tavener was hit on the 10th, and died of wounds the following day. On the 11th 2nd Lieuts. E. M. Hannah, and J. K. Mylius were wounded, the latter dying next day. At 2 p.m. on the 12th the attack commenced, the battalion being in support of the 2nd York and Lancs. The assault was successful, and, although hung up by hidden machine guns for some time, the battalion reached its objective. During the attack Lieut. J. M. L. Grover and C.S.M.'s Jones and Johnson were wounded. The battalion was relieved on the evening of the 12th, and moved back to the reserve trenches north of Ginchy. On the 19th the battalion was relieved again, and marched back to billets in Meaulte, moving on the 21st to Daours. On the 23rd the battalion moved again via Bailleul to Bethune, where they arrived on the 28th and joined the I Corps, 1st Army. The battalion remained at Bethune till the end of the month. During October the following officers were sent to the Field Ambulance: Captain F. R. H. Maunsell, 2nd Lieuts. Bird and Thomas. 2nd Lieut. A. G. W. Browne left for the 16th Brigade Trench Mortar Battery. Lieut. F. K. Symonds-Taylor rejoined, and the following officers joined: 2nd Lieuts. H. H. Buckley, W. C. Beckett, A. O. Kersey, R. I. Comins, L. D. Chambers, A. G. W. Browne, A. V. Mackenzie, M. R. Featherstonhaugh, T. W. M. Wolley, N. B. Saunders and B. E. Gracie. Lieuts. R. S. Whitmore and F. K. Symonds-Taylor, both of the Special Reserve, were promoted Captain. The following were awarded the M.C.: Captain E. V. T. A. Spink, Lieut. C. R. Young, R.A.M.C. (attached), and C.S.M. Denyer. Drafts amounting to 184 were received, including 154 men from the Denbigh Yeomanry. Total casualties for the month, other ranks: 14 killed, 63 wounded.

The battalion remained in comfortable billets at Bethune until the 27th of November, when they marched to the support-line trenches in the village of Le Plantin, west of Givenchy, relieving the 14th R. Warwicks, in a quiet sector of the line. During November Lieut. R. L. H. Green left the battalion sick, and 2nd Lieut. W. C. Beckett for training duties at the base. 2nd Lieut. F. L. Platt rejoined, and 2nd Lieuts. T. G. H. Rooper, G. Wildig, J. G. Lumley and E. S. de V. Thomas joined on first appointment. Ptes. Jenks and Lundie were awarded the Military Medal and L.-Corpl. Teale received a bar to his medal. Drafts amounting to 37 other ranks were received. On December 1st Major Winterscale took over command from Lieut.-Colonel Murray, appointed to Divisional Schools.

The battalion remained in support until the night of December 2nd, when they moved up into the front line at Givenchy, relieving the 2nd York and Lancs. The battalion stayed in the line, which remained quiet, until the 6th, when they were relieved and proceeded to billets in Le Quesnoy, returning to the front line on the 10th. Alternate reliefs between the front line, support line and reserve billets at Le Quesnoy continued until Christmas time, Christmas Day being spent in billets at Bethune. On December 27th the battalion relieved the 1st E. Yorks in the support trenches north-east of Vermelles, a quiet sector in which they remained until the end of the month. During December 2nd Lieut. L. D. Chambers left the battalion for training duties at the base, and 2nd Lieut. A. Avery was transferred to a Trench Mortar Battery. Reinforcements amounting to 136 other ranks were received. Total casualties for December: other ranks 1 killed, 10 wounded.

THE FIRST BATTALION. FEBRUARY, 1917

On January 1st, 1917, the battalion moved up into the first-line trenches north-east of Vermelles, relieving the 1st Buffs. The New Year's Honours List included the following awards: Major (temp. Lt.-Colonel) B. E. Murray, D.S.O., to be Brevet-Lt.-Colonel. Corpl. Kettle the D.C.M., Captain Harris, Lieut. Mylius (since died of wounds), and R.S.M. J. Skirving mentioned in despatches, and Lieut. and Quartermaster J. W. Smith awarded next highest rate of pay. The line in this sector was still quiet and the battalion continued the routine of four days in the line, four days in support and four days in reserve billets at Noyelles, throughout January. During the month 2nd Lieut. T. W. M. Wolley went to the Field Ambulance and 2nd Lieut. Busby and 50 N.C.O.'s and men proceeded to La Beuvriere to form a fifth, or training, Company under Lt.-Colonel Menzies of the 14th D.L.I. The following officers joined during January: 2nd Lieuts. L. S. Pilbrow, R. W. Kirby, P. J. Hudson, T. R. Hearne, J. N. Hilditch and C. E. Evans. Drafts amounting to 20 other ranks were received. Casualties during the month were light. and inflicted mostly by snipers, Lieut. T. G. H. Rooper being killed by a sniper on January 18th. Casualties other ranks: 5 killed, 3 wounded.

The same routine was continued until the end of the first fortnight in February when the 16th Brigade was relieved, on February 14th/15th, by the 110th Brigade, 21st Division, and the battalion marched back to billets in La Bourse, moving to Robecq on the 16th. Here they remained until February 25th. when they marched to Chocques, remaining there till the end of the month. During February Major W. J. Brooke, second in command, left for the Field Ambulance, and 2nd Lieut. Beckett rejoined from training duties at the base. The following joined on first appointment: Captain L. H. Morris, 2nd Lieuts. L. Burland, H. V. O'Meara, A. E. Lewis and G. V. Blake. 2nd Lieuts. Lewis and Blake were posted to the 6th Divisional Training Company, under command of Lieut. J. H. Busby. Drafts amounting to 51 other ranks were received. The only casualties for the month were one man killed, and C.S.M. (acting R.S.M.) Griffiths, who was badly wounded by a bomb dropped from an enemy aeroplane.

On March 1st the battalion marched to billets in Les Brebis, between Lens and Bethune, spending two nights at Petit Sains on the way. On the 8th the battalion returned to the trenches south-south-east of Loos, relieving the 2nd York and Lancs. During the relief the enemy was very active with granatenwerfer (aerial darts), and 2nd Lieut. M. R. Featherstonhaugh was wounded. On the 15th the battalion was relieved and occupied the defensive works in Loos village, returning to the trenches on the 20th. On the 26th the battalion was relieved again and returned to billets in Les Brebis, where it remained until the end of the month. During the month Captain R. S. Whitmore and 2nd Lieut. H. H. Buckley (Lewis-Gun Officer) left for the Field Ambulance. 2nd Lieut. Rogers was attached to Brigade Head-quarters for instruction in staff duties, and 2nd Lieut. P. J. Hudson and 25 other ranks left to join the newly formed Brigade Pioneer Company. The following officers rejoined: 2nd Lieuts. A. E. Lewis and G. V. Blake from the Training Company, 2nd Lieuts. H. E. B. de Gruchy, H. H. Scott and T. W. M. Wolley from the base. Lieut. D. W. Jackson and 2nd Lieuts. C. H. O. A. Chester and J. G. Davies joined on first appointment. Lt.-Colonel Murray. Commandant of the 6th Division School, was wounded whilst attending a demonstration. Total casualties for month: other ranks 9 killed, 16 wounded. On March 31st C.S.M. G. E. S. Denyer was appointed to a regular commission as Lieutenant, and posted to A Company.

The battalion moved back to the trenches south of Loos on the 1st of April for seven days, returning on relief to the defences of Loos. On the 13th, in consequence of the successful attack from Arras on Vimy Ridge, the enemy withdrew from the right of the 16th

Brigade front, and the 2nd York and Lancaster Regiment advanced and occupied the high ground from the Double Crassier to the Lens–Bethune road, encountering little opposition. Loos village was heavily shelled on the 14th and Lieut. H. H. Buckley was killed, and Captain Symonds-Taylor and Lieut. W. H. M. Roxby were wounded, the former dying of wounds on the 17th. A further advance by the 16th Brigade, planned for the 15th, failed, and the 1st K.S.L.I. in reserve were not called upon. On the 16th the battalion moved up and relieved the 1st Buffs in the new trenches at Cité St. Auguste, two miles east-south-east of Loos. At 5 a.m. on the 18th A and C Companies attacked, after a heavy preliminary bombardment, and gained their objective—the old German front line. During this advance 11 other ranks were killed, and 2nd Lieut. C. E. Evans and 25 other ranks wounded.

On the 19th B and D Companies continued the advance, reaching their objective and capturing 18 prisoners. 2nd Lieuts. T. W. M. Wolley, N. B. Saunders and G. Wildig were wounded. On the following day the battalion was relieved by the 11th Essex Regiment (18th Brigade) and returned to Loos. On the 22nd the 11th Essex Regiment attacked at 5 a.m., and at 10 a.m. C Company K.S.L.I. moved forward in support. At 12 noon D Company was sent up, followed by B Company at 5 p.m. The attack, which reached its objective in the morning, failed on account of a heavy counter-attack with strong artillery support, which forced a retirement during the evening to the original line. The battalion was relieved on the night of 22nd/23rd, and marched to billets in Philosophe. On the 23rd the 1st K.S.L.I. returned to the trenches, relieving the 2nd Sherwood Foresters (71st Infantry Brigade) on the left of the Divisional line north of Hulluch. On the 28th the battalion was relieved and returned to billets in Philosophe, where they remained for the rest of the month. During April Captain F. L. Hulton-Harrop rejoined, and Captain J. Jones was attached from the 2nd D.L.I. Drafts amounting to 73 other ranks were received. Total casualties, other ranks: 17 killed, 79 wounded. For gallantry in the severe fighting south-east of Loos on April 13th/28th, the following N.C.O.'s were awarded the Military Medal: Sgt. D. Williams, Sgt. H. Kennedy, and L.-Corpl. J. Harris. Sgt. L. Hockenhull was awarded a bar to his Military Medal.

On May 3rd the battalion left Philosophe and relieved the 1st Buffs in the trenches in the right sector of the Brigade front between Loos and Hulluch. The enemy was active with trench mortars and aerial darts, and on the 8th Captain A. Fox, commanding A Company, was killed. On the 11th the battalion was relieved and marched to billets in Mazingarbe. On the 15th the battalion returned to the trenches, and on the 17th Lieut. D. W. Jackson was wounded, dying of his wounds on the following day. On the 19th the battalion was relieved, and marched to billets in Fouquieres, spending one night at La Bourse on the way. On the 23rd the Corps Commander presented medal ribbons to Lieut. G. S. E. Denyer, 2nd Lieut. J. F. Addy, and Sgt. Hockenhull.

On the 26th the battalion marched back via La Bourse to the trenches at Hulluch, where they remained without incident till the end of the month. During May Captain H. A. R. Hoffmeister re-joined, and took over the duties of second in command from Major Jones, D.L.I. (attached), who left to join the 8th Bedfords. Captain Whitmore rejoined from the base. The following left for the Field Ambulance: Captain Hulton-Harrop, 2nd Lieuts. T. R. Hearne and G. V. Blake. Captain Morris left to join the 1st Army School.

At 2 a.m. on the night of June 1st a very successful raid on the enemy trenches was carried out under the direction of Captain Spink. The attacking force was organized in four parties under the command of 2nd Lieuts. W. C. Beckett, A. V. Mackenzie, J. G. Davies and C.S.M. Pugh, the whole force having had nine days' special training for the event. Each party succeeded in entering the enemy trenches and inflicting heavy casualties, sixteen Germans being killed and several machine-gun posts destroyed. Many identifications were secured, but no prisoners taken alive. The raid appeared to have been expected, otherwise the results might have been still better. During this raid 2nd Lieut. J. G. Davies was killed and 2nd Lieut. W. C. Beckett and C.S.M. Pugh were wounded, and 3 other ranks killed and 11 wounded. A similar raid on the same sector was carried out at 2.45 a.m. on June 4th with the object of securing prisoners. The raid was organized in two parties, each twenty strong, under command of 2nd Lieuts. A. V. McKenzie and J. G. Lumley. The time allowed was only ten minutes, which proved too short. The two parties succeeded in entering the enemy trenches, but met with strong opposition. Both officers became casualties at once, and at the end of ten minutes, when the signal was given to return, no prisoners had been captured. Our casualties were 2 officers wounded, and 3 other ranks killed and 12 wounded. On the night of June 4th the battalion was relieved by the 8th Bedfords and moved back to billets in Mazingarbe. The following awards were made in respect of the raids of June 1st and 4th. The Military Cross: 2nd Lieuts. A. V. Mackenzie, W. C. Beckett and P. J. Hudson (attached 16th Brigade Pioneer Company). Bar to Military Cross: Captain C. R. Young, R.A.M.C. (attached). Distinguished Conduct Medal: Sgt. L. Hockenhull, L.-Corpl. H. L. Crittenden. Military Medal: Ptes. T. Thomas, G. Aspinall, L. Cartwright, A. Thwaites (attached 16th Brigade Pioneer Company), G. Rowson (attached 16th Brigade Pioneer Company) and Pte. R. Draper (attached 16th Brigade, T.M.B.). On June 9th the battalion relieved the 1st Buffs in the right sector of the Brigade front south-west of Hulluch. On the following day the 9th Suffolks (71st Brigade) on our left carried out a successful raid under cover of a smoke screen. The battalion executed a dummy raid, as a diversion, which succeeded in its purpose. During this operation 2nd Lieut. L. D. Chambers was wounded. The battalion was relieved on June 16th, and returned to billets at Mazingarbe and Fouquieres until the 29th, when it relieved the 1st Buffs in the front line. During the month Captain A. C. L. D. Lees joined and took over command of A Company. 2nd Lieuts. J. H. Corbet and C. B. Andrews joined and 2nd Lieut. R. I. Comins left on transfer to the Indian Army. Casualties, other than those referred to above: other ranks, 1 killed, 5 wounded. Reinforcements: 9 other ranks.

On July 7th at 2.55 a.m. a strong enemy raid was made on the sector held by the 1st K.S.L.I. After a severe bombardment, lasting for a quarter of an hour, a party of the enemy, about sixty strong, attempted to enter D Company's trenches. The raid was repulsed by rapid rifle fire and the assistance of two Lewis guns; the losses, however, were severe, amounting to 20 killed and 15 wounded. Later in the day 2nd Lieut. J. P. Hudson was wounded. In recognition of the gallant manner in which D Company held their line the following awards were made: Bar to Military Medal, Corpl. A. Murray. Military Medal, Corpls. H. Turner and H. Hewson, Ptes. E. Dix and J. R. Cooke (R.A.M.C. attached). 2nd Lieut. A. G. W. Browne (attached 16th Brigade, T.M.B.) was awarded the Military Cross. The battalion was relieved on the night of the 7th and returned to billets at Mazingarbe. The battalion returned to the trenches on the 12th, the sector remaining quiet until the 22nd, when the 6th Division was relieved by the 46th, and the battalion marched back to Houvelin and Rocourt, near St. Pol, to rest. During the month of July the following officers joined the battalion: 2nd Lieuts. F. W. A. Carter, D. Ractivand, J. M. Yarwood, B. E. Carter, S. T. R. Lloyd, D. B. Hasler, C. E. Parker. Major H. R. Mc-Cullagh, D.L.I., was attached as second in command. The following officers left the battalion during the month: Major H. A. R. Hoffmeister, on appointment as Brigade Major 4th Brigade, R.F.C., 2nd Lieut. C. H. O. A. Chester, on appointment as Town Major of Le Brebis, and 2nd Lieut. B. E. Carter to the Field Ambulance. On July 17th 2nd Lieut. R. W. Kirby was slightly wounded in the trenches at Hulluch. During the month Captain R. S. Whitmore, commanding D Company, and Lieut. T. S. Lanyon were awarded the Military Cross, and C.S.M. Derbyshire and Ptes. Hargreaves and Brown (R.A.M.C. attached) the Distinguished Conduct Medal.

During the first three weeks of August, 1917, the 6th Division were at rest, during which training was carried on vigorously. At the 6th Divisional Rifle Meeting the battalion distinguished itself by winning the Officers' Revolver Team Competition, in which Lt.-Colonel Winterscale, Captain Morris and 2nd Lieuts. Denyer, Kersey, Corbet and Busby represented the battalion. Sgt. A. V. Gough won the silver cup for the highest aggregate in the individual competitions, and Sgt. J. Blud the Running Man (individual) Competition. In all the 1st K.S.L.I. carried off thirty prizes.

On August 23rd the battalion returned by march route from Houvelin via Houchin to Mazingarbe, and on the 25th took over the village line in reserve north of Loos. On the 26th the battalion relieved the 4th Canadian Mounted Rifles in the front line at Hill 70, north-east of Loos, which, after the recent severe fighting, now became a quiet section of the line. During the month of August the following officers rejoined the battalion: Lieut. W. H. M. Roxby and 2nd Lieuts. J. N. Hilditch and N. V. Webber. 2nd Lieuts. M. H. Wright and L. W. Symonds joined on first appointment. 2nd Lieut. A. O. Kersey left for transfer to the Indian Army. Drafts amounting to 61 other ranks were received.

The first fortnight of September was spent in the reserve and front-line trenches north-east of Loos, and was one of hard work for all ranks building up the trench system and consolidating after the battle of August 15th–25th. Except for a raid on B Company's sector on the 6th, which was easily repulsed, the enemy remained quiet. On the 14th the battalion was relieved and marched via

Le Brebis into billets at Vaudricourt. On the 21st the battalion moved south via Bracquemont to trenches north of Lens on the Hill 70 front, where on the 28th 2nd Lieut. A. E. Lewis was killed in action. On the 30th the battalion withdrew in Brigade support to cellars in Cité St. Pierre. During the month of September, 1917, Lieuts. R. G. Thomson and J. Deedes joined the battalion, and 2nd Lieut. J. H. Corbet left on transfer to the R.F.C. The battalion continued in support at Cité St. Pierre, and in the trenches north of Lens, until October 17th. On the 8th, 2nd Lieut. J. H. Busby, the transport officer, was wounded at the ration dump, and on the 16th the enemy attempted a raid on A Company, otherwise the sector remained quiet. On the 17th the 6th Division was withdrawn for rest to the St. Hilaire area west of Lillers, and a week later commenced its march south to join the Third Army for the battle of Cambrai. The battalion proceeded via Le Brebis, Nœux-les-Mines, Honenghem and Ostreville to rest at Ivergny, arriving on October 30th. During the month Lieut. E. S. de V. Thomas was admitted to the Field Ambulance.

Time at Ivergny was spent in practising attacks with tanks until November 15th, when the battalion entrained at Bouque Maison for Peronne. From Peronne the battalion marched north to Moislans, arriving at 2.30 a.m. on the 16th, continuing the march at 6 p.m. to Dessart Wood, one mile north-east of Fins, where they encamped for the night.

BATTLE OF CAMBRAI, 1917

On the 19th the battalion left the camp in Dessart Wood and took up its assembly position for the attack timed for 6 a.m. on the 20th. The Hindenburg line, Banteux–Havrincourt–Mœuvres, in front of Cambrai, formed a salient at Havrincourt. The 6th Division, with the 20th Division on their right, and the 51st on their left, attacked on the front Villers–Plouich–Beaucamps, in the southern sector of the salient, with Ribecourt, and the spur to the south-east, as their first objective, an advance of some 3,000 yards. The final objective was the support system some 1,000 yards beyond. The Brigade attacked in three waves, the 2nd York and Lancs and 8th Bedfords, in the first wave, drove in the enemy outpost line, and reached the Hindenburg front line. At 6 a.m. the second wave, consisting of one Company the Buffs, on the right, and C Company K.S.L.I. on the left, passed through the first and established itself in the Hindenberg front line. Little opposition was encountered, though the Company came under heavy machine-gun fire from the direction of Ribecourt, when nearing its objective, which caused about 40 casualties. Three enemy machine guns were captured during the advance. At 7.10 the third wave, consisting of the remaining companies of the Buffs on the right, and K.S.L.I. on the left, continued the advance and reached the final objective—the Hindenburg support line. Captain Whitmore, commanding D Company, was killed, and Captain L. H. Morris, commanding B Company, and 2nd Lieut. Symonds, A Company, were wounded. About 20 other ranks became casualties. At 9 a.m. the 29th Division passed through the 6th and captured Marcoing. B Battalion of the Tanks, consisting of 36 tanks, advanced with the Brigade, and contributed greatly to the success of the attack.

The battalion moved forward on the 21st to a position 500 yards north-west of Marcoing in Brigade Reserve, whilst the Buffs, with the assistance of the Tanks, were clearing the villages of Premy Chapel and Noyelles. On the 27th the battalion was relieved by the 2nd Sherwood Foresters, and withdrew to Divisional Reserve in the Hindenberg support line. On the 30th a heavy enemy counter-attack was launched on the whole of the Third Army front. Gouzeaucourt was lost and retaken, and the 16th Brigade took up a position on the road between Gouzeaucourt and Villers. On the night of the 30th an attempt was made to gain the high ground between Gonnelieu and La Vacquerie. The battalion advanced,

but was checked by heavy machine-gun fire from Gonnelieu on the line of the railway between Villers Plouich
and Gouzeaucourt. The 2nd York and Lancs, on the
right, and the Buffs, on the left, were similarly held up.
Both flanks being now in the air, the battalion was forced
to fall back on its original line. At 6.30 a.m. the Guards,
with the assistance of tanks, succeeded in reaching the
high ground and capturing half of the village of Gonnelieu. On the night of December 1st/2nd the battalion
was relieved and returned to the Hindenburg support line.
At 10 p.m. on the 2nd the battalion relieved the 1st
Border Regiment (29th Division) on the east side of the
St. Quentin Canal, east of Marcoing railway station. The
whole position astride the canal was a salient subject to
shell, rifle and machine-gun fire from north, south and
east. The K.S.L.I. held the north of the loop across the
canal, the 14th D.L.I. the south. At 10.30 a.m. on the 3rd,
after an intense bombardment, the enemy attacked our
position in strong force, but was repulsed by rifle and
machine-gun fire. A second attack followed an hour later,
and after severe hand-to-hand fighting succeeded in
penetrating the line held by the 14th D.L.I. Shortly
afterwards the enemy succeeded in entering C Company's
lines, and the situation became extremely critical. The
enemy was in force on our right rear and the bridges over
the St. Quentin Canal had already been partly destroyed.
Orders were accordingly issued to withdraw to the west
bank of the canal at 2 p.m. Fighting with desperate
gallantry the battalion managed to extricate itself, many
officers and men swimming the canal, and finally rallied at
dusk in the Hindenburg support line. Our casualties were
heavy and included: 2nd Lieut. G. V. Blake killed,
Lieut. T. S. Lanyon missing. Captain Spink and 2nd
Lieut. O. Price (S.W.B. attached) shell shock, 20 other
ranks killed, 30 wounded and about 40 missing.
At 4.30 on the morning of December 4th the battalion
took up a position in Brigade Reserve on the Premy
Chapel ridge, one thousand yards west of Marcoing.

During the next two days, under Corps orders, the line was gradually withdrawn to the Hindenburg support line, which became our front line, and on December 9th the 6th Division was withdrawn to rest in the Basseux area south-west of Arras. The battalion proceeded via Sorel to Courcelle-le-Comte, five miles north-west of Bapaume, arriving on December 11th and being accommodated in huts. On the 17th, the 16th Brigade having been placed at the disposal of the 3rd Division to relieve a Brigade on the Bullecourt front, the battalion proceeded to Mory, and on the 20th relieved the 1st West Yorks Regiment in the front line south-east of Bullecourt. The sector was quiet, and on relief, two days later, the battalion returned by march route to rest at Courcelles-le-Comte, where they remained till the end of the year. Late in November 2nd Lieut. J. M. Yarwood left the battalion for the Field Ambulance, and in December Captain and Adjutant R. Bryans left to take up a staff appointment, Captain F. L. Platt taking over the duties of Adjutant. The following officers joined during December, 1917: Lieuts. J. D. G. Lewis, F. C. Armitage, G. P. Lloyd, S. G. White, A. C. Welbourne and 2nd Lieut. W. R. Green. The following awards in connection with the operations in November were announced: Bar to Military Cross, Captain R. Bryans, M.C.; Military Cross, Lieuts. F. W. A. Carter, H. E. B. de Gruchy, N. V. Webber and A. B. Rogers; D.C.M., C.S.M. A. Knight and E. T. Jones, Ptes. R. S. Orris and E. Lewis; M.M., Corpl. J. H. Watkins, L.-Corpls. White and Ryder, and Ptes. F. Chirgwin, G. Wells, C. Taylor and J. Leah. Mentioned in Despatches, Lt.-Colonel Winterscale, Brevet-Lt.-Colonel B. E. Murray, D.S.O., Captain and Qr.-Master J. W. Smith, C.S.M. A. Knight and Sgt. J. D. Moran.

On January 1st, 1918, the battalion left Courcelles-le-Comte and proceeded by march route to billets at Bailleulval, where they continued training until the 20th, when they returned to Courcelles-le-Comte. On the 21st, the 6th Division having relieved the 51st on the Hermies–

Boursies front, the battalion marched to Fremicourt, and five days later relieved the 2nd Sherwood Foresters (71st Infantry Brigade) in the right sector of the divisional front between Demicourt and Boursies. Quiet days followed and nothing noteworthy occurred until the battalion was relieved on February 3rd and proceeded to billets in Fremicourt. During January 2nd Lieuts. O. B. Haseler and O. Price left for the Field Ambulance, and the following officers joined: Captain F. T. Nott, 1/4th Herefords, 2nd Lieuts. F. E. A. O. Davenport and H. Christmas. Early in February, 1918, owing to shortage of man power, the Infantry Brigades were reduced from four battalions to three, and many battalions were disbanded, the 16th Brigade losing the 8th Bedfords. On February 15th Lt.-Colonel H. M. Smith, arrived from the disbanded 5th K.S.L.I. to take over command of the 1st K.S.L.I. from Lt.-Colonel Winterscale, who had been in command since late in 1916. The following officers from the 5th K.S.L.I. also joined during the month of February: Captain E. G. R. Lloyd, Captain H. T. Colbourne and 2nd Lieuts. H. B. Humbeck, L. A. T. Speer, E. H. Oldham and drafts amounting to 151 other ranks. On February 10th the battalion moved north, and on the 12th relieved the 8th Border Regiment in the trenches at Lagnicourt. On the 21st the battalion was relieved, and spent the remainder of the month in billets at Favreil. During the month 2nd Lieut. J. C. Jackson-Taylor joined the battalion.

On March 1st, 1918, the battalion was back in the line in front of Lagnicourt. The weather was fine but cold, and the sector exceptionally quiet. It was the lull before the storm, the enemy being fully occupied in organising for their last desperate effort. On March 3rd B Company, under 2nd Lieuts. O. B. Andrews, and W. H. Morris, with 50 men, raided an enemy post, known as " Magpie's Nest." The enemy fled, leaving the post unoccupied. The raiding party captured a machine gun, and during the return 2nd Lieut. Andrews was slightly wounded. The sector remained unusually quiet, but reports from enemy deserters that we were to be heavily attacked persisted; all kinds of rumours were current, and the battalion was constantly " standing to." The 6th Divisional front was on a forward slope opposite and south of the villages of Quéant and Prouville on a line Noreuil–Lagnicourt–Morchies. No Man's Land averaged about three-quarters of a mile, and the country was down land particularly suitable for tanks. Our trenches were on the ground wrested from the enemy in the battle of Cambrai of November, 1917, and having been hastily improvised were very imperfect for defence. The 16th Brigade, now only three battalions strong, was on the left of the Division, covering a front of some 1,500 yards. Each Brigade was covering its front with one battalion, with two battalions held in depth in the battle zone.

THE FIRST BATTLES OF THE SOMME, 1918

After a nerve-wracking fortnight of expectancy the German offensive began at 5 a.m. on March 21st with an intense bombardment which lasted for five hours. The infantry attack, launched with great dash and an overwhelming superiority of numbers, drove back the 59th Division, on the left of the 16th Brigade, into the outskirts of Noreuil, leaving the left flank of the 1st K.S.L.I., which was opposite Quéant and on the extreme left of the Division, in the air. The battalion had A and B Companies in the line, disposed along the front in posts, consisting of eight to ten men, some seventy yards apart. These two companies, in common with the garrison of the forward system all along the line, were almost annihilated in the first hour and a half of the bombardment, and by 7 a.m. the enemy was reported to be through. An hour later the enemy were reported through on our right. Lt.-Colonel Smith, commanding, went forward to D Company in reserve to lead a counter-attack, and Captain Platt, the Adjutant, went to investigate the position on the right. No news of A, B or C Company (in support) was received, all forward communication being cut, and on arrival at D Company the Colonel found them heavily engaged. Captain Platt was not seen again, and at 10 a.m., with both flanks in the air, the battalion was in a desperate situation. Sending back Lieut. Moody, 1st Buffs, and some thirty men of that battalion, to cover the retreat, Lt.-Colonel Smith decided to retire. Lieut. Moody was killed soon after leaving the Colonel, fighting to the last and refusing to surrender. Lieut. Jackson-Taylor, sent to ascertain whether Lieut. Moody's party was in position, was also killed, and when D Company commenced to retire they found the enemy already in their rear. Those of the battalion who had not already been killed at their posts were thus caught in a trap and surrounded. Without bombs or machine guns, the remnants of the 1st K.S.L.I. endeavoured to break out through the open with the bayonet, few being successful. When darkness fell the remnants of the battalion, less than 100 strong, were in the Corps line to which the whole Divisional front had been forced back. At 7.30 a.m. the survivors of the 16th Brigade, in the Haig line, were again heavily attacked, and fighting desperately the seventy odd survivors of the battalion under Lieut. A. B. Rogers, wedged between the 1st Buffs and the 2nd York and Lancs, were forced back on to Vaulx. At dusk the battalion (if such it can be called) received orders to retire to the G.H.Q. line behind Vraucourt. On the morning of the 23rd the battalion was relieved and, under Major H. de R. Morgan of the Buffs, proceeded to Achiet-le-Grand, and from thence, on the following day, by train from Puissieux to bivouac in the citadel at Doullens. On the 24th the battalion entrained at Doullens for Rousbrugge, seven miles northwest of Poperinghe, and marched to Chauny camp, where they arrived at 6.30 in the morning of the 26th for rest.

Unfortunately figures for the casualties in the 16th Brigade during the fighting of March 21st/22nd, 1918, are not available. Of the other two Brigades of Infantry in the Division it is recorded that, out of a strength of 1800 all ranks in each Brigade, the survivors in 18th Brigade numbered 8 officers, 110 other ranks; in 71st Brigade, 11 officers and 279 other ranks. Of those who took part in the fighting in the 1st K.S.L.I.. 77 other ranks survived on the evening of March 22nd. On arrival at the rest camp on March 25th the total strength 1st K.S.L.I. was 13 officers and 272 other ranks. Casualties in the battalion killed, wounded and missing for March 21st/22nd amounted to 21 officers and 492 other ranks.

The rest at Chauny, which the survivors of the 1st K.S.L.I. were anticipating, was denied them, for on the 25th the remains of the 6th Division was ordered north to join the Second Army in the Ypres salient, and on the 27th, the day following their arrival in the rest area, the battalion marched via Watou and Poperinghe to Hussar Camp in Potijze Wood, where it arrived on Saturday, March 30th, on the eve of Easter Day.

During March the following officers joined the battalion: Major H. P. Osborne, 1st Middlesex Regiment, and 2nd Lieut. T. Dutton. A draft of 14 other ranks was received. The following officers left the battalion during the first three weeks of March: Major A. C. L. D. Lees and Lieuts. W. H. M. Roxby and J. F. Addy, all to England for six months' home duty, and 2nd Lieut. H. Christmas to England, on transfer to the Machine Gun Corps. Officer casualties during March 21st included, killed: Captain F. L. Platt (Adjutant) and 2nd Lieuts. J. C. Jackson-Taylor and F. E. A. Davenport. Wounded: Lieut. R. G. Thomson, 2nd Lieut. H. V. Tucker, H. E. B. de Gruchy and 54 other ranks. Prisoners of War: Lt.-Colonel H. M. Smith, Major H. P. Osborne (Middlesex Regiment attached), Captain Bird, Captain Deedes, Lieuts. G. P. Lloyd (Hereford Regiment attached), A. C. Welbourne, N. V. Webber, S. G. White and 2nd Lieuts. L. A. Speer, W. H. Morris, H. W. D. Evans, M. Hatfield-Wright, A. W. Lepper, G. M. van Humbeck, and 388 other ranks. Those captured were marched from the line about 5 p.m., without food or water, by roundabout ways to Marc. One party, including Lieut. G. P. Lloyd, marched 50 kilometres and was 40 hours without food.

The first five days of April, 1918, were spent training in the camp in Potijze Wood. On April 3rd Lt.-Colonel G. Meynell arrived to take over command of the battalion from Major Morgan, who rejoined the 1st Buffs. On April 6th C and D Companies and Head-quarters relieved Head-quarters and two companies of the Buffs at Tokio and Retaliation Farms in the support line, being joined by A and B Companies two days later. On the 11th the battalion moved up to the front line, 2nd Lieut. D. B. Haseler and 2 other ranks being wounded during the relief. The front line here was really an outpost line, and on the night of the 15th/16th the line was withdrawn to the battle zone. The movement was successfully carried out, all stores being removed, water tanks destroyed, and the interior of " pill boxes " dismantled. The 1st K.S.L.I. withdrew to the support line in the ramparts at Ypres, and the trenches connecting with them. Whilst in the support line the battalion suffered severely from a number of heavy bombardments with gas shells. On the 23rd the battalion relieved the Buffs in the front line. On the night of the 26th/27th a further withdrawal was made to a line—west end of Zillebeke Lake—White Château. The remainder of the month, and the first few days of May, were spent in the support and reserve trenches under continuous shell fire, 2nd Lieut. F. H. Davies, S.W.B., attached, being wounded on the 28th. During the month of April, 1918, the following officers rejoined the battalion: Captain E. A. Freeman, Lieut. J. M. L. Grover and 2nd Lieuts. D. B. Haseler, J. D. G. Lewis, F. C. Armitage and O. B. Andrews. The following joined on first appointment: 2nd Lieuts. W. P. Bodman, A. Taffs, E. J. M. Corfield and 14 officers from the S.W. Borderers and Pembrokeshire Yeomanry. The following officers left for the Field Ambulance: Captain F. T. Nott, Major E. G. R. Lloyd, and 2nd Lieuts. B. E.

Carter, O. B. Andrews, and 2nd Lieut. W. G. Davies (S.W.B. attached). Drafts amounting to 427 other ranks were received. Casualties, other than those referred to above, amounted to other ranks: 3 killed, 104 wounded. The majority of the casualties were caused by gas from the gas shells.

On May 2nd Captain C. E. Parker, who had been acting Adjutant since March 22nd, was appointed Adjutant, and Captain E. A. Freeman took over the duties of second in command. On May 11th the 6th Division side-stepped into the II Corps area, in the southern sector of the salient, and after ten days in Divisional Reserve, during which they were working on the Vlamertinghe line, generally under fire, the battalion relieved the 11th Essex Regiment in the Zillebeke trenches on May 24th. Casualties during the period May 13th–24th included Captain G. P. Roch, Pembroke Yeomanry, killed on the 21st, and 2 other ranks killed and 4 wounded. The battalion remained in the trenches at Zillebeke, enjoying a comparatively quiet period, until the end of the month. On May 26th Lt.-Colonel G. Meynell left the battalion for the Field Ambulance, and was succeeded in temporary command by Captain E. A. Freeman. The following officers also left the battalion during the month: Captain D. H. Leslie, for attachment to the York and Lancs Regiment, and Captain Colbourn, and Lieuts. Taffs and Adams-Posner, to the Field Ambulance. 2nd Lieut. Rogers from 4th K.S.L.I. and 2nd Lieut. E. R. Wall, Welch Regiment, joined during the month.

The battalion was relieved in the line on June 7th, 1918, and the 6th Division went out to rest. Major D. H. Leslie rejoined from the York and Lancs Regiment and took over command from Captain Freeman on the 9th. After four days at School Camp, in the vicinity of St. Jan Ter Biezen, the battalion entrained at Proven on June 12th for St. Omer, and marched from there to Cormette Camp. After four days, spent on musketry at Cormette, the period of rest was unfortunately cut short, and on the 16th the battalion entrained again for Proven and marched to Ransford Camp, moving on the 21st to Dirty Bucket Camp for work on the Poperinghe Defence Line. On June 26th the 6th Division passed to the XIX Corps and relieved the 46th French Division (Chasseurs) in the Dickebusch sector, an unpleasant spot due to the dominating position of the enemy on Kemmel Hill. The battalion took over support trenches which remained quiet until the end of the month. During the month the following officers rejoined the battalion: Captain F. T. Nott and Lieut. J. D. G. Lewis from the base, 2nd Lieut. T. Dutton from Area Commandant Brandhoek, Lieut. F. C. Armitage from hospital, 2nd Lieut. D. Ractivand from 16th Trench Mortar Battery, and 2nd Lieut. E. J. M. Corfield and 29 other ranks from the Brigade Pioneers. The following joined: Lieut. J. A. Shelley and 2nd Lieuts. C. Stone, G. Matthews and A. T. Green. The following officers left for the Field Ambulance: Major E. A. Freeman, Lieuts. A. B. Rogers, and F. W. A. Carter, 2nd Lieuts. Oldham, Dutton and Scott. Casualties for the month of June: other ranks 2 killed, 4 wounded. The following were mentioned in despatches during the month: Lt.-Colonel G. Meynell, Lt.-Colonel C. F. B. Winterscale, Brevet-Lt.-Colonel B. E. Murray, Captain and Qr.-Master J. W. Smith and Sgt. T. G. Gardiner. A Divisional Order announced that the 1st K.S.L.I. headed the twelve units of the Division for good salvage work done during May. C.Q.M.S. Turner and Sergt. Blud received prizes as the best shots in the Brigade during the musketry training at Cormette Camp, and the battalion carried off eight out of thirteen prizes at the Brigade Sports.

The battalion remained in the southern neck of the salient (Kemmel–Dickebusch sector) throughout July whilst preparations were going forward for the recapture of Kemmel. On July 5th a German prisoner of the 174th Regiment surrendered to A Company, and generally speaking the enemy were " tails down," and there was little activity. On July 17th Lt.-Colonel Leslie left for the Field Ambulance, and Major Freeman took over command. About this time rumours of an impending attack by the enemy were current and our artillery was very active. Enemy retaliation caused some casualties, but no attack was made. Several more enemy prisoners surrendered during the month, and although all spoke of an impending enemy attack, none was made. On the 25th one company of the 27th American (New York) Division was attached to the 1st K.S.L.I. for instruction, and soon made themselves popular. Heavy work was put in by the battalion during the month on the Ouderdom line, and lack of sleep and rest caused a great deal of sickness. On July 23rd Major Freeman left for the Field Ambulance and Captain H. T. Colbourn, who had rejoined on the 14th, took over temporary command. On the 24th 2nd Lieut. D. Jones (S.W.B. attached) was killed and 2nd Lieut. C. Stone wounded during an enemy bombardment of the line. During the month the following officers left the battalion for hospital: 2nd Lieuts. E. A. Wall, H. J. Bunker (S.W.B. attached) and G. Matthews. The following rejoined: Captain L. H. Morris, and 2nd Lieuts. E. H. Oldham and T. Dutton. The following joined on first appointment: 2nd Lieuts. C. I. Goodfellow A. G. Beer, A. Bamber, W. E. Mason and L. B. Pritchard. Drafts amounting to 96 other ranks were received. Casualties for the month, other than those referred to above, amounted to 2 other ranks killed, and 2nd Lieuts. A. E. Martin, H. E. James (accidental) and 28 other ranks wounded.

The battalion was relieved on August 2nd and went into billets on the outskirts of Poperinghe, in Divisional Reserve, for a week. On August 8th Lt.-Colonel C. H. Cautley took over command of the battalion, which the same evening relieved the 2nd York and Lancs in the Ouderdom line. On the night of the 12th/13th the battalion moved up to the front line, relieving the 2nd Battalion of the 106th American Infantry Regiment, in the left sub-section of the Brigade front at Dickebusch. One platoon of A Company, 1st Battalion 107th American I. R., was attached to each company 1st K.S.L.I. for instruction. In the early morning of the 13th the enemy captured a post of A Company on the left of the line, consisting of an N.C.O. and 6 men. The post was re-occupied at dusk. Captain F. C. Armitage was wounded during the day. The enemy was very active in this section of the line, his sniping and Trench Mortar fire being very effective. Major-General J. F. O'Ryan, commanding the 27th American Division, visited the battalion in the line on the morning of the 14th. The battalion was relieved on August 19th by the 1st Battalion, 107th A. I. Regiment. Major L. H. Morris, with 1 officer per company and 1 N.C.O. per platoon, remaining in the line. On the 21st the 6th Division began to move south, being transferred again to the XIX Corps (1st, 6th, 32nd and 46th Divisions), and by September 3rd was concentrated in the Heilly–Ribemont–Franvillers area, on the River Ancre, south-west of Albert, in G.H.Q. Reserve. The 1st Battalion entrained at Remy siding at 1.45 in the morning of the 22nd, on the light railway running to Winnezeele. Here they re-entrained at seven in the morning for St. Momelin, three miles due north of St. Omer, arriving about 11 a.m. From St. Momelin the battalion marched to Quelmes, a very trying march in view of the heat and after the fatigue of the previous forty-eight hours, one man dying on the road. On the 28th the battalion marched via Licques to Tilques, where it arrived at 9 p.m. on the night of August 1st. Next day it moved to Arques and there entrained for Heilly in the rest area. At Licques, on August 29th, Lt.-Colonel Meynell rejoined and took over command again. During August, 1918, the following officers rejoined: Lieut. R. G. Thomson and 2nd Lieuts. R. C. Adams-Posner, J. H. Rees (Pembroke Yeomanry) and D. Ractivand and 30 other ranks from the R.E. course. The following joined on first appointment: 2nd Lieut. A. A. Evans (from 7th Battalion) and 2nd Lieuts. C. Sheppard and T. Brown. The following left the battalion: Captain C. E. Parker, the Adjutant, for attachment to 18th Brigade Staff, being succeeded in the duties of Adjutant by 2nd Lieut. G. S. E. Denyer, Captain C. M. Burmester and Lieut. J. P. Shelley (Cheshire Regiment) to the Field Ambulance. A draft of 48 other ranks was received. Casualties during the month: other ranks 11 killed, 40 wounded, 7 missing. Casualties amongst U.S. troops attached, other ranks 1 killed, 3 wounded.

The battalion spent the first ten days of September at Heilly practising attacks, and became quite skilful at training in open warfare. It was soon plain to all ranks that a " break through " was expected from the impending allied offensive, and there was a general feeling that victory was in sight. The battalion moved on the 11th to Aubigny, and on the 14th to Trefcon preparatory to the attack.

THE BATTLES OF THE HINDENBURG LINE

The Australian Corps and 32nd Division had won back the ground gained by the Germans in the March offensive, and during August had forced back the enemy on this front to Holnon Wood, three and a half miles west of St. Quentin, thus clearing the way for an attack on the Hindenburg line. The position to be attacked was one of great natural strength, as had been conclusively proved more than once before. On the 16th the 18th Brigade attacked and gained Holnon Wood, but failed to clear the village of Holnon east of the wood. Holnon Wood covered practically the whole of the 2,500 yards of the 6th Divisional front, and was so drenched with gas shells, and cut up by trenches and works, that the 16th and 71st Brigades had to make a detour round it to attack. The 16th Brigade advanced from the north of Holnon Wood with its right on the crest of the high

ground, where stood a strong point, known as the
" Quadrilateral " (similar to the one on the Somme
captured two years before), and its left on Fresnoy.
The attack opened at 5.20 a.m. on September 18th,
with the 2nd York and Lancs in the first wave, and with
the 1st Buffs on the right and the 1st K.S.L.I. on the left
in the second wave. The night was very dark with heavy
rain, and in the morning a thick mist obscured all land-
marks. The entire brigade became hoplessly mixed. An
advance of some 3,000 yards was made, but the attack
failed to establish itself in Fresnoy-le-Petit, which was
very strongly held. During the day Captain R. G. Thomson and 2nd Lieut. R. C. Adams-Posner were killed, and
Lieut. E. R. Wall, and 2nd Lieuts. W. James and H.
Gittins were wounded. Meanwhile the 71st Brigade on
the right of the 16th, and the French on their right, were
even less successful, making the position of the 16th
Brigade more difficult. At 1.30 a.m. on the 19th orders
were received to renew the attack on Fresnoy-le-Petit at
5.30. The battalion, hastily entrenched in an exposed
position, had great difficulty in circulating the necessary
operation orders in time. In spite of all difficulties, however, the attack was made, and B Company most gallantly
fought its way into the village. All officers became casualties and the Company, in isolated posts, remained in the
village, cut off from the battalion, and resisted throughout
the day all attempts to surround and capture them. At
dusk the survivors of B Company rejoined D Company,
now on the left of the battalion front. The following
casualties occurred on the 19th September. Wounded:
Captain R. A. Hoare, 2nd Lieuts. C. Shepherd, A. G.
Beer and E. J. M. Corfield. Casualties amongst other
ranks during 18th/19th amounted to approximately 176.
Although the situation on the evening of the 19th may
have seemed to the fighting troops disappointing, in actual
fact overwhelming difficulties had been met and in many
instances overcome, with the greatest courage and resolu-
tion. The " Quadrilateral " dominated the whole of the

ground, and the attack on the 19th, contrary to expectations, was anticipated by the enemy, and met with a carefully prepared artillery resistance of unsuspected intensity. In other words, the enemy was fully prepared to stand his ground instead of, as was supposed, fighting a rear-guard action. The Army Commander (General Rawlinson) wired on the 20th: " Please convey to the " 6th Division my congratulations and warm thanks for " their success of yesterday. Though all objectives were " not gained they carried through a difficult operation " with great gallantry and determination. I offer to all " ranks my warm thanks and congratulations." Owing to the severe losses and general disorganization, it was decided not to renew the attack for a few days, but to devote the interval to a thorough artillery preparation, and the reorganization of the infantry. Accordingly our guns put a thousand shells a day into the " Quadrilateral," and the 1st K.S.L.I. re-formed companies and consolidated their line. On the 21st Pte. Austin of B Company, three times wounded, crawled into the K.S.L.I. lines from Fresnoy-le-Petit. He reported that the Germans were killing our wounded in Le Fresnoy, he himself having been twice fired upon and hit after calling for help.

On September 24th the attack was renewed, and the 18th Brigade, on our right, advanced up to the face of the " Quadrilateral," while the 1st Division on our left attacked Fresnoy. The 1st K.S.L.I., with the 2nd York and Lancs on its left, worked round to the north of the " Quadrilateral," capturing 64 prisoners. That night the battalion was relieved by the 1st Buffs and withdrew into Brigade Reserve. Meanwhile at 11 p.m. the 18th Brigade launched a final and successful frontal attack on the " Quadrilateral." After desperate fighting the garrison surrendered, and by midnight on September 25th/ 26th the " Quadrilateral," a position of such strength that the German officers of the garrison regarded it as impregnable, was in our hands.

Casualties in the battalion during the advance on the 24th were, killed: Lieut. J. D. G. Lewis, 2nd Lieut. A. A. Evans and 12 other ranks. Wounded: Captain H. T. Colbourne, 2nd Lieuts. S. Adams, G. Matthews, E. T. Green and 64 other ranks. During the relief on the night of September 24th/25th Major L. H. Morris, commanding, was sent for by the G.O.C. 16th Infantry Brigade to receive his congratulations upon the " magnificent fighting " of the battalion during the day. The battalion remained in Brigade Reserve until the 29th when they were relieved by French troops, and proceeded to Tertry for rest. During September the following officers rejoined: Captain Colbourne, Lieut. F. W. A. Carter, 2nd Lieuts. G. Matthews, H. J. Bunker and A. Evans. The following left the battalion: 2nd Lieut. W. P. Bodman for traffic control duties, and 2nd Lieut. H. C. Brooke, as Town Major of Athies.

In the last days of September the 46th Division had broken the Hindenburg line north of St. Quentin, and forced the enemy over the canal. Pursued by the 32nd Division the enemy had fallen back to stand on a line Sequehart–Ramicourt, six miles north-east of St. Quentin. Meanwhile the French had taken St. Quentin. After a brief rest, spent by the 1st K.S.L.I. at Tertry, the 6th Division moved up to relieve the exhausted 32nd Division. The battalion left Tertry on the 4th and marched to shelters on the west bank of the St. Quentin Canal, in the neighbourhood of Bellenglise. On the following night it relieved the 1st Gloucester Regiment at Precelles Farm, 2nd Lieut. J. H. Rees being wounded during the relief. The 16th Brigade with Méricourt as their objective attacked at 5 a.m. on the 8th. The 1st K.S.L.I. formed the first wave of the attack, and getting to their work with great dash secured their objective (a sunken road east of " Mannikin Hill ") before six o'clock. According to plan the 1st Buffs then passed through, and later were passed by the 2nd York and Lancs, who made the final assault on Méricourt. Although the attack of the French and the 18th Brigade, on our right, was held up for some hours over the difficult task of capturing Bellecourt Farm and "Mannikin Wood," by 3 p.m. the right of the attack broke through, and by nightfall all objectives had been gained, and Méricourt was in our hands. Casualties during the day—Killed: 2nd Lieuts. J. A. Harrop and W. C. Duckworth (Welch Regt. attached). Died of wounds: Captain C. M. Burmester (S.W.B. attached) and 2nd Lieut. C. Pye. Wounded: Lieut. H. E. B. de Gruchy, 2nd Lieuts. T. Brown, T. Grant (S. Staffs), S. Walduck (S. Staffs), W. J. Reeves (S. Staffs) and 110 other ranks. Congratulatory messages were received from the Army and Corps Commanders on the brilliant successes achieved.

BATTLE OF CAMBRAI, 1918

At midnight on October 8th/9th orders were received that the battalion was to attack again at 5 a.m. in a new sector, on the 30th American Divisional front, on the left. With barely time to circulate the necessary orders, the battalion managed to reach the assembly positions just in time to attack at the time stated. A heavy mist made it difficult to keep direction, but by 6.30 the battalion had gained its objective, meeting but little opposition. Only scattered parties of the enemy remained, and when patrols were pushed forward the village of Fresnoy-le-Grand was found unoccupied, except for a remnant of the civilian population, which was sent back. The village, previously undamaged, was heavily shelled by the Germans at 10 a.m. Patrols were pushed forward along the Fresnoy–Bohain railway, and at nightfall the 71st Brigade on the left, working round by the north, captured Bohain, liberating some 4,000 inhabitants and capturing vast quantities of war material but comparatively few prisoners. On the evening of the 9th Lt.-Colonel Meynell left to assume command of the 171st Brigade, and Major L. H. Morris took over command. Captain J. M. L. Grover was wounded during the day, which left the battalion with only 6 officers: Major Morris, Lieut.

Denyer, the Adjutant, 2nd Lieut. Mason, A Company, Lieut. Carter, B Company, 2nd Lieut. Bannerman, C Company and 2nd Lieut. Pritchard, D Company. The 16th Brigade was in Divisional Reserve from October 10th–16th and the battalion enjoyed a brief period of rest. A congratulatory message was received from G.O.C. 6th Division on the success of the action of the 9th, which stated: "The difficulties were very great owing to "darkness, fatigue and the necessarily short time available, "and the disorganization after yesterday's battle, but they "were successfully overcome by the energy of Battalion "and Company Commanders."

BATTLE OF THE SELLE

On October 17th the battalion attacked from the south-east corner of Busigny Wood, and gained its objective without much difficulty, though suffering severely from enemy artillery fire, especially gas shells. The Buffs, and York and Lancs carried on the attack, followed by the units of the 2nd Infantry Brigade (1st Division). The attack was entirely successful. Casualties for the day amounted to about 25 per cent, including 2nd Lieut. H. J. Taylor (The Buffs, attached) killed, and Captain Young, the M.O., and Lieut. Carter gassed. The battalion remained in the captured trenches, moving to Regnicourt on the 18th and to billets in St. Martin Riviere and St. Souplet on the following day. The 18th Brigade attacked again on October 23rd, with the 16th Brigade in reserve, and on October 24th the 16th Brigade continued the advance in the Mazinghien sector. The battalion attacked with the 2nd York and Lancs on the left and, after stiff fighting, gained its objective. Lieut. G. Wildig was wounded, dying of his wounds a fortnight later. On the night of 24th/25th the battalion was relieved and moved to billets in Basuel, two miles south-east of Le Cateau. During the 26th, 27th and 28th, the 16th Brigade pushed forward with patrols as far as the village of Ors, encountering little opposition. The battalion

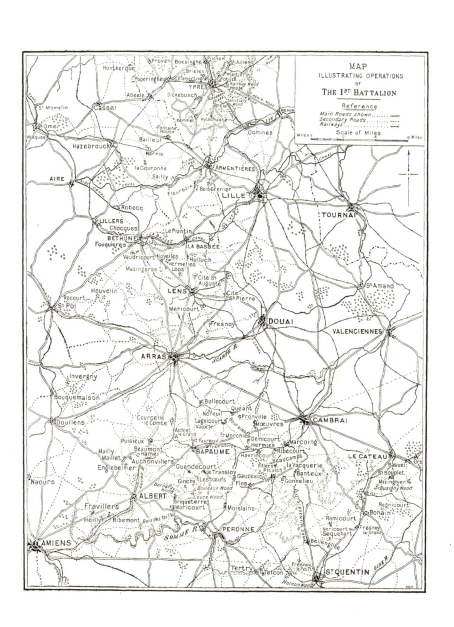

MAP
ILLUSTRATING OPERATIONS
OF
THE 1ST BATTALION

Reference
Main Roads shown.........
Secondary Roads.........
Railways.........
Scale of Miles

spent the 25th, 26th and 27th in Brigade Reserve, resting in billets at Basuel. On the 28th news of the unconditional surrender of Austria was received, and the end appeared to be in sight. At three o'clock in the afternoon the battalion relieved the 2nd York and Lancs in the front line. Patrols were sent out along the bank of the Ors canal, and three strongly situated enemy posts on the west bank were located. At three in the morning of the 30th three fighting patrols left the battalion lines to attack these enemy posts, two of which were vacated by the enemy, and the garrison of the third, consisting of three or four men only, was killed. This proved to be the last fighting the battalion was to see, for the 6th Division was relieved, and the 1st K.S.L.I. left the line on the night of October 30th for the last time, and marched via St. Souplet to Fresnoy-le-Grand, arriving on the evening of the 31st. During the first few days of October the following officers rejoined: Captains Burmester, Rogers and Parker, Lieut. de Gruchy and 2nd Lieut. Ractivand. On October 19th: Lieut. G. Wildig rejoined and 2nd Lieuts. J. T. W. Poole, L. R. Earp, A. T. Lawrence, H. Fellows, H. W. Wilson, F. Rampton, H. V. Lees, D. T. Harper, A. H. Woodland, E. G. Drew, C. V. Lightfoot, J. Maynall and E. E. Tyler joined on first appointment. On October 23rd Lieut. Roxby, and 2nd Lieuts. Ryder and Green rejoined. On October 2nd a draft of 209 other ranks from 10th K.S.L.I. and 2/5th Gloucester Regiment was received. During October 1918, the 1st K.S.L.I. captured 6 officers and 287 other ranks, 3 heavy machine guns, 24 light machine guns and 2 automatic rifles.

A further draft of 269 other ranks joined the battalion at Fresnoy-le-Grand on November 1st, and training was continued. On the 5th the battalion moved to Bohain, where they remained until after the Armistice. There was no special demonstration to celebrate the announcement of the cessation of hostilities on November 11th, only a general feeling of satisfaction

—possibly too deep to be lightly expressed—at having " finished the job," and beaten the Germans. After the Armistice the 6th Division passed to the 2nd Army, and joined in the advance into Germany. The battalion crossed the frontier at Malmedy on December 16th, and arrived at Fussenich, in the occupied territory, on December 23rd, remaining there until March, 1919. On March 22nd, 1919, the 6th Division, B.E.F. ceased to exist, and the 16th Brigade became the 2nd Midland Brigade. On April 18th, 1919, the 1st K.S.L.I. returned home.

The following served with the battalion throughout the war :—

Lieut. G. S. E. Denyer   Pte. W. Dobinson
R.S.M. J. Skirving   ,,   C. Bonehill
R.Q.M.S. T. Lloyd   ,,   R. Whitney
Sergt. J. Blud   ,,   F. Williams
   ,,   D. Moran   Bugler A. Williams

CHAPTER II

THE SECOND BATTALION

THE outbreak of the Great War in August, 1914, found the 2nd Battalion of the King's Shropshire L.I. serving at Secunderabad in India.

They sailed for England from Bombay, in the s.s. *Neuralia*, on the 13th October, forming part of an imposing convoy of forty-six transports, escorted by three British men-of-war. The following morning twenty-nine transports joined the convoy from Karachi. Since the German cruiser *Emden* was still at large, the convoy was forced to sail with due precautions, and no lights were allowed at night. Passing through the Mediterranean escorting warships were provided by the French, who were relieved again by the British Navy at Gibraltar.

After a good voyage the battalion landed at Plymouth in November, and since the warm clothing, sent out from England, for some reason missed connection at Aden, the troops were obliged to land in their thin Indian drill, and suffered considerably from cold. From Plymouth they moved to Winchester by train, and went into camp on Mourne Hill outside that town. On arrival they were cheered by a good breakfast, most kindly provided by the Duke of Cornwall's Light Infantry.

At Winchester they joined the 80th Infantry Brigade under General The Hon. C. G. Fortescue, C.B., C.M.G., D.S.O., in whose column in South Africa a detachment of the battalion had served in 1902. The Brigade consisted of:—

The 2nd Battalion King's Shropshire Light Infantry,
The 3rd Battalion King's Royal Rifle Corps,
The 4th Battalion King's Royal Rifle Corps,
The 4th Battalion The Rifle Brigade,
Princess Patricia's Canadian Light Infantry,

and formed part of the 27th Division, commanded by General T. D'O. Snow, C.B. A month was spent at Winchester, the time being taken up in route marching

F

and drawing war equipment and transport. The battalion was now organized into four companies. The colours were placed in Winchester Cathedral with those of other battalions of the Brigade. A draft was received from the 3rd (Special Reserve) Battalion, then at Edinburgh. The weather at Winchester was atrocious, the camp a sea of mud, and all ranks were glad when the order to proceed to France arrived.

The following is the list of Officers who went to France with the battalion :—

Lt.-Colonel R. J. Bridgford, D.S.O.
Major J. H. Bailey.

A Company

Captain C. E. Atchison
Lieut. J. S. Skinner
2nd Lieut. J. H. Mansfield
2nd Lieut. A. Davies

B Company

Brevet-Major C. A. V. Wilkinson
Lieut. L. J. B. Lloyd
Lieut. C. Holman
2nd Lieut. R. J. H. Green
2nd Lieut. F. H. Harris.

C Company

Captain C. W. Battye, D,S.O.
Captain C. F. B. Winterscale
2nd Lieut. H. Beacall
2nd Lieut. G. C. Bannister
2nd Lieut. T. Lloyd
2nd Lieut. A. J. Talbot

D Company

Captain H. G. Bryant, D.S.O.
Captain C. M. Vassar-Smith
Captain J. C. Plowden
2nd Lieut. E. V. T. A. Spink
2nd Lieut. V. H. Crane

Adjutant
Quartermaster
Transport Officer
Machine Gun Officer
Medical Officer

Captain F. J. Leach
Captain E. Lewis
Lieut. W. E. Shaw
2nd Lieut. G. D. Farrer
Lieut. D. Bell, R.A.M.C.

The battalion marched from Winchester to Southampton on the 20th December, 1914, and embarked for France, on the s.s. *Maidan*, the same afternoon. Shortly before sailing it was discovered that three men, who had been ordered to remain with the Details, had smuggled themselves on board, without any arms or accoutrements. Their keenness was appreciated and they were allowed to sail.

Disembarking at Havre the following day, the battalion moved up to Aire by train on the 23rd, and went into billets about Blaringhem for twelve days, where the time was occupied digging trenches, usually in the rain.

Colonel Bridgford, Major C. A. V. Wilkinson and other officers were taken up in buses, and shown round the trenches by the Suffolk Regiment in front of Kemel.

Sir John French and Sir Horace Smith-Dorrien inspected the battalion. The latter, in whose 19th Brigade the battalion had served in the South African war, expressed his pleasure at having the 2nd K.S.L.I. under his command again. The 27th and 28th Divisions had now been formed into the V Corps commanded by Sir Herbert Plumer. This corps joined the 2nd Army under Sir H. Smith-Dorrien. On January 5th, 1915, the battalion marched to billets about Strazeele, and the next day to Meteren, *en route* for the front line.

Before following them into the trenches it is necessary to say a few words concerning the state of the front about to be taken over from the French by the 27th Division. The weather had been atrocious; heavy rains, frost and gales of wind had succeeded each other without a break. The ground was so sodden that movements of troops had become almost impossible, and the trenches well-nigh uninhabitable. As a result the men were going sick in large numbers with trench feet, and other ailments. To crown all the St. Eloi sector, which we were about to take over, was perhaps the worst on the whole of the British front. Such was the prospect facing the 27th Division, composed of men who had just come from India.

To return to the battalion, they marched on January 9th from Meteren to Dickebusch, and thence to Kruisstraathoek, where they were posted in support of the rest of the 80th Brigade, already in the trenches. On the 8th the battalion had its first taste of shell fire. About midday the enemy started shelling, and companies were forced to leave their billets and take refuge in ditches and trenches. One private was killed and 15 wounded. At dusk the battalion moved to Vormezeele, and took over trenches in front of the village from the 4th Rifle Brigade.

During the move up to the line the battalion became strung out in the pitch darkness, owing to French guns and transport forcing their way along the road at the same time. The noise of their wheels on the *pavé* was deafening, and it was impossible, when trying to get the companies together, to distinguish whether a man belonged to B, C or D Companies. For this reason Colonel Bridgford altered the distinguishing letters of the companies to W, X, Y and Z, by which letters they are still known.

The relief was successfully accomplished, and two days were spent in the trenches, standing knee-deep, and often nearly waist deep, in mud and water, in bitterly cold weather. Shelling on the first day, and the usual sniping, were the only hostile activities experienced, but exposure to cold and wet were to prove far more deadly than the enemy's attentions. On the night of the 10th the 2nd Gloucesters took over the trenches, and the battalion returned to billets at Dickebusch.

It was a pitch-dark night and very wet, the German Véry lights providing the only light. In spite of their fitful illumination, however, Colonel Bridgford took an involuntary cold bath in a " Jack Johnson " shell hole. The next day the battalion marched to Boescheppe, and was billeted in the church, a cold and comfortless home. Although only forty-eight hours had been spent in the trenches, some three hundred officers and men were unable to march owing to frost bite, and many of these were not fit again for several months. The 12th January

THE SECOND BATTALION. FEBRUARY, 1915

was spent resting, and all ranks enjoyed a hot bath. The next day the battalion returned to Dickebusch, but now only 500 strong, the sick and the lame being left behind under command of Major C. A. V. Wilkinson, who became Town Major of Boescheppe, commonly called " Bo-peep."

After another tour of the trenches, the battalion returned on the 16th for a week at Westoutre. Westoutre was then looked on as a kind of earthly paradise, where hot baths and many other comforts were obtainable. Battalion Head-quarters enjoyed the hospitality of the nuns in the convent, who showed them every kindness in their power.

On the 24th the battalion was in the trenches again, in billets at Dickebusch on the 27th, back in the trenches for another forty-eight hours' spell on the 28th. During this last tour Captain C. E. Atchison, Lieut. A. N. Davies and 4 other ranks were wounded. Captain C. E. Atchison, one of the soundest and most popular officers who ever served in the regiment, was evacuated with his wound never to return to the battalion, and later died, gallantly leading a service battalion of the Yorkshire Light Infantry, in the Third Battle of Ypres.

On the 31st the battalion relieved the P.P.C.L.I. in the trenches at St. Eloi, which was soon to become the centre of a grim struggle. In forty-eight hours they were relieved by the 4th Rifle Brigade, and after spending a day at Dickebusch returned to rest billets at Westoutre until the 9th of February. That evening they relieved the Argyll and Sutherland Highlanders in the line, where they remained till relieved by the 4th Rifle Brigade forty-eight hours later. During this tour Captain J. S. Skinner shot a German sniper in the top of a tree. He reported that the Hun came down with a most gratifying thud.

The St. Eloi front was now becoming more lively as the casualties, since the 1st of February, amounting to 5 other ranks killed, Lieut. J. O. Farrer and 10 other ranks wounded, testify. Lieut. E. V. T. A. Spink was also wounded while passing through Vormezeele but refused to leave his men. The 13th February was spent at Dickebusch, where a draft of 180 N.C.O.'s and men was received.

On the evening of the 14th the 82nd Brigade carried out a counter-attack, and succeeded in retaking four trenches, near St. Eloi, which had been taken by the enemy the previous night. The 80th Brigade was ordered to support this operation, the battalion " standing to " all night at a farm near Dickebusch. On the 15th they relieved the 4th Rifle Brigade in the trenches for another forty-eight hours, during which their casualties were 5 killed and 14 wounded.

On the 17th another draft of 164 N.C.O.'s and men was received, these drafts helping to make good the heavy losses from " trench feet." The 20th and 21st again saw the battalion in the trenches, where, on the 21st, the 28th Division, which was on the left of the 27th, had a good deal of hard fighting, losing and regaining several trenches. In spite of these incidents in their neighbourhood, the battalion's losses during this tour were but 2 killed and 3 wounded. On the 23rd the 2nd K.S.L.I. returned to Westoutre until the 26th, being back again at Dickebusch on the 27th. The next day the P.P.C.L.I. carried out a very dashing attack, capturing a German trench, which they levelled and made untenable. During this action the battalion stood to arms at Dickebusch, ready to support the attack if required.

During the first ten days of March, 1915, the battalion had three tours of duty in the trenches at St. Eloi, which took heavy toll, the casualties totalling 3 officers, Lieuts. W. D. Vyvyan, G. R. Venables and F. C. Bird killed; 3 officers, Captain W. J. Brooke, Lieuts. A. C. P. Biddle-Cope and C. Holman wounded ; 20 other ranks killed and 52 wounded. Lieuts. Vyvyan and Bird both fell gallantly leading bombing attacks in an effort to regain a trench which had been lost on our left. Lieut. Venables, who had joined from the 3rd Battalion on the 5th February, had made himself deservedly popular with all ranks. Many of these losses were caused by a heavy trench mortar the enemy had brought up, which did a lot of damage to our line, and rendered some of the trenches untenable

On March 10th the battalion temporarily withdrew from the foremost trenches to enable our artillery to carry out a heavy bombardment of the enemy trenches. During these tours several reports were sent in by the battalion that the enemy was mining under its position. Unfortunately these reports were disbelieved, being apparently attributed to " nerves." They were correct, however, and the mine was about to cost us dear.

About this time an amusing incident occurred. Lieut. L. J. B. Lloyd was having breakfast in the front line, whilst the enemy was making a nuisance of himself with bombs. Annoyed at the constant interruptions, Lieut. Lloyd threw a half empty tin of marmalade into their trench. The enemy, taking this for one of our jam-tin bombs, was heard scuttling away down his trench, and no further interruptions occurred.

On the 10th March the British attack at Neuve Chapelle started and led to three days' heavy fighting, with the result that the British remained in possession of considerable gains, in spite of heavy German counter-attacks. On the 14th the enemy attempted a counterstroke at St. Eloi to avenge this defeat; the 82nd Brigade holding the line there at the time. To the south-east of the village of St. Eloi there was a mound some seventy feet long and twenty high. This mound commanded the flat ground all round, and with trenches on either side of it formed part of our defensive system. After a short but heavy bombardment the enemy exploded a mine under the mound. His infantry attack, which followed, succeeded in capturing the mound, together with several fire and support trenches in the neighbourhood, as well as the southern end of the village.

THE KING'S SHROPSHIRE LIGHT INFANTRY

At 7 p.m. the battalion was called out and marched up to Dickebusch. A counter-attack by two battalions of the 82nd Brigade had made some progress, but was held up by machine-gun fire from the mound and trenches on each side of it. About 4.30 on the morning of the 15th the 80th Brigade was called on to attack the mound, and neighbouring trenches. It moved forward with the 4th Rifle Brigade leading on the right, and Princess Patricia's Light Infantry on the left. The battalion and the 3rd K.R.R.C. followed in support. The Canadians could accomplish little against the machine-gun fire from the mound, but, on the right, the Rifle Brigade regained several trenches, all their efforts against the mound, however, were unavailing. W and Y Companies of the battalion were then brought up. Day was already breaking, however, and their advance was stopped in its turn by the enemy's machine guns. Captain C. M. Vassar-Smith was severely wounded at the head of his company, when close to the enemy's position; it was impossible to get him in until the following night, and his leg had subsequently to be amputated. Other casualties were 4 killed and 24 wounded. Later in the morning Colonel Bridgford was ordered to retake the mound with the battalion during the following night. These orders were, however, countermanded in the afternoon, and the enemy was left in possession until the Battle of Messines in June, 1917, when he was blown up in turn by our mines.

On the 16th the battalion relieved the D.C.L.I. in the trenches, being relieved in turn by the Rifle Brigade on the 18th. During this tour Lieut. L. H. Torin (employed at Brigade Head-quarters) and 13 other ranks were wounded, and 4 other ranks killed. Battalion Head-quarters was in the well-known Bus House, so named from a derelict motor bus stranded on the road just outside. One evening the enemy took a special dislike to the Bus House and rendered it untenable with his shells. The garrison, consisting of the Adjutant, R.S.M., signallers and orderlies, led by the Colonel, who acted as section Commander, retired, extended to six paces, giving a fine display of how to retire under fire. On re-occupying the house later a curious mixture of kit, rations, and debris was found.

The night of the 19th was spent digging trenches at St. Eloi, the 20th and 21st in the trenches again; this tour costing 19 casualties. On the 24th the battalion marched back to rest at Reninghelst until April 5th. Here the time was spent at company drill, musketry, machine gun and grenade training. The battalion was inspected by Sir Horace Smith-Dorrien and Sir Herbert Plumer, the former in his address saying that he knew well with what difficulties the 27th Division had had to contend during the last three months—such difficulties as probably no other division had had.

On April 5th the battalion left Reninghelst and, on the 7th, entered the Ypres salient, relieving the Argyll and Sutherland Highlanders, and the 268th French Infantry, in the trenches at Polygon Wood. The next fortnight was passed in tours of 48 hours in the line, alternating with spells of 48 hours in billets in Ypres. Casualties during these tours amounted to 6 other ranks killed and Lieuts. L. J. B. Lloyd, D. Bell, R.A.M.C., and 23 other ranks wounded. In addition to these losses Lieut. G. Holman, a most promising young officer, was unhappily killed by a shell in the front line on April 9th.

The battalion also had the misfortune to lose its popular and efficient Adjutant, Captain F. J. Leach. He was not often allowed to go round the front line, but on this occasion he asked leave to go, and the Commanding Officer, who had himself just returned at 3 a.m. from a tour of the line, consented. Captain Leach having completed his round started back in the early morning twilight across country, instead of along the communication trench. He was spotted by a German sniper and received a wound in the head, to which he succumbed a few days later in a hospital at Boulogne. Lieut. H.

Beacall, who was with Captain Leach, made a gallant effort to drag his body under shelter, the Germans on this occasion chivalrously withholding their fire.

THE BATTLES OF YPRES, 1915

On April 22nd, 1915, began the Second Battle of Ypres, which opened with the great German gas attack. The allied front in the neighbourhood of Ypres was occupied as follows: The Belgians held the Yser Canal to Bixschoete; from there French Territorial and Colonial troops carried the line eastwards to the Ypres–Poelcapelle Road. Here they were joined to Plumer's V Corps, consisting of the Canadians on the left, the 28th Division in the centre and the 27th Division on the right, holding a line which passed a mile north of Zonnebeke and circled round outside Polygon Wood to where it joined up with the 5th Division, which held Hill 60. The average distance of this line from Ypres was about five miles.

The opening of the battle found the battalion with three companies in the support dug-outs in Bellewaerde Wood, and Z Company at Polygon Wood. At 5 p.m. the enemy started with a terrific bombardment of the French line, and the left of the Canadian Division. At the same time jets of whitish vapour were seen to issue from the German trenches. These grew into a considerable cloud, which, driven by a northerly wind, drifted swiftly across the space separating the two lines. The French Infantry were overwhelmed by this diabolical agency; many gasped out their lives where they stood, others rushed madly out of the devilish cloud retiring behind the canal or to Ypres. The Germans meanwhile advanced and took possession of the trenches now only defended by the dead and dying. By 7 p.m. there was a gap of five miles in the allied lines.

The enemy, who had passed through this gap, turned eastwards to roll up the Canadian line. The left brigade of the latter, realizing their danger, threw out a new flank to the south-west; reserves and supports counter-attacked, the guns swung round from north to west, and poured shrapnel into the advancing masses at a range of 200 yards. All night the Canadians held their original front, while fighting this new enemy on their flank and rear, so that by daylight on the 23rd, the enemy had only penetrated to a depth of two miles through the five-mile gap. The Germans were now faced by a weak British line, with many gaps in it, stretching from near St. Julien, which had become the centre of a dangerous salient, to about a mile south of Boesinghe where we had regained touch with the French.

BATTLE OF ST. JULIEN

The battalion, sent across from Bellewaerde Wood, occupied a portion of this line, digging themselves in near Verlorenhoek and holding, with two companies of the 4th Rifle Brigade, a front of nearly a mile and a half. The enemy, however, not realizing what slender forces stood between him and his goal, failed to press his advantage. Further reserves of the 27th and 28th Divisions were hurriedly collected and sent north, not only to strengthen the overstretched line, but with orders to attack the enemy so as to gain time for reinforcements to arrive from other parts of the British line. The battalion also received orders to attack the Vaal Capelle Ridge, but these were cancelled. By the evening of the 24th the battalion was again collected in Bellewaerde Wood with Z Company in Polygon Wood. On the 25th it marched to Verlorenhoek as escort to the guns and spent the day digging trenches.

The fighting had now extended southwards and the trenches of the 28th Division were heavily attacked. The battalion was lent to the 85th Brigade of that Division. In the evening of April 25 X Company, Captain Pound, and Z Company, Captain Bryant, the whole under Major G. Meynell, were sent up to the extreme apex of the salient, near Broedesiude, to retake a communication trench in the 28th Division area, which the enemy had captured from the East Surrey regiment in the middle of our front line. They reached a sunken road, half a mile beyond Zonnebeke, and here it was decided, after a reconnaissance had been made, that the attack should be undertaken by two platoons of Z Company. No. 13 (Lieut. C. R. Blackett) led, with No. 14 (Lieut. E. V. T. A. Spink) in support. Lieut. A. C. P. Biddle-Cope with his machine guns co-operated.

The enemy was too strong and the attack failed with the loss of all the officers engaged. Lieut. Biddle-Cope, who was killed, was last seen standing on the German parapet, with a revolver in each hand, firing into the trench, having gallantly left his machine guns, and rushed forward to join in the assault. Captain Bryant, who had a high standard of duty and was absolutely without fear, also went over with his company, and reached the German line, where he was shot down. He succumbed later to his wounds in a German Hospital, his widow afterwards receiving a letter from the German Staff praising his bravery. Lieut. Blackett, another gallant officer, was killed, and Lieut. Spink wounded.

Captain J. R. Pound's company then made an equally gallant but unsuccessful attempt. Lieut. R. du B. Evans led this attack, and actually reached the enemies trench, where he was wounded and taken prisoner. Our casualties among other ranks amounted to 32. It was found that the enemy had connected the captured trench up to his own line, making it an exceedingly strong position, well garrisoned with machine guns. The attackers, after deploying on a front of barely fifty yards, had to advance over very rough ground, and at an angle to their line of deployment, making it very difficult to keep the correct direction. Artillery support was practically non-existent, owing to the shortage of telephone wire, and the impossibility of registering the batteries. Efficient bombs and trench mortars were unfortunately not available at this period of the war.

X and Z Companies now took over the trenches, adjoining the communication trench they had just attacked, from the East Surrey Regiment. Here Captain J. R. Pound, who had left his desk at Shrewsbury School to fight, was killed.

The battle continued on the 26th with unabated fury about St. Julien, and along the front of the 28th Division. W and Y Companies were occupying the trenches near Verlorenhoek which they had dug the previous day. About 10 a.m. they were ordered to take up a position on a ridge, about a mile to the front, as the enemy were advancing. They were heavily shelled with gas and high-explosive shells during the advance, but it was not until they reached, and occupied, some shallow trenches on the top of the ridge that they began to suffer. The cover given by these trenches was very slight, and little could be done to improve them under the heavy shell fire. About 5 p.m. the two companies, together with the 6th and 7th Battalions of the Durham Light Infantry, which had only arrived from England the day before, all under the command of Colonel Bridgford, were ordered to advance to the aid of our front line, a portion of which was said to be cut off and surrounded by the enemy. The advance was carried out under heavy shell fire, W Company leading. No hostile infantry was met with, and the post, which was supposed to be in need of succour, was found holding its own quite unconcerned. W and Y Companies were withdrawn to Zevecoton for the night, their casualties amounting to 4 other ranks killed, Captain C. W. Battye, Lieuts. H. D. Beadon and E. D. Collins, and 37 other ranks wounded.

On the evening of the 27th Colonel Bridgford received orders to attack the same communication trench which X and Z Companies had already attempted to carry. By 11 p.m. W Company, 140 strong, under Lieut. L. J. B. Lloyd, and Y Company, 90 strong, under Lieut. F. W. Voelcker, had arrived at the Head-quarters of the East Surrey Regiment. Here they halted to make the necessary arrangements for the attack. Artillery support was arranged for, and each company was given its portion of the enemy's trench to attack. Communication trenches led up to within 100 yards from the enemy, and were utilised as " jumping-off places " from which to assault. By 2.30 a.m. all was ready, and at 2.40 a.m. the signal to attack was given. Both companies climbed out of their trenches, and rushed forward simultaneously. The enemy appeared to reserve his fire until they were some thirty yards distant, when a very heavy rifle and machine-gun fire was poured into them. Several officers and men reached the German parapets, but were unable to get into the trenches, and eventually the attack fell back. Apart from the strength of the enemy, the probable cause of the failure was the early loss of all the leaders, and the light of the moon, which made the attackers plainly visible. Later on a whole brigade failed to capture this same position. The losses of the two companies amounted to 23 other ranks killed and missing, Lieut. A. H. Walker and 28 other ranks wounded. In addition Lieuts. L. J. B. Lloyd and F. W. Voelcker were reported missing. The former, a capable and popular young officer, was later found to have been killed, the latter became a prisoner of war.

On the 28th the battalion returned to the 80th Brigade, and were concentrated in support in Bellewaerde Wood, where they were kept busy digging a new line of trenches until 2nd of May. After leaving the 85th Brigade, Colonel Bridgford received the following letter from Br.-General A. J. Chapman:—

" Will you please convey to your officers, N.C.O.'s and " men the high appreciation of myself and all the 85th " Infantry Brigade for their gallant conduct and work " whilst attached to this brigade, especially with refer- " ence to the gallant attempt to retake the trench in the " East Surrey trenches on the night of the 27th instant. " Your losses in officers and men are deeply deplored, " and all of us deeply sympathise with your regiment in " your great losses.

" As regards yourself I shall for ever feel indebted to
" you for your great assistance and help in a very trying
" time."

On the 3rd of May the enemy renewed his attack on the
28th Division, and on its neighbours on the left, now
the 4th Division, which had relieved the remnants of the
Canadians. The battalion was moved up north of Potijze
as a precaution, but did not come into action. That night
the British line was readjusted, the chief retirement
taking place on the front of the 27th Division, which was
still holding the trenches it occupied at the beginning
of the battle.

The battalion was ordered to occupy the new front line
at Bellewaerde, and allow the P.P.C.L.I. to retire through
them. These orders were however cancelled, and the
battalion was sent up towards St. Julien, where, with
battalions of the Cameron and Argyll and Sutherland
Highlanders, it covered the retirement of the 28th
Division. The retirement, though in some places from
within a few paces of the enemy's lines, was accomplished
successfully. The Battle of St. Julien was now at an end.
Probably troops have never been more highly tested.
Gas, a new terror, and a most serious one for troops who
were without respirators, heavy artillery bombardments, to
which our guns could make no corresponding reply, and
overwhelming machine-gun fire, all contributed to the
odds our men had to face. The enemy it is true had gained
ground, but the road to Ypres was still barred.

During this battle the total losses of the battalion
amounted to 11 officers and 153 other ranks killed,
wounded and missing.

By the evening of the 4th May the adjustment of the
British line was complete. The order of battle from north
to south was the French Corps on the left, and the 4th,
28th, 27th and 5th British Divisions; the 80th Brigade
holding the line on the Ypres–Menin road by Hooge
Château.

That evening the 2nd K.S.L.I. relieved the P.P.C.L.I.

in the trenches opposite Westhoek. The shelling was exceptionally severe, the enemy using gas as well as high-explosive shell. Casualties on the 5th amounted to Lieut. Turner slightly wounded, 29 other ranks killed, 32 other ranks wounded. On the 6th 30 other ranks were killed and wounded. That evening the battalion was relieved by the P.P.C.L.I. and was withdrawn to G.H.Q. line at Potijze, which it was set to repair, losing 12 other ranks killed and wounded during the day.

BATTLE OF FREZENBERG RIDGE

By the 8th of May the enemy's preparations were complete and the Battle of the Frezenberg Ridge, which was to last for six days, commenced. At first this consisted almost entirely of an artillery attack, which raged with remorseless fury along the front of the 4th, 28th and 27th Divisions. A ceaseless rain of huge shells fell with deadly precision, smashing in the trenches and burying their defenders. At the same time great drifts of gas came over. After a day of this terrible pounding an infantry attack developed, the chief weight of which fell on the 28th Division in the Frezenberg trenches. Their losses from shell fire had been very heavy and the line was too weak to resist. Their right was forced back, opening a gap between the 27th and 28th Divisions. The left of the 27th Division was held by Princess Patricia's Canadian Light Infantry, who firmly held their ground though their flank was turned.

The battalion and a party of the 4th Rifle Brigade were sent up to reinforce them and fill up the gap between the two divisions. A defensive flank was organised and held, under very heavy shell fire, and all attempts by the enemy's infantry to exploit their success were frustrated. Meanwhile reserve battalions of the 4th and 28th Divisions were collected to counter-attack. They were partially successful and re-occupied the village of Frezenberg, but the nett result of the battle was a further restriction of the area held by the British. The casualties of the bat-

talion were Lt.-Colonel J. R. Bridgford, Lieuts. W. E.
Shaw and T. C. N. Hall wounded, 10 other ranks killed,
and 25 wounded. Lieut. W. E. Shaw, who died of his
wound, was the battalion transport officer, who had been
put in command of a company, owing to the shortage of
officers. He had quickly proved his worth in the trenches
and his loss was deeply deplored. Major J. H. Bailey now
assumed command of the battalion.

On the night of the 8th of May the battalion was
ordered to hold the trenches from Bellewaerde Farm to
the Railway. As this line proved to be too extensive,
a portion of it, on the left, was occupied by a battalion
of the Royal Fusiliers. On the 9th about 6 a.m. the enemy
started shelling our line and continued until 2 p.m.,
all firing then ceased for about half an hour, when it
suddenly recommenced with increased intensity working
systematically up and down the line. Soon after four
o'clock the shelling developed into an absolute furnace
of fire. For twenty minutes this rain of shells continued.
Shells of every description, from " Jack Johnsons " to
9-pounders, fell in and about our trenches. Suddenly it
ceased. It was obvious that an infantry attack was coming, and an order to clean rifles was passed along.

Almost at once a line of Germans appeared over the
crest of the hill some 250 yards in front. This line was
followed by a second and then a third. On they came,
shoulder to shoulder, their lines stretching right across
the front. The troops hailed this apparition with deep
satisfaction; here at last was something they could deal
with. The enemy was met with a heavy and accurate
fire. His lines melted away, some lay down, some turned
and ran. Then it was seen that many of the enemy were
wearing British uniform, and these came on shouting to
our men. The battalion took no notice, but continued to
fire. The Royal Fusiliers, however, ceased firing, though
only for some twenty seconds, but it was twenty seconds
of valuable time lost.

The enemy rallied and came on again over the ridge.

He was again met by a heavy fire, which he could not face, but turning round fled in disorder. This brought to an end a really satisfactory infantry fight, which made up to the troops for a great deal of their sufferings under the appalling bombardment they had endured.

During this bombardment Lieut. H. Beacall, a promising young officer, was killed. He had on a previous occasion been recommended by Colonel Bridgford for the V.C., but, owing to the lack of surviving eye-witnesses to his bravery, this decoration could not be awarded him. The following messages were received:—

" The Corps Commander wishes to express to all ranks " his admiration for the gallant stand they have made to-"day, of which he has informed the Commander-in-Chief."

Later the Division wired:

" The Corps Commander has just been here and is lost " in admiration for the way in which the Shropshires, " 3rd and 4th K.R.R.C. and the Rifle Brigade are sticking " this heavy bombardment."

On the 10th the enemy continued his bombardment of our trenches, though not with the same intensity as on the previous day. In the evening Majors W. J. Rowan Robinson, C. A. Wilkinson and Lieut. A. H. St. G. Hamersley arrived at Battalion Head-quarters. This was a most welcome reinforcement, as there was a very serious shortage of senior officers.

On the 11th and 12th the enemy continued shelling our trenches. On the latter day a very heavy bombardment was opened on Railway Wood, in which Battalion Head-quarters were posted, and on the support trenches. Head-quarters evacuated their dug-out, and sought a more sheltered locality. Later on, when the shelling slackened somewhat, Majors Rowan Robinson and Wilkinson returned to get their equipment. While in the dug-out a shell came through the roof and burst inside, killing them both, together with four other officers and four men of other units who were there. This was a great loss to the battalion, as both were exceptionally capable and experienced officers.

Major Rowan Robinson had served with the 1st Battalion during the first few months of the war. Major Wilkinson, a particularly keen soldier, who had seen considerable service in South and West Africa, had foreseen this war, and prepared himself for it by hard study and training in peace time, and would doubtless have risen to high rank had his life been spared. The losses of the last four days, chiefly incurred on the 9th, amounted to 122 other ranks killed and wounded, in addition to the officers already mentioned, bringing the battalion's total losses for this battle up to 7 officers and 282 other ranks. Lieut. A. H. St. G. Hamersley succeeded Lieut. Beacall as adjutant.

The fury of the battle of Frezenberg was now dying down, and the road to Ypres was still securely barred to the enemy. On the evening of the 12th the battalion was relieved by the 6th Cavalry Brigade, and withdrew to bivouac between Ypres and Vlamertinghe. The following day a draft of 97 other ranks under Lieuts. J. S. H. Beamish and J. C. F. Lister joined. On the 15th, the 3rd K.R.R.C. was relieved in the trenches near Bellewaerde Lake by the battalion, which was relieved in turn, on the 17th, by the Queen's Bays and 5th Dragoons. This tour cost a casualty roll of 5 killed and 17 wounded. A draft of 130 was received from the Base on the 16th.

The battalion was now withdrawn to rest at Busseboom, where they were inspected by the Commander-in-Chief, Sir John French, who in a speech to the Brigade said:

" The 80th Brigade have had a very hard time, and
" I want to tell you how much I appreciate what you
" have done. You held on to your trenches in the most
" magnificent manner under a more severe artillery bom-
" bardment than has ever been known, and in doing so
" you have been of the greatest assistance to operations
" which the British Army was carrying out at the time.

" Men who have merely to lie down and wait under
" a fire like that are apt to think they are undergoing war
" rather than making war, but I want to tell you that by
" doing what you did you were really making war, or what
" will be known in the future as a great battle—the
" Second Battle of Ypres.

" By holding on to your trenches you prevented the
" Germans from attaining an object which it was very
" necessary for them to attain. They wanted to take
" Ypres, and to be able to tell the whole of Europe and
" America that they had taken Ypres, and if they had
" done so this would have done us a lot of harm.

" This might have had the effect of keeping neutral
" nations out of the war, but I can tell you that Italy
" will to-day declare war on behalf of the Allies.

" You prevented them from taking Ypres by your
" tenacity, and besides that you drove off German forces
" attacking you, and so considerably helped the Allied
" advance from the south at Arras.

" To remain in the trenches under a heavy artillery
" bombardment, to keep your heads and your discipline,
" and to be able to use your rifles at the end of it, require
" far higher qualities of personal bravery than actively
" to attack the enemy when everybody is on the move and
" conscious of doing something.

" I see before me famous old regiments whose battle
" honours show that they have upheld the British Empire
" in all parts of the world in many famous battles, but
" I tell you that the battle you have just fought will rank
" higher than any that your regiments have to show on
" your colours."

The General Officer Commanding the 27th Division
also sent a message of congratulation to the Brigade.
The letter to the Officer Commanding ran :—

" The G.O.C. Division wishes me to express his admira-
" tion at the way you and your Brigade have fought and
" endured during the past four weeks' operations.

"Twice the Brigade has found itself in a position with
"its left flank turned, and on both occasions there has
"been no retirement, but the exposed battalions have
"fought it out on the ground, thereby inflicting enor-
"mous losses on the enemy.

"The manner in which the officers and men stuck to
"their trenches in the face of a terrific bombardment is
"the admiration of all.

"The G.O.C. deeply deplores the heavy losses incurred,
"but units will find comfort in the fact that they have
"taken part in an episode which will figure in and rank
"with any in their regimental history. He is proud to
"have command of a Division which includes such a
"'stonewall' Brigade as the 80th have proved themselves
"to be. He congratulates you and your Brigade, and the
"Brigade on its Brigadier."

At Busseboom Colonel Bridgford returned, and yet
another draft of 130, under Lieuts. H. A. Robinson and
R. B. L. Persse, joined, and on the 23rd Captain D.
Leslie also arrived. Throughout the Second Battle of
Ypres, thanks to the large drafts of men sent out by the
3rd Battalion, there was no shortage in the ranks, but
officers became casualties far quicker than they could be
replaced, and companies were often commanded by very
junior officers. The rest of the battalion at Busseboom
was soon cut short by the opening of the Battle of Bellewaerde Ridge on the 24th May.

BATTLE OF BELLEWAERDE RIDGE

At dawn that morning, a beautiful summer's day, the
enemy launched a cloud gas attack, accompanied by a
terrific drum-fire from his artillery, on our front from
Langemarck to Bellewaerde Ridge, thus involving the
4th, 28th, 27th and Cavalry Divisions. The gas and artillery attack was soon followed up by an infantry advance
which was in part beaten off, but which succeeded in
penetrating our position in some places. At 5.10 a.m.

the 8oth Brigade got under arms and at 6.30 a.m. moved forward round the south side of Ypres. About 4.30 p.m. orders were received to retake trenches about Bellewaerde Ridge, and Railway Wood, which had been lost by the remnants of the 28th Division. The Brigade Commander was away, having been summoned to 28th Divisional Headquarters. Colonel Bridgford and the other Commanding Officers held a consultation, and decided to advance in two columns. The K.S.L.I. leading on the left, supported by the 4th K.R.R.C., and the 3rd K.R.R.C., leading on the right, supported by the 4th Rifle Brigade. These two columns moved forward along the Ypres–Menin road towards Bellewaerde and Railway Wood, picking up parties of the Royal Fusiliers, Suffolks and Buffs, who had orders to co-operate. The advance was slow and occupied the greater part of the night. There was no opportunity for reconnaissance, but at length the battalion arrived within striking distance of its objective.

X Company, led by Captain D. Leslie, and Y Company, led by Lieut. E. A. Williams-Freeman, assaulted. Captain Leslie was soon disabled by a severe wound in the leg, but Y Company, advancing through Railway Wood, captured the enemy's front line, and established themselves in it. Efforts to take the enemy's second line failed, owing to heavy machine-gun and rifle fire from the front and both flanks. It was now getting light, and the enemy was reinforced. Y Company's position, thrust forward into the enemy's line, was obviously untenable, and they were accordingly withdrawn, and the battalion dug itself in along the road west of Whitteport Farm, to the Ypres–Menin road.

An extraordinary incident occurred here. Although the enemy was close at hand, a motor-car drove along the road between us and the Germans, picked up the kits of some cavalry officers, which had been abandoned there the day before, and got away safely.

After holding the newly constructed line during the following day, the battalion was relieved and moved back to Busseboom by bus. During the relief the enemy favoured them with an extra heavy shelling by way of farewell. Casualties during this Battle of Bellewaerde Ridge included Lieuts. D. G. Hazard and C. Steward killed, Captain D. Leslie, Lieuts. E. A. Williams-Freeman, J. C. F. Lister, J. S. H. Beamish, G. Mardlow and H. A. Robinson wounded, and 192 other ranks killed, wounded and missing.

After the battle the following letter was received by Colonel Bridgford from the Officer Commanding the 1st Battalion the Welch Regiment.

" I am writing to bring to your notice the gallant
" conduct of one of your officers and the splendid way
" your men behaved in the attack on Railway Wood.

" We had just captured the trench at the top of the
" hill after very heavy casualties, when one of your
" officers came charging through the wood followed by
" his men amid a hail of bullets. He shouted to his men
" to charge the second trench, when he was unfortun-
" ately hit and I fear killed outright.

" The men of your regiment behaved splendidly,
" keeping up the fire on the German trenches in front until
" the last moment when we were compelled to retire
" owing to our own artillery plastering us with shrapnel."

Unfortunately the name of the officer is not mentioned.

At Busseboom a draft of four officers, Lieuts. J. C. D. Hill, J. Deedes, J. L. M. Grover and R. B. S. Munn, with 24 other ranks, was received.

On the 30th of May orders were received for the transfer of the 27th Division to the III Corps at Armentières, and at 4.30 the following morning the battalion marched south, bidding good-bye to the Ypres salient where for five long months they had endured the worst that the enemy and the climate could do, and in which they had left for ever many a gallant comrade.

Halting for a night at Dränoutre, and another at

Steenwerck, the battalion arrived at Armentières, and relieved the North Staffords in the trenches on the evening of the 2nd of June. The trenches at Armentières were a very welcome change after those of the Ypres salient. They were comparatively dry and comfortable, and conditions were altogether more peaceful. The town had not been knocked about like the unfortunate Ypres, and afforded comfortable billets with many of the amenities of civilised life. The battalion remained in this section until September 14th.

The war diary for these two and a half months is a record of normal trench warfare. Reliefs, working parties and occasional shelling. No heavy fighting occurred. Regimental sports, football matches and rifle competitions are also mentioned. A Divisional horse show was held in which the battalion did well, winning competitions for the best turned-out company cooker, and the best limber. They also carried off first and second prizes for pack ponies, and did well in the wrestling on horseback competitions, beating the K.R.R.C. and only being beaten by the P.P.C.L.I. in the finals after a hard struggle.

On the 13th July Colonel Bridgford was promoted to command the 18th Infantry Brigade, and left the battalion, which he had piloted through so much storm and stress, to the deep regret of all ranks. Major J. H. Bailey took over command.

The following casualties occurred in the Armentières section: Lieut. A. A. Tippet killed, Captain R. E. Holmes à Court, Lieuts. J. M. L. Grover, R. H. Booth and C. P. Hazard wounded, 13 other ranks killed, and 60 wounded.

On September 14th the battalion marched from Steenwerck at 8 p.m., arriving at Borre at midnight, and camping in the fields round the village. On the 17th the Corps Commander, General Pulteney, made a farewell speech to the 80th Brigade, complimenting them on the good work done in improving the trenches.

On the 18th the battalion marched to Hazebrouck

88

and entrained for Guillacourt. From there they moved by bus to Mericourt and marched into billets at Froissy. On the 19th they marched to Cappy and from there relieved the 123rd French Infantry in the trenches on the 20th. The war diary for the next month again records a period of normal trench warfare, with its alternate tours of duty in the front line, and spells of rest and training in rear. During these spells of rest large working parties were found for work on reserve and communication trenches.

Casualties during this month were light. Lieut. M. A. Koch was killed on September 22nd, and Captain F. R. H. Maunsell and 9 other ranks were wounded.

On the 25th of October the battalion was relieved in the trenches by the 113th French Infantry Regiment, and marched back to Pissy, where they arrived on the 28th, having halted on the way at Mericourt, Avancourt and Boves. A fortnight was spent at Pissy, during which training was carried out. On the 8th the P.P.C.L.I., who had proved themselves the stoutest of comrades and magnificent fighters, left the Brigade.

The 27th Division was now ordered to Macedonia, and the battalion entrained for Marseilles on October 16th at Longeau. Arriving at Marseilles on the 18th, it embarked on H.M.T. *Huntsgreen*, and arrived at Salonica on December 4th after an uneventful voyage.

During the next six weeks the battalion passed through a very difficult period, continually moving from place to place in the vicinity of the town of Salonica and Lembet Plain, the time being occupied chiefly by entrenching, wiring, road making and the furnishing of guards. These duties, though sounding simple in themselves, were rendered more arduous by the fact that the regimental transport did not arrive for some weeks after the disembarkation of the battalion ; consequently everything had to be carried on the man. At one time, during this period, every man was carrying a bivouac sheet and pole, a blanket, a greatcoat and a pick and shovel, in addition to his ordinary fighting equipment, and all under the most miserable climatic conditions imaginable ; added to this was the general uncertainty, felt by all ranks, concerning the attitude of the Greek Army, which was also concentrated in the same area. It was at this time that Captain J. C. Plowden joined the battalion and took over the duties of Adjutant.

On January 17th, 1916, the battalion moved to the village of Kireckoy. Here orders were at last received for a move forward, which commenced on January 20th and continued until January 27th, when the battalion took over a section of the Rendina Defences from the 10th Battalion Hampshire Regiment. Here it remained until June 26th, when another forward move was made to Kar Tasle Derbend on the shores of the Gulf of Orfano, where work was continued on roads and water supply until July 27th. During this period the services of two valuable officers were lost, namely, Major C. W. Battye, and Lieut. G. K. Lloyd, the former leaving to take over command of a battalion in Egypt, the latter dying of appendicitis on February 21st.

On July 28th the battalion moved forward to Neohori at the mouth of the River Struma, and three days later, with the 3rd K.R.R.C., crossed the river and took up a position on the Neohori Plateau, where work was at once commenced on new defences, roads and paths. The Brigade was now holding the whole of the eastern sector of the Allied front from Lake Tahinos to the Gulf of Orfano.

It was soon after taking over this sector of the line that the battalion first experienced the ravages of malaria, which so quickly and so sadly depleted its ranks, and which from that time onwards became one of its chief enemies.

On August 26th small parties of the enemy were observed moving on the hills about a mile to the north of our position ; these soon began to consolidate, and by September 4th a regular system of trench warfare had set in once more, and intermittent shelling continued day after day, followed by patrol actions at night. In these trenches the battalion remained continuously until July 17th, 1917, during which period two minor operations were carried out in the nature of " demonstrations " in order to hold the enemy to his ground while attacks were being made by other troops on our left.

The first of these demonstrations took place on September 10th, when the battalion, in co-operation with the 3rd K.R.R.C., advanced about 1,000 yards, and then withdrew to our own line. The operation lasted about four hours. Casualties : 13 other ranks wounded.

The second was a raid on a large scale against the enemy's trenches on the Hog's Back on October 31st, again in conjunction with the 3rd K.R.R.C. Casualties : 1 other rank killed, Lieut. R. W. O. J. Bruce and 4 other ranks wounded.

On November 29th Lt.-Colonel J. H. Bailey left the battalion to take over command of the 82nd Brigade, and Major J. S. Skinner assumed command until January 15th, 1917, when the former returned, and proceeded on leave, almost immediately, with the first leave party to England. On February 20th a second party, consisting of Major J. S. Skinner, R.S.M. S. J. C. Baikie and 7 other ranks, followed, all of whom were lost at sea, their boat being torpedoed off Mudros. A few days after his return from leave on March 21st, 1917, Lt.-Colonel Bailey again left the battalion to take over command of the 80th Brigade, with which he remained until June 18th, Major J. C. Plowden assuming temporary command of the battalion.

During the night of July 16th the battalion was relieved in the trenches by the 4th Battalion Rifle Brigade, and moved into Brigade reserve on the further side of the river, remaining there until October 18th, when it returned to the trenches and relieved the 4th Battalion Rifle Brigade. This tour of duty in the trenches proved less tedious than the last, for at the beginning of December a general relief between the 80th and 82nd Brigades commenced, which lasted some days. On December 4th the battalion was relieved by Lovat's Scouts, and marching by half-battalions along the southern shores of Lake Tahinos arrived at the village of Badimal, where it found itself in Divisional reserve billeted in and around the village.

New conditions and scenery undoubtedly had a very beneficial effect on all ranks after having lived continuously for two years in the Neohori trenches. Billets and hutments were nearly always available in the new area, except in the front line, which consisted of a series of redoubts and bridge-head fortifications along the River Struma. The task of keeping in touch with the enemy by means of patrols and raiding parties was allotted to what was known as the " Offensive Company." This company was furnished in turn by each battalion in the Brigade, and was billeted in old broken-down houses in front of the line of redoubts.

The battalion remained in this area until March 26th, 1918, when it was relieved by the 1st Regiment of the Greek Army (which army was now beginning to take over part of the Allied front), and marched to Orljak, where it took over yet another sector of the river line from the 2nd Buffs, 28th Division. This march will live long in the memory of those who took part in it, on account of the severe blizzard which set in just as the village was sighted, and which lasted for several days. Short respite only was allowed in this sector, for on June 6th the battalion was again relieved by the Greeks (1/38th Evzones) and marched to a place called Four Tree Hill about fifteen miles behind the line, where it remained in bivouacs until June 25th. On that date the battalion moved by march route and lorry combined to Guvesne, a village quite close to Salonica, which was reached on July 3rd, and where orders were received to entrain on the following day for an unknown destination.

On July 8th the battalion was once more in the trenches on the Vardar front near the village of Mayadag,

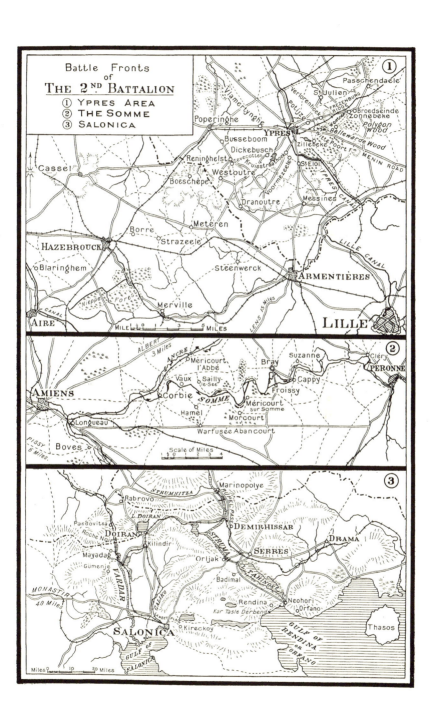

Battle Fronts
of
THE 2ND BATTALION
① YPRES AREA
② THE SOMME
③ SALONICA

having relieved the 2nd Regiment of Zouaves. Unfortunately these trenches were in an insanitary condition, and the result was an immediate increase in the number of cases of dysentry.

In spite of the hilly and broken nature of the country, the distance between the enemy front line and our own was in places not more than forty yards. Intermittent shelling continued during the day, whilst patrol activity gradually increased by night.

On September 1st two companies were detached from the battalion and came under the orders of the 82nd Brigade, with which they took part in the attack and capture of the Roche Noir salient. No casualties were sustained, and the two companies rejoined the battalion on the following day. On September 10th Major J. C. Plowden took over command of the battalion on his return from leave, Lt.-Colonel J. H. Bailey having left some few days previously.

On September 19th the battalion went into the trenches for its last and final "tour of duty," for as a result of reports received from various patrols on the general withdrawal of the enemy, an advance was ordered during the night of September 23rd, which continued practically unceasingly until the 26th, when a day's rest was ordered at Rabrovo. From here a move was made eastwards to Marinopolye, thence southwards through the Rupel Pass to Demirhissar, after which the battalion found itself back in its old haunts in the Struma valley. After various peregrinations by road, lorry and train, a resting-place was at last found on November 24th in hutments and dug-outs at a place called Gugunchi, about twenty miles from Salonica.

It is interesting to note that during these operations the battalion covered more than 100 kilometres on foot, 57 of which were completed in four days over roads of the worst description, in addition to which practically every man was suffering from either the present or after-effects of malaria—in spite of all not one single man in the battalion fell out on the line of march during the whole operation.

Early in December, 7 officers and 464 other ranks of the 8th Battalion were absorbed, and on December 12th a reconstituted battalion left camp for Salonica, whence it sailed on December 16th on H.M.T. *Katoomba*. In December 23rd the battalion arrived at Batoum, on the east coast of the Black Sea, where a large force of Turks was found in occupation of the whole province. This force was soon evacuated to Turkey in Europe without any untoward event, and forthwith the administration of the whole province was gradually taken over by the various units of the 27th Division, of which the battalion still formed part.

The battalion remained continuously in billets in the town of Batoum, performing normal garrison duties, and furnishing two detachments at Tchakwa and Artvin respectively until the end of April 1919. On June 17th the cadre, under command of Major O. S. Benbow Rowe, embarked at Chanak for England, arriving at Shrewsbury on July 2nd, 1919.

CHAPTER III

THE FOURTH BATTALION

THE eve of the outbreak of war found the 4th Battalion at the annual training at Glan Rheidol, Aberystwith. On Sunday, August 3rd, 1914, camp was broken up and the battalion returned to its various headquarters. Instructions were issued to the men to go back to their homes and await orders. Excitement ran high, and at many of the out-stations the drill halls were crowded with men who preferred to spend the night there in order to keep in touch with any development which might arise. At 4 p.m. on August 4th the one word "mobilize" arrived, and after a busy day at Shrewsbury the battalion, under the command of Lt.-Colonel J. H. Howard MacLean, with Captain J. C. Hooper as adjutant, left for its war station, Barry Docks, Cardiff, in two special trains. At Cardiff the battalion was billeted in two large schools at Cadoxton, Barry Docks. It was almost inevitable in face of a new situation, and amidst the stress of greater events, that there should be a certain amount of confusion in the administrative services. It was five long days before the blankets and camp kettles arrived, and in the meanwhile the men were largely dependent on the kindness of the local inhabitants for their food. In a few days, however, things began to straighten out, difficulties disappeared and the battalion settled down to its duties in connection with the Severn Defences, then commanded by Lt.-Colonel V. P. East, who was given the local rank of Brigadier. The days were devoted to manning the defences and training, and amidst the general air of excitement the discomforts were disregarded by all ranks.

On September 3rd telegraphic instructions were received to move to Sittingbourne, Kent. Early on the morning of September 4th the train journey was completed, but, owing to some mistake, the battalion which was to be relieved had not vacated its billets, accordingly temporary accommodation was found in the neighbouring village of Milton Regis. Bad as the billets had been at Barry Dock, here they were infinitely worse, especially one rat-ridden, deserted jam factory.

Shortly after the arrival at Milton all the N.C.O.'s of the permanent staff, with the exception of R.S.M. Hinde and Col.-Sgt. Whitney, were drafted to the 42nd E. Lancs Division. On September 13th the battalion moved into Sittingbourne proper, where the quarters were much more suitable, though survivors of G Company will probably still remember with disgust their billets in the old Cinema. During this period an appeal, calling for volunteers for service abroad, was made. A battalion parade was held and after an address by the Commanding Officer over 85 per cent of the men came forward.

On October 13th Major Garrett, who was to assume command of the battalion on the retirement of Lt.-Colonel MacLean, was ordered to go to the War Office to see General Sir E. Bethune, Director-General of the Territorial Forces. General Bethune said that Lord Kitchener wished to know if the County Territorial Battalions would go to India if required, and that as he had always regarded the 4th K.S.L.I. as a typical County Battalion he had sent for Major Garrett to ask this question. Major Garrett assured him that his battalion—although the men expected to go to France— was ready to go to any part of the world where it was wanted. General Bethune left the room and on returning expressed Lord Kitchener's thanks, and later on the same day the battalion received orders to be ready to sail for India at an early date. Four days' leave was at once given to every man by half battalions.

On October 15th Major Garrett took over the command of the battalion from Lt.-Colonel Howard McLean, whose period as C.O., which had already been extended for two years, had just terminated.

On October 26th the battalion, together with three other territorial battalions, was reviewed by His Majesty The King, who was accompanied by Lord Powis, the

Lord-Lieutenant of Shropshire. At the conclusion of the inspection His Majesty personally bade farewell to the C.O.'s, and wished all ranks the best of good fortune. Subsequently at a regimental parade Lord Powis presented Lt.-Colonel Garrett with the T.D.

At midnight, October 28th, the battalion left Sittingbourne and embarked next day at Southampton on H.M.T. *Deseado*. The strength on embarkation was 31 officers and 805 other ranks, and included :—

Commanding	Lt.-Colonel A. B. Garrett, T.D.
Second in command	Major H. P. Harris-Edge, T.D.
Adjutant	Captain J. C. Hooper
Medical Officer	Captain W. C. Scales, R.A.M.C.
Quartermaster	Lieut. A. E. Ayling

COMPANY COMMANDERS

A (Shrewsbury)	Captain L. H. Morris
B (Wem. & Whitchurch)	Captain E. S. Hawkins
C (Wellington)	Captain H. E. Wace
D (Ironbridge)	Captain W. G. Litt
E (Shifnal)	Captain R. Haslewood
F (Bridgnorth)	Captain W. H. Westcott
G (Ludlow)	Captain W. G. Lane
H (Oswestry)	Captain W. C. Shearer

On December 1st the battalion arrived at Bombay, where it disembarked and entrained on the 3rd for Calcutta, which was reached on December 6th. Here it re-embarked at once on the *City of Marseilles* and arrived at Rangoon on the 10th. One and a half Companies, D and half of H, were immediately sent to the Andaman Islands to relieve regular troops stationed there. On the 15th the whole of the Rangoon Garrison was reviewed by Br.-General A. A. J. Johnstone, Commanding the Rangoon Brigade. Whilst at Rangoon the first casualty occurred, Sergeant H. Tudor of H Company dying of heart failure shortly before Christmas.

On the evening of January 21st, 1915, at about 11 p.m.

an urgent message was received from G.H.Q. ordering the C.O. with his Adjutant to go at once to report to the General. It had just been discovered that a native Infantry Battalion of the garrison was on the verge of mutiny. The 4th K.S.L.I. was ordered to disarm it, peaceably if possible, but if necessary force was to be used. The Native Infantry Battalion was stationed in three forts on the riverside, one company in each, whilst the 4th Company was in the Native Infantry Barracks with a guard at Government House. Colonel Garrett detailed one company to disarm the mutineers at each of the three forts, the remaining companies being sent to the Native Infantry Barracks and Government House. Those of the sick in hospital, who could hold a rifle, were ordered to stand to and be prepared for emergencies. The arrangements worked with the utmost smoothness, and all the prospective mutineers were disarmed by 5.30 a.m. without a shot being fired. The promptitude with which the operation was carried out averted without doubt an outbreak, at least as serious as that which subsequently occurred at Singapore, as it was discovered that the mutiny was timed to take place at dawn on the following day. For this service the battalion subsequently received the cordial thanks of the Indian Government, to which the Commander-in-Chief added a hearty endorsement.

On February 4th a column of about 250, all ranks, under Major Harris-Edge, was sent out on an eighteen days' route march up country through the In Sein district between Rangoon and Mandalay. The primary object was to make a demonstration, as the annual dacoity unrest was reported amongst some of the natives. The remainder of the battalion stayed at Rangoon. Despite considerable difficulties with regard to water, the column was successfully fulfilling its mission, when news of the Singapore outbreak arrived at Head-quarters.

On the evening of February 6th an urgent message was received from Delhi ordering the battalion to embark at

3 p.m the following day. Difficulties regarding transport were solved by the provision of motor lorries, and by 2.30 p.m. 600 men of the battalion were on board H.M.T. *Edavana*, 500 rounds of ball ammunition per man having been issued. After a record voyage of seventy-two hours from quay to quay the *Edavana* reached Singapore. On arrival the Governor, Sir Arthur Young, with Admiral Sir Martyn Jerram, Commander-in-Chief China Station, and General Ridout, G.O.C., Singapore, were found waiting on the P. and O. Quay. The battalion was inspected on board by the Governor, who summarized what had happened in a speech to all officers in the saloon.

It appeared that a few days previously the 5th Light Infantry had mutinied. The mutineers broke up into small parties, murdering every European whom they happened to meet, and in some cases Chinese and Malay civilians also. At first the situation was dangerous since, with the exception of some artillery and the local volunteers, there were no other troops in Singapore at the time. With great promptitude General Ridout requested the Captain of H.M.S. *Cadmus*, then in the harbour, to land a detachment ninety strong to attack the mutineers. The first party that was met was headed by a native officer who was the prime instigator of the mutiny and the only capable organiser. By a lucky chance he was killed by one of the first shots fired, and the rebels then dispersed. Further detachments were landed from allied warships in the harbour, and by the time the battalion arrived the situation was in hand, though some seventy Europeans, including several women, had lost their lives.

As it was now nearly 8 p.m. the Governor decided that disembarkation should not take place until the following morning, the men sleeping on board fully armed and equipped ; E Company (Shifnal) under Captain Haslewood being detailed to act as an " inlying picquet." At 2 a.m. this picquet was called for and stood to arms but, though heavy firing was heard at no great distance, it was sent back on board again at 4 a.m. At 8 a.m. the battalion disembarked, A Company being sent to the island fortresses of Pulu Brani and Blakan Mati, B to Fort Canning, and the remainder in motor-cars to Tanglin Barracks. The day was spent in taking over charge of captured mutineers and patrolling, but the mutiny was practically over and no actual fighting took place, except for desultory encounters in the jungles of the island.

On the 23rd February the first of the executions took place. Colonel Garrett was in command of these parades, at which upwards of forty of the mutineers were shot outside the gaol, in the presence of large crowds.

A definite scheme of operations was put into force with the object of rounding up as many of the rebels as possible. Singapore Island was divided up into areas of roughly six miles by four. The mutineers were usually in parties of about twenty, and when one of these was located every available man of the battalion was sent out and, ably assisted by the Singapore Volunteers, the party was surrounded. The country was extremely difficult, consisting of rubber and pineapple plantations, mangrove swamps, virgin jungle and, worst of all, ground that had been cleared during the rubber boom but allowed to lapse, and which was covered by dense growth to a height of eight feet. The night work was done in reliefs, officers and men off duty getting what sleep the mosquitoes allowed, in plantation sheds, motor-cars, or any available shelter. At 4 a.m. tea was served out and at dawn every man was ready for the day's drive. The drive usually lasted until 9 or 10 p.m., but few captures were made as a rule, owing to the impenetrable nature of the cover, and to the fact that the mutineers preferred to surrender to the native police, rather than to the battalion or to the Singapore Volunteers.

On the 15th March Colonel Garrett, with the Quartermaster, left for Rangoon to collect details left behind and the regimental stores. On April 4th the Ironbridge and Half Oswestry Companies, which had been at the Andamans, also arrived at Rangoon, and on Monday, April 5th, the whole party started on the journey to Singapore on R.I.M.S. *Mayo*, arriving on the 10th. During the absence of Colonel Garrett a party from B and C Companies, about 250 strong, had been sent to Hong Kong under Major Hawkins. This detachment was shortly afterwards made up to 400 by the addition of B and H Companies. Another party of forty, under Lieut. Butler, had also sailed for Australia as escort to German prisoners, and a further party left shortly afterwards on the same duty under Captain Haslewood. These two detachments were the first British troops seen in Australia since the inauguration of the Commonwealth, and whilst there were detailed to act as bodyguard to the Governor-General.

On May 2nd an urgent message was received at Singapore from the British settlement at Kelantan, about 400 miles to the north on the east side of Malaya, near the Siamese border. A sudden rising had taken place, several Europeans had been murdered and Government buildings had been burnt. A detachment consisting of 160 men of the battalion under the Adjutant, Captain Hooper, with 100 details, was ordered to embark within five hours, the whole force being under Colonel Brownlow, R.G.A. The Kelantan column was away for fifteen days, though there was practically no fighting, as the rebels invariably disappeared into the bush on its approach.

On the 23rd May both the Australian detachments returned, and as the battalion, with the exception of the Hong Kong wing, was now concentrated and the local troubles had subsided, a period of intensive training was begun which continued uneventfully until the departure for England.

During this period the battalion was reorganized into four companies: A and G becoming C, F and E becoming B, B and H becoming D, and D and C becoming A.

Through casualties and the departure of time-expired men, the strength of the battalion gradually fell to no more than 720, but in May, 1916, a draft of 8 officers and 460 other ranks arrived from home. This reinforcement brought the numbers up to some 1200, which was amply sufficient to find the garrisons for Hong Kong and Singapore, and to provide instructors for the local volunteer forces in the Straits Settlements as far north as Penang, 400 miles away.

On the 24th May, 1916—Empire Day—the whole of the European garrison of Singapore was reviewed on the general parade ground and, at the conclusion of the parade, the battalion was publicly thanked by the Governor, Sir Arthur Young, on behalf of the Indian and Straits Settlements Governments for the prompt embarkation at Rangoon in February, 1915, and for the energy displayed in the subsequent rounding-up of the mutineers.

In December information arrived from the War Office that the battalion was to be relieved by the 25th Middlesex in January, 1917. Considerable delay was caused however, by the *Tyndareus*, which was carrying the Middlesex, being damaged off Cape Agulhas to such an extent that the battalion had to be taken back to Cape Town. Towards the end of February, 1917, however, the 25th Middx. arrived on the *Ingoma*, though, as the ship was in quarantine, disembarkation was delayed ten days. Despite the protests of the C.O., Lt.-Colonel John Ward, M.P., who disliked the idea of dividing his battalion, two companies were ordered to stay at Singapore and the remainder, with the Battalion Head-quarters, sailed for Hong Kong a few days later to complete the relief. On April 13th the *Ingoma* returned from Hong Kong with D and A Companies on board, and on the next day the rest of the battalion embarked.

The excellent impression made by the battalion both at Singapore and Hong Kong was illustrated by the farewell address of the Governor, and by articles in all the local papers.

Accommodation on the *Ingoma*, which was escorted by

the Japanese cruiser *Tone*, was considerably crowded, as she had been fitted to carry about 800 all ranks, whereas the strength of the battalion at this time was over 1,100.

On arrival at Colombo on the 19th April a delay occurred pending the arrival of a fresh escort. Four days later A and B Companies disembarked and went into camp at Rifle Green, and on the 26th the whole battalion moved to Dywatalawa Camp some 250 miles by train from Colombo, and at an altitude of over 6,000 feet, a welcome relief from the sweltering heat of the town and harbour. Early on the morning of May 1st a telegraphic communication was received to the effect that the *Ingoma* was to sail on the 3rd. After some difficulty caused by the line being blocked by a landslide, A and B Companies left that night, the remaining two companies travelled down next day, embarking immediately on arrival.

On May 23rd the *Ingoma* reached Durban whence, after a short stay waiting for an escort, the battalion sailed in a storm for Cape Town, arriving on the 30th. Here orders were received to disembark and go to Wynberg Rest Camp for an indefinite period.

The first night proved extraordinarily trying to a unit straight from the tropics, for the bitter cold was accompanied by torrential rain, hail and sleet and, as a result, there were between 150 and 200 fever cases next day. The battalion, however, soon settled down to the ordinary routine of training and garrison duties. At this period it was probably smarter than at any time since its embodiment, and the greatest rivalry existed between those portions which had formed the garrisons of Hong Kong and Singapore. On June 25th orders arrived to embark for England four days later in the *Walmer Castle*.

Owing to the South African Government taking over their own defences, the 4th K.S.L.I. was the last complete unit of Imperial troops engaged in the Cape defences, and with the departure of the battalion the new order came into operation.

The voyage to England, except for a torrid stay of a week in Sierra Leone harbour, was uneventful, and on July 27th, 1917, the battalion reached Plymouth. Here a great disappointment was in store. Instead of being granted leave, as had been hoped and expected, the battalion was ordered at once to Southampton to sail the same night for France. This disappointment, which was aggravated by the fact that no mails had been received for over six months, was borne by the men with the same discipline and cheerfulness which they had shown in all their wanderings, and by 9 o'clock on the following morning the battalion landed and entrained. On arrival at Southampton the stores and baggage were loaded on the ship which was to carry the battalion to France, and immediately loading operations were finished the battalion embarked and reached Havre at 3 a.m. on 29th July, 1917.

The strength on landing was 27 officers and 1,115 other ranks, including the following :—

Lt.-Colonel A. N. B. Garrett   In command
Major H. E. Harris-Edge   2nd in Command
Major E. S. Hawkins

Captain W. C. Shearer	Captain H. E. Wace
,, R. J. R. Haslewood	,, W. G. Litt
Lieut. W. D. Roberts	Lieut. D. M. Marston
,, T. H. Butler	,, W. Atherton
,, E. R. Litt	,, G. L. Peace
,, C. H. Greene	
2nd Lieut. G. Morley	2nd Lieut. F. A. Parker
,, R. K. S. Exham	,, E. E. Corser
,, A. Solomon	,, F. J. K. Smith
,, H. Collins	,, G. W. Bright
,, E. H. C. Lloyd-Davis	,, H. E. O'Meara

Lieut. G. F. Bright   Adjutant
  ,, A. E. Ayling   Quarter-master
Captain W. C. Scales, R.A.M.C., Medical Officer.

After disembarking, the battalion marched to No. 2 Rest Camp, Havre, and on the next day moved to No. 1 Rest Camp at San Vic on the north side of the harbour; the appearance of a battalion, over 1,100 strong, dressed in tropical khaki, causing considerable excitement amongst the inhabitants of the town. Here the battalion was re-equipped and rearmed, as all rifles had been left behind at Singapore. Transport and horses were also issued. The issue of clothing was especially necessary to an unit which had come straight from the tropics, and which was still wearing drill on arrival in France. There was also daily instruction at the training school in wiring, bombing and gas—subjects which there had been no opportunity to learn in the East.

Whilst at San Vic Camp a telegram arrived from the War Office, signed by the Secretary of State for War as follows :—

" Please convey to the Officer Commanding and all " ranks 4th K.S.L.I. my admiration for the soldier-like " behaviour of the battalion under the recent trying cir- " cumstances. It was unfortunately impossible to grant " leave owing to shipping arrangements after the absence " of two and a half years abroad, and when the decision " came the whole battalion accepted it without a sign " or murmur of disappointment, and worked willingly " and well at loading their ship, an attitude which " reflects the highest credit upon the Commanding " Officer and all under his command.—DERBY."

On the 23rd August orders were received to join the 190th Brigade 63rd (R.N.) Division, to which the battalion had previously been posted. After a long journey the battalion went into billets at Maroeuil, near Arras, and for the first time heard the sound of guns in action, and saw the results in various shell-holes in the walls of their billets. Here a special leave allotment was granted at the rate of twenty a day, whilst the battalion underwent a period of intensive training in the various necessary technical subjects. During this period the battalion went into the front line for the first time, one platoon from each company successively being attached to another unit of the Brigade and taking over a short sector. All officers also went up for two days each with other battalions. The Brigade, the other units of which were the 1st Artists' Rifles, 7th Royal Fusiliers and 4th Bedfords, was holding a comparatively peaceful frontage, the Divisional sector extending southwards through Oppy Wood and thence east of Arras.

On October 2nd the Brigade entrained at Magnicourt for the north and arrived at Hazebrouck at about midnight. It was here discovered that the battalion's rest billets were at Hardifort, some twelve kilometres away to the north. It was pouring with rain, and by the time Hardifort was reached at 4 a.m. every officer and man was dead tired and soaked to the skin. Next morning, whilst all ranks were busily engaged in drying their clothes, the 7th Battalion K.S.L.I. came through the village on their way from the salient to the Somme. Here Major Harris-Edge was invalided home with blood poisoning, and Major Hawkins became second in command.

The stay at Hardifort was, however, not a long one, and on October the 4th the battalion left by march route, arriving at Houtkerque on the 7th. Here the halt was of longer duration in order to undergo special training for future operations in front of Ypres.

On the 24th the Brigade set off again by bus, and after one night's halt at Dampre Camp marched to the canal bank at Ypres on the 25th. During the stay here it was noticed that the water was rapidly increasing, and on the 28th a sudden rise of two feet brought matters to a climax. Every dug-out was flooded and a considerable amount of equipment and clothing lost. This flood necessarily caused the evacuation of the canal bank, so on the same night the battalion moved to Irish Farm, four miles north-east of Ypres.

Leaving Irish Farm at 9 p.m. on the 29th the battalion

arrived at Albatross Farm at 11.45 p.m. No casualties were suffered until the allotted positions were reached, but during consolidation some 30 occurred, including Lieuts. Greene, Charlton and Lowe, who were hit by overhead shrapnel whilst waiting to deploy.

THE SECOND BATTLE OF PASSCHENDAELE

At 1.30 p.m. on the following day orders were received to send two companies to attack Source Trench, and thus fill a gap in the line near Varlet Farm, and also to place another company at the disposal of the Canadian Brigade on the right at Kronprinz Farm.

The two companies (A and D) for the attack on Source Trench under Major Litt moved off at 2 p.m. via Kronprinz Farm, where a Canadian officer was allotted to them as a guide. The attack lost direction slightly in the appalling mud, but though all the original objectives were not gained the gap between Source Farm and Varlet Farm was closed. The general behaviour and steadiness of the men must have set at rest any uneasiness that may have existed in the minds of the higher authorities concerning the reliability of a Territorial battalion, straight from the East, under fire for the first time in France under trying circumstances. When the order to advance in attack formation was given, N.C.O.'s could be heard checking intervals and dressing despite the fire, and the lines moved forward as accurately as on parade.

The third company (B) had in the meantime been ordered to Kronprinz Farm and was thence directed by the O.C. 5th Cape Mounted Rifles to take up a position near Source Farm in support of one of his companies, which had suffered heavily. B Company lost severely in doing so, but after dark got into touch with A and D Companies on the left and from that time onwards acted in concert with them, all being placed under the command of the Canadian Brigadier. During the night a line of posts was established connecting the right of the Canadians with the left of the remainder of the 160th

Brigade, and in this position the battalion remained until relieved by the Nelson Battalion after dark on October 31st.

The total casualties in this their first action in France were: Officers killed 1 (Lieut. C. S. Coakley, 1st Battalion K.S.L.I., attached 4th), wounded 8; other ranks killed 21, wounded 106, missing 1.

The day following the relief, the 4th K.S.L.I. marched to Poperinghe, where it was congratulated by the Divisional Commander personally, and on behalf of the Corps Commander, for the steadiness and bravery shown by all ranks. On the 3rd of November the battalion was ordered to Brielen, near Ypres, to work on the light railway which was being constructed from St. Julien to Langemarck. This work was most arduous; the men leaving camp at 4 o'clock each morning, marching three miles to the entraining point, thence going by railway trucks towards Langemarck or to any other point of the line which might have been destroyed during the night. In addition, both the working parties and the camp were continually bombed and shelled. Only two casualties, however, occurred, though the preceding unit had lost over 100 men in twenty-four days.

On the 23rd November the battalion moved by bus to the Eringhem area and thence by march route to Houtkerque on the 28th. Here the battalion stayed doing company training until December 10th when, after entraining at Goedswaervelde, it marched into the line on Welch Ridge, opposite Marcoing, on the 16th, halting for brief periods at Miraumont, Rocquigny and Metz-en-Couture. This portion of the line was comparatively quiet at the time and nothing beyond the normal events of trench life happened until December 30th when a heavy bombardment, which severed all telephonic communication, was opened on the front trenches at 6 a.m.

ACTION OF WELCH RIDGE

At about 9 a.m. a runner reached Battalion Headquarters from the front line with a message to the effect that the trenches held by the unit on the right had been rushed, and that a defensive flank had been formed by the right company (D) of the 4th K.S.L.I. At about 10 a.m. the Brigade Major arrived with information that the counter-attack battalion, the 1st Artists' Rifles, was moving up to retake the lost trenches and that the two support companies were to co-operate with them. The initial counter-attack was only partially successful.

The situation was eventually restored owing to the exceptionally gallant and resourceful action of Lieut. G. H. Morley. This officer had only returned from a bombing course the night before, and it was actually the first time that he had been in the line. Heading a party consisting of about 10 men of A Company, he made his way along the captured trench, bombing the Germans back yard by yard until his stock of bombs was exhausted. He had, however, noticed a dump of German stick bombs and, sending one of his party back for a supply, he continued his advance until the trench was completely cleared of the enemy, large numbers of whom were killed. Lieut. Morley was unfortunately killed by a stray bullet after the completion of his task on his way back to Battalion Head-quarters. For his gallantry and successful initiative he was recommended for the V.C., and though this posthumous honour was not awarded, his gallantry was recorded in despatches.

In the afternoon Colonel Garrett decided to reinforce the front line with the support companies and, after a few half-hearted attempts, the resulting enemy attack died away and the shattered trenches were restored and the wire repaired.

In addition to Lieut. Morley the battalion suffered a severe loss by the deaths of Lieuts. W. Atherton and N. L. Smith, two of the most efficient and popular subalterns. For their gallantry in this most successful action no fewer than 17 N.C.O.'s and men received the D.C.M. or M.M.

On the 3rd of January, 1918, the battalion was relieved

and went back to huts in Havrincourt Wood, returning to the line again on the 10th. The sector now occupied was also on Welch Ridge, but to the right of that sector in which the action of the 30th December had been fought. There was little enemy activity, but the men suffered very severely from the terrible weather and the melting snow which flooded the trenches inches deep, with the result that over 180 cases of trench feet occurred in the fortnight they were in this part of the line, despite every precaution. Whilst in this sector the opportunity was taken of erecting crosses over the graves of the officers and men killed on 30th December, who were buried in the little cemetery near the Marcoing road.

On January the 18th, 1918, the battalion was relieved, going back into Divisional Reserve at Beaulencourt for rest and refit. The battalion was now taken out of the 63rd Division and transferred to the 56th Brigade, 19th Division, the other units of which were the 8th Battalion Staffordshire Regiment and 9th Battalion Cheshire Regiment. A draft of 2 officers and 107 other ranks from the 5th Battalion K.S.L.I., which had been broken up, arrived on the 4th of February.

On the 5th February the battalion was back again in the line on Welch Ridge, and after an uneventful tour of trench duty was relieved and went back into rest billets at Bouzincourt, where, to the delight of all ranks, Colonel Howard-MacLean was found installed as Town Major. The next move was to Beaulencourt on March 7th. Whilst here several reconnaissances were made of the country towards the front line in view of a counter-attack when the expected German offensive should take place. Working parties were constantly employed on the Haig line in the vicinity, and whilst digging this line a somewhat remarkable incident happened. An officer of the R.E. arrived and closely questioned a working party of the battalion as to the nature of the work on which they were engaged. Though some of the questions in the light of subsequent events seemed suspicious, not much notice was taken of him; however, next day a secret order from the Brigade arrived to the effect that he was to be arrested if seen, as he was an enemy spy. However, nothing further was heard of him.

FIRST BATTLE OF BAPAUME

At 6 a.m. on March 21st the order came to stand by in readiness to advance and at 12.30 the battalion moved towards the front line. At 5.30 p.m. A Company was ordered to relieve a company of the Wiltshire Regiment in a beet-root factory near Lebucquiere on the Bapaume–Cambrai road, the remaining companies being dug in in Gaika Copse, Le Velu, in close support to the 57th and 58th Brigades, which were in readiness to make a counter-attack. From this position the battalion, except A Company, was withdrawn at 11.30 p.m., arriving at Fremicourt at 3 a.m. on the 22nd and occupying a trench in the east of Fremicourt Wood as reserve to the 56th Infantry Brigade, who were in support of the 58th Brigade then defending Beugny. At about midnight 22nd/23rd the battalion moved in accordance with orders to Lebucquiere to take up a position in support of the then front line, and here it was rejoined at about 3 a.m. by A Company from the beet-root factory. At 10 a.m. the Division on the right of the sector occupied by the battalion, was seen to be withdrawing across the Bapaume-Cambrai road followed by large numbers of the enemy. As this retirement left the right flank of the Brigade exposed, and as a previous " S.O.S." from the front line had produced no response from the artillery, the battalion received orders to retire fighting to the Green Line in rear of the Cheshire Regiment and 8th North Staffordshire Regiment. At 1.15 p.m. a fresh attack was seen to be developing from the direction of Beugny, orders were received to retire to Bancourt to reorganize and to occupy trenches on the next day in support of the Green Line.

Here instructions arrived to the effect that Lt.-Colonel W. A. Bowen was taking over command of the battalion, as Colonel Garrett had gone on leave on the 19th of March, and Major Hawkins who had been temporarily in command had been wounded.

At 5 p.m. on March 24th a further retirement to the south-east outskirts of Baupaume was made and by 8 a.m. on the 25th the battalion had taken up a line on the Bapaume–Albert road, with the 2nd Division on the right and a battalion of the Welch Regiment on the left.

By 11 a.m., March 25th, following persistent enemy attacks the right flank became practically enveloped, casualties were heavy and another withdrawal became essential if annihilation was to be avoided. This was effected by 3 p.m. through the 62nd Division, and a new line was occupied west of Miraumont, the battalion being the last unit of the British Army in Bapaume for many months. Orders were received late at night from the G.O.C. 56th Brigade to withdraw further and rendezvous at Hebuterne. This was effected and, in the early hours of the morning of the 26th, officers and men of the now greatly reduced battalion were looking for billets in the hopes of, at any rate, a short period of rest. At about 6.30 a.m. General Jeffreys, G.O.C. 19th Division, rode through the streets with his Staff. When this party reached the eastern exit of the village it was seen to turn about and gallop back, as it had ridden right into a party of the enemy who were on the point of entering the town. The remains of the Brigade, about 250 strong, fell in, fixed bayonets and doubled in fours down the main streets in the direction of the enemy, who were seen advancing over a crest about 800 yards away. Covered by the fire of the N. Staffords and Cheshire Regiment the battalion, now reduced to under 50 men, charged with the bayonet headed by Colonel Bowen, whereupon the enemy took to flight without awaiting an actual collision.

At 10 p.m. on the same day the Division was relieved by an Australian Division, and the battalion withdrew to Sailly-aux-Bois. Here a halt for one day was made. The next move was by march route to Candas, where the battalion entrained for Caestre, arriving at 1 a.m. on the 30th. The ultimate destination, Cable Camp, Wulverghem, was reached next day by bus, after a halt by the way at Kemmel. Here the 19th Division rested and reorganized until April the 10th, on which day an order to stand-by arrived at 5.30 a.m., and by 12 noon, in accordance with further orders, the battalion took up a position on the western slope of Hill 63, in support of the 17th Brigade.

BATTLE OF MESSINES, 1918

At 1 p.m. the enemy attacked heavily from the right rear and, after a company under Captain H. E. Wace, who was killed four days later, had been sent forward to counter-attack, a defensive flank was formed. Here, too, fell Lieut. G. D. McAlister, whose courage and cheery optimism had endeared him to all ranks.

BATTLE OF BAILLEUL

At 9 p.m. orders to withdraw arrived, and two hours later a fresh position was occupied in the Army line between the Wulverghem—Neuve Eglise road and another road some thousand yards to the right. Several minor enemy attacks were driven off by rifle and machine-gun fire, and at 8 a.m. on April 13th small parties of the enemy were seen penetrating Neuve Eglise village. These, however, were immediately driven out by a gallant counter-attack by elements of the 4th K.S.L.I., K.O.Y.L.I., York and Lancs and R.E., hastily collected by Major Wingrove, who was then acting as second in command of the battalion.

In the evening orders to take over a line north of the Neuve Eglise road, then held by the 4th Battalion York and Lancs Regiment, were received from the G.O.C. 148th Brigade, to which Brigade the battalion was attached. This movement was carried out by 9.45 p.m. Next morning the line was very heavily shelled and the battalion was withdrawn to a line running parallel to the Neuve Eglise road. At the same time the enemy re-occupied part of the village. On the following evening, owing to severe trench-mortar shelling, the line was further withdrawn and a defensive flank was formed.

On April 15th the battalion, now consisting of 9 officers and 279 other ranks, was ordered to retire to Rossignol Camp, where it was reorganized and eventually placed in reserve under the orders of the G.O.C. 56th Brigade. On the 18th operation orders arrived for relief by the 28th French Division. By dawn next day the relief was completed, and the battalion, after concentrating at Canada Camp, marched to Wippenhoek. After resting here until the 21st, it moved by march route to Tunneler's Camp and thence to Ouderdom on the 25th. Here it remained training and reorganizing until the 1st May, 1918, when it relieved battalions of the K.O.Y.L.I. and Bedfordshire Regiment in the front line near Dickebusch. The only incident worthy of record occurring in this part of the line was the capture of a German limber by D Company under Captain Peace. This limber had evidently lost its way and was coming down the road, drawn by two Russian ponies and accompanied by two men, straight for our lines. It was speedily seized and was found to contain papers for a German light-gun team, and two jars of rum. The papers were sent on to Battalion Head-quarters, the rum was not.

After two short periods one in the front line and one in support the battalion received orders on May 16th to march to rail-head at Waayenbure, where it entrained southwards for Chalons on the next day. On the 18th it detrained at Vitry-la-Ville and marched to billets in Omey. The next ten days were spent in training and reorganization till on the 28th sealed orders arrived and the battalion " embussed," eventually being billeted in a slaughter-house near Chaumuzy, ten miles south-west of Reims. From Chaumuzy it moved to Chambrecy and took up a position north-north-east of Sarcy on the afternoon of the 29th, B, C and D Companies being in the front line with A in support.

BATTLE OF THE AISNE, 1918

At 11 a.m. the next day the enemy attacked under a heavy bombardment, and by 2 p.m., after the flanks had been forced back, a withdrawal was made to the ridge east of Aubilly. Here a reorganization was effected behind some French troops who were holding the ridge. The losses incurred in this action were: 6 officers and 180 men. By ten o'clock that night a position in support of the French, north-west of Bligny, was occupied, the battalion moving up in close support next day. At 4 p.m. on May 31st the enemy attacked and the French were forced back. A counter-attack was immediately ordered. and at a loss of about 6 officers wounded, one of whom, 2nd Lieut. W. L. Owen, 1st attached 4th, died of wounds on June 12th, and 80 other ranks, the position was regained and the situation restored. After this successful counter-attack the enemy attacks died away and by 6 p.m. the line was organized, the 8th N. Staffordshire Regiment on the left, the 4th K.S.L.I. in the centre and the 53rd French Regiment on the right.

BLIGNY

On the 5th of June the battalion withdrew to the Chaumuzy line as counter-attack battalion. The trenches were far from elaborate and consisted of disconnected shallow slits which had been hastily dug in the ploughed fields and which were then covered with growing corn about two feet high, still green. At 1.30 a.m. a heavy enemy barrage descended, a new form of gas shell, subsequently identified and known as " Green Cross," being chiefly employed. The conditions were trying in the extreme, and as the morning wore on it became increasingly difficult to prevent the young soldiers from taking off their masks, though any relaxation was at once followed by violent sickness. Gradually the character of the bombardment changed. At daybreak on June 6th high explosive was substituted for gas shell, and it became obvious that a serious attack on Bligny Hill was in progress. At about 6.30 the barrage lifted on to the support trenches, but luckily, despite the inadequacy of the cover, casualties were few, as the standing corn, though it undoubtedly held the gas, masked the position very considerably. Wounded men began to trickle through, and from their accounts it was evident that the enemy were attacking in great strength.

At about 9.30 the N. Staffords and Cheshires, who were holding the ground immediately in front, were observed to be retiring down the hill, fighting over every yard of the ground and finally holding on to a position at the bottom of the nearer slope. At 12.45 orders were given by Colonel Heath, Commanding 56th Brigade, for an immediate counter-attack. The senior officer then present was Lieut. G. W. Bright, and it was under his arrangements that the counter-attack was organized. The objective was nearly a mile away, and the advance had to take place for the most part up hill, over practically open country without a vestige of dead ground or cover of any sort. In contradistinction to the miserable weather in which most of the operations in France took place, the brilliant sunshine and almost tropical heat was a further disadvantage. The battalion, now less than 200 strong, advanced in four waves at 100 paces distance and, though it came under a terrific fire from every form of ordnance the enemy possessed, and in spite of casualties, dressings and intervals were preserved throughout the attack. There was no artillery support, though it was afterwards discovered that it had been intended that the advance should have been preceded by ten minutes' intensive bombardment, but owing to an error in timing and the rapidity with which the attack went forward, the supporting guns did not open until the hill had actually been captured. That casualties were fewer than could reasonably have been expected was almost entirely due to the splendid dash of the troops, many of whom were boys of eighteen. When the remnants of the N. Staffords and Cheshires were reached, a short pause took place. Five minutes after, the advance was resumed and Bligny Hill was regained at the point of the bayonet, a machine gun and 40 prisoners being captured. The casualties were 2 officers (wounded), and 75 other ranks.

The remainder of the day was spent in consolidating. As the battalion, now reduced almost to vanishing point as far as numbers were concerned, was holding a frontage previously held by a Brigade and in addition was enfiladed on both flanks, an enemy attack in strength must have meant annihilation. Luckily, however, no counter-attack took place, and at 11.30 p.m. a Brigade of Northumberland Fusiliers arrived in relief.

The Montagne de Bligny was undoubtedly the key position in this area, and its permanent capture by the enemy would have forced a withdrawal on a considerable scale. The importance of this successful counter-attack was speedily recognised, and shortly after gaining the position a message from the G.O.C. 19th Division was signalled: "The Divisional Commander congratulates "the K.S.L.I. on their very gallant performance." A little later fifteen Croix de Guerre arrived from the French General commanding the Corps.

On relief the battalion went back to Bois de Courton. By reason of the heavy losses it had suffered, the 56th Brigade was here reorganized into the 56th Composite Battalion commanded by Colonel Koebel, N. Staffordshire Regiment, the 8th N. Staffords forming A Company, the 4th K.S.L.I. B Company and the 9th Cheshires C Company. On the 10th the Divisional Commander presented Croix de Guerre to Lieut. G. W. Bright, Sgt. Poole and Pte. Greaves for their gallantry at Bligny. On June 11th the 56th Composite Battalion moved into the line north-west of Chaumuzy, where it remained, under comparatively peaceful conditions, until the 18th, when it was relieved by an Italian unit. The Italians were obviously picked troops, well provided with interpreters, and were commanded by a descendant of the famous Garibaldi. Next day the 56th Battalion moved back to Hautvillers Wood, where it was broken up again into its component units. On the following day the Brigade marched to Le Mesnil, fifteen miles away, and the fact that not a man fell out was a noteworthy illustration of the spirit and discipline possessed by all ranks, despite the extreme hardships that had recently been undergone. On the 21st another move was made in lorries to Oyes, and thence next day to Broussey le Petit. Here the battalion stayed, training and reorganizing until the 2nd July, when it marched to Azincourt and thence to Vercouch on the 7th, where a reinforcement of 2 officers and 134 other ranks arrived.

The next move was to Lieres on the 14th, where the battalion was gradually built up to establishment again by almost daily drafts, until on the 6th of August, after "embussing" at La Bouverie, it moved up to the La Bassee Canal on the 7th, and on the 10th relieved the 8th N. Staffordshire Regiment in the front trenches near Locon. In this sector the comparatively heavy casualties suffered were due to the fact that the front line ran through standing corn which was drenched with gas each night by the enemy.

On August 17th, after being relieved by the 9th Cheshires, the battalion moved back to rest billets at Annezin. On the 25th it was back again in the front line in relief of the 8th N. Staffordshire Regiment. The enemy defence was at this time beginning to crumble and, giving him no rest, our positions were pushed forward upwards of a quarter of a mile, until on the 30th the 56th Brigade was relieved and went back by light railway to Chocques. Here on the 4th September information arrived that the battalion as a whole had been awarded the Croix de Guerre et Palme for its gallantry at Bligny on the 6th of June. This was conveyed in a special order of the day, a translation of which runs as follows:—

" General Order No. 371 by the General Commanding
" the 5th French Army, dated 21st August, 1918.
" On the 6th June, 1918, when the right flank of an
" English Brigade, which had been heavily engaged, was
" threatened by the enemy's advance, the reserve bat-
" talion—1/4 Battalion of the King's Shropshire Light
" Infantry—was ordered to deliver a counter-attack
" against an important position from which the garrison
" had been driven. With magnificent dash the 1/4
" K.S.L.I. advanced to the assault of the hill which had
" been occupied by the enemy, scattered death in his
" ranks and, after heavy fighting, took one officer and
" 28 men prisoners. Thanks to this vigorous and heroic
" recovery of a position which was the key to the whole
" line of defence, it was possible to re-establish the line
" and maintain it intact. By its rapid advance, its initia-
" tive and its superb valour, the 1/4 K.S.L.I. contributed
" in no small degree on this memorable occasion to the
" re-establishment of a position which had become ex-
" tremely critical.

"(Signed) Le General Commandant

" La Vme. Armee, BERTHELOT."

On September 5th the battalion entrained on the light railway for Le Touret, and eventually relieved the 9th Sherwood Foresters (47th Division) " in the line of retention " west of Richebourg St. Vaast. As the enemy was gradually retiring, the line kept moving forward, touch being maintained by active patrols. On the 9th the battalion relieved the 9th Battalion Cheshire Regiment, the left battalion of the 56th Brigade, near Bois Biez. In this position it stayed patrolling and consolidating until the 17th when, after being relieved by the 3rd Battalion Worcestershire Regiment, it went back to

Locon to rest. On the 21st the battalion was back in the line again relieving the 2nd Battalion Wiltshire Regiment.

In preparation for an attack on the enemy's position in the immediate future, patrolling was at this period very active with the object of discovering the strength of the posts in front and the extent to which our bombardment had been successful in cutting the wire. The attack which took place at 7.30 a.m. on September the 30th was completely successful, and by 7.45 the primary objective, La Laies Ditch, had been captured. Later in the day " Notion Trench " was also captured and consolidated. The casualties were, however, heavy, including Lieuts. W. Harty and R. E. H. Leech killed, and Lieut. H. E. A. Marindin who died of his wounds a week later. Next day the battalion was relieved by the 8th Battalion North Staffordshire Regiment and marched to another line of trenches in front of Lacoutre, where it was relieved on October 2nd by the 15th R. W. Fusiliers. The fact that the enemy had retired behind the Aubers ridge caused considerable delay, but eventually the battalion reached rest billets at Chamblain Chatelain on the 3rd. Two days later it moved to Bavincourt, thence to Graincourt on the 7th and then to Proville on the 10th, where billets vacated by the retreating enemy were occupied. The next few days were spent in clearing up the battlefield area until, on the 12th, Cambrai was entered. Here on the 13th the battalion had the honour of being selected to form the Guard of Honour to the French Premier. The town itself also had a considerable sentimental interest to the survivors of 1917, who had seen it in the distance for so many weeks from Welch Ridge.

As the enemy continued to retreat the battalion moved forward on the 17th to Avesnes les Aubert and thence on the 26th to Cagnoncles. It is significant of the change which had come over the general situation that the manœuvre most practised during this period of training was an advanced guard in open warfare.

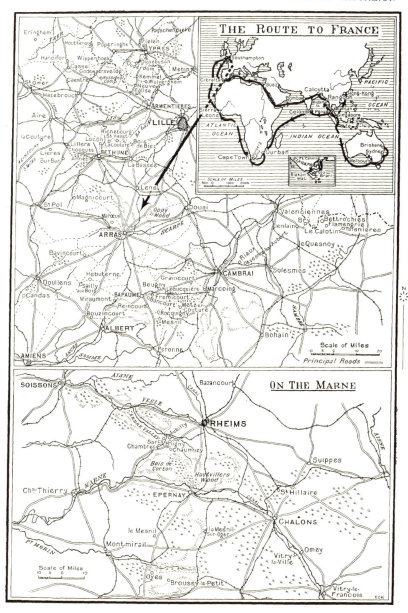

BATTLE OF THE SAMBRE

On the 3rd of November the battalion came under fire for the first time for nearly a month, and next day went into action for the last time in France. The enemy rearguards were holding a line west of the river between Jenlain, five miles south-east of Valenciennes, and Wargnies-le-Grand. At six o'clock on the morning of the 4th the position was attacked through Jenlain and captured. Casualties were, however, severe, amounting in all to 110, and including Captain L. O. Jordan, Herefordshire Regiment, killed. Next morning the battalion passed through the 8th N. Staffordshire Regiment and, continuing the attack to Le Calotin, eventually consolidated a position on the high ground east of La Flamengrie, having suffered little loss. During this operation in an advance of a few miles, the Belgian frontier was twice crossed, so tortuous is the line of demarcation hereabouts. On the morning of November 6th reconnoitring patrols reported machine guns active in the direction of Bettrechies, and a stream in front of the enemy position, 6 feet wide and 4 feet deep, which necessitated bridges, if a rapid crossing was to be made. Touch was maintained during the day till in the evening the battalion was relieved by a battalion of the Worcestershire Regiment and marched back to billets at Bry. Here, unfortunately, it came under long-distance shell fire and the last casualties sustained in France occurred, Lieut. R. Hibbard and 2 other ranks being killed and 8 other ranks wounded.

The rapid retirement of the enemy on the Divisional front led to a further forward movement, and on November 7th an advance was made to Tasnieres, a distance of some eight or nine miles. Despite the fact that alternate fighting and marching had taken place almost continuously for the previous six days not a single man fell out.

On reaching Tasnieres patrols were sent out which failed to gain touch with the enemy, and later in the evening news arrived from the cavalry that the enemy had retreated beyond the railway running north and south between Maubeuge and Mons. Next day, the 19th Division was drawn out of the pursuit, and the battalion returned to Bry. At 9.30 a.m. on the 11th intimation arrived that hostilities would cease at 11 a.m.

The first few days after the Armistice were spent in cleaning up, checking deficiencies and salving the huge quantities of stores left behind on the battlefield until, on the 15th, the battalion marched to Rieux, moving thence to Cambrai on the 25th, to Rubempre on the 29th, and to Villars l'Hospital on the 15th December. Here a halt was made until May 4th, 1919, when the cadre left for England, eventually arriving at Southampton on the 18th.

From October, 1917, until the Armistice the battalion was engaged in almost continual fighting, and few of those who sailed for the East in 1914 remained until the end. It is, however, pleasant to be able to record that there are several officers and N.C.O.'s still serving in 1924 in the 4th K.S.L.I. who were with it at the outbreak of war.

Casualties in France were :—

Officers killed 11, wounded 77; other ranks 253 killed, 1260 wounded. In addition some 170 were taken prisoner, three of whom died in captivity.

CHAPTER IV

THE FIFTH BATTALION

ON the 6th August, 1914, two days after the Declaration of War, Captain G. A. Delmé-Murray, Captain R. Fort, 2nd Lieut. R. H. Shears and 30 other ranks of the 1st Battalion K.S.L.I. left Tipperary to form the nucleus of the 1st Service Battalion. Major H. M. Smith, Commanding Depot, was appointed to the command, and the men were accommodated in hutments at Blackdown Camp, Aldershot. The battalion left the depot by companies, the last company leaving on August 27th. 1914.

There was no recruiting in the ordinary sense of the word, merely a printed notice signed " Kitchener, Field-Marshal," informing everyone who chose to read that Our King and our Country needed its able-bodied men in this great emergency. The call was not in vain and thousands from Shropshire, Herefordshire and the bordering Welsh counties flocked to the Regimental Depot at Shrewsbury in order that they might have the honour of being chosen for the First Service Battalion of the County Regiment. This was designated the 5th K.S.L.I., and allotted to the 42nd Brigade of the 14th Light Division. The Brigade Commander was Br.-General C. J. Markham, and the other battalions of the Brigade were the 5th Ox. and Bucks L.I., the 9th K.R.R., and the 9th R.B. The Division was commanded by Major-General V. Couper.

Drafts arrived at Blackdown at intervals of a few days, and companies were formed—A Company first, and the other three as the numbers arrived. At first the men were without rifles, equipment or uniform, and there was great excitement when C Company arrived from the depot fully dressed in khaki, and with rifles and equipment complete. Alas! this did not last long, the losses of the retreat from Mons had to be made good, and in a few days all this panoply of war was taken away to be sent to France for the fighting men there.

The weather was beautiful and training began at

once. The keenness of all ranks was intense. From morning till night, Sundays included, drilling went on, but after a fortnight or so it was recognized that the pace was too hot to last, and Sunday became to some extent a day of rest, and the work on week-days was modified to the capacity of the men.

The raw material of all ranks was excellent. Some of the officers came from the O.T.C. of Shrewsbury School, but with few exceptions all were ignorant of military matters. Officers and N.C.O.'s who had to instruct learnt their work by teaching, and the progress of the battalion was rapid. Some sergeants of the Marines were lent to the battalion as instructors and did good service, and M. H. White and J. H. Tombling, two schoolmasters from Shrewsbury School, spent their holiday helping. In a short time the battalion was over establishment and Lt.-Colonel S. G. Moore was given the surplus to form the 6th Battalion.

From Blackdown the Brigade proceeded to North Camp, Aldershot, the battalion sharing Malplaquet Barracks with the 5th Ox. and Bucks. Here a strong feeling of comradeship sprang up between the two battalions, which lasted till the 5th Battalion was broken up.

With the approach of winter the battalion marched on the 27th November sixteen miles to Chiddingfold in Surrey, where they occupied billets. The people of Chiddingfold were exceedingly good to all ranks, and many still carry grateful recollections of this beautiful village. Here training of a more advanced type began, and the clothing and equipment of the men were gradually completed.

On 23rd January, 1915, the battalion, together with some thousands of other troops, was inspected near Witley by Lord Kitchener and a representative of the French Government. As it was thought advisable that the French should know how well equipped the troops were, great coats were not allowed to be worn, and few who attended this parade will ever forget it. It snowed all the time and the cold was bitter. However, the French General was heard to say " C'est magnifique," and the praise was certainly not undeserved.

About the 8th March the Brigade returned to Aldershot, and the 5th K.S.L.I. shared Salamanca Barracks with the 5th Ox. and Bucks. Their Majesties The King and Queen inspected the troops at Aldershot and also attended a cross-country running competition in which Pte. D. Stewart of the battalion came in first. H.M. The Queen presented the prizes. Training continued and included a course of musketry.

Early in May measles having broken out in the battalion, it was moved to Watts Common under canvas, and severe weather and much snow made conditions most unpleasant.

All ranks now knew that the great day when they would move to France was approaching, and when, on 9th May, 1915, Lieut. P. Bellasis left for duties at the port of disembarkation, and the battalion was placed on a war footing, hope grew high, but another week passed before the advanced party left Aldershot for Southampton. Here, on the 19th May, Major J. G. Forbes with Lieut. S. G. Beaumont, Lieut. J. C. B. Firth, 109 other ranks, 79 horses and mules, and the whole of the transport embarked and sailed for France. On the following day 28 officers, 797 other ranks, under Lt.-Colonel H. M. Smith, left Aldershot in two trains at 5.20 and 5.45 a.m. and proceeded via Folkestone and Boulogne to Osterhove rest camp, on the outskirts of Boulogne. The advanced party entrained at Havre on May 20th, and after a night journey arrived at Pont de Bricque at 9.30 a.m. on the 21st, where the battalion was found drawn up ready to join the train. In five minutes all were aboard on the way to Cassel.

The following are the names of the officers who crossed to France :—

Lt.-Colonel H. M. Smith, Commanding
Major J. G. Forbes, 2nd in Command
    „   R. A. A. Y. Jordan, D Company
    „   G. A. Delmé-Murray, A Company

Captain T. Avery
    ,,   W. L. Herd, B
        Company
    ,,   C. J. French
Lieut. N. T. Porter
    ,,   R. S. Clarke, Sig-
        nalling Officer
    ,,   J. C. B. Firth, Trans-
        port Officer
2nd Lieut. E. G. R. Lloyd,
        Bombing Officer
    ,,   C. W. Mould
    ,,   R. F. Taylor
    ,,   R. G. Budgen
    ,,   A. C. L. Ward
    ,,   V. D. French

Captain T. E. Moore-Lane
        C Company
    ,,   H. E. Measor
    ,,   R. Meynell
Lieut. H. G. Booker
    ,,   B. H. Ellis
    ,,   S. Beaumont
    ,,   P. J. Bellasis

2nd Lieut. F. H. W. Hunt
    ,,   H. W. G. Ripley
    ,,   R. G. W. Stark
    ,,   P. C. Owen
    ,,   F. C. Roden
    ,,   F. S. Holt

Lieut. Qr.-Master P. Bradshaw
Lieut. J. Penny, R.A.M.C.

Captain R. Fort, the Adjutant, was left behind with measles, and the Rev. W. Amery, R. C. Chaplain, joined on the journey.

Arrived at Cassel, a long and tiring march was made to Erkelsbrugge, where the companies were billeted in farms. Here the battalion remained until the 27th May, 1915, being inspected on the 24th by Br.-General Stopford, after which a move was made to Eecke, a march of sixteen miles.

It was fairly clear by this time that our destination was to be the Ypres salient, and on the 30th A and B Companies, and the transport, proceeded to Dickebusch, and next day the whole battalion now concentrated was addressed by Major-General Sir Charles Ferguson to whose Division it was attached for instruction.

The same day two companies moved to some dug-outs near Ypres and in the evening, 31st May, the battalion came under fire for the first time. Some new trenches were being constructed at Zillebeke, not far from

Hill 60, and Colonel H. M. Smith went up with 550 other ranks to do the digging. This was done at night, by the light of the Véry lights which the Germans threw up all the time. Although the diggers were not visible to the Germans, the enemy kept up a constant unaimed rifle fire with the result that Sgt. A. R. Diss was killed and 3 other ranks wounded. The neighbourhood of the dug-outs was shelled on the 1st and 2nd, but there were no casualties.

On the 3rd June the battalion went back to Canada Huts near Dickebusch till the 6th, and on every night during this time a portion of the battalion was employed on digging with the result that 2 other ranks were killed and 10 wounded, in addition to those mentioned above. Dickebusch at this time was still a town with shops and cabarets, although it was not particularly " healthy " even then, as German shells fell into it, or near it, several times a day.

Having had instruction in digging under fire, it was now time for the battalion to learn something of life and discipline in the trenches, so on the 6th June it marched to Locre. The line in front of Locre was held by a Brigade of Sherwood Foresters (T.F.), with the Head-quarters of the Brigade at Locre. The Brigade band played in the evening, and after the experience of the Ypres district this seemed a peaceful sport. C and D Companies went up past Mount Kemmel to the trenches, D Company being attached to the 6th, and C to the 8th Sherwood Foresters—and for two days saw all that could be seen in the time of trench routine. Then A and B Companies relieved them on the third evening and underwent the same instruction. A post occupied by B Company was attacked by bomb throwers, but these were driven off by rifle fire. The casualties during the week were 3 other ranks killed and 5 wounded.

On the 11th June A and B Companies returned to Locre from the trenches and on the next day the battalion marched back to Canada Huts, and on the 14th to huts just south of Vlamertinghe. On this day the 1st Battalion passed through Vlamertinghe on its way up to the trenches, and, word having been received that it was coming, the 5th lined the streets to receive them. The 1st Battalion was halted for a few minutes and there was a hurried greeting of old friends. The first draft, of 99 men, arrived in the evening.

FIRST ATTACK ON BELLEWAERDE, 1915

On the 16th June the 42nd Brigade took part in an attack which was made by a Territorial Division on the German trenches. The battalion on the night of the 15th dug itself in near the Ypres–Roulers railway line south-east of, and just outside, the walls of Ypres, and on the morning of the 16th, after listening to two hours' bombardment of the German trenches by our guns, marched at ten o'clock to support the attack. It was intended to support the centre, but on debouching from the railway cutting at " Hell-Fire " Corner the battalion came under a heavy fire of high explosive and other shells, and in consequence was diverted to the right. The two leading platoons of A Company did not receive the order to retire, and continued their way under heavy fire in the open to the original objective, a sunken road.

The remainder of the battalion, on reaching the high ground near Gordon House, came under heavy gun fire from the direction of Hill 60, and the platoons lost touch with one another. The trench which passes Gordon House being discovered, most of the battalion entered this and passed along it. It was already packed with men of all regiments taking part in the attack, and after reaching the low ground near and across the Menin Road it was so crowded that it was impossible to move.

About four o'clock a movement was made to retire, but no orders having been received it was impossible to know if the order which was passed from mouth to mouth was genuine. A heavy but fortunately inaccurate fire from the German guns was being directed on the trench, and some men trying to leave the trench and run across the open were instantly shot down by the enemy. By degrees men of the various units crowded together, were sorted out and reorganised and in groups made their way back to their starting-place. A few hours after daybreak of the 17th the survivors of the battalion were back at Vlamertinghe. The casualties in this fight were as follows: Captain T. Avery, Lieut. B. H. Ellis and 11 other ranks killed; 2nd Lieut. V. D. French, 2nd Lieut. R. G. W. Stark and 57 other ranks wounded, 1 other rank missing. 2nd Lieut. French died next day and was buried at Dickebusch. The 17th and 18th were given over to rest and refitting. On the 19th a draft of 82 men arrived from England and the battalion went into the trenches for the first time on its own, taking over from the Suffolk Regiment. Gordon House, the Battalion Head-quarters, was a shattered farmhouse with a deep cellar. A pump in what remained of the scullery was a great asset, water being scarce in the trenches. On the first night there was considerable rifle fire by our own troops on each flank of the battalion, and heavy shelling by the Germans kept the battalion under arms all through the second night. On the 21st there was again heavy shelling, and on the 22nd Lieut. E. G. R. Lloyd and the battalion bombers took part in an attack made on our left by the 5th Ox. and Bucks. On the 23rd there was some firing, and on the morning of 24th one of the support trenches occupied by C Company was wrecked by shells.

The casualties for the tour of five days were 3 other ranks killed and Lieut. H. G. Booker and 42 other ranks wounded.

The battalion was relieved on 24th at 10 p.m. by the 10th D.L.I. The relief took place without casualties and with very little firing, but it was not till 6 a.m. 25th that all the companies reached Zwynland, one mile south-west of Poperinghe, and bivouacked in and about a farmhouse there. A hot meal had been provided in a field east of Vlamertinghe on the way back, but despite this the men were exhausted on reaching their bivouac.

The battalion remained at Zwynland for a fortnight and a pleasant time it was, except for the trench digging, the weather being fine and warm. A cricket match against the R.A.S.C. was played. The amenities of Poperinghe, as yet little damaged by the enemy, were appreciated greatly. Here a civilized meal could be obtained at a restaurant, and the men revelled in the hot baths provided for them at the Poperinghe Brewery. On the 5th July the 1st Battalion came on a route march through our camp and halted for an hour, and on that same evening there were sports. The principal drawback to this life was the continual trench digging. A party of from 100 to 400 would parade at 6 p.m., march to the outskirts of Poperinghe where London buses, with the glass taken out and replaced by boards, and painted khaki colour, would arrive and into these the party would get. The men soon discovered that the rule that each bus should only carry a certain number was strictly adhered to, and that any surplus had to be sent back to bivouac, so after the first journey they did not press to be the first in. In these buses they were taken to some R.E. " dump " and handed out picks, shovels and sandbags, and marched in the dark, guided by a R.E. N.C.O., to some spot in rear of the firing line and given tasks. The darkness was of short duration at this time of the year, and hardly was the task commenced than it was time to knock off work and get away before the light of dawn should give the Hun the chance of a shot. Then back to the dump, into the buses, back to Poperinghe and march to bivouac, arriving at about 6 a.m.—a twelve hours' outing and possibly less than two hours' digging. The casualties during this fortnight were 2 other ranks wounded with the first party that went up.

On the 1st July a draft of fifty men under Captain E. J. E. Tunmer arrived; he, however, returned to the base on the 3rd. On the 8th the Brigade went into the line again, the 5th Ox. and Bucks and 9th R.B. to the trenches, with the 9th K.R.R. and 5th K.S.L.I. in reserve in the ramparts of Ypres. The same night a carrying party of 600 men went up to the trenches with rations, water and engineering material for the 5th Ox. and Bucks. The regimental transport brought the rations and water as far at the ramparts, arriving after dark to avoid the enemy fire. The rations were in sandbags, so many rations in each bag. The water was in petrol tins, and all this was unloaded at the Battalion H.Q., whence it had to be carried by hand to the H.Q. of the battalion in the trenches. The nights, as stated above, were very short and the distance to the 5th Ox. and Bucks Battalion H.Q. at Railway Wood was over two miles and, after leaving the Menin Road, through narrow and tortuous communication trenches, often with a foot or so of water in them, so that it was not easy to get back before it was light. It was a dangerous proceeding, for, even in the dark, the Hun occasionally made a lucky shot, and it was a duty that required great faithfulness in performance. Time in the ramparts was spent carrying for the Ox. and Bucks by night, and clearing up the streets of Ypres (Ypres was shelled practically every day), and improving the dugouts in which the men lived by day. On July 9th the Germans shelled the ramparts and vicinity of the Menin gate with gas shells and wounded 2nd Lieut. F. S. Holt and 3 men. In addition during our stay here 2 men were wounded carrying rations, and Pte. A. D. Harford, M.G. Section, was killed by a shell and buried by the Ox. and Bucks in Railway Wood.

On the 13th July the battalion took over the trenches from the 5th Ox. and Bucks about Railway Wood, being relieved on the 18th by the D.C.L.I. machine gunners, signallers and bombers and the Somerset L.I. The relief was not completed till 2.45 a.m. on the 19th, and it was a hustle to get out before daybreak

The casualties during this tour in the trenches were 4 other ranks killed (1 accidental), 40 other ranks wounded, of which 2 died of wounds. During this tour Lt.-Colonel

H. M. Smith was wounded by a splinter from a " Whiz-bang," but the wound being slight he remained on duty. Owing to the lateness of the relief it was 5.30 a.m. before the battalion got to their bivouac at Busseboom, two and a half miles south-east of Poperinghe.

Working parties now became the order of the day and night on a redoubt near Vlamertinghe and at the White Château, a very " unhealthy " place, but fortunately there were no casualties. At 7 p.m. on the 19th July we saw from our bivouac the explosion caused by blowing up the mines which had been made under Hooge Château, and heard next day that the operation had been success-ful and that the crater had been occupied by our troops. On 22nd July Lt.-Colonel H. M. Smith, who had been more seriously hurt than he would acknowledge, had to go to hospital to the regret of all ranks, and Major J. G. Forbes succeeded to the command.

On 26th July, the battalion reinforced by a draft of 40 other ranks which had arrived on the 23rd, returned to the ramparts and took over from the Somerset L.I. The usual routine of carrying started again ; two mules were killed and a limber waggon was damaged by shell fire in Ypres when on ration duty. On the 30th Lieut. F. T. Burrough arrived, and on the same day the Germans attacked and captured the crater which had been formed by the blowing up of Hooge Château on the 19th July. In consequence of this attack the order which had been given for the battalion to relieve the Ox. and Bucks in the trenches at Railway Wood was cancelled. A counter-attack being made by the 9th K.R.R., Lieut. Lloyd and his bombers were sent to assist. The companies were ordered to various trenches in support one after another on the night of 30th July and the morning of 31st July. On the morning of 31st orders were received to relieve the 9th K.R.R.C. in the front trenches by daylight, but this was found to be impossible and it was not till midnight that the relief was complete.

A B and C Companies were in trenches in the front

line near the culvert and were placed under the command of Colonel Villiers Stuart, 9th Rifle Brigade.

On the 2nd August the 8th K.R.R.C., under Colonel Green, came up and took over from Colonel Villiers Stuart, A, B and C Companies remaining with him. Battalion Head-quarters was moved to H.Q. lines and the " New General's Dug-out " handed over to Colonel Green. Captain R. Fort, who had remained behind sick, arrived and took over the duties of Adjutant from Lieut. R. Taylor. On the 4th August, 1915, the battalion was relieved by the 1st K.S.L.I., which had come up for an attack on the German lines with the 16th and 18th Brigades, and proceeded to some dug-outs near the *Ecole* just east of Ypres, with A and B Companies in the H.Q. trench north of Menin Road. Here a reinforcement of 40 other ranks arrived. On the 6th, the 5th K.S.L.I. relieved the 5th Ox. and Bucks in the trenches about Railway Wood. Colonel Cobb, 5th Ox. and Bucks, was in command of this (left) sector.

For the next three days the trenches underwent a severe bombardment. What was called the " apex of the salient," which was on our immediate right and occupied successively by two companies 9th K.R.R.C. and two companies 9th R.B., was intensely bombarded and the trenches wrecked.

LAST ACTION OF HOOGE

On August 9th the attack on the German lines by the 16th and 18th Brigades took place ; it was preceded by a bombardment of the German trenches which lasted from 2.45 a.m. till 3.15 a.m., and was supported by the rifle and machine-gun fire of the 5th K.S.L.I. The attack was successful and resulted in the capture of the Hooge crater and other German trenches. This relieved the situation and on the night of the 10th, after a quiet day, the battalion was relieved by one platoon 10th Durham L.I. and the 6th Somerset L.I., and arrived in bivouac west of Vlamertinghe and north of Brandhoek early next morning.

The casualties between the 26th June, when the battalion went to the Ypres ramparts, and the 10th August, when it was relieved at Railway Wood, were: Lieut. R. F. Taylor and 27 other ranks killed. Captains H. E. Measor, R. Meynell, W. L. Herd, T. E. Moore-Lane, P. J. Bellasis, Lieut. E. G. R. Lloyd and 129 other ranks wounded, 4 other ranks died of wounds. When in this bivouac 2nd Lieut. W. F. W. Shields and 40 other ranks arrived from the base. On the 17th Major J. G. Forbes and Major R. A. A. Y. Jordan left for England, and Lieut.-Colonel O. C. Borrett, King's Own R.L. Regiment, took over command. About this time Br.-General C. J. Markham also left and Colonel Cobb of the Ox. and Bucks took over command of the Brigade. The battalion remained in this bivouac till 20th, finding many working parties, but only losing one man wounded.

On the 19th there was an inspection of the battalion by the Brigadier in the morning, and in the evening the G.O.C. 5th Corps addressed the officers and said that the regiment had a very fine name and that he was proud to have one of the battalions under his command. On the same day 2nd Lieut. H. D. E. Elliott joined with a draft of 55 other ranks. On the 20th the battalion moved into hutments about half a mile north-west of Vlamertinghe as Brigade Reserve, and on the 22nd the following officers arrived: Lieut. T. G. Bonnyman, Lieut. J. H. Llewellyn, 2nd Lieut. R. S. Foster, 2nd Lieut. C. C. Smith, 2nd Lieut. E. C. Faulkner and 2nd Lieut. W. L. Davis.

On the 23rd Captain E. J. E. Tunmer and Lieut. F. T. Burrough were wounded while visiting the trenches preparatory to the battalion taking over that night the line held by the 5th Ox. and Bucks. During this tour Lieut. R. G. Budgen was killed by a sniper's bullet and Lieut T. G. Bonnyman and 13 other ranks wounded; and 2nd Lieut. A. O. Egerton joined on the 26th. The battalion was relieved on the 29th by the 6th D.C.L.I.

From the 30th August to 6th September the battalion

was bivouacked north of Brandhoek, half-way between Vlamertinghe and Poperinghe. Here Lieut. J. T. Smeall, R.A.M.C., and 40 other ranks reported for duty. On 7th September the battalion returned to the trenches near Ypres, C and D Companies in H.Q. trench, north and south of Menin Road, with H.Q. and A and B Companies . in dug-outs near the *Ecole* east of Ypres, and on 11th H.Q., A and B took over the front trenches from 5th Ox. and Bucks; 4 other ranks were wounded during the tour. On 15th September the battalion was relieved by a Yorkshire battalion and on the way back to bivouac D Company was shelled, losing 2 other ranks killed and 12 wounded. At this bivouac, which was two miles north-west of Poperinghe, the battalion was inspected on the 17th. by General Plumer, the Army Commander. Here rehearsals for an attack were gone through, and on the night 23rd/24th of September the battalion in fighting order, strength 17 officers, 780 other ranks, moved up to Ypres by train. The trenches in Railway Wood were occupied by the battalion in preparation for the attack which was to be made on the following day with the object of holding back German troops from the Battle of Loos.

At 3.50 a.m. on the 24th September our guns bombarded the enemy trenches till 4.20 a.m. Retaliation immediately followed and a bombardment of our trenches was maintained throughout the day, resulting in Captain S. G. Beaumont being killed and 8 other ranks wounded. At 3.50 a.m. on 25th our artillery again intensely bombarded the enemy trenches and at 4.5 a.m. the battalion was in position for the assault. A and D companies and half B Company with two machine guns and signallers were in company column in front of our own trenches, and half B and C Companies in support in the trenches.

At 4.20 a.m. the assault took place and, as far as the battalion was concerned, was successful in that it carried out its allotted task and reached the second line of enemy trenches. The battalions on the right and left, however, were not able to reach their objectives, and consequently, when the Germans brought up fresh troops for the counter-attack, the position of the 5th K.S.L.I. became untenable, and there was nothing to do but to retire to the original line—or what was left of it—as the trenches had been filled in almost everywhere by the German shell fire. This retirement was effected about 8.15 a.m., the losses being very heavy, so much so that later in the day it was necessary to reinforce the remnants of the battalion by two platoons of the 6th Somerset L.I. The Germans bombarded the trenches heavily up till 1 p.m., and again from 9 p.m. till midnight. Just before midnight the battalion was relieved by the 6th D.C.L.I. and returned to billets near Poperinghe.

The casualties during the attack were 7 officers killed and 5 wounded, 41 other ranks killed, 280 wounded, 100 missing, 7 wounded and missing. Names of officers killed: Capts. R. S. Clarke, C. W. Mould, F. H. W. Hunt, Lieut. W. F. W. Shields, 2nd Lieuts. P. C. Owen, C. C. Smith, and A. O. Egerton.

Wounded: Major G. A. Delmé-Murray, Capt. R. Fort, Lieuts. H. W. G. Ripley, R. S. Foster, and J. C. B. Firth. The only officers untouched were Lt.-Colonel O. C. Borrett and Captain N. T. Porter. Many of the missing, however, reported later, some after wandering about for three or four days looking for their unit. On the 26th the V Corps Commander paid a visit and congratulated the battalion on its good bearing on the 25th inst., and said it could rest assured that it had drawn considerable forces of the enemy towards Ypres, and prevented him from reinforcing down south. It could therefore be said that the battalion had materially assisted in the victory round Arras.

The battalion remained in billets till October 12th. On the 13th it returned to the trenches, with H.Q. near the *Ecole* just outside Ypres, in relief of the 7th R.B., and on the 17th, owing to increased enemy activity, the battalion moved up to support the 5th Ox. and Bucks. On the 18th it relieved the 8th R.B. in A Sector, a new

part of the line, with H.Q. at Potijze Wood, remaining
till relieved on 21st by the 1st Leicesters. There were no
casualties during either of these tours.

On the 22nd the battalion proceeded to billets at
Houtkerque, north-west of Poperinghe, where two reinforcements of 10 and 22 other ranks joined.

On 27th October, 1915, His Majesty The King was
present when the Army Commander inspected selected
detachments of the VI Corps at Abeele. Lt.-Colonel
O. C. Borrett was in command of a Composite Battalion,
and the detachment of the 5th K.S.L.I. consisted of
Captain N. T. Porter and 25 other ranks, of whom 9,
namely, Sgt. Gittins, Sgt. Williams, Corpl. King, L.-
Corpls. Wilson and Parsons, Ptes. Lloyd, Crawshaw,
Jordan and Lloyd, had been recommended for honours
and awards.

On the 18th November the battalion relieved the West
Yorkshire Regiment in the trenches near Ypres with
H.Q. at Potijze Wood, and on relief by the 5th Ox. and
Bucks on the 21st marched to huts at Brandhoek. The
casualties for this tour were 2nd Lieut. E. W. Partridge
and 2nd Lieut. V. B. Hoskins and 1 other rank killed,
and 5 other ranks wounded; a reinforcement of 20 other
ranks arrived on 19th.

The winter had now set in and at this time of the year
there are a few places in Europe more unpleasant than
Belgium. And it was Belgium at its worst, the country
water-logged, and the numerous shell-holes filled with
muddy water. The men, however, made light of these
hardships and their general health was good.

From November, 1915, until February, 1916, the
battalion remained in the northern sector of the Ypres
salient occupied with tours in the trenches and in reserve
in huts at Brandhoek. During the winter the period of
duty in the front line was shortened and averaged about
four days. A welcome rest came at Christmas time when
the battalion moved out of the line from 16th to 29th
December into billets at Houtkerque. During this

period Major G. A. Delmé-Murray and Captain H. E. Measor rejoined the battalion, and the following officers, with a draft of 150 other ranks, reported for duty: 2nd Lieuts. L. A. Jones, R. A. Butt, C. S. Underhill, H. G. P. Bulmer, R. Brooke, R. B. D. Malden, W. F. Sheather and Captain O. Skulley (R.C. Chaplain).

The casualties for the period were 2nd Lieut. R. A. Butt killed, 2nd Lieut. C. S. Underhill (died of wounds), 43 other ranks killed and 89 other ranks wounded.

The winter dragged itself on and the discomforts were telling to a certain extent on the men when on the 11th February, 1916, a new Division arrived in the salient, and curiously enough the battalion was relieved in the trenches by the 6th K.S.L.I., a chance meeting which caused great pleasure. During this relief the enemy attacked one of the trenches with bombs, but was driven away by our bombers and machine gunners. Casualties in the relief amounted to 10 other ranks killed and 17 other ranks wounded. Three machine gunners were reported missing and believed killed, but they returned to the battalion on the 14th with their machine gun. On relief the battalion marched to billets at Hout-kerque, and on the following day to Wormhout, where it remained for ten days, being inspected on the 17th by the 42nd Brigade Commander. While at Wormhout 2nd Lieut. R. G. W. Stark rejoined and the following officers, Lieut. F. W. Rhodes and 2nd Lieuts. T. E. Burke, R. R. Lawrence, W. J. G. Yeomans and G. C. Sharp, and 28 other ranks, joined the battalion. Two officers and 33 other ranks left the battalion to form a Brigade Machine-Gun Company.

At last, after nine weary months, news was received that the battalion was to leave what was generally considered the most unpleasant spot in Europe, and on the 21st February, wishing their successors the best of luck, the 5th K.S.L.I. turned its back on Ypres and the salient in the hope never to return again. Leaving Wormhout the battalion entrained at Esquelbecq at 9 a.m. and reached

Longeau just outside Amiens at 8 p.m., where buses conveyed the men to billets at Berteaucourt-les-Dames which was reached in the early morning of 22nd.

Here the battalion remained till the 25th, when it marched to Grand Rullecourt. A heavy snowstorm made the conditions so difficult for men and animals that the march was not completed till 7.30 a.m. on the 27th. Leaving Grand Rullecourt on the 29th Sombrin was reached the same day and on the 1st March the battalion moved to Berneville. Here they remained three days and on the 5th marched to Arras, in or near which town they were destined to remain for many months. These marches were a great test of endurance to men who had been so long in water-logged trenches, and the battalion came out of them with every credit. Not only had they to compete with heavy snowstorms, but, on one of the longest marches, a French division was encountered on the move, and the transport of our Allies became hopelessly mixed with ours, which consequently, owing to the treacherous state of the road, had to be man-handled for practically a whole day's march.

All ranks were much impressed by the beauty of Arras in spite of the fact that by this time many of its finest buildings had been much damaged, but the chief cause of delight was the extremely comfortable billets. The next few days were spent in getting a general idea of the trench system and the defences of the town.

On the 7th ten men of a party carrying rations to the 9th R.B. in the trenches were accidentally wounded by the explosion of a French bomb which was lying on the road over which they were marching.

Captain E. J. E. Tunmer rejoined on this day and a draft of 60 other ranks was received. On the 13th the battalion commenced its first tour of duty in the trenches of the new area. The distribution of the battalion was three companies in the line and one company as battalion reserve with Head-quarters at Ronville, a small suburb of Arras within 800 to 1,000 yards of the front line.

Despite this proximity the houses had been little damaged, and many of the gardens looked as if they had been cared for quite recently. The trenches handed over by the French were extremely good, with deep dug-outs and beautifully dry. Considerable damage was done to one of the front trenches on this tour by German artillery, to which our artillery replied. A draft of 41 other ranks joined for duty on the 18th, and the casualties for the tour were 3 other ranks killed, 13 other ranks wounded.

On the 22nd the battalion went into billets at Simencourt till the 29th, during which time Captain R. Fort, 2nd Lieut. W. J. Milton and Captain N. T. Porter rejoined, and Captain C. D. Harris and 30 other ranks joined the battalion.

The usual tours of duty in the trenches now commenced. Sometimes a certain amount of artillery fire took place, chiefly on the back areas, but more often there was little of interest to report. Whilst in billets drafts of officers and men constantly arrived from England. These newcomers brought with them wonderful reports and rumours which though highly improbable, and usually without the slightest foundation, yet gave rise to interesting discussion which helped to pass the few days of rest. It must not be thought that " rest " meant literally doing nothing, as short parades were constantly taking place whenever the ground and the enemy allowed such exercise, and in addition there were many brigade and battalion rifle meetings when far away from the line.

During April Captain S. Clarke (R.C. Chaplain), 2nd Lieut. A. Hyndman and 71 other ranks joined, and Captain P. J. Bellasis, Captain T. E. Moore-Lane and Lieut. E. G. R. Lloyd rejoined the battalion. The casualties for the month were 4 other ranks wounded.

In May the battalion was in trenches on the anniversary of its landing in France, but on relief it went to Bernville where battalion sports took place. During the month 1 other rank was killed and 1 wounded. Lieut.

J. C. B. Firth rejoined, and 2nd Lieut. J. H. Quirk, 2nd Lieut. H. J. Kendall and thirty other ranks joined the battalion.

In June 2 other ranks were killed and Lieut. C. B. Firth (Transport Officer) and 7 other ranks wounded. 2nd Lieuts. H. T. Hughes, C. V. Holder, M. I. Machell and 8 other ranks joined the battalion.

On the 15th July, 1916, the Commanding Officer, Lt.-Colonel O. C. Borrett, was transferred to the command of the 1st Battalion of his own regiment, the King's Own R. Lancashire Regiment. His departure was regretted, for he was both an able and popular Commanding Officer. Major Delmé-Murray succeeded to the command. On 1st July the great Battle of the Somme which was destined to last for many months commenced. Early in the month it became known that the battalion would take part therein. When therefore the battalion was relieved on the 27th July by the 9th Battalion Lancashire Fusiliers, and marched to Agnez-Les-Duisans, no one was surprised to hear that the march to the battle had commenced.

BATTLES OF THE SOMME, 1916

The battalion was certainly not lucky in the weather for its marches; it was now extremely hot, even for July, and after a prolonged period of comparative inactivity the strain of marching fully equipped was very great. Fortunately the marches were not too long, and the billets at Grand-Rullecourt, Barly and Candas, where halts were made, were extremely good, and the villagers always gave the men a hearty welcome. From Candas a long train journey was made to Mericourt, and after about two miles' marching Buire-Sur-L'Ancre was reached on the 7th August.

During July the casualties were 3 other ranks killed and 30 wounded. The following 2nd Lieuts, joined the battalion, R. C. M. Elliott, N. P. d'Albuquerque, V. J. Simpson, W. L. Faber, H. Atkinson, J. C. Thompson,

141

THE KING'S SHROPSHIRE LIGHT INFANTRY

N. R. Cosgrove, J. A. Lee, A. W. Parsons, J. W. Jackson, J. Higginson and W. H. Jones.

On the 12th August the battalion marched to bivouac near Fricourt. On the 18th a portion of the battalion was lent to the 43rd Brigade, who were making an attack on the enemy, as reserve, and 5 other ranks were wounded.

BATTLE OF DELVILLE WOOD

On the 24th the 42nd Brigade made an attack. On the 21st the battalion had taken up a line of trenches on the edge of Delville Wood and a continuous bombardment of the enemy's lines was kept up on the 22nd and 23rd. The 5th K.S.L.I. was in the centre with 9th K.R.R. on the right and 5th Ox. and Bucks on the left.

At 5.45 a.m. the attack began, and so far as the battalion was concerned was successful, the enemy being cleared from the edge of the Wood, but the success was only temporary, for the right flank being unsupported the battalion was obliged to withdraw to its own trenches, and eventually to the second line. During this action the battalion captured 2 machine guns, 2 officers and 115 other ranks.

Casualties: Captains P. J. Bellasis, J. H. Llewellyn, and 2nd Lieuts. R. C. M. Elliott, W. L. Faber, C. V. Holder, R. R. Lawrence, and V. J. Simpson killed, and 194 other ranks.

The following congratulatory messages were received:

From the 4th Army on 26th October, 1916.

" The Army Commander congratulates all ranks on " their gallant attack on 24th inst."

14th (Light) Division Special order.

" On completing our first tour in the Battle of the " Somme, the G.O.C. wishes to express to all units and " all ranks his great appreciation of the discipline, hard " work and cheerfulness shown by the Officers, N.C.O.'s " and men of the 14th (Light) Division. . . ."

After this the battalion went back to the bivouac near Fricourt, about four miles from the scene of action.

On the 28th August, 1916, it was again in the trenches in Delville Wood in relief of the 6th K.O.Y.L.I. The weather was now very bad with incessant rain, and this, combined with the heavy shelling, made the holding of the line particularly onerous. Delville Wood at this time, although much damaged, still gave considerable protection from view, and this turned out to be rather a snare, as it was difficult to realize that trees were a very small protection against shell fire or even rifle bullets.

The casualties for the tour were 8 other ranks killed, 32 other ranks wounded and 4 missing.

On the early morning of the 31st the battalion was relieved by the 8th R. West Kent Regiment and returned to bivouac near Fricourt, whence after a few hours' interval for rest it was conveyed by motor-buses to Mericourt station and entraining at about 6 p.m. arrived at Airaines at 10.15 p.m. From here a march of about five miles brought it about 2.30 a.m., 1st September, to Vergies, a pretty little village many miles beyond the sound of the guns.

On the 19th August 2nd Lieut. J. Reynolds reported for duty.

The battalion rested here for eleven days, and refitted for its next effort in the great battle that was for ever calling for fresh regiments and new leaders. Now for the first time since the battalion was formed it received drafts from units other than its own. The first of these drafts was composed of 1/6th and 1/7th (T.F.) Notts and Derby Regiment, and it brought home the appalling wastage of human material in war.

While at Vergies Lieut. J. C. Jinks and his Lewis-gun section, which had been unable to leave the trenches on August 31st, rejoined the battalion. The G.O.C. 72nd Brigade and the G.O.C. 42nd Brigade both wrote appreciative letters referring to the good work done by this section.

During the time the battalion was at Vergies forty-eight hours' leave was granted to several parties of men

143

to proceed to Ault, the 4th Army seaside resort, and a draft of 150 other ranks was received.

BATTLE OF FLERS-COURCELETTE

On the 11th September, 1916, the battalion returned to the battle area and arrived in camp near Mericourt at 6 p.m., marching next day to tents. On the 11th 2nd Lieuts. N. Naylor and J. Chapman joined, and on the 13th Lieut. T. G. Bonnyman, rejoined. On the 15th the 14th (Light) Division in conjunction with other Divisions of the 4th Army made a combined attack on the enemy defences between Morval and Martinpuich with the object of seizing Les Bœufs, Gueudecourt and Flers. The line allotted to 5th K.S.L.I. was practically straight to Gueudecourt, but as a preliminary movement the battalion had to get through or round Delville Wood to link up with the battalions on the right and left. This move was successfully accomplished, and after passing the Wood the battalion moved in extended order for about two miles almost without a break. When slightly to the north-east of Flers, they were held up for the first time. The village was held in some force, and there were also field guns and a line of snipers directly in front. At this period the troops acting on the right flank lost direction, owing to a considerable force of the enemy being located at Les Bœufs. This caused the whole attack to be held up, but even then, had there been any reinforcements in the vicinity, it would have been possible to have reached Gueudecourt, as it was not till late in the evening, that is, hours after the attack was stopped, that the Germans could be seen taking up their positions in front of the village not more than a mile away. It was understood that a large force of cavalry was on our right rear, and although officers were collecting information as to the probable strength of the enemy, no move was made. It seemed a pity, as the country in front was peculiarly suitable for action by cavalry. No doubt there were good reasons for not using this force, but to those on the spot it appeared as if a golden opportunity of breaking through the enemy's line was missed.

On this occasion the battalion captured the three or four field guns which had been firing point-blank at them. This good work was carried out by C and D Companies, to whom the greatest credit is due for the determined nature of their attack. The following message shows that this capture was not made without loss.

" Three field guns were captured by 5th K.S.L.I. at
" 12 noon, on September 15th, 1916, in Bull's Road,
" between point N.13.D.10.8 and point N.31.D.6–9.
" One machine gun (not water cooled) was also captured
" here. It was impossible to bring this out, as when
" relieved I had only 7 men of the regiment left un-
" wounded, and these carried out 3 wounded men.

" (Signed) F. W. Rhodes, Lieut.,
" O.C. C Company."

In addition to the enemy guns 50 prisoners were captured, while our casualties were 2nd Lieut. M. I. Machell and 34 other ranks killed, 11 officers, 184 other ranks wounded and 34 other ranks missing.

This day is memorable as the first occasion on which Tanks were used in warfare. Four were in action with the 14th Division; three out of the four were very early casualties, but the fourth reached Flers and did splendid work.

On 16th after being relieved by the 6th D.C.L.I. and having eleven hours' rest in the Montauban area, the battalion was again in the trenches in relief of the 8th K.R.R.C. An order which was received to capture Gueudecourt having been cancelled and the battalion being relieved, it marched back to the camp from whence it had started on the 15th.

The casualties for 16th September were 2nd Lieut. J. A. Lee, 2 other ranks killed and 8 other ranks wounded.

Many congratulatory letters and messages referring to operations of 15th September, 1916, were received,

L

and the G.O.C. 14th Division issued the following Order of the Day:—

" General Order of the Day.

" On completing our second tour of duty in the Battle " of the Somme, the G.O.C. congratulates all ranks of " the 14th (Light) Division on the high character they " have earned for dash, discipline and hard work.

" The Division has proved that the New Army is in no " way behind the Old Army in fighting qualities, and the " names of the famous regiments represented in the " Division, have, by the hardships endured and sacrifices " triumphantly made, acquired new and undying honours.

" (Signed) V. Couper,

" Major-General Commanding 14th (Light) Division."

" *24th September*, 1916,

After this action the 14th Division was retransferred from the 4th Army, and the battalion left the Somme area on 19th September and moved back to the Arras sector. The following farewell letter was received from General Rawlinson :—

" 42nd Infantry Brigade.

" Letter. Fourth Army, No. 350 (G).

" 14th Division.

" It is with very sincere regret that I hear the 14th " Division are leaving the 4th Army, and before they do " so I desire to convey to every officer, N.C.O. and man " my gratitude and congratulations for the admirable " work they have done. Both in Delville Wood and in the " attacks of the 15th and 16th of September they dis- " played a fighting spirit and a dash which is worthy of " the best traditions of the British Army, whilst their " discipline and self-sacrifice has been beyond praise.

" The artillery support has on all occasions been adequate " and well directed, and is the result of careful and " thorough training.

" I have been struck by the keenness and good comrade-

" ship which exists amongst all ranks in the 14th Division.
" It is a most valuable asset in War, and shows that both
" Staff and Regimental Officers are working in harmony.
" At some future date I trust it may be my good
" fortune to again find them under my command.

        " (Signed) Rawlinson, General,
                " Commanding Fourth Army.
" H.Q. Fourth Army,
   " *20th September,* 1916."

The battalion marched by easy stages and in wet weather
to Grand-Rullecourt, where it was billeted for two
nights. A draft of 33 other ranks joined there and on the
25th the battalion proceeded in buses to Warlus, and the
next day relieved the 8th R. Fusiliers as Brigade Reserve
at Agny.

From the 26th September to the 25th October the
battalion divided its time between reserve at Agny, rest
billets at Dainville, and the trenches in " G Sector."
Except for intermittent trench mortaring by the enemy,
a quiet time was spent in the line, and casualties were
light. Monsieur Pierre Durnevin joined to replace
Monsieur Charbonnel, the interpreter, killed at Delville
Wood. Captain T. C. Tanner, Major C. R. B. Wingfield,
2nd Lieuts. A. P. Webb, H. T. Clarke, G. R. Mather,
A. W. Keight and 15 other ranks arrived. On the 25th
October the battalion was relieved by the 11th Battalion
Middlesex Regiment at Agny, and proceeded in buses
to Wanquentin and next day by a march of about 8 miles,
A Company to Blavincourt and B, C and D Companies
to Lignereuil, to refit and train recruits who had recently
joined. A regular course of training in drill, bayonet
fighting, physical drill and musketry was done here and
at Ivergny, to which place the battalion marched on the
7th November. During the time the battalion was at
Ivergny horses and mules were lent to the inhabitants
to assist them in their farm work. The battalion did not
go near the line for about a month, till the 23rd November,

when it was back in billets at Dainville, having reached this place by a march of over fifteen miles. Here it remained till the 8th December, finding working parties for the Corps lines.

On the 29th November, 2nd Lieuts. W. A. Preshowe, T. Onslow and F. Buckley joined for duty. There were no casualties during this month.

On the 8th December the battalion moved to billets at Gouy-en-Ternois, a march of about fifteen miles, where it stayed till the 15th and took part in a 14th Divisional musketry competition. On the 16th it was back again in Brigade Reserve at Agny.

From this time until March, 1917, a regular winter's programme was carried out with but little change, the troops being kept in the line as short a time as circumstances permitted. The last three months of 1917 were extremely cold, but the health and spirits of the men were well maintained, considerable credit being due to the medical officer, Captain J. T. Smeall, R.A.M.C.

During December 182 other ranks joined the battalion and 1 other rank was wounded.

While in the line on January 6th, 1917, the 43rd Infantry Brigade on the left raided the enemy trenches, and in order to assist them the battalion made a smoke screen with smoke bombs, receiving the thanks of the G.O.C. 43rd Brigade for their " very effective co-" operation."

The casualties to the battalion were 2nd Lieut. T. Onslow and 2 other ranks killed.

During January Captain C. S. Smith, Lieut. H. T. Colbourn, 2nd Lieuts, A. J. Radcliffe, D. H. Lloyd, C. M. I. Hamer, A. C. Bernard, W. J. G. Yeomans and 132 other ranks joined the battalion. In addition to the casualties mentioned above, 1 other rank was wounded.

In February the battalion occupied the trenches in " H Sector " and on relief acted as Brigade Reserve at Ronville, which was followed by a period of rest at Dainville.

The following officers, Major M. C. Richards, Lieut.

H. S. Griffin, 2nd Lieuts. A. W. Groves, W. S. Garton,
J. H. Ikin and P. W. Lee, arrived for duty. Lieut. S. G.
Budgett and 2nd Lieut. G. P. Bulmer left to join the
R.F.C. and Captain J. T. Smeall, R.A.M.C., was relieved
by Lieut. R. Lee, R.A.M.C.

On the 2nd March the Germans sent about 12 shells
into Dainville and 3 other ranks were wounded. The same
succession of trenches, Brigade Reserve in "H Sector"
and rest at Dainville continued through March. Certain
suspicions of the enemy's plans were beginning to be
formed during this month, and a close watch was kept
on him. There was a series of unaccountable fires in his
back areas and explosions also were heard and everything
seemed to point to some fresh move on his part, so that
when, on March 18th, patrols from A and C Companies
were sent into his line, they were not surprised to find
that he had departed. The trenches up to his fourth
line were promptly occupied and the work of consolidation and the making of communication trenches commenced. The trenches were in a dreadful condition,
partly as a result of rain on top of a severe and lengthy
winter frost, and partly on account of shell fire.

The enemy, as usual on these occasions, heavily shelled
his former lines at intervals for some days, and the consolidation was much delayed thereby and many casualties
occurred. To add to our discomfort many ingenious little
mechanical contrivances were found, upon touching
which a violent explosion occurred. Such things as helmets, water-bottles, etc., which the men were likely to
pick up as curios, were left lying about to which were
attached grenades with the pin partially out. There were
also clockwork arrangements which caused explosions in
the dug-outs several days after the Germans had evacuated
them.

On March 22nd the battalion was relieved in these
trenches and went to Dunedin Cave. Our casualties
for this tour were 12 other ranks killed and 49 other
ranks wounded.

Dunedin Cave was a portion of a much larger work extending for some miles around Arras and finally leading up to the German front line. This extraordinary mining feat had been going on for some months, yet the secret was so well kept by the men at work that the caves were quite unknown to those who passed to and fro almost daily. This work was performed by skilled miners of the Australian and New Zealand contingents aided by men from Pioneer Battalions. Each separate cave could easily billet a battalion, and it was complete in every way like a barrack and was lighted with electricity. The whole length was connected up by a light railway.

There were many advantages in being billeted here, including complete immunity from the heaviest shell fire, but there were also disadvantages, one being that whenever the temperature rose the walls dripped with water, and another that the very security of the place had a bad effect on the moral of the troops. For this reason the practice was to keep troops billeted in the caves for a few days only, and accordingly the battalion moved out on the 24th and returned to billets at Dainville, moving on the 28th to huts at Fousseux. During the month of March, Major C. R. B. Wingfield left to take over the command of the VII Corps Lewis-gun School, and 2nd Lieut. H. W. B. Evans joined the battalion.

The battalion moved to Simencourt on 3rd April. Both here and when at Fousseux a severe course of training, made necessary by the constant changes in battalion organization and methods of attack, was proceeded with, the programme being greatly interrupted by bad weather.

The following Order of the Day was issued by the G.O.C. 14th Division on April 8th:—

" The G.O.C. wishes to convey to all ranks his great
" appreciation of the amount of hard and difficult work,
" which has been accomplished by the R.E., Infantry and
" Pioneers of the Division in pushing our lines forward
" to within assaulting distance of the enemy. The

" determination and good spirit shown is a good augury
" to the operations now about to be carried out.

" As everyone is doing his best, then it is certain that
" the Division will accomplish the task which has been
" set to it and maintain the name and reputation gained
" during the Battle of the Somme.

"(Signed) G. D. Bruce, Lt.-Colonel,

" General Staff,

" 14th Light Division."

THE BATTLES OF ARRAS, 1917

On the 8th April the battalion was again in the trenches,
in relief of the 9th K.R.R.C., prior to taking part in the
Battle of Arras on the 9th April. The ground allotted
to the battalion was south of Tilloy from a point about
half-way between this village and Telegraph Hill to about
300 yards south of the latter. The enemy was caught
unawares, in many cases asleep in the dug-outs, consequently a large number of prisoners was taken with their
arms and ammunition. In our line of advance there was
a very strong work known as " The Harp " on account
of its singular shape, but thanks to the accurate bombardment which had preceded the attack, not much of
this was left and the battalion had little difficulty in
reaching its objective. The second phase of the attack
which had been planned was the capture of the village
of Wancourt and the line immediately west of the point,
but this was not persevered with. A considerable body of
our cavalry was concentrated later on in the day near
Telegraph Hill, but they were not able to help the
situation much for various reasons.

The weather on this occasion added much to the difficulty of the troops, there being a series of violent snowstorms. Nevertheless the bearing of all ranks was excellent, and it was good to see the undoubted superiority
of our men over the enemy.

THE KING'S SHROPSHIRE LIGHT INFANTRY

BATTLE OF VIMY RIDGE

The part played by the battalion is contained in the following report, rendered to 42nd Infantry Brigade :—

" I was in command of B Company 5th K.S.L.I., " operating on the right flank of the battalion and detailed " to capture the Cojeul Switch from Eye Lane to Dog " Lane inclusive. On obtaining objective I was to take " charge of battalion front on Blue Line.

" The battalion was formed up in assembly trenches " by 2 a.m. and the men were made to lie down to avoid " observation by the enemy. The assembly trenches were " not shelled. At 7.34 a.m. our barrage commenced, and " the battalion advanced.

" At this time there were two tanks just in front of " assembly trenches, and two just behind, the condition of " the ground seemed to make their progress very slow and " in my line of advance I saw nothing more of them, " and they played no part in the operations. The enemy " barrage which appeared to be fairly heavy was drawn " through the crest of Telegraph Hill immediately west " of Telegraph Work. At this point the attacking line " also came under heavy machine-gun fire from the " direction of Neully Trench and Tilloy. Slight resist- " ance was encountered in Telegraph Hill Trench, and " Head Lane, but this was immediately overcome and " my company captured between 50–75 prisoners here. " No resistance was offered in Pole Trench, but enemy " fired a machine gun from Nouvion Lane. On a patrol " being sent forward, the enemy abandoned Nouvion " Lane and ran to the rear, but were shot down by our " Lewis-gun fire. One enemy machine gun was captured. " The D.L.I. of the 43rd Brigade had converged slightly " into my area, but I occupied a part of Pole Trench " and had established communication with the D.L.I. " on my right by 8.45 a.m. Germans in dug-outs were " cleared out by 9.10 a.m., and work was forthwith " started in consolidating the line. I captured and con- " solidated this line with the remnants of A, B and C

" Companies. D Company had meantime obtained their
" objective in Silent Work, and by 10 a.m. communica-
" tion had been established with the Suffolks on their
" left and the Ox. and Bucks L.I. in the String and
" Negrine Trench. At 1.15 p.m. the R.B. passed through
" my line to establish an outpost line in advance. They
" appeared to encounter no resistance whatever.

" *Total casualties** in the battalion as far as can be
" ascertained at present amount to 12 officers and 189
" other ranks.

" *Trophies.* Only one enemy machine gun was captured,
" but the trench system is so smashed up by our artillery
" fire, that it is very possible several others are buried in
" the debris, also I needed every man in my final objec-
" tive and could not send men back to search Telegraph
" Hill Trench, the enemy's front line. We have secured
" several hundred rifles and a large quantity of bombs
" and equipment.

" *Prisoners.* I would estimate that the prisoners taken
" by the battalion numbered over 300.

" (Signed, O. S. Benbow-Rowe,
" Captain, 5th K.S.L.I."

The following complimentary order was issued by the
G.O.C. 42nd Infantry Brigade.

" The Commander-in-Chief has personally requested
" me to convey to all ranks of the 14th (Light) Division
" his high opinion of the excellent fighting qualities
" shown by the Division.

" The commencement of the great offensive of 1917
" has been marked by an initial success in which more
" than 11,000 prisoners and 400 guns have been taken
" on the first day alone.

" The Division has taken a prominent part in achieving
" the success and maintained the reputation gained last

* The battalion lost the following officers killed on April 8th and 9th,
1917:—2nd Lieuts. J. K. Chapman, P. W. Lee, A. P. Webb and W. J. G.
Yeomans. Capt. T. E. Burke died of wounds on April 14th, and
2nd Lieut. H. S. Griffen on the 9th.

" year on the Somme, and added to the laurels of the
" gallant regiments of which it is composed."

On the day following this battle, when the battalion
was in the captured German trenches on Telegraph Hill,
our old Commanding Officer, Lt.-Colonel H. M. Smith,
who had commanded the battalion originally, arrived
and took over the battalion from Major Delmé-Murray,
and next day, the 11th, the battalion left the line for Liencourt via Wanquentin and Noyellette arriving on the
14th. Here it rested in billets and underwent a course
of training in offensive action until the 22nd, on which
date it left Liencourt and returned to the Harp Trench,
one of those captured on the 9th. On the 25th the
battalion moved to support trenches near Wancourt.

During April, 2nd Lieuts. R. Morgan and E. G. Faithorn, Captain R. Johnson and 133 other ranks joined the
battalion, and on 21st Major G. A. Delmé-Murray left
to join the 7th K.S.L.I., and Captain E. P. Carey, 8th
R.B., joined as temporary second in command.

On the 28th April the battalion proceeded to Niger
Trench near Wancourt in relief of the 9th K.R.R.C. and
from there took part in an action by the Brigade, the object
of which was to straighten out the line by the capture of
a German trench called Ape Trench. On May 3rd the
Brigade moved forward, the battalion being detailed to
occupy Ape Trench on its capture by the assaulting
troops, and to hold it at all costs. The troops of the
Brigade became considerably mixed after the attack, but
all objectives were gained and the battalion remained in
possession of Ape Trench until relieved on the night of
4th May by the 6th Somerset L.I.

From the 4th May till the 24th when the battalion relieved the 8th K.R.R. in the front line the battalion was
employed on working parties improving and altering the
old German defences to suit the new situation, and during
part of the time was under the tactical command of the
41st Brigade.

On the 25th the 18th Division on our right put over gas

154

which, owing to the unfavourable wind prevailing at the time, blew back into our trenches causing several casualties. On the same day Lieut. A. Gittins was killed in action. There was heavy shelling on our line on the night of the 26th, and on the 27th a party of about fifty of the enemy attempted a raid on B Company's front, but were repulsed by rifle and machine-gun fire. A message received from 42nd Infantry Brigade on the 28th ran as follows:—

"The G.O.C. Brigade directs me to say that he is very "pleased with the manner in which your battalion re-"pulsed a hostile raiding party last night, by means of "rapid rifle fire. Please convey appreciation of their good "work to those concerned."

On the 29th May the battalion was back in support trenches near Wancourt. While here on the night of the 1st May the enemy fired a large number of gas shells, but caused no casualties. On the 1st June a reinforcement of 23 other ranks arrived. On being relieved by the 6th K.O.Y.L.I., the battalion proceeded to the Divisional support area at Neuville Vitesse, and then on the 4th June to Divisional Reserve area near Beurains. While here R.Q.M.S. F. H. Grimley was appointed Hon. Lieut. and Qr.-Master and posted to the 5th K.S.L.I.

From here the battalion proceeded to Puchvilliers by march route, halting for the night of the 9th at Monchiet, and for the night of the 10th at Saulty and Gombremetz.

On reaching Puchvilliers on the 11th June, Lt.-Colonel H. M. Smith proceeded to H.Q. and assumed command of the 42nd Brigade. On the 13th Major C. E. Atchison, (K.S.L.I.), joined and assumed command of the battalion. A whole month was spent here, during which a programme of training was carried out, and rifle, football and other competitions were held and a Divisional horse-show took place.

While at Puchvilliers a complimentary order was received from rhe G.O.C. 42nd Brigade, dated July 10th, paying a tribute to the excellent behaviour of the troops during the past months. No complaints had been received from the civilian inhabitants, but only words of thanks and praise. This he regarded as a great tribute to the discipline of the Brigade. The following officers joined whilst the battalion was at Puchvilliers: Captain C. B. Buckley, R.A.M.C. (vice-Captain F. E. Johnson, R.A.M.C., to 42nd Field Ambulance), Lieut. C. W. Strong, 2nd Lieuts. R. B. D. Malden, H. D. Corbet and 38 other ranks. Major C. R. B. Wingfield went to a senior officers' course at Aldershot, and 2nd Lieut. L. G. Macklin left the battalion to join the R.F.C.

Before leaving Puchvilliers Lt.-Colonel H. M. Smith resumed command of the battalion and Major C. E. Atchison left to take over command of the 6th K.O.Y.L.I. on 19th July. On 12th July the battalion marched to Candas and entraining there at 6.50 a.m. reached Bailleul at 1.50 p.m., from here they proceeded to camp one and a half miles north-west of Bailleul, arriving at 2.30 p.m. The battalion remained in this camp till the 6th August, during which time training was continued, and on the 26th July General Sir H. Plumer, Commanding 2nd Army, inspected the 42nd Infantry Brigade.

On the 6th August the battalion marched into the Cæstre area, where it remained until 15th.

During the time it was at Bailleul and in the Cæstre area 2nd Lieuts. W. R. Weston, L. Burland, G. H. Hughes, W. Stanley, B. E. Sheldon, W. Bullock, A. H. Day, Lieut. F. R. Dymond and 129 other ranks joined the battalion, and Lieuts. J. C. Thompson and C. C. Abraham left to report for duty with the R.F.C.

THE BATTLES OF YPRES, 1917

On the 15th August the battalion left the Cæstre area for the Ypres salient. After a journey by bus and route march it arrived in camp near Ouderdom and next day marched to Dickebusch. On the nights of the 17th and 18th August the Division took over " the most important " part of the line on the present Flanders battle-front," and the battalion went to dug-outs at Halfway House, and were shelled next evening, resulting in the following casualties: 2nd Lieuts. B. E. Sheldon and L. Burland, and 9 other ranks wounded, 1 other rank killed. On the 19th there was more shelling and 2nd Lieut. B. Morton and 5 other ranks were wounded. On the 20th the battalion relieved the 5th Ox. and Bucks in the line and were again shelled by the enemy, both on their way up and when in the trenches, losing in casualties 5 other ranks killed and 19 other ranks wounded.

On the 22nd the battalion took part in an advance by the 14th Division on the Stirling Castle–Glencorse Ridge, being on the right of the Brigade front with the K.R.R. on its left, and the 43rd Infantry Brigade on its right. The 43rd Brigade was to advance 600 yards and the battalion was to advance so as to join up with the 43rd Brigade on the right, and the K.R.R. who were to remain where they were on the left.

The following report of the operation was rendered to the 42nd Infantry Brigade.

" Report of action of August 22nd, 1917, carried out " by the 5th Battalion King's Shropshire L.I. to the east " of Ypres. The objective to be reached and held ex- " tended from the right of the trenches held by the King's " Royal Rifles on our left, who were to remain stationary, " to a point level with the ' L ' Farm on our right, where " we were to connect with the left battalion of the 43rd " Infantry Brigade who were also advancing (600 yards). " Prior to the attack I disposed of my battalion as follows: " Two companies (B on the right and A on the left) " under Captain O. S. Benbow-Rowe, M.C., were " situated in Jargen Trench with strong outposts to their " front in Glencorse Wood. One company (D company) " under Captain E. G. R. Lloyd was situated as a support " in Jargen Switch, one company (C Company) under 2nd " Lieut. H. W. B. Evans was situated as battalion reserve " in Ignorance Trench. Zero hour was given as 7 a.m. " and the advance was to take place simultaneously with " the 43rd Brigade on our right.

THE KING'S SHROPSHIRE LIGHT INFANTRY

ACTION AT ZERO AND AFTERWARDS

" Immediately on zero going A and B Companies
" advanced in small section column through the wood and
" quickly obtained their objective throughout the line,
" with the exception of the right flank, which was refused
" in order to maintain connection with the 43rd Brigade,
" whose progress was held up by machine-gun fire from
" ' L ' Farm. Within five minutes of the advance all the
" officers of the right company (B) became casualties and
" only one junior officer remained with the left company
" (A). Considerable opposition was encountered during
" the advance, especially by machine-gun fire. D and C
" Companies carried out their instructions for action in
" zero, and on my being informed of the officer casualties
" in A and B Companies, I ordered Captain Lloyd for-
" ward from D Company to take charge of the two
" assault companies. (This occurred at 8.25 a.m.) Cap-
" tain Lloyd found on arrival that B Company had with-
" drawn from its advance position, and owing to lack of
" leaders the line had lost connection in several places ;
" he at once reorganized the line and again advanced B
" Company, effectually establishing communication with
" A Company, though touch with the 43rd Brigade,
" which had been lost, was not regained. About this time
" the enemy was observed in the sunken road occupying
" dug-outs, and we attacked him by means of rifle
" grenades ; result of the procedure could not be ascer-
" tained. At 10.20 a.m. I personally directed 2nd Lieut.
" J. D. Evans, Commanding C Company, to send 2nd
" Lieut. Cooke to the assistance of Captain Lloyd, in
" view of the officer casualties in A Company, and later
" wired my O.C. details for all officers at the camp to
" be sent up to me immediately. At 12.20 p.m. I wrote
" to O.C. C Company Ox. and Bucks L.I. asking him to
" hold the company of his that was at my disposal in the
" trench on the north side of Menin Road, and to report
" to me at my H.Q. I did this because I realized that at

" least a fourth of my battalion had by this time become
" casualties, and wished to be prepared adequately for any
" counter-attack which might follow. At 12.48 p.m. I
" received information from Captain Lloyd that con-
" nection had been established with the 43rd Brigade,
" and this was maintained until the relief of my battalion.
" On the morning of the 23rd inst., at about 4.30, a
" heavy counter-attack was launched against the 43rd
" Infantry Brigade, but it was only on my extreme right
" that our Lewis gunners were able to participate in re-
" pelling it, and considerable execution was done by them
" in the enemy's ranks, firing half right. We continued
" to hold the ground gained on the battalion front until
" relieved by the 5th Ox. and Bucks L.I. on the night of
" the 23rd and 24th inst.

"(Signed) H. M. Smith, Lt.-Colonel
" Commanding 5th K.S.L.I."

Casualties, killed: 2nd Lieut. C. P. Cooke and 19 other
ranks.

Wounded: Captain O. S. Benbow-Rowe, Lieut. H.
Atkinson, 2nd Lieut. M. Cutler, 2nd Lieut. M. S. Porter
and 107 other ranks; missing: 12 other ranks.

On relief the battalion returned to the dug-outs at
Halfway House till 25th. The casualties while here on
23rd and 24th were Lieut. F. R. Dymond and 21 other
ranks wounded. On 25th the battalion marched to Café
Belge for the night, and next day proceeded in buses to
billets and camp near Abeele. On the 28th the battalion
moved to billets and camp in the Thieushouk area, where
they remained till the 1st September.

On the 27th August 2nd Lieuts. D. I. Price,
F. W. R. Francis, H. A. Turner, C. R. T. Shepherd
and 16 other ranks joined, and on 31st 2nd Lieuts.
H. C. Trumpler, T. E. Flynn, C. W. Jeffreys and 94
other ranks joined, and Lieut. D. E. G. Preece rejoined
the battalion.

THE KING'S SHROPSHIRE LIGHT INFANTRY

The following was received from the Division with reference to the action of the 22nd August.

" All Units, 14th Division.

" The following has been received from 5th Army.

" The Army Commander wishes to thank all ranks " 14th (Light) Division for gallant work they have done " while with 5th Army.

" Despite difficulties of ground, bad weather and de- " termined resistance of the enemy, they made valuable " progress along ridge on 22nd August, and maintained " position in face of heavy shell fire and repeated " counter-attacks, inflicting heavy losses.

" Division has maintained its high reputation in some " of the heaviest fighting on this front.

" (Signed) G. D. Bruce, Lt.-Colonel, General Staff.

" 14th (Light) Division."

On the 1st September the battalion marched to camp in the Neuve Eglise area, and next day to support lines immediately north of Messines in relief of the 18th Battalion Manchester Regiment. Here Captain F. R. Burton joined for duty, and on the 6th the battalion relieved the 9th K.R.R.C. in the front line, remaining in the trenches till the 10th September.

During the tour there was considerable activity with aeroplanes, gas and other shells, machine-gun fire and snipers, and 5 other ranks were killed and Lieut. R. C. Morgan and 18 other ranks wounded.

On relief by the 8th R.B. the battalion proceeded to billets at Neuve Eglise, remaining there till the 15th, when the 42nd Brigade relieved the 43rd Brigade as reserve to the 57th Division, which was holding the line Fleurbaix–Bois-Garnier–Armentières, in the Doulieu area.

During the stay in billets, 2nd Lieut. W. H. Powell joined for duty. On 18th it removed to hutments at Canteen Corner, where 2nd Lieut. L. A. T. Speer, 2nd Lieuts. J. C. Jackson-Taylor, T. A. Allen and T. Wilde

joined for duty, and 2nd Lieut. W. J. C. Wood rejoined the battalion from hospital.

During the time the battalion was at Canteen Corner
parties were sent out to Wulverghem and other places
to work on the trench tramways. On the 23rd an anti-
aircraft shell which had been fired at an enemy aeroplane
failed to explode in the air, and fell on one of the huts
occupied by H.Q. signallers and caused casualties to the
number of 2 other ranks killed and 12 other ranks wounded.

On 28th the battalion moved again into support lines
north of Messines, and on the 3rd October into the front
line in relief of 9th K.R.R.C. till the 8th October, when
it was relieved by the 3rd Battalion Scottish Rifles and
proceeded to huts at Kortepyp. The casualties for this
tour were 2nd Lieut. A. T. Clarke and 1 other rank
wounded. Reinforcements of 37 other ranks joined during
the tour.

The battalion next marched to Ridgewood, staying one
night in the Berthen area on the way. From 12th to 15th
October the battalion was in huts at Ridgewood and two
reinforcements totalling 107 other ranks arrived. On the
16th the battalion moved up to support trenches north of
Menin Road (near Fitzclarence Wood) in relief of 8th
Battalion K.R.R.C., and on the 21st went into front-line
trenches in relief of the 5th Ox. and Bucks till 24th. When
taking over the support trenches the enemy's artillery fire
was heavy, and the following casualties occurred : 2nd
Lieut. C. W. Jeffreys and 11 other ranks killed and 29
other ranks wounded, and 2nd Lieut. R. J. Shepherd was
admitted to hospital. During the whole tour, in addition
to the above, 19 other ranks were killed and 2nd Lieut.
C. Strong and 74 other ranks wounded, and Captain
K. W. Groves and Lieut. H. C. Trumpler were admitted
to hospital.

While in these support trenches on the 17th October a
hostile aeroplane fell near Battalion H.Q., brought down
by anti-aircraft gun fire. The observer and pilot, whose
names were not ascertained, were buried by men of the

5th K.S.L.I. where they fell. Reinforcements of 12 other ranks arrived during the tour. On relief by 9th Devons and 2nd R. W. Kents on the 24th, the battalion proceeded to billets in the Berthen area. On the 26th October Lt.-Colonel H. M. Smith, D.S.O., left to assume temporary command of the 42nd Brigade, and Major G. Turner took over command of the battalion in his absence.

After a day or two of rest a programme of training was carried out, which included physical drill, bayonet fighting, extended order drill, musketry, wiring, night outposts, rapid loading and gas drill. On 5th November Lt.-Colonel H. M. Smith returned and resumed command of the battalion, which on the following day moved to the Canadian Corps' forward area for work under the 1st Canadian Division, east of Ypres. The battalion was encamped half-way between St. Jean and Potijze, and from the 7th to the 28th, with the exception of the 17th, when the battalion spent the day bathing, large working parties were found for road making behind the front line, which by this time was far away from where it had been. During the stay in this camp Lieut. C. M. I. Hamer was admitted to hospital, Captain H. Atkinson rejoined and 37 other ranks joined for duty. Casualties, 2 other ranks killed and 13 other ranks wounded. Aeroplanes were active on both sides.

On 29th November the battalion was relieved by the 1/1st Battalion Herts Regiment and proceeded to Ypres, where it entrained at 11 a.m., arriving at Godewaersvelde at 12.40 p.m. From there the battalion marched to billets in the Eecke area, arriving at 1.30 p.m.

The battalion remained but two days in billets at Eecke, moving by route march to a hutted camp at Brandhoek. On December 9th the battalion relieved the 6th Somerset L.I. in the support line, moving to the front line in the trenches north of Paschaendale on the 12th, where they remained for three fortunately quiet days. On the night of the 15th the battalion was relieved by the

10th D.L.I. The relief was difficult owing to the wet state of the ground, and the enemy's artillery being fairly active 1 other rank was killed and 5 other ranks wounded. One other rank was also killed on the 14th. On relief A, B, C and H.Q. proceeded to Capricorn Camp, and C and D to California Camp south of St. Julien in reserve.

On the 19th December the battalion under Major G. Turner (Colonel Smith being away on short leave to England) went into support trenches at Bellevue and Vine Cottages west of Paschaendale. Artillery was active during relief and 2 other ranks were wounded. On the following day 2nd Lieut. H. A. Turner was wounded, but on the 22nd, although enemy artillery was active with gas shells during the relief, no casualties occurred. From 23rd to 25th the battalion was at Junction Camp near St. Jean, where working parties were found for the R.E.

On the 25th the battalion left the Ypres salient, entraining at St. Jean Station for Wizernes whence, after hot coffee and biscuits, it marched to billets at Longuenesse, near St. Omer, arriving at 10 p.m. One other rank was wounded by shell fire before entraining in the morning.

On 1st January, 1918, the battalion left Longuenesse for the 5th Army area. It entrained at 7.20 p.m. at St. Omer Station for Edge Hill and arrived there at 9.20 the following morning, and, after cocoa and biscuits, marched at 10.30 a.m. about eighteen kilometres to Suzanne, getting into billets about 3 p.m. Here it remained for about three weeks and was exercised in musketry and other training. On the 4th Lt.-Colonel Smith returned from leave, and on the 18th the Regimental Transport won a 42nd Brigade Transport competition.

On leaving Suzanne the battalion moved to Monterescourt, being billeted on the 22nd at Rosiere-en-Sauterne and on the 23rd and 24th at Guerbigny; from near this place they were conveyed by motor lorries to Berlancourt and marched to Beine, where they billeted for night of 25th, and next day reached Monterescourt by route march and were immediately warned for the trenches. On the 27th January the battalion took over the trenches of the French 413th Regiment, and here they remained till 2nd February, enjoying a quiet time with nothing unusual to report. Whilst here all ranks were staggered by receipt of instructions, on 2nd February, 1918, for the immediate disbandment of the battalion.

The explanation of this sudden order was a change of organization of the Army, made necessary by the shortage of man power, and whereby brigades in future were to consist of three battalions instead of four.

The Commanding Officer Lt.-Colonel H. M. Smith, wrote the following farewell order:

" I regret to inform the battalion that we are all being " disbanded to-morrow. The only bright spot is that we " are all going, to different battalions it is true, but still " to the same regiment.

" In bidding good-bye I wish to tell you a little of the " work you have done—you have fought gallantly and " never lost a trench, or failed to do what was required " of you.

" You have often been hungry and thirsty, had to " endure intense cold and rain, mud and discomfort, have " had to work and march in the course of your duty till " you had hardly strength to stand. You have done all this " without a murmur, and with a cheerfulness which has " been beyond all praise.

" I know full well you will carry on the same splendid " work in the other battalions of the dear old Corps you are " going to. No regiment in the British service has a finer " record, and remember this, it is each one of you who " help to keep that record unsullied and its honour " bright. It has been the proudest and happiest time of " my life during which I have had the honour of com- " manding you, and I still hope I may continue to soldier " with you.

" I wish especially to thank the staff of the battalion

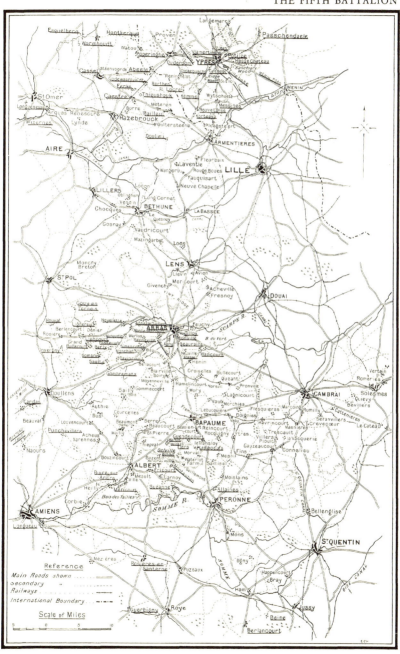

" for their unfailing devotion and the loyal way in which
" they have always supported me. The Orderly-room
" Staff, the Qr.-Master Staff, Medical Staff and stretcher
" bearers, the Transport (who have recently won fresh
" laurels), the Orderlies and Battalion Cooks have each
" and all helped to make the battalion what it is to-day.

" Words fail me to thank you adequately for what you
" have done.

" I wish you all the best of luck and happiness in the
" future, and may God bless you all.

" (Signed) H. M. Smith,

" Lt.-Colonel Commanding 5th K.S.L.I."

The battalion on relief marched into billets at Jussy,
and the next day, 3rd February, paraded at 7.30 a.m.
The above order was read, the roll was called, and each
company dismissed and proceeded in buses to its new
battalion, A Company to the 6th, B to the 7th, C to
1/4th, and D to 1st K.S.L.I.

The Battalion H.Q. signallers, and the regimental
transport remained behind at the disposal of G.H.Q.

The battalion had ceased to exist.

On the 4th February, the Battalion H.Q. received the
following letter :

" To Lt.-Colonel H. M. Smith, D.S.O., Officers,
" W.O.'s, N.C.O.'s and men of the 5th K.S.L.I.

" It is with great regret that I have to write this letter
" to you. It is a hard blow to both you and the 42nd
" Infantry Brigade that a battalion, which was one of the
" first hundred thousand, has been ordered to disband.
" My confidence in the battalion has always been great,
" and when I say this I am certain that I can speak not
" only for myself, but for my predecessor and the other
" three battalions of the Brigade.

" When I state that I have always considered you, in
" slang terms, a battalion of ' stickers,' I wish you to take
" it as one of the greatest compliments that can be paid

" you—you have always been so both in attack and de-
" fence, and have always done what you have been called
" upon to do.

" This disbandment is hard on you, but your con-
" solation must be that it is being done for the best for our
" beloved country's sake, and I hope you will take it in a
" cheerful spirit, in the same spirit you have always shown
" when we have had bad times.

" I wish you all the best of luck wherever you go, and I
" hope you will always remember with pride that you
" belonged to the 42nd Infantry Brigade.

" I am very sorry to lose you, and I thank you *all* for
" the loyal support you have always given me at all times.

" (Signed) G. M. B. Forster, Br.-General
" Commanding 42nd Infantry Brigade."
" 2/2/18."

Although the battalion had ceased to exist it was a consolation to all ranks to remain with the regiment. Each individual carried away with him the fine spirit of the 5th Battalion, and the pride of having served with the Senior Service Battalion of the K.S.L.I.

CHAPTER V

THE SIXTH BATTALION

THE 6th Service Battalion K.S.L.I. was formed, by companies, at different towns in the county and left the Depot for Blackdown on 10th September, 1914, under Lt.-Colonel S. G. Moore commanding, with Major B. Cotton as Second in Command, and Lieut. G. V. Breffit as Adjutant. Lieut. J. Lovelock was appointed Quartermaster, and 2nd Lieut. R. E. O. L. Green, Transport Officer.

On leaving Blackdown the battalion marched to Cowshot, where the process of forming companies continued, A Company under Major E. A. Wood, B Company under Captain S. F. Eyre, C Company under Captain C. E. Ward and D Company under Major H. E. Welch. The C Company, raised by Mr. Stuart Asbury of Shrewsbury, was composed solely of Shrewsbury " Pals," which fact much interested H.M. The King when he inspected the battalion. Later this experiment proved a wise step, and the C.O. often expressed his high appreciation of the intelligence, keenness and loyalty to their officers and comrades shown by this company.

Recruits poured in so rapidly that the greatest difficulty was experienced in clothing and equipping them. No uniform was available until November, when a suit of emergency blue was issued to each man. A certain number of old rifles for drill purposes became available about the same time, but poles, stakes and pit-props had to be served out to make up the numbers. Companies paraded in emergency blue uniform, mufti of all descriptions, sweaters and jerseys of every hue; bowler and straw hats of all shapes and kinds, most of which had seen better days.

With the exception of the officers named above, none had served in the Regular Army. With this sprinkling of Regular officers and N.C.O.'s wonders were achieved, thanks to the excellent material raised in Shropshire and Herefordshire. The enthusiasm of the men knew no bounds, but their patience was sorely tried. For example, so few rifles were available that only one company at a time could fire its musketry course, handing over the rifles to the next company waiting to fire.

A special word of praise is due to Regimental Sergeant-Major Williams, who, with his long military experience and soldierly qualities, was a model to all ranks. The one desire of the men was to learn their job and get out to France. The battalion returned to Blackdown where service dress was issued, and drills, musketry, tactical exercises, digging trenches in a sea of mud, and lectures crowded the training programme. Later the battalion moved to Larkhill, Salisbury Plain, where after further intensive training the battalion became a unit of the 60th Brigade, and on 21st–22nd July, 1915, entrained at Amesbury, under Lt.-Colonel Moore, at 4.30 p.m., for Folkstone *en route* for Boulogne. After a very rough crossing in drenching rain the battalion disembarked at 12.50 a.m., and was guided to Osterhove Rest Camp, on the outskirts of Boulogne, arriving about 3 a.m. No one will ever forget that cold morning with its drenching rain, mud and chaos. The Salvation Army hut alone afforded a little comfort. At 12 noon all were glad to march on to Pont de Brique railway station, where the entraining was most expeditiously carried out by the R.T.O., and by 3 p.m. the battalion was on its way to St. Omer via Calais.

On arrival at St. Omer General Dawkins (of the K.S.L.I.) the D.Q.M.G., G.H.Q., met the battalion and gave them a short address, after which they proceeded to billets at Zoudousque, five miles south of St. Omer. The following is a list of the officers that proceeded overseas with the battalion:—

Lt.-Colonel S. G. Moore	Major E. A. Wood
Major B. Cotton,	Captain and Adjutant
Second in Command	G. V. Breffit
Major H. E. Welch	Captain C. E. Ward

THE SIXTH BATTALION. AUGUST, 1915

Captain S. F. Eyre	Lieut. L. E. Gielgud
„ F. Latham	„ A. E. Laurence
„ S. F. Thomas	„ M. J. Hellier
„ T. A. Higginson	„ G. K. S. Kerr
„ D. J. MacLeod	2nd Lieut. R. E. O. L. Green
Lieut. and Quartermaster	„ I. W. Garnett
J. Lovelock	„ R. A. M. Lutener
Lieut. M. Boddington	„ S. H. Hyndman
„ P. S. Rendall	„ J. F. Sidebotham
„ W. P. Hawkins	„ H. M. O'Connor
„ R. C. Craigie	„ S. R. Marshall
„ L. Owen	„ C. Wilson

Lieut. H. A. Ford (R.A.M.C.)
Regimental Sgt.-Major Williams

Route marching over the cobbled roads, in full marching order, was most trying at first, but in time the men's feet became hardened.

On July 26th the battalion joined the 60th Brigade at Arques, and next day the Brigade, picking up the other infantry units at Renescure, marched to Borre. When passing through L'Hoffand the G.O.C. 20th Division inspected the battalion.

On the 30th the Brigade arrived at Outersteene and came into the III Corps area, where intensive training was continued. General Sir Douglas Haig (Commanding 1st Army) inspected the battalion at this time and was much struck with its physique and general smartness.

On the 11th August, when a party was sent up to the trenches held by the West Yorks Regt. (8th Div.) for instructional purposes, the battalion registered its first casualty in Sgt. E. S. Williams of A Company, who was seriously wounded by an " egg " bomb. Platoons from each company, M.G. sections and bombers went into these trenches for twenty-four hours, and during the next few days the whole battalion by companies. All ranks of the West Yorks Regt. took great pains in showing the battalion the ropes.

On the 21st August our medical officer, Lieut. Ford, was replaced by Lieut. J. L. P. Bennett, whose very gallant services were gratefully appreciated by all ranks during the rest of the war. About this period we had the experience of riding in the Piccadilly buses, without payment, to visit the trenches near Laventie, where later we relieved the 6th Wilts and certain fortified posts held by the Garhwal Brigade. The names of Masselot-Wangerie, Road-Bend, Fauquisart-Eglise and Elgin will be familiar to the 6th K.S.L.I.

On August 29th keen interest was taken in the report, given by a Hun deserter, that an attack on the right of the line held by the Brigade was contemplated. That night about 8 o'clock the transport, coming up with supplies, was badly knocked about by machine-gun fire near Wangerie Post. No further developments took place, however, and the battalion was relieved by the 12th R.B. and retired to rest billets, sending up working parties for the trenches, and carrying on with intensive training. The casualties since going into the trenches had been light, but on 19th September the battalion lost a gallant young officer of much resource in the death of Captain T. A. Higginson, who was killed by the falling in of the roof of his dug-out in the front line.

On the nights of September 23rd and 24th, under a heavy bombardment from our Divisional artillery, a strong party under Captain S. F. Thomas worked strenuously, running a sap from the sector held by the 12th K.R.R.C., where the German line ran out into a sharp salient, protruding into a wider re-entrant in our own line. It was intended, in the case of an advance of our troops, to continue this sap through the German line and make a fire trench of it, so connecting up the line already held with the ground newly won.

On the eve of the battle of Loos our very gallant Padre, the Rev. J. Bulstrode, met the Battalion Signalling Officer, Captain Stewart Marshall, in the front line and asked, " Are you prepared ? " The reply was, " The

signalling lines are as complete as I can make them."
An innocent misunderstanding of the purport of the
Padre's inquiry.

THE BATTLE OF LOOS

In supporting the 12th R.B. in their attack D and A
Companies of the 6th K.S.L.I. (D Major Welch, A Major
Wood) entered the sap referred to above and on emerging
the former extended to the right, whilst the latter extending to the left entered the Hun trenches at the apex
of the salient in close touch with the 12th R.B. The
Rifle Brigade continued the advance, but were driven back
by a counter-attack, and streamed through the two companies of the 6th K.S.L.I. back to the original front line,
losing heavily. Lieut. Gielgud, B Company, 6th K.S.L.I.,
was badly wounded, and whilst being brought back was
left with many other wounded on a stretcher on the surface. This was due to the press of troops advancing up the
main communication trench, which obliged the bearers to
place the stretchers with their wounded on the surface
under very heavy gunfire. The two companies of the 6th
K.S.L.I. were still in possession of the enemy front line,
and did much slaughter during the German counter-
attack. Later, much to their surprise, the company
commanders received orders, first to advance south-east
and connect up with the Bareilly and Garhwal Brigades,
then another order to retire back to the original line;
here the gallant Colonel Moore was seen on our parapet
under heavy fire, waving his stick and shouting for the
companies to fall back, on orders received from the
Brigadier. A and D Companies of the battalion were
thankful that the sap existed, otherwise their casualties
would have been heavy across " No Man's Land." Major
Wood, who spoke Hindustani fluently, was able to collect
together over 300 of the Indian contingent, which having
lost most of its officers had rushed in confusion to the
rear. 2nd Lieut. S. H. Hyndman, B Company, gallantly
rescued several wounded in " No Man's Land," bringing

them into the sap, on which his company was hard at work, under a galling fire. At 2 p.m. the 6th K.S.L.I. was back in its own front line much depleted. The operations had been successful in this sector, only so far as they held the enemy to his ground, and thus prevented him from sending reinforcements to the scene of the main attack. The battalion lost 4 officers and 59 other ranks. Lieut. W. P. Hawkins, who behaved with the greatest gallantry, died of his two wounds later in hospital. The battalion stretcher-bearers, under Corpl. F. Lovekin, worked splendidly, bringing in all the killed and wounded.

This was the battalion's first engagement of importance, and it would be invidious to mention names when all ranks behaved with gallantry. No further demonstration took place, and the battalion was withdrawn to rest on the 26th, the 20th Division side-stepping on the 28th to the right, which brought the right flank to a sunken road about half a mile north-east of Neuve Chapelle, and the left to a point some quarter of a mile north of Rouge Bancs.

On the 6th October Lt.-Colonel G. S. Moore handed over command of the battalion to Major E. A. Wood, who was promoted Lt.-Colonel commanding, and Major B. Cotton having been evacuated sick, Major H. E. Welch became second in command. Losing our Commanding Officer, who had created the battalion and licked them into shape, was a great blow to all ranks. He went home to do good work at the M.G. school at Grantham.

With the idea of still holding the enemy to his ground a demonstration, in which the 6th K.S.L.I. took part, was made by the Division on the 13th October. The ruse adopted was to use dummies made of sacks stuffed with straw and clothed with old salvaged great coats and caps, lent by the men. Boxes of phosphorus had been put out over night in No Man's Land, and by means of smoke bombs the front was covered with thick smoke for nearly two hours. As it cleared the dummies were used so effectively that the Hun S.O.S. brought down a heavy artillery barrage on the dummies as they were put over the parapet, rolled over as if shot, and then pulled back by strings when the smoke became thick again. Meanwhile the enemy manned his parapet to meet the dummy attack and was freely peppered by our machine guns and artillery. One man of A Company coolly got over the parapet into No Man's Land to fetch his " doll," the string having broken. A German *communiqué*, dealing with this incident, came later into our hands; it ran: " A strong attack by the enemy was stopped at his trenches."

On the night of the 31st October particularly fine work was carried out by the battalion in completing the portion allotted to it of a new breastwork to straighten off a re-entrant near Duck's Bill, only 70 yards from the enemy front line. The experienced coal miners of the K.S.L.I. finished their work hours before the other battalions of the Division. For the next two months the battalion continued to take its tour of duty in the trenches, being relieved in the different sectors by the 6th Ox. and Bucks, 12th King's Liverpool Regiment and 3rd Grenadier Guards. On the 29th December 2nd Lieut. E. A. Walker, a very promising officer, was killed in action. The 20th Division then went into Divisional Reserve.

Suddenly on the 20th January, 1916, the Division was ordered to move north to the 2nd Army, having been selected to form part of the new XIV Corps. Strenuous times followed in holding the canal bank, and the lake of mud and water below Pilkem Ridge. The trenches were knee-deep in water, and many of the " grouse butts " held in the front line were mere islands made of two or three sheets of corrugated iron, upon which the men were obliged to sit during the day, and were able to stand up only when night came. The casualties were heavy and no retaliation from our guns was afforded to these isolated posts.

On the 12th February at 2 a.m., whilst holding the

canal bank, the battalion came under very heavy enfilade fire from enemy artillery. A large Nissen hut in the canal bank collapsed under several 5·9 shells, killing Lieut. J. F. Sidebotham, 2nd Lieut. I. W. Garnett, 2nd Lieut. F. O. Lloyd, 2nd Lieut, J. R. E. Barnes, and Sgt.-Major J. E. Barrett, with 19 other ranks killed in other parts of the sector and 46 wounded. Many men were buried under the debris and only rescued after many hours of digging. Sgt. Davidson and his pioneers did wonders, working under heavy fire all through the night.

On the 19th the Battalion Transport Officer, 2nd Lieut. R. E. O. L. Green, a very capable and gallant officer, was killed on a working party. The usual rest—working parties—reliefs in line with occasional raids, made up the life of the battalion for the next few weeks and brought the usual casualties.

On the 6th April 2nd Lieut. R. A. M. Lutener was killed in the front line whilst sniping. This young officer had organized and trained the battalion snipers to a very high standard of efficiency, and his good work was brought to the notice of the Corps Commander, Lord Cavan, who ordered the other units composing the corps to work on the lines adopted by him. Under his highly-trained snipers the companies holding the front line enjoyed a greater measure of security. On this occasion Lutener, finding that one of his best snipers was unable to account for a Hun sniper, who had bagged three of our men, took his place, and was shot through the head as he opened the shutter in the shield. Four had thus fallen to the German sniper in twenty minutes.

On 27th the battalion entrained for Calais for a month's rest and intensive training, which benefited the men greatly, and a battalion band was formed which proved a godsend throughout the war. On the 20th May the battalion took up quarters in Ypres, relieving the Scots Guards.

On 25th the 6th K.S.L.I. took over the trenches in Railway Wood, and came under very heavy shell fire the following day. The Hun amused himself by blowing up mines daily in the front line, causing huge craters, which he failed to occupy. On the right at Railway Wood was the Canadian Corps; on the left, the 6th Division. In front of the 6th Battalion the German salient was only 70 yards away.

BATTLE OF MOUNT SORREL

On the 1st June, 1916, the Hun artillery bombardment was continued with great activity, and on the 2nd was concentrated on the whole of the battalion front. Lachrimatory shells were used in large numbers, and the damage to communication trenches was great. The battalion was under intense fire, but held its ground most gallantly. The enemy's intention soon became evident. He tried to advance on the left of the Canadians in " Y " Wood, and to wipe out the 6th K.S.L.I. on the high ground, but Lt.-Colonel Wood, who was in the front line, waited until they had left their parapet, when he called upon the Divisional artillery, which brought down a barrage annihilating the advancing enemy in No Man's Land. Further attempts to advance were made only to be met with devastating fire. Our artillery, which was always splendid, did wonders on this occasion. The Hun, badly shaken, and having failed to gain Railway Wood held by the battalion, kept quiet until dusk, when he put up a grand pyrotechnic display that eclipsed all his efforts in this line within the experience of the battalion. One could read pencil messages in the light of the bursting shells. By 10 p.m. the main attack developed, and the Canadians were rushed, losing the whole of their front to a great depth, including Hill 62. The 6th K.S.L.I. most gallantly supported the Canadians by repeatedly driving the enemy back from determined attacks on the Canadian left. The battalion was continually under very heavy fire for thirty-six hours, but never wavered, and accounted for most of the enemy as they left their parapet. High praise was given by the Corps Commander, the G.O.C. of the Division, and the Brigade Commander, and the G.O.C. 3rd Canadian Division, was most enthusiastic in his praise. The 6th Battalion was proud of having been afforded the privilege of helping their sister battalion, the Princess Patricia's Canadian Light Infantry, which is closely associated with the K.S.L.I., the officers being honorary members of the officers' mess. On this occasion the 1st Battalion K.S.L.I. were with the 6th Division, which was held up at the Quadrilateral in front of Les Bœufs on the Somme, and the 6th K.S.L.I. found itself fighting side by side with the 1st Battalion. Thus no less than four Shropshire battalions, 1st, 5th, 6th and 7th, were within less than a mile of each other during this engagement.

On the night of 29th/30th June two parties of 42 each, A under Lieut. H. M. O'Connor and B under Lieut. D. S. A. McKimm, carried out raids on the enemy trenches after a most successful artillery preparation. These companies had carefully rehearsed the work to be done on a model of the Hun trenches specially made in the back areas. Captain Latham and Corpl. Cross gained very valuable information, bringing in samples of the enemy barbed wire and full details of the sector about to be raided. At 11.45 p.m. the two companies were brought up fresh from the practice ground and placed under cover in the front-line trenches which had been very considerably thinned out, most of the garrison going to ground. Accordingly when the enemy brought down their curtain of fire on the front and support lines, our casualties were only 4 men slightly wounded. It was originally intended to precede the assault with a gas attack but, since the wind was only fair, the gas officer wished to postpone letting off the gas; the Colonel decided to cancel the gas attack and adhere to the kick off at 12.3 a.m. At this hour the two parties, lying at the appointed places in No Man's Land, advanced. The enemy was found in dug-outs, and no quarter was given —bombs and bayonets were freely used, accounting for scores of dead and wounded and 70 prisoners. At the given signal Lieut. O'Connor and Lieut. McKimm withdrew their parties to our lines after twenty-five minutes' stay with the Hun. At the very moment our artillery bombardment was raised to come down on the support trenches our two parties entered the enemy trenches, taking him absolutely by surprise, for no one was found on the surface, not even a look-out man. All ranks of A and B parties behaved most gallantly, each unit carried out its allotted task to the letter. A party lost 1 killed and 3 wounded. B party 2 killed, 9 wounded. The following awards were made : M.C. to Lieut. D. S. A. McKimm. M.C. to Lieut. M. O'Connor and 2nd Lieut. J. P. Shaw for commanding and leading with great courage a raiding party on 29th/30th June, M.C. to 2nd Lieut. K. J. H. Lindop for gallant conduct in repelling a counter-attack in above-mentioned raid. The D.C.M. to Corpl. R Richards for very gallant conduct in continuing to lead his party when wounded. The M.M. to Pte. Thomas Jordan for gallantly holding a trench single-handed after his two comrades were wounded ; Sgt. G. Price, Pte. W. D. Jackson, Pte. P. A. Forsythe and Pte. A. H. Maiden for gallant conduct in driving off a counter-attack.

Captain M. Boddington, commanding D Company, was killed in the line on 1st July, and Lieut. D. McLeod was wounded. Capt. Boddington was a very gallant and keen officer, beloved by all ranks. On the same date Captain F. T. Burrough, a very capable officer, met his death in the trenches with 9 other ranks. On this occasion 2nd Lieut. D. G. Smith was awarded the M.C., and Corpl. F. Phillips and Pte. G. E. Osborne the M.M. for gallantry.

Many moves were made during the next few days, and on 14th July the battalion took over the trenches at Fleurbaix, on the left of the 5th Australian Division, whom the battalion supported whilst they attacked the enemy on the 19th. The 6th K.S.L.I. was thanked by

N

the G.O.C. 5th Australian Division for its help in bringing out the Australian wounded on the morning of the 20th.

On the 24th July the battalion was in the Somme area, and once more the 20th Division was in the XIV Corps. The 6th K.S.L.I. went into the trenches opposite Serre and found them waist-deep with our dead, the stench was appalling, and the battalion worked day and night to bury the bodies that had been lying there for eleven days. The rest of July and August was spent in trenches, and in rest and intensive training in and around the craters close to the Carnoy-Montauban road. After strenuous work in the Guillemont area, preparing for the great attack on that town, the 60th Brigade, which included the 6th Battalion K.S.L.I., had been so seriously reduced in numbers that the Corps Commander decided to withdraw it into reserve, but the 6th Ox. and Bucks, who could muster 550 rifles, were attached to the 59th Brigade as a fifth battalion. Later when the attack was made, and the 7th Division troops had been driven back to their own trenches, the 60th Brigade was brought up from the craters to relieve the 47th Brigade in the line.

BATTLE OF GUILLEMONT

The 6th K.S.L.I. approached the village of Guillemont at 2 a.m. on Sept. 4th, and joined in the battle until the 7th. Lt.-Colonel E. A. Wood, having been gassed on the 4th, was evacuated to England, Major H. E. Welch taking over command of the battalion. The casualties from 3rd to 7th were 7 officers wounded, 2nd Lieut. J. P. Shaw missing, 11 other ranks killed and 23 wounded. On the 7th the battalion marched to Bois Les Tailles, and next day into billets at Corbie for rest. The battalion next moved to Carnoy, and thence on the 16th back to the trenches in front of Waterlot Farm. A large number of the enemy, split up in small groups, made a bombing attack on the left of the battalion front at 1 p.m. on the 17th, but were easily driven back by a bombing party under L.-Corpl. Lockey. Supported by heavy artillery and machine-gun fire, the enemy made several more attempts to enter our trenches, only to be driven back with heavy loss. Our casualties during this twenty-four hours were 20 killed and 42 wounded. There was a heavy bombardment during the night, and the enemy attacked again on the 18th, but was unable to get near our trenches. This day we lost 2 killed, 21 wounded and 3 missing.

On the 20th, when in support, Battalion Head-quarters was heavily shelled, 2 men being killed and 6 wounded. The signal communication throughout the battle of Guillemont was especially good under the able supervision of Captain S. Marshall, who worked incessantly day and night during the whole period, as he had always done in the past. The capture of Guillemont was a fine achievement. The Commander-in-Chief, the Commanders of the 4th Army and of the XIV Corps all sent messages of congratulation to the 20th Division. The co-operation of the Divisional artillery with the infantry was perfect, the success being in no small measure due to the battalion commanders of the Division, who were at all times in or out of the line in close touch with their comrades of the artillery. When covered by the 91st, 92nd and 93rd Brigades the 6th K.S.L.I. went into action with the greatest confidence.

After the operations at Guillemont the Division went back for a short period of rest. On the 25th September the Brigadier-General, Leslie Butler, presented certificates for gallantry to the following N.C.O.'s and men :—

Sgt. C. A. Fletcher	Pte. W. Meeson
L.-Corpl. Sheldon	„ R. Bruson
Pte. T. Melia	„ G. Davies
„ W. Mathews	„ E. Royce
„ F. Hicks	

L.-Corpl. J. Peake, killed in action 17.9.16, was also awarded a certificate for gallantry.

BATTLE OF THE TRANSLOY RIDGES

The battalion next marched to Morval and relieved the 15th R. War. Regt. During this relief the enemy shelled the battalions moving up for fifteen minutes. The 6th K.S.L.I. lost 17 wounded and missing before being relieved by the 33rd Battalion French Infantry. The battalion returned to Carnoy, and later moved to Mons Wood, where on the 3rd October 2nd Lieut. D. C. Hair was killed. On the 3rd and 4th October the 60th Brigade moved up into the line, relieving the 61st Brigade. The 6th K.S.L.I. was in reserve on the 7th when the enemy attacked in order to establish a position on top of the ridge overlooking Le Transloy and Beaulencourt.

On the 13th October Lord Cavan, the Corps Commander, inspected each of the three Brigades of the 20th Division, and highly commended all units, adding in conclusion, " I have asked the Army Commander and " the Commander-in-Chief not to take away the 20th " Division if they can help it, and they have promised to do " their best. I would not lose the 20th Division for crowns " and crowns." During the whole of this period on the Somme Captain C. W. Webb worked indefatigably as Adjutant, and Captain Lovelock, the Quartermaster, was a veritable Moses in feeding, clothing and re-equipping the battalion. He worked his department under undreamt-of difficulties, and the battalion never went short of anything. Delightfully hot cocoa and coffee were always ready half-way out of the trenches, and on arrival in camp a hot supper. His good work was reflected in the physique and morale of the battalion, which was always of the best.

The following N.C.O.'s and men were awarded medals and certificates for gallantry in the recent operations:—

Sgt. W. Dixon, D.C.M.
L.-Corpl. E. Lockley, D.C.M.
L.-Corpl. G. Sheldon, D.C.M.

THE SIXTH BATTALION. JANUARY, 1917

Pte. T. Jordan, Bar to M.M.
Corpl. G. Edwards, M.M.
Pte. G. W. H. Nock, M.M.
Pte. J. W. Jones, M.M.

From 9th October to 9th December the Division was out of the line resting, training and bringing the much-reduced units up to establishment again.

The 1st of November found the battalion at Cavillon, west of Amiens. Here much time was given up to recreation of all kinds—football, cross-country and boxing competitions were organized, and several very successful race meetings were held. The C.O. (Lt.-Colonel E. A. Wood) got up pig-sticking with service lances, and improvised hog spears with bayonets attached, the forest country providing the wild boars, and all ranks joining in as beaters. Under the able management of Corpl. Fletcher, a concert party and pierrot troupe was formed, arrayed in Clarkson's best. One of the " star turns " was " Marcel Wave " Shaw, so well known in Shrewsbury for close " shaves." Captain Latham with Corpl. Cross preferred living in No Man's Land—it was reported that the former wanted to improve his knowledge of German.

On the 9th December units of the 20th moved forward to relieve the 29th Division. The weather was so bad that units only did two days in the front line. Here on the 23rd December 2nd Lieut. N. A. Howell, Lewis-gun officer, was killed by enemy machine-gun fire.

Christmas Day was spent at Ville-sur-Ancre amidst much good cheer. Works of art were produced by way of Christmas cards by Captains Breffit and Marshall. These sold in thousands and the proceeds were sent home for the Widows' and Orphans' Fund of the Shropshires.

On 27th Dec., Co. Sergt.-major H. Turner was promoted 2nd Lieut. and left for England.

By the 4th January, 1917, the Division took over from the Guards between Saillisel and Sailly-Saillisel. The front line consisted of isolated posts, in some cases only

181

thirty yards from the enemy. With the terribly cold weather, registering twenty degrees of frost, and heavy falls of snow the tour of duty was most trying. Our patrols in No Man's Land adopted white suits over their khaki in order not to show up against the snow. No action of importance took place during January, and on the 28th the Division moved back to Heilly.

On the 5th February the battalion was selected to give a demonstration to the Division on "Attack on a Strong Point." It was a great success and most interesting to all ranks. The G.O.C. 20th Division and the three Brigadiers expressed their entire satisfaction. The undermentioned N.C.O.'s and men were awarded the M.M. for bravery in the field since the 1st January, 1917:—

Pte. E. Andrews	Pte. A. G. C. Cockle
Sgt. C. A. Fletcher	Sgt. E. Gilbank
C.Q.M.S. S. Greatwich	Sgt. T. Hambleton
Sgt. F. O. Hayward	Pte. J. Hicks
Pte. H. J. Meredith	Sgt. J. Saunders

On the 11th, 2nd Lieut. C. H. W. Pugh was wounded, and on the 15th Captain F. Stanier became Adjutant. On the same day the 60th Brigade came out of the line to Carnoy. That afternoon, when most of the officers and men were attending football matches, or the pierrot performance given by the "Véry Lights," a terrible explosion took place, destroying the whole of the camp of the 12th King's Liverpool Regiment and many other huts. Three officers were killed and 52 other ranks wounded. It appears that a large German store with tons of high explosives was buried in underground tunnels, unknown to the troops, whose camp was quite near. It is thought that the explosion was caused by a party of men who, whilst ratting with dogs, saw some huge rats that infested the camp go to earth, and who threw down gun-cotton into a small hole and thus blew up the camp.

Rumours pointed about this period to a general retreat

by the enemy to the new Hindenburg line, and on the 17th March the retreat began whilst the 6th K.S.L.I. were holding the front line at Sailly-Saillisel. The enemy was at once followed up, and the 6th Battalion were hot on their heels across the Peronne–Bapaume Road to the town of Le Transloy—occupying Rocquigny, Bapaume and Le Mesnil. The number of infernal machines hidden in walls, doors and floors caused several casualties, the enemy expending much ingenuity in concealing these traps. All ranks showed great eagerness in following up the retreating enemy, who fought his rearguard actions in a most determined manner. The country traversed was pitted with shell holes, and the going was very difficult. The battalion continued to be engaged frequently with the enemy as he was driven back. A welcome rest came with the few days in Havrincourt Wood, although skirmishing continued east of the wood.

On the 22nd April the battalion advanced with the 12th R.B., and occupied the village of Trescault. After the capture of Bilhem the Division had finally driven the enemy on its front into the Hindenburg defences. It then became necessary to organize the line as a defensive position in order to safeguard the ground which had been gained. In re-siting the trenches, after the capture of Trescault and Bilhem, the battalion, together with the others of the Brigade, dug and wired in twelve days a good trench, five feet deep and six feet wide, throughout the whole Brigade front, a distance of 3,000 yards. It was now May and the weather perfect.

On the 19th the Division left the 4th Army to go further north. The Corps Commander, Lt.-General Sir John du Cane, addressing the Division on the 20th, said that the 20th Division had driven back the enemy from the trenches in front of Morval and Lesbœufs to the Hindenburg line, a greater distance than that achieved by any other division on that front. The 20th had seen much hard fighting and had never failed to gain its objectives. The Army Commander wrote a farewell message full of the highest praise, and hoped the Division would soon return to his command.

On 20th June R.Q.M.S. B. C. Reynolds, a very efficient N.C.O. of the old army, was awarded the Meritorious Service Medal.

On the 23rd the Division was in the Fifth Army and in the IV Corps. Three weeks of active trench warfare followed in the Noreuil–Lagnicourt–Morchies sector, after which, on June 29th, the Division moved to Domart to refit, train and rest.

At Domart intensive training in open warfare was the order of the day, and all ranks took a keen and intelligent interest in the new exercises. On 21st July the battalion arrived at Proven, and the 20th Division once again joined the XIV Corps, 5th Army, and for the rest of the month remained in corps reserve behind the 38th Division. The new German gas, in which it was possible to work for some hours before the effects of the gas were felt, was first used on the 25th. This gas, which could not be seen, and could be detected only by a faint smell of sour apples, was very deadly, but our casualties were few, thanks to the efficiency of our gas helmets and the special rattles provided to give timely warning. On the 6th August the 20th Division was given the task of capturing Langemarck. As a preliminary operation it was necessary to gain command of the Steenbeek Valley to reach the ground on the far side of the stream, where the leading waves might form up for the attack. On the front of the 20th Division there was a very strong work of reinforced concrete at Au Bon Gite, 300 yards beyond the east bank on the Langemarck road. On both sides of the stream there were several more concrete pill boxes, commanding all approaches, but Au Bon Gite was the key to the enemy's defences in this sector.

On the 11th August the 59th Brigade was ordered to force the Steenbeek, with artillery support, but they were overwhelmed by the enemy on the east bank and had to retire. A similar fate met the attack on the 14th, Au Bon

Gite being the stumbling-block. The casualties were heavy, consisting of about a dozen officers and over 200 other ranks. Next day another attack on the same objective had to be abandoned, because the forces were unable to reach their jumping-off ground owing to the enemy barrage.

BATTLE OF LANGEMARCK, 1917

On the 16th August the 60th and 61st Brigades were ordered to take Langemarck. The 60th Brigade was to attack the first and second objectives on a one battalion front with the Ox. and Bucks L.I.; the 6th K.S.L.I. and the 12th K.R.R.C. were then to advance to the final objective. On the night of the 15th/16th the attacking troops formed up, the 6th K.S.L.I. were met after midnight by Captain Dugdale, who had laid out the tapes, marking the forming-up place. The greatest credit is due to this gallant officer for the able manner in which he carried out the very hazardous task under heavy shell fire. From midnight to zero hour at 4.45 a.m. the enemy rained shells as he had never done before, and his machine-gun fire from the pill boxes, whilst the battalion lay in the open, 150 yards from the enemy, was deadly. Our artillery barrage, accurate and beautifully timed, fell like a curtain, and close behind it the leading waves of infantry moved forward to the attack. Au Bon Gite, with its garrison of one officer and fifty men, was captured. Once across the Steenbeek all movement was very difficult, the ground was nothing but a swampy field of craters right up to the final objective. In order to gain the first objective the only possible formation for the troops was a series of small columns, which wound their way, in single file, between the deep pools of mud and water. The Battalion Commander, whilst leading the battalion with Captain Dugdale on his heels, sank up to his waist in the mud. The battalion advanced, mopping up all shelters and dug-outs they passed, killing scores of the enemy and taking 46 prisoners. Alouette, a second Au Bon Gite, was captured by the battalion and later made their head-quarters. They then formed up east of the second objective, having cleared Langemarck, ready to advance. At 7.20 a.m. the whole line advanced to the final objective, the 6th K.S.L.I. on the right deploying 100 yards east of Alouette Farm under heavy machine-gun fire from Rat House and White House.

Strong opposition was met from parties of the enemy concealed in hedges, ditches, concrete dug-outs and fortified houses, and as the attack advanced the battalion came under an intense machine-gun fire from the right flank—the troops of the Division on the right having been held up. The battalion accounted for many killed, and captured 135 unwounded prisoners. By 7.45 the final objective was taken and held. The three companies came into the line and consolidated, throwing out a screen 150 yards in front with three Lewis guns. The enemy was driven out of Kangaroo Trench and made for the small wood behind White House. Lieut. E. M. Hannah and eight men rushed this fortified house, killing 9 Huns and taking 5 unwounded prisoners. Lieut. Hannah, whilst shooting through the loopholes, was shot dead. For this gallant attack he was specially mentioned in despatches. Enemy aeroplanes appeared over the battalion firing machine guns from about 100 feet or less. The map issued by Army Head-quarters showed that the 6th K.S.L.I. held its portion of the final objective further east than the troops on right or left—having to make a defensive flank, on its right, back to the 2nd objective, with Rat House still held by the enemy. The battalion captured the officer commanding Langemarck. The line was held from right to left by the 6th K.S.L.I., 12th K.R.R.C., 12th King's and the 7th D.C.L.I. These battalions quickly consolidated the position ready for the enemy counter-attack. Whilst forming up for counter-attacks to the right front of the battalion the enemy presented a fine target and was mowed down by machine-gun fire from sixteen guns; no further forming up took place in front of the battalion, but from midday onwards the enemy crept up and attacked the junction of the two Brigades about Schreiboom and drove back the 12th K.R.R.C. and 12th King's for a distance of 200 yards. The 6th K.S.L.I. lent the 12th K.R.R.C a platoon with four Lewis guns, two Vickers and one trench mortar with fifteen boxes of S.A.A. to restablish connection—this platoon did excellent work driving the enemy out of the cemetery. The morale of the battalion was good in the advance, but improved very considerably as all ranks saw each enemy force, assembling for the counter-attack, annihilated. The C.O. gave the exact position of his front line, but as it appeared incredible that so much ground had been gained, in view of the 11th Division being 250 yards in rear of the final objective, the G.O.C. Division sent up a senior staff officer to clear up the situation. It was, however, not until two corps staff officers, and two more staff officers from the 5th Army Headquarters had verified the facts that the report of the Commanding Officer was accepted.

Our casualties were as under:—Died of wounds, Captain H. M. O'Connor, Lieut. D. G. Smith, 2nd Lieut. Hannah. Wounded, 2nd Lieut. V. C. Hares, and 2nd Lieut. T. J. Hannon. Other ranks:—Killed in action 39, wounded 147, missing—drowned in mud 5.

In this battle the battalion advanced to the attack under very heavy fire in as perfect order as if on Salisbury Plain; nothing could have been finer. On the 18th/19th the battalion was relieved by the 10th Battalion Welch Regiment, when the situation was normal, and returned to Proven for rest and training.

On the 5th September the Divisional Commander, Major-General Sir W. Douglas-Smith, presented medal ribbons and awards to the following officers, N.C.O.'s and men of the battalion :—

Lt.-Colonel E. A. Wood	Bar to D.S.O.
Captain R. C. Craigie	M.C.
A/Captain O. R. Lloyd	M.C.

THE KING'S SHROPSHIRE LIGHT INFANTRY

C.S.M. F. O. Hayward	D.C.M.
Sgt. J. Clark	D.C.M.
Sgt. W. Beddoes, M.M.	D.C.M.

The Military Medal was given to :—

Sgt. J. Brammer	Corpl. A. E. H. Halford
L/Corpl. J. W. Lewis	Pte. W. Caswell
Pte. W. H. Carter	Pte. H. Payne
Pte. J. Melia	Pte. E. Salmon
Pte. P. Coleman	Pte. W. Northwood
Pte. E. Acton	L/Corpl. W. H. Barrett
L/Corpl. H. Cope	L/Corpl. W. Madeley
Pte. A. J. Broome	

The following three weeks were spent in preparing for the next operations, whilst the enemy was busy organizing shell holes as posts and strong points. With September the weather improved, making life more bearable.

On the 11th September the 20th Division relieved the 38th Division, and the 60th Brigade held the line 1000 yards east of Langemarck, in a north-westerly direction to the railway. The fighting strength of the battalion at this period was only 350 all ranks, and was under the command of Major H. E. Welch, Lt.-Colonel E. A. Wood, having been evacuated sick. The objective in the forthcoming attack included Goed ter Vesten Farm and the enemy trenches to the south-east from the farm west to the railway, involving, on this flank, only a short advance. On the right the attack was to be made in two bounds, but on the left there was an intricate network of trenches, which it was considered better to capture without any pause.

BATTLE OF THE MENIN ROAD RIDGE

The 6th K.S.L.I. formed up on the 19th September at Alouette Farm, and the operations began at 5.40 a.m. on the 20th. D Company (right) Captain McKimm, and A Company (left), advanced, in artillery formation, in support of the 12th R.B. and 6th Ox. and Bucks respectively.

C(right), B(left) remained in assembly position in support. D Company reached White Trench, coming under heavy machine-gun cross fire from Eagle Trench. Since the battalion on the left appeared to be deflected by White Trench, one platoon of D Company advanced to fill in gaps between Eagle and White Trench, where there were no assaulting troops, and opened fire. Two platoons and Company Head-quarters took up positions as ordered in shell holes about the White Trench and Windmill at 6 a.m. Lieut. Kimpster returned over 180 yards, under heavy machine-gun and rifle fire, to report situation. Captain McKimm asked for barrage to be dropped back before any action could be taken, and then reorganized his position to cover his front and advanced into old Shropshire Trench, under covering fire of 2nd D.L.I. at White Mill. A Company advanced in support of 6th Ox. and Bucks and, finding them hung up by machine-gun fire from Eagle Trench, advanced and dug in, suffering several casualties. Communication to this company was practically impossible. C and B Companies were heavily shelled, suffered casualties and moved forward 100 yards to avoid the enemy barrage. During the morning Major Welch went forward with the Officer Commanding the 12th R.B. to reconnoitre; on reaching White Trench the situation became apparent. At 2 p.m. the 6th K.S.L.I. and one company 12th K.R.R.C., under the C.O. of the former, were ordered to attack Green Line. Under heavy fire the runners carried the orders to the companies. After discussion with the G.O.C. on the telephone, Major Welch was ordered to attack with the 6th K.S.L.I., and one company 12th K.R.R.C., the Red Dotted Line (White House, Louis Farm, Cemetery, Eagle Trench). Lieut. Kimpster, again under heavy machine-gun and rifle fire, delivered the C.O.'s orders to the Company Commanders. From 5.30 to 5.45 O.C. D Company reported enemy advancing in open order on Kangaroo Trench, and later the troops of the Division on the right were observed retiring. At 6.30 our barrage was put down, and ten minutes later Captain McKimm, O.C. D Company, advanced his storming party for Eagle Trench up to the barrage. At 6.44, D Company 6th K.S.L.I. assaulted Eagle Trench and a party attacked Louis Farm, taking on the companies of the R.B. to these objectives and meeting with stiff opposition. Corpl. S. Williams of D Company with fifteen men took Louis Farm, the garrison surrendering, and went on to consolidate beyond. Meanwhile the storming party of this company, under C.S.M. Barlow, advanced on Eagle Trench, but were held up by a tornado of bombs. Captain McKimm seeing this at once secured one of the D.L.I. anti-aircraft Lewis guns, rushed it into position and firing himself cut down the opposition, enabling the storming party to advance. C.S.M. Barlow advanced and cleared the trench, while Captain McKimm bringing forward the gun established himself in a pill box, covering the attacking party and mowing down the enemy bombers. One man of the D.L.I. gallantly acted as the No. 2 on this gun. The attack up Eagle Trench progressed until No. 13 platoon K.S.L.I., under Lieut. Kimpster, and a party of Ox. and Bucks cut off the fire of the supporting gun. A set-back in Eagle Trench followed until Corpl. Collins established a block together with the D.L.I. gunner. Captain McKimm waved forward the mixed troops coming up, and finally succeeded in getting them along Eagle Trench, and in through the cemetery, thus clearing the ground between that and Louis Farm. Captain Craigie advanced his company (C), and with the R.B. secured the ground south of Louis Farm, on the Red Dotted Line, as ordered, joining up with the 51st Division. A Company on the left, with some of the Ox. and Bucks, made a most gallant attempt in co-operation to rush the trench frontally. In this attempt Captain O. R. Lloyd, a most gallant officer, fell mortally wounded. All objectives having been gained, work of consolidating went on all night, no counter-attack being attempted.

On the 21st an enemy patrol, attempting to gain touch,

bombed the front line south of Louis Farm. Corpl. Smith of C Company 6th K.S.L.I., advancing from the support line together with a man of the 12th R.B., bombed the patrol in shell holes, killed the officer and brought in as prisoners eight Sturmtruppen. The battalion was relieved, going into support, but left Lieut. Banks and twenty-five men behind to hold the cemetery flank, and later that evening 2nd Lieut. Simon was lent to the 10th R.B., whose head-quarters he reached with compass bearing on a very dirty night over very difficult ground.

In the attack made by the 10th R.B. on the 23rd, 2nd Lieut. Morris advanced over the open, from the cemetery flank, and did excellent work with his party in helping the 10th R.B.

The battalion was then relieved by the D.C.L.I. The four days' fighting provide a glorious record of gallant achievements by the battalion. So fierce had been the fighting, and so important had been the results of the capture of Eagle Trench, that the following message was sent by the Army Commander, General Sir Hubert Gough :—

" The tenacity, gallantry and skill which your Division
" showed over the operations round Eagle Trench are very
" fine. Please accept my congratulations and expressions
" of admiration for you and all ranks of your gallant
" Division."

On the 1st October the battalion entrained for Bapaume.

Before leaving another congratulatory message was received from the Army Commander, as follows :—

" The Army Commander wishes to thank all ranks of
" the 20th Division for the part they played in the Third
" Battle of Ypres. The Division may well be proud of the
" capture of Langemarck on August 16th, and the taking
" of Eagle Trench on September 23rd. While holding
" the line of the Steenbeek during a prolonged spell of
" bad weather the Division showed a good soldierly

" spirit under difficult conditions. The Army Com-
" mander is sorry to lose such a good fighting Division."
On the 30th September the undermentioned N.C.O.'s
and men received the Divisional Commander's Congratulatory Certificates for specially good work:—

Co. Sgt.-Major F. O. Hay-ward	Sgt. W. Beddoes
	Corpl. A. E. H. Halford
Sgt. J. Brammer	L.-Corpl. J. W. Lewis
L.-Corpl. W. Madeley	Pte. H. Payne
L.-Corpl. H. Cope	Pte. W. Caswell
Pte. P. Coleman	

The battalion moved to several rest camps, and on 5th
October relieved the 14th Argyll and Sutherland Highlanders in the left sector of the Divisional front, facing
the Hindenburg line, south-west of Cambrai. The Division
was now in the III Corps of the 3rd Army. The battalion was employed on work in the front line at Villers
Pluich, where the following N.C.O.'s and men appeared
in Battalion Orders for awards for bravery in the operations between 19th and 23rd September:—

A.-Sgt. W. L. John	M.M.	Pte. N. Lees	M.M.
L.-Corpl. C. E. Jones	,,	L.-Corpl. J. Robley	,,
L.-Corpl. J. Adamson	,,	L.-Corpl. A. Jones	,,
Pte. N. Childs	,,	Pte. I. Jones	,,
Pte. J. Povall	,,	Pte. F. Dunn	,,
Pte. W. R. Nicholas	,,	Pte. W. Badrock	,,
L.-Corpl. S. Tonks	,,	A.-Sgt. W. J. Meeson	
L.-Corpl. D. Johnson	,,		Bar to M.M.
L.-Corpl. H .C. Darlow	,,		

Training, reliefs in front line and general work went on
as usual for the rest of October. For the recent operations,
19th and 23rd September, Major H. E. Welch and Captain
D. S. A. McKimm received the D.S.O. A bar to his
M.C. was awarded to Captain R. C. Craigie.
2nd Lieut. W. A. Kimpster, 2nd Lieut. H. M. Morris

and C.S.M. H. Barlow received the Military Cross, and the D.C.M. was awarded to: Corpl. S. Williams, Corpl. J. Smith, and Corpl. H. Gollins.

Preparations for the attack on 20th November were begun on 29th October, and continued under the greatest secrecy. The battalion went into the back areas for tank demonstration. On November 5th Lt.-Colonel Wood was promoted to command of the 55th Infantry Brigade, handing over command to Major Welch, and the following order was issued as an appendix to Battalion Orders dated 7th Nov., 1917 :—

"The Commanding Officer has received the following message from Br.-General E. A. Wood, D.S.O., and wishes it conveyed to all ranks :—

" In relinquishing Command of the 6th K.S.L.I. I wish " to convey my sincere thanks to all ranks for their most " loyal support during the last three years.

" I have no doubt that the high esprit de corps will " continue and support my successor equally well.

" The battalion has covered itself in glory and proved " itself second to none in the British Army.

" I look forward to co-operating with the battalion in " the future.

" Owing to the relief yesterday and being urgently " wired for, I extremely regret that I have been unable " to see all ranks personally, as was my intention when I " came up to the support line.

" I wish you now, in writing, the best of luck and a " speedy return home.

" (Signed) E. A. Wood, Br.-General."

On the 14th the Commander-in-Chief, Field-Marshal Sir Douglas Haig, with the Divisional Commander watched the battalion at a practice attack with tanks and expressed his great pleasure. On the 16th the battalion marched to the specially built camouflaged camp, and all ranks were strictly confined during daylight.

THE KING'S SHROPSHIRE LIGHT INFANTRY

BATTLE OF CAMBRAI, 1917

On November 19th, tuned up to the highest fighting standard, the battalion took up position in support of the 6th Ox. and Bucks L.I. north-east of Villers Plouich. The first wave of tanks moved forward at 6.10 a.m., and at 6.20 the artillery barrage opened along the whole front. The attack went exactly as planned from beginning to end. The 60th Brigade carried the Welch Ridge defences. The 6th K.S.L.I. then attacked the second objective and gained it, capturing many prisoners, guns and other war material—only when nearing the Hindenburg support line was there much opposition. The tanks unfortunately lost direction, bearing far too much to the right, and thus losing touch with the 12th R.B. The leading platoons of the 6th K.S.L.I. and 12th R.B. abandoned these tanks, and followed those going in the right direction through the wire of the support line. A party of the enemy here made a determined resistance opposite C Company. Lieut. T. B. Sampson, commanding the company, and 2nd Lieut. R. Turner were killed before the crest of the hill was taken. On the appearance of the tanks on the skyline an intense artillery fire from a battery of field guns about 600 yards away was opened over open sights, and several tanks were knocked out by direct hits. This locality became very unhealthy for the companies advancing down the reverse slope towards Marcoing. At this stage B Company reinforced C, who had lost all but one of their officers, and eventually took their place in the front line. The situation became easier as the enemy abandoned the field battery mentioned above. A Company met with strong opposition, its commander, Captain Lewis, a very gallant and dashing officer becoming a casualty. B Company, under Captain Hellier, with their flanking fire helped A to take the position, whilst C.S.M. Barlow distinguished himself by taking several prisoners. The enemy on seeing a tank about this time fell back on Marcoing and the firing quietened down. The battalion at once set to work reversing the fire trenches they had captured in the Hindenburg reserve line, which now became our main line of resistance, and dug outposts within 400 yards of Marcoing. A battery of 5·9 howitzers fell to the battalion and many machine guns. Amongst other booty several cases of German M-V rations and Tommy Cookers proved most acceptable. An hour after the final objective was taken the cavalry passed through our infantry towards Cambrai, but soon retired. The night passed quietly.

On the 21st the battalion was moved to the right to a point on the Masnières Road in support to the 59th Brigade. At close of the action companies were commanded as follows:—

A—2nd Lieut. Kinchin-Smith, B—Captain Hellier, C—2nd Lieut. Hamer, and D—2nd Lieut. Bygott.

All the above officers and Lieuts. Banks and Pugh, with C.S.M. Barlow, did especially good work.

Battalion Head-quarters was situated near four abandoned enemy anti-aircraft guns, mounted on farm waggons and of primitive make—probably captured from the Russians.

On the night of the 21st/22nd the battalion relieved a battalion of the 59th Brigade in the deep salient opposite Crevecœur, and during the next two days the Hun treated the battalion to some very heavy shelling. On the night of the 24th/25th a strong patrol of C Company was sent out to reconnoitre the position at Revelon Château, and found the enemy holding a strong line of posts in front of the Château, covering the canal crossings.

THE GERMAN COUNTER-ATTACKS

By the morning of the 30th the Divisional front was held by two Brigades. None of the battalions had a fighting strength of 400, and some were well under 300. The relief of the 60th Brigade by the 59th Brigade was not complete when the Germans launched their great counter-attack. The enemy opened a bombardment on the front of the 55th and 12th Divisions on the right. This spread to the 20th Division about 7.30, when three barrages, which included smoke and mustard gas shells, fell simultaneously between the outpost line and the sunken road from La Vacquerie to Masnières. At 8 a.m. the Germans advanced on the whole of the 20th Divisional front, under cover of a thick fog, and managed to break through. At 9 a.m. the 60th Brigade was ordered forward, the 6th K.S.L.I. and 6th Ox. and Bucks L.I. to the ridge running south-west from Gonnelieu, but the news had got back that the front was broken, and the above order was cancelled, the two battalions being directed to take up a position in the Hindenburg line north-east of La Vacquerie. However, by the time the new order was received, the battalion was heavily engaged with the enemy, south-west of Gonnelieu, and could not be withdrawn. The Ox. and Bucks, standing fast, reported the situation, and later was ordered to attack the ridge. Both battalions made some progress, but were unable to gain the crest, and eventually dug in on the north-west slope. At midday a very fine attack by the Guards drove the enemy out of Gouzeaucourt. At the same time the 6th K.S.L.I. made a second attempt to clear the high ground south-west of Gonnelieu. Owing to heavy machine-gun fire, and to the obscure situation on the right, one company had to be sent towards Gouzeaucourt; the rest of the battalion was unable to gain the crest, but the right company fired into the flank of the Germans, mowing them down as they retired before the Guards. Another attempt to seize Gonnelieu and the ridge was made that night. The battalion was to work down the railway to a point east of Gouzeaucourt, and then turn left-handed, while the Ox. and Bucks attacked in conjunction with the 12th R.B. Unfortunately the attack was unable to gain ground, owing to very heavy machine-gun fire.

Captain R. F. Smith and Lieut. Mathews behaved with conspicuous gallantry, under heavy machine-gun fire, in gaining and bringing back information concerning the situation during this period. Special mention must also be made of the work done by Lieut. Butt, the Battalion Transport Officer, who succeeded in getting all stores and munitions safely away during the enemy counter-attack. During this attack 3 officers were killed and 4 wounded, 90 other ranks killed and 70 wounded.*

On the 3rd December the battalion was relieved and proceeded by bus to Varennes. From there they marched to Albert, and entrained for Behurainville and thence marched to Ergny, where they embussed to Lynde, and joined the IX Corps. On 16th the battalion moved by train to Dickebusch, and later to Wardrecques, where the usual programme of intensive training was carried out.

The 20th Division was now in the 4th Army. At 4.45 a.m. on January 10th, 1918, a party of thirty to fifty of the enemy attempted to raid the left company of the battalion in the left sub-sector of the Brigade front. The forward posts were temporarily driven in, but the positions were quickly retaken, and though the enemy failed to capture any K.S.L.I., they left two of their own party prisoners in our hands.

The undermentioned officers and other ranks were awarded decorations for bravery during the operations round Cambrai between November 20th and December 2nd, 1917:—

Bar to the Distinguished Service Order :
Lt.-Colonel H. E. Welch.
Bar to the Military Cross :
A.-Captain R. F. Smith
The Military Cross :
Lieut. G. W. T. Butt, A.-Captain R. H. Banks,
2nd Lieut. C. H. W. Pugh
The Distinguished Conduct Medal :

C.S.M. H. Barlow	Sgt. H. Simpson
Sgt. W. E. Kingstone	Corpl. J. Holmes

* 2nd Lieut. T. J. Hannon died of wounds on December 1st, 1917.

THE KING'S SHROPSHIRE LIGHT INFANTRY

The Military Medal:

A.-Corpl. W. A. Watson	Corpl. G. Garmston
Corpl. R. Stevenson	Pte. F. Williams
Pte. N. J. Aldridge	L.-Corpl. H. Griffin
Pte. T. Hodgson	Pte. H. Hollis
Pte. J. S. Leighton	

On the 20th January the battalion was again in the trenches, and continued the usual reliefs in and out of the front line for the rest of the month. When out of the line the battalion was accommodated at rest in Tor Top Tunnels. Shortly after the battalion joined the 4th Army the following memorandum was issued by the Army Commander: " The area of the Army Battle Zone about " the Menin Road is probably the most important on the " whole Army Front, and it rests with the IX Corps to " make it as nearly impregnable as possible." This then was one of the tasks which the 20th Division had to undertake. The weather was atrocious, the front-line trenches being flooded so deeply that they had to be evacuated; posts were established which were constantly patrolled to prevent the enemy from occupying them. Being on the forward slope of the ridge, a great deal of the position was in full view of the enemy. The whole of the ground was a mass of shell holes, and the only approaches to the front line lay along duck-board tracks, which the Germans regularly shelled. The journey to the front line and back, along these slippery tracks, was a very unpleasant and dangerous business; and as a Brigade relief took place every six days, and battalions remained in the front trenches only forty-eight hours, and sometimes only twenty-four, it had to be made very often. Tor Top Tunnels, a huge underground cavern, lit by electric light, held the whole of the battalion in reserve to the left Brigade. Not even a match was allowed to be struck in these tunnels, for there were only four exits, and a fire would have made them a death trap. This lesson was learnt from the fate met by the 61st Brigade in the

Hedge Street Tunnels, when several officers and men were burnt to death.

On the 31st the 20th Division was transferred from the IX to the XXII Corps. Under the new organisation of the Division it had been decided to reduce all infantry Brigades to three battalions each. The 6th K.S.L.I. was fortunate in being selected to remain in their Brigade, instead of being split up amongst the other Shropshire battalions. After this the 20th Division was transferred to the 5th Army south of the Somme.

The 6th K.S.L.I. with the 60th Brigade was billeted in the Ham area, and during the rest of February, and first three weeks of March, the battalion worked on the defences behind the battle zone. On the 20th March the battalion received the order to man battle stations, the battalion being then billeted in Cugny. On 21st at 3.15 p.m. the battalion moved out of Cugny, and occupied quarries round about Bray St. Christophe.

BATTLE OF ST. QUENTIN

At 1.30 p.m. on March 22nd the enemy attacked, and drove in the regiments holding the line in front of the battalion. The 6th K.S.L.I., under Lt.-Colonel H. E. Welch, on the right, made a fine stand west of Happencourt with the enemy on both flanks. As the Germans came down, shouting and singing, they were surprised by Lewis-gun fire from the battalion, and were completely routed. Most of the fighting occurred on the 60th Brigade front. At 11 p.m. the Germans, who had crept up close to the position, under cover of a dense mist, drove a wedge between two companies of the 12th K.R.R.C., and got into the trenches of the 6th K.S.L.I., cutting off practically the whole of B Company, and taking many prisoners. Colonel Welch led a counter-attack with his own battalion head-quarters, but was driven back by overwhelming numbers. The companies retiring in different directions became separated from the Brigade until the afternoon of the 24th.

On the 28th the battalion was relieved by the French, and concentrated with the Brigade east of Hangest. The Brigade was soon reformed and on the 29th marched to Rifle Wood. The same day the battalion went to the support of the 59th Brigade, which was heavily attacked round Meziers. About 2.30 p.m. Lt.-Colonel Welch was mortally wounded by a piece of shrapnel, and died a quarter of an hour afterwards near Villers. A more gallant officer and true gentleman never wore the King's uniform.

On the 31st the Division was again heavily attacked, and the 6th K.S.L.I., coming up from a position southeast of Domart to protect the right flank, succeeded in stopping the enemy advance for a time and in causing him severe loss. The cavalry came up on this occasion and secured the right flank—the 6th K.S.L.I. and 11th D.L.I. being put under the command of the G.O.C. Cavalry until the Division was relieved on the 2nd April.

The incessant fighting in March, and the extremely heavy losses suffered, left the Division unfit to take the field. Large reinforcements came to the 6th K.S.L.I., and no time was lost in reorganizing the battalion. On the 1st and 3rd May the battalion was with its Brigade in the Avion and Lens sector. In this area patrolling was somewhat unusual in character as No Man's Land consisted almost entirely of loose bricks and rubbish, and the noise made was great, though drowned to some extent by a raucous chorus from the huge frogs and waterfowl on the lake. A patrol of C Company had a curious experience. Going out to silence an enemy machine gun, which had become a nuisance, they took a Lewis gun with them, but unfortunately used a drum of "tracer" bullets which brought down a heavy fire from the enemy trench mortars and machine guns.

On the 15th Lt.-Colonel R. E. Boulton assumed command of the battalion, being succeeded shortly afterwards by Major S. F. Thomas. The Division was now in the 1st Army area.

On the 25th the undermentioned N.C.O.'s and men were awarded the Military Medal for bravery during the periods March 22nd to 1st April, 1918:—

A.-C.S.M. T. Tozer	Pte. L. H. Donnelly
Corpl. H. Parker	Pte. H. T. Clarke
Corpl. J. H. Lovatt	Pte. W. Davies
Corpl. C. Minton	Pte. T. Ferrington
Corpl. A. Redford	Pte. J. Matton
L.-Corpl. R. Davies	Pte. J. H. Clay
L.-Corpl. W. V. Birchall	Pte. F. Owen
L.-Corpl. H. Tebby	Pte. F. G. Baker
L.-Corpl. D. Johnson, Bar	Pte. W. Davies
to M.M.	Pte. W. Mills
Pte. A. Thomas	Pte. H. Morris

On the 20th the battalion was relieved in the trenches by the 2nd Scottish Rifles and moved to Alberta Camp. There were eight casualties from gas during the relief.

The following officers and N.C.O.'s were awarded decorations for gallantry during the operations March 21st to April 1st, 1918:—

Bar to the Military Cross :
Lieut. K. J. H. Lindop

The Military Cross :
2nd Lieut. A.-Captain A. E. Kinchin-Smith
,,   A.-Captain E. Faithorn
,,   H. B. Davies

Bar to the Distinguished Conduct Medal :
Sgt. J. Smith.

The Distinguished Conduct Medal :
Sgt. W. Price
Sgt. T. Fletcher

A marked characteristic of the Lens sector was the frequent shelling with mustard gas which the enemy poured into Lièvin. During the rest of May, and well into June, the battalion was employed in patrols and raids, and lost heavily. On June 10th, 2nd Lieut. L. A. Cox was killed, and on the 16th 2nd Lieut. H. G. Hughes wounded, with three other ranks killed, and 16 wounded. Intensive training was still carried on whilst at rest. Meanwhile the enemy continued to seek a decision in various parts of the southern battle front, but the turn of the tide came when, on 18th July, Marshal Foch delivered the counter-attack, and from that date the history of the war is an unbroken record of Allied successes.

Here a few words of the excellent salvage work of the battalion may be put on record. The system adopted by the battalion in 1915 proved a great success throughout the war, and the 6th K.S.L.I. invariably headed the list in the monthly total of salvage by the Division.

On the 2nd August Q.M.S. F. Thomas was accidentally killed. This N.C.O. had proved himself a keen and trustworthy worker in the interests of his company. The weather improving, the trenches became dry and work continued merrily, notwithstanding the fact that the enemy were very active with their gas shells and machine-gun traversing fire. At " Crumps " Corner an enemy aeroplane dropped a light bomb, causing seven casualties.

On the 14th the battalion embussed at Alberta Camp, and thence marched to the front line to relieve the 1st Sherwood Foresters. That night 620 gas projectors were discharged from the battalion front. On the 27th the battalion relieved the 2nd Royal Berks in the Acheville section front line with Battalion Head-quarters on the edge of Vimy Ridge. On the 30th, when in reserve, sports were held, C Company proving the champions with thirty-nine points, A Company second with thirty-six points. On the 31st the battalion relieved the 12th K.R.R.C. in the left sub-section of the Méricourt sector.

Early in September the enemy began to show greater activity and kept our patrols constantly on the alert. The Germans held on to most of their positions opposite the Division, the artillery using gas shells. Fighting patrols of the 6th K.S.L.I. had to overcome determined opposi-

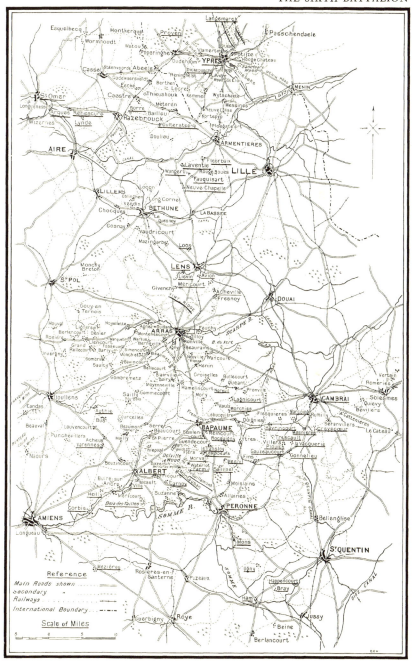

tion before they could gain a footing in the enemy's line between Acheville and Méricourt. Two platoons of A Company moved forward against the German line south of Méricourt on 3rd October, but coming under heavy machine-gun fire could not get further than the enemy front line before dark. There they remained until the next morning when the Company Commander took over his two other platoons, accompanied by a section of the Light Trench Mortar Battery, and established himself in the front line. In the course of the fighting one of the enemy was shot, and later Sgt. Naylor, at great personal risk, went over and secured the identification. Contrary to expectations the enemy was everywhere putting up a determined fight. One platoon of C Company lost nearly every man. Eventually a patrol of the battalion succeeded in entering the support trench, and joined up with the Scottish Rifles near Méricourt. The positions won were held, and on 5th/6th the battalion was relieved. Casualties between 3rd-5th October were 7 other ranks killed, 27 other ranks wounded.

Intensive training was carried on until 30th October, when the battalion entrained for the Cambrai area and came under the 3rd Army.

Little remains to be said. On the 7th November the battalion marched to Jerilain, and next day to Feignies. The enemy had evacuated these villages, and the inhabitants welcomed the British most enthusiastically.

Here ended the fighting days of the glorious 6th K.S.L.I. It had fulfilled its rôle; its record is one of which it may well be proud. Before the cadre of the battalion went home for final demobilization Br.-General Duncan presented the King's colour at Authie.

Lt.-Colonel S. F. Thomas brought home the cadre to Shrewsbury, where they received a great welcome from the Lord-Lieutenant of the County and the Mayor and citizens of Shrewsbury, being fêted by all. Finally the Battalion Old Comrades Association was formed, and meets annually with a reunion dinner.

CHAPTER VI

THE SEVENTH BATTALION

THE 7th Service Battalion was formed at the depot, Shrewsbury, on September 22nd, 1914, and left the depot at 4.30 in the morning of Saturday, September 26th, for Codford, Wilts. The battalion as it marched off consisted of four officers (Lieut. H. Linton, 2nd Lieut. W. H. Ingrams, 2nd Lieut. W. L. Lloyd and 2nd Lieut. W de B. Wood) and 750 men, and on arrival at Codford was accommodated in camp. The following officers were awaiting the arrival of the battalion at Codford: Major Sir Robert Cockburn, Bart., who was appointed to command, Lieut. and Qr.-Master E. H. Bennett, and 2nd Lieut. F. Johnston. The battalion was in camp with the 76th Brigade, which at that time consisted of the 10th Royal Welch Fusiliers, the 6th South Wales Borderers, the 10th Welch Regiment (Rhondda Battalion) and the 7th K.S.L.I., and was commanded by Br.-General H. Archdale (R.W.F.). It was at once apparent that the battalion contained a number of men of superior education, many of whom, after some persuasion, applied for and were granted commissions within a few months of joining.

The men arrived clothed in motley, about 60 per cent had red coats, and the rest civilian suits. A few had service dress, but no overcoats other than civilian ones. Hats were very various and included every form of civilian headgear. There were no rifles and no equipment. The effect, on parade, of a man in a red coat, drab trousers and a bowler hat defies description.

There was a great shortage of N.C.O.'s, those the battalion had were either re-enlisted soldiers, promoted at the depot, or ex-N.C.O.'s, rejoining as instructors, and for home service only. Many of the latter were elderly men who had been out of the service anything from ten to twenty years, actuated by the highest motives, but with a scanty knowledge of the "new drill." The word "platoon," for example, was a novelty, and was variously rendered "pathoon," "pontoon" and even "spitoon."

The Regimental Sgt.-Major was T. Lillis (late Signalling Sgt. of the 1st K.S.L.I.), and the Regimental Qr.-Master-Segt. A. P. Lunam. The camp at Codford was badly sited, a fact not so much apparent at this time, since the weather for the first fortnight was splendid. Had the local farmers been consulted much discomfort could have been avoided. In fact, the first intimation received by the owner of the land (the late Dr. Yeatman-Biggs, then Bishop of Worcester) that troops were encamped at Codford St. Mary was in the form of complaints from his tenants. Hurrying down there he encountered a battalion cook (not of the K.S.L.I.) sawing up one of his best oak fences. " You seem to be making yourself very much at home," expostulated the Bishop. " Yes," said the man, " the old cock what owns this place won't know it again." 2nd Lieuts. J. G. Hopcraft and H. S. Hopcraft joined in the evening of September 26th, and 2nd Lieuts. H. M. Pendlebury and R. G. Smithard on September 28th, bringing the strength of the battalion up to 11 officers and 750 other ranks. Lieut. H. Linton was appointed to the duties of Adjutant. There was no stationery available for the orderly room, and no Army Forms. The first three weeks were devoted to squad drill without arms. " D.P." Rifles were issued about October 20th.

The first battalion orders were issued by Major Cockburn on September 29th, 1914, and dealt almost exclusively with details of camp discipline, concerning which the men knew nothing.

On September 30th the companies were formed as follows :—

A Company, 2nd. Lieut. Ingrams
B Company, 2nd Lieut. H. S. Hopcraft
C Company, 2nd Lieut. Johnston
D Company, 2nd Lieut. Lloyd

The following officers joined on the 30th, 2nd Lieuts. H. N. D. La Touche, J. K. Mylius and F. M. C. Houghton. On the 1st of October the Rev. F. H. Roach of Shrewsbury, a chaplain in the Territorial Force, was attached to the 76th Brigade temporarily, and joined the officers' mess 7th K.S.L.I.

2nd Lieut. N. M. Hughes-Hallett joined for duty on October 5th. About this time the battalion was frequently practised in night work and in short route marches. The step set was never less than 140 to the minute, there being a superstition that this was the correct light infantry pace. The men were, of course, without arms. These route marches were usually about five miles, and served to get the men into condition, and to introduce the officers to such elementary matters as the care of the men's feet and the fit of their boots. With the exception of the Commanding Officer and Adjutant, who had both had militia service, and the Quarter-master, who had been Regimental Sgt.-Major in the 2nd K.S.L.I., all the officers were in their first few weeks of service. Discipline was admirably maintained. Those gazetted on September 14th were scrupulous in addressing those gazetted on September 11th as " Sir." All officers, except Head-quarters, were drilled and exercised in word of command for four hours every morning under a colour-sergeant of Marines. The men, actuated by a keen desire to learn, were gluttons for work ; the naïve ignorance of the majority of all things military, however, provided many amusing incidents. One man, checked by a sergeant for failing to salute the Adjutant, replied with some indignation at the unjust rebuke, " Why, I 'ardly knows 'im! " At this date, October 10th, the battalion was officered by one major, two lieutenants and twelve 2nd lieutenants; the latter, with the exception of Wood, Johnston and Smithard, being all under twenty years of age, having joined straight from school. All were from public schools, five being from Shrewsbury. The evenings were devoted to the earnest study of " Infantry Training," and the discussion of drill problems. Thus, even in the earliest days, few, if any, of these very young officers failed to realize the heavy responsibility of what was likely to be expected of them. Work on the parade ground began at daylight and continued, with one hour's break for dinner, until dark. Invariably on first parade at dawn, looming out of the mist, would be seen the figure of the Brigadier. On October 14th the bad weather began. The men had no tent boards, and all approaches to the camp became knee-deep in mud. At the supply depot one subaltern of the R.A.S.C., and eleven civilians, with such transport as they could raise locally from the farmers, were engaged in rationing 14,000 troops. Small wonder if the bread did not always arrive to time, or if the rations were received spoilt by the rain.

A vacancy at the School of Instruction, Chelsea, having been allotted to the battalion, the names of all officers present in camp were placed in a hat, 2nd Lieut. Johnston drew the lucky number and proceeded to a fortnight's course at Chelsea on October 19th. On October 20th all the men were provided with " Kitchener's blue " suits, and uniformity in dress, at least, was insured on parade. On October 24th Lieut. E. C. R. Bailey from the Territorial Force joined, and on the 26th Lt.-Colonel W. J. Newell (Indian Army retired) arrived and took over command.

Early in November the weather got steadily worse. From October 25th until November 10th it rained in torrents every day. Roads to the camp became impassable, and training was suspended. Even route marches were impossible, the troops being soaked through before the last man of the company had struggled through the mud on to the road. The men, of course, had no change of clothing, and no washing accommodation. There was nothing to be done day after day but to lie, in an indescribable state of mud, in tents without floor boards, listening to the rain beating on the canvas. Rumours of other battalions training in billets in their home towns affected some of the troops in the Brigade to such an extent that mass meetings were held, and cases of men refusing to go on parade by companies occurred. One regiment of South Wales miners marched away, and it was supposed that they had gone to train in their home counties, but this was not the case. The rest of the Brigade remained cursing the rain and Codford.

On November 1st, Captain C. W. Daubeny joined for duty, and on November 4th, the following message was circulated from the G.O.C.-in-Chief Southern Command to be read out to all troops. " Let your men know we are " doing all we can for them." The same day notice was received that the whole of the 25th Division would move into billets in Bournemouth.

The 76th Brigade was allotted the district, situated in north Bournemouth, known as Winton. The inhabitants of the neighbourhood viewed the coming of the troops with mixed feelings. The battalion under Lt.-Colonel Newell moved into Bournemouth on November 12th, 1914. Lieut. Ingrams acted as Adjutant, and Lieut. Linton, who was not fit for active service, returned to duty at the depot. Immediately after arrival in Bournemouth, all ex-soldiers (i.e. trained men) were ordered to be sent to the 3rd (Special Reserve) Battalion K.S.L.I. for drafts for overseas. There were only 50 of these all told.

Training at Bournemouth was slightly less strenuous, owing to the short days. The battalion at this period was at company training; the surrounding country affording very good facilities for this, but, being in billets, and each company being left largely to itself, the battalion, as such, did not progress as quickly as it might otherwise have done.

There were two Brigade tactical exercises early in December, consisting of a defence of the coast at Bournemouth. The number of chines along the coast to the west of Bournemouth made the exercise rather monotonous.

On December 18th Colonel Newell left the regiment, on sick leave, and died suddenly at his home two days later.

At the close of the year the regiment was officered as follows:—

Major Cockburn, Commanding; Captain Daubeny; Lieuts. Ingrams, Johnston, Wood, Bailey, Rangecroft and Bennett; 2nd Lieuts. Smithard, Caesar, Pendlebury, J. G. Hopcraft, H. S. Hopcraft, Lloyd, Hughes-Hallett, Hopkinson, Robinson, Silvester, Shaw, Rust, La Touche and Mylius. A total of 22 officers.

On January 1st, 1915, Major A. V. Weir from the 1st Royal Irish Rifles took over the command. He appointed Lieut. Wood Adjutant and handed D Company over to 2nd Lieut. Lloyd. The new Colonel, being the one and only serving officer of the regular army who was ever in the 7th K.S.L.I., previous to proceeding overseas, improved rapidly the standard of training. Battalion parades were frequent, and the regiment began to feel its feet as a unit.

Battalion training commenced in February and Colonel Weir had the battalion out for the day, two or three times a week, and on parade every morning. The men were learning very quickly, and their intelligence, keenness and good behaviour were most striking. The officers all worked hard, with a full realization of the responsibilities attaching to the duties they were learning to perform. In short, all ranks were concentrated on one purpose—to fit themselves to play their part over in France.

The battalion was first inspected by Br.-General Vizard, an Inspector of Infantry, on February 1st, 1915. The battalion was still but half-equipped, having only "D.P." rifles, and not a sufficient number of these. He reported favourably on the battalion, and, at the earnest request of the Colonel, added a recommendation that senior officers might be sent to the battalion, which still remained without any officers with previous service in the regular army. The War Office, however, was not able to supply any.

2nd Lieut. E. A. Helmore joined for duty at Bournemouth on January 29th, 1915. He was with the regiment only a few months, leaving the 7th K.S.L.I. to take up a cadetship at the R.M.A., Woolwich, on May 13th. 2nd Lieut. Walker joined on January 18th, 1915. Early in February 2nd Lieuts. E. W. Rigby and D. D. Bowie joined from a school of instruction, the former having come from the Malay States, and 2nd Lieut. Mylius left for the R.M.C., Sandhurst. About this time the appointment of specialist officers began. Lieut. F. N. Rust, assisted by Sgt. Galliers, undertook the training of battalion signallers, and very soon had a most efficient signal section, there being two or three postal telegraphists in the regiment. Lieut. J. G. Hopcraft was appointed transport officer and Sgt. W. H. Roberts transport sergeant, as soon as the horses began to arrive in January, 1915. From the outset Lieut. Hopcraft set a very high standard of efficiency, and his horsemastership earned the praise of Major-General Ventris, commanding the 25th Division. Lieut. Ingrams with a dummy machine gun, made of wood, undertook the training of a machine-gun section.

The 6th S.W. Borderers left the 76th Brigade early in the year, becoming a pioneer battalion. The 8th K.O.R.L. had come into the Brigade at Codford in October, replacing the 10th Welch Regiment, and the 13th K.L.R. now joined the Brigade in place of the 6th S.W.B. 2nd Lieut. H. N. D. La Touche, having experience of mining engineering, was transferred to the 6th S.W.B.

On March 1st, 1915, Lt.-General Sir William Pitcairn Campbell, G.O. C.-in-C. Southern Command, inspected the Division and saw the 7th K.S.L.I. at a tactical exercise. He spoke of the advent of rifles that would shoot, and of an early move to France. The men were delighted at the news, which unfortunately proved an optimistic forecast. Those N.C.O.'s who had re-enlisted for training purposes—mostly over forty-five and some over fifty-five years of age—left the battalion, being redistributed to " younger units " on March 15th, 1915.

There were twenty-two of these and the majority had performed useful work. On their departure the battalion was able to promote its own N.C.O.'s from a large amount of excellent material available. Captain R. E. Negus from the Inns of Court O.T.C. joined the battalion on April 15th and took over command of C Company.

Towards the end of the month the battalion suffered a severe blow through the recalling of Lt.-Colonel Weir to join the Expeditionary Force. He left on April 29th to command his regiment then fighting at Hill 60 in the Ypres salient. Major J. H. Barber, second in command of the 8th K.O.R.L., was promoted to command and took over on May 1st.

On May 2nd, 1915, the battalion left Bournemouth. The streets of Winton were lined with the kind friends who had taken the Shropshire men to their hearts, and there could be no mistake about the genuineness of the feelings of regret on both sides at this leave-taking. The battalion marched to Romsey, spending the night at Ringwood on the way. Here they remained three weeks under canvas, during which time they were again inspected by Br.-General Vizard, who found the battalion much improved and all ranks smarter and more soldierly. From Romsey the battalion marched via Flowerdown and Alton to Odiham, where the men had their first experience of close billets. On May 25th Major Cockburn and Captain Daubeny, both being over the age limit at that time fixed for service overseas, left to join the 9th K.S.L.I., a farewell dinner being held in their honour. A rearrangement of the company commands was made, Captain Negus taking over A Company and Captain Johnston C. The battalion left Odiham by march route for Aldershot.

The battalion reached Aldershot on June 3rd, 1915, and was quartered in Albuhera Barracks, sharing the same with the 13th King's (Liverpool) Regiment. Brigade and Divisional training was resumed. The equipment, still very deficient, began to be made up soon after arrival. Transport was completed to establishment by the middle of July, and the battalion was confidently expecting to go overseas within a few weeks. Unfortunately there were no rifles forthcoming. A bugle band was formed under Corpl. Richards, and soon became a great asset.

Orders were received about July 15th to make up the officers to war establishment (29) and to post surplus officers to the Reserve, and on July 30th the Rev. P. E. Lee joined the mess as chaplain to the battalion.

Br.-General E. St. G. Pratt took over the 76th Brigade on arrival at Aldershot in June from Br.-General Archdale, and Major-General C. B. Doran succeeded Major-General Ventris in command of the 25th Division.

Rifles arrived and musketry courses began throughout the Division in the last week of August. Lord Kitchener inspected the 25th Division on August 12th, 1915, and the men proceeded on final leave as from the following week.

H.M. The King inspected the 76th Brigade on the road near Aldershot, when returning from a tactical exercise, about September 5th. The four months' training (June 1st–September 25th) at Aldershot was very strenuous and included a Divisional entrenching scheme on Hartford Bridge flats, which occupied about ten days.

The troops became exceedingly fit, often marching ten miles out and ten miles back from an exercise without feeling any strain. Some of the exercises began as early as five in the morning, finishing at six or seven in the evening. This strenuous training had the effect of weeding out the unfit from all ranks. The march discipline of the battalion was splendid, and it was no uncommon thing for the battalion to be out all day on an exercise, marching twenty to twenty-five miles, without a single man falling out. Very special attention was given to care of feet to achieve this result. This good march discipline was later to stand the battalion in good stead.

The whole battalion was put through its musketry in

three weeks, coming out first in the Brigade and third in the Division. Lieut. and Qr.-Master E. H. Bennett and Regimental Sergt.-Major T. Lillis, were found medically unfit for service overseas and were transferred to the Reserve. The units of the 76th Brigade going overseas were commanded as follows:—

General Officer Commanding	Br.-General E. St. G. Pratt.
Brigade-Major	Captain G. T. Keith
Staff Captain	Captain H. L. Cowlard
Aide-de-Camp	2nd Lieut. R. J. Davies, 7th K.S.L.I.
13th King's	Lt.-Colonel Gibbons
8th K.O.R.L.	Lt.-Colonel Thorn
10th R.W.F.	Colonel Beresford-Ash
7th K.S.L.I.	Lt.-Colonel Barber

The Brigade embarked for France September 23rd–27th, 1915.

The following officers proceeded overseas with the battalion, September 27th, 1915.

Lt.-Colonel J. H. Barber	Commanding
Major R. E. Negus	Second in Command
*Major G. S. Rangecroft	Commanding A Company
Captain W. de B. Wood	Adjutant
„ E. W. Rigby	Commanding D Company
„ F. Johnston	Commanding C Company
„ F. N. Marcy	Commanding B Company
„ F. N. Rust	D Company
„ R. G. Smithard	Intelligence Officer
„ H. M. Pendlebury	Asst.-Adjt. for Musketry
„ G. F. Silvester	B Company
Lieut. E. L. Wright	A Company
„ N. M. Hughes-Hallett	C Company
„ *R. E. Philp	Pioneer Officer]
„ W. L. Lloyd	D Company
„ J. G. Hopcraft	Transport Officer

* Commissioned from the ranks 7th K.S.L.I.

Lieut. E. H. Robinson	Machine-Gun Officer
„ C. B. O. Walker	A Company
„ C. P. Caesar	A Company
2nd Lieut. D. D. Bowie	A Company
„ W. N. Legg	C Company
„ W. A. Pilkington	Signalling Officer
„ G. C. Smythe	Bombing Officer
„ *L. M. Dell	Scout Officer
„ *A. W. Johns	Bombing Officer
„ W. A. N. Baker	A Company
„ H. C. Tweedale	Machine Guns
„ C. V. Townsend	Sniping Officer
Lieut. and Quartermaster	W. T. Calthorpe
Medical Officer	Lieut. C. S. Gideon, R.A.M.C.

Regimental Sergeant-Major, H. Ellis; †Regimental Quartermaster-Sergeant, G. Clarke; ‡Company Quartermaster-Sergeant, M. J. Parker; Company Sergeant-Majors: A Company F. Lenton, B Company E. Cross, C Company J. Caddick, D Company R. Hall.

The 7th K.S.L.I. entrained at Aldershot at 8 o'clock on the night of September 27th and disembarked at Boulogne at 2.30 a.m. on 28th. The battalion marched to Osterhove Rest Camp on the heights above Boulogne, bedding down about 4 a.m. on 28th. The transport under Major Negus, with Lieuts. J. G. Hopcraft and E. H. Robinson, disembarked at Havre on September 27th. The battalion, less transport, entrained at Pont de Briques at 10.30 a.m. on 29th in pouring rain. Strength: Officers 26, other ranks 839 (3 officers and 110 other ranks were with the transport embarked via Havre). Total: Officers 29, other ranks 949. The battalion detrained at Hazebrouck in Flanders about 4 p.m. The transport had detrained at Steenwerck. The battalion had orders to march to Merris and set out in a heavy rainstorm carrying, in addition to full equipment, a good deal of material

* Commissioned from the ranks 7th K.S.L.I.
† Acted as Orderly-room Sergeant.   ‡ Acted as R.Q.M.S.

which normally would have been on the transport. After two hours' march in the rain, a cycle orderly arrived on the road with an order changing the destination to Meteren. As night fell the Véry lights from the trenches could be seen, and the sound of the guns distinctly heard. About 9 p.m. the battalion arrived at Meteren to find that no arrangements had been made for billets, and it was some hours before all the men, who were now wet through, were under cover. The transport meanwhile had been ordered to Merris, and there were no rations for anybody that night. The transport arrived in the afternoon of September 30th, having been away from the battalion for four days.

The battalion moved from Meteren to Outtersteene at 3 p.m. on the 31st. The news from the front was very good, and an Order of the day, by Lord French, announced that the big offensive of September 25th had broken through to the German third line, and was still continuing. Officers and men of the 24th Division, encountered passing through our camp at Outtersteene, had grim tales to tell of their part in the Battle of Loos. The battalion moved from Outtersteene to Bailleul on Monday, October 4th, 1915. Strength: 29 officers, 924 other ranks. In Bailleul the battalion left its band instruments, fondly imagining that some day they would be collected again. On the night of October 4th/5th, a fleet of Zeppelins was observed flying over the town *en route* for England. The 25th Division was detailed to relieve the 1st Canadian Division holding the line at Ploegsteert Wood.

The battalion left Bailleul on October 7th and moved into camp at Papot, four and a half miles north-west of Armentières, and about two miles west of Ploegsteert Wood. The C.O., Adjutant and Company Commanders visited the Canadian trenches on the same day for a preliminary reconnaissance of the line. However, before the battalion was due to take over, news was received on Saturday, October 9th, that the 7th K.S.L.I.

was transferred, with the 13th K.L.R., to the 8th Brigade, 3rd Division—then with the V Corps, 2nd Army. Major-General Doran came to say good-bye, and expressed himself as very sorry to lose the battalion. He had no information as to whether the transfer was temporary or permanent ; in fact, it was permanent. The 3rd Division was at this time in the Ypres salient.

On October 9th the battalion moved from the neighbourhood of " Plugstreet " to camp at Bousseboom in the Ypres salient, via Bailleul. On October 11th the right half battalion, under Major Negus, left camp at twenty minutes' notice to move into the trenches for forty-eight hours' instruction. The right half battalion moved off to time, but without adequate provision for rations and water. The battalion was attached for instruction to what was left of the 1st Gordons (9th Brigade).

On the 13th October, Head-quarters (including the Rev. P. E. Lee, the very popular chaplain) and the left half battalion moved up to replace the right half in Sanctuary Wood (three miles south-east of Ypres), leaving camp at five and arriving about 9.30 p.m. Battalion Head-quarters was in Maple Copse. The battalion was shelled on the way up, but had no casualties. On 15th October A and B Companies came up again, and the battalion took over the trenches from the Gordons, who went out to rest. The first casualties, Ptes. Smout and Cooper, killed, and Ptes. Pugh, Lacey and Fellowes, wounded, occurred on the night of October 13th/14th, 1915.

The trenches in Sanctuary Wood were in poor condition and needed constant attention. They were badly enfiladed, and enemy snipers were very active in the day, and fixed rifles were going all night. The battalion settled down comfortably and soon got used to being shelled from both flanks and the rear. They held this sector until October 21st, when they were relieved by the 10th Sherwood Foresters from the 17th Division.

The 3rd Division was due for rest, and the 17th Division had just arrived to take over from them. On the night of 21st/22nd the battalion marched to Bousseboom, a distance of twelve miles, arriving about 3 a.m., but, finding no camp accommodation available for them after their long march from the trenches, officers and men slept on the roadside. On the following night the battalion marched back to Steenvoorde, where the 3rd Division was to have its month's rest after three months in the salient.

Casualties for the first tour in the trenches, October 13th–21st: other ranks 2 killed and 8 wounded. In addition 2 officers were invalided—Captain F. N. Rust with trench feet, and Lieut. R. E. Philp, pioneer officer, with pneumonia.

The battalion, being inexperienced, suffered a good deal from minor discomforts that seasoned troops had learnt to avoid. During the ten days' tour many men got very little sleep, not having as yet acquired the art of sleeping on the fire-step. The trenches on the left of the sector were waterlogged. Very few men got any sleep at all on the night of 21st/22nd, and the following night was spent in the march to Steenvoorde. The battalion bore the fatigue excellently, and the high spirits of the men proved irrepressible; when the trenches were being shelled they seemed happiest. 2nd Lieut. C. V. Townsend at once got to work with his snipers and was able to account for several Germans. Major Negus did some useful reconnaissance work, appreciated by the Divisional Intelligence Staff. Both officers and men enjoyed the novelty and excitement of patrolling No Man's Land at night.

Lieut. Philp, formerly Corpl. Philp, D Company, 7th K.S.L.I., worked day and night with the pioneers, draining and revetting the trenches, and building up the parapet which, in many places, was far from being bullet proof.

The period of rest at Steenvorde was spent in training and refitting. Fearsome-looking short fur coats of goatskin, which smelt abominably, were issued to the men and caused much amusement. The battalion, as a new-comer to the 3rd Division, was inspected in turn by the Divisional Commander, General Haldane, the Corps Commander, General Allenby, and the Army Commander, General Plumer. On each occasion the battalion was informed that the 3rd Division would remain throughout the winter in the Ypres salient, and that there would be no leave. On November 23rd the battalion marched into camp at Reninghelst, where 2nd Lieut. F. S. Loft joined, and Lieut. C. P. Caesar was invalided as the result of an accident at football.

The camp in tents at Reninghelst was well situated, but a long way from the trenches, the sector of the line the battalion was to hold (known as the " U " trenches, between St. Eloi and Hill 60) being ten miles from the camp. The route via La Clytte, Dickebusch, Café Belge, Kruisstraathoek, "Shrapnel Corner" and "Kingsway" was, for the last three miles, over heavily shelled and broken roads, often very congested with traffic at night. Considering that the transport had to make this long journey to and from the trenches every night, it is surprising that the animals kept so fit. The ration "dump," whence rations and water, in petrol cans, had to be carried to the trenches, was yet another mile from the front line, making the work of the fatigue parties very heavy. The new sector was situated just south of the Ypres–Commines canal in the southern neck of the salient, the line facing roughly south-east. Head-quarters was situated in " Spoil Bank," and the feature known as " the Bluff " was on the opposite bank of the canal.

The composition of the 8th Brigade at this time was as follows :

Br.-General J. D. McLachlan, Cameron Highlanders, Commanding.

2nd Royal Scots.	5th Middlesex.
13th King's Liverpool Regiment.	1st London Rifle Brigade, and 7th K.S.L.I.

The new trenches were in a very bad condition. The first line, over the sector held alternately by 1st North'd Fus. and 7th K.S.L.I., was not consecutive, some portions being isolated and inaccessible in daylight, having no communication trench. The Head-quarters' dug-outs in Spoil Bank alongside the canal, however, were fairly good.

The sector held was roughly 1,000 yards frontage. At this time these trenches were quiet, there being a little shelling every morning and evening, but usually quiet nights, with very little sniping activity. Our guns were, of necessity, not much in evidence, due to shortage of ammunition.

Casualties for the first three tours averaged about 4 killed and 12 wounded each tour. Wastage from sickness, however, was considerable. This was due to the bad state of the trenches, necessitating continuous heavy fatigue work unceasing night or day. Also the long march of over nine miles to and from the trenches, and the heavy fatigues carrying up rations and trench materials. As one of the battalion grousers was heard to observe, " It ain't the war I complains of—it's the way up to it."

As the weather got worse it was found almost impossible to improve the trenches in any way, it being only just possible by unceasing work to keep the line intact. The dug-out accommodation in reserve here was very inadequate. The tour of duty was seven days in the line and seven days in rest camp. Due to a shortage of men the seven days in the rest camp were spent on continuous fatigues; the battalion having to furnish from 50 to 500 men daily.

During November Lieut. W. L. Lloyd was injured in a bombing accident at the Grenade School and left the battalion for a time.

On December 13th Lt.-Colonel Barber, who had been in poor health for some time, was invalided home. Major Negus was promoted to command of the battalion

219

from that date; Major Rangecroft was appointed second in command and 2nd Lieut. E. L. Wright was appointed to command A Company.

The weather in early December was very bad and there was a large number of cases of trench feet in the Division. The 7th K.S.L.I. had as many as forty-three cases in one week. Energetic measures on the part of all ranks, and the issue of gum-boots and anti-frostbite grease, reduced this number to four or five cases a week. Twenty-five of the new steel helmets were issued to the battalion and allotted to the Machine-gun Section.

About December 17th all troops in the salient were warned of an impending gas attack by the Germans. On the night of 19th/20th December a heavy bombardment began about three in the morning and continued till dawn. The 76th Brigade on our left opened fire, but no target was presented on our front. The gas attack, which lasted from 5.30 till 6.15 a.m., was launched by the Germans in the north of the salient in the neighbourhood of Pilkem, and a north-east wind carried the gas well behind the 7th K.S.L.I. trenches. Some slight effect was felt by reason of gas shells in our reserve line. Casualties from the phosgene gas occurred as far back as Poperinghe, over eight miles from the point where the gas was launched. The attack was a failure, although there was a considerable number of casualties from the gas among the troops on our left. The battalion was delighted to hear the news that the 1st K.S.L.I. had distinguished itself on this occasion. The infantry attack following the gas was repulsed.

The battalion continued to hold the same sector of the line, relieving the 1st North'd Fus., up to Christmas. Christmas Day was spent in the rest camp—the North'd Fus. being in the line that day—the officers dined together in the evening. The men had plenty of good cheer from home and the day was a great success.

New Year's Eve was spent in the trenches. The night was quiet and a piano could be faintly heard somewhere about the German third line. About 11 p.m. 2nd Lieut. Smythe took a small party out and threw some bombs into the German first line, which appeared very thinly held. A small concentration of troops was heard and the 41st Battery sent over six rounds to this spot, three being direct hits on the German parapet. By twelve o'clock midnight all was quiet again.

On January 3rd Captain H. M. Pendlebury and 2nd Lieut. W. A. Pilkington were wounded, and on the 12th 2nd Lieut. W. N. Legg was hit whilst on duty at the ration dump, dying of his wounds two months later.

Early in February, 2nd Lieut. Smythe was wounded in a bombing accident and 2nd Lieut. Johns was appointed bombing officer.

The battalion remained in the same sector until February 2nd, 1916, when the 3rd Division went back to the neighbourhood of Eperlecques, about six miles north-west of St. Omer, to rest.

During the period of rest battalion training was resumed under Lt.-Colonel Negus. Sport of all kinds was encouraged; a battalion cross-country run was arranged in which every available officer and man, from the C.O (who came in third) to cooks and sanitary squad, participated. The 7th K.S.L.I. worked their way into the final of the 3rd Divisional Association Football Cup, being beaten therein by the R.A.M.C. The 8th Brigade cross-country run was won by the 7th K.S.L.I. on February 26th. During the month 2nd Lieut. H. S. Hopcraft, A. C. Hetherington, G. H. Richmond and R. O. Huyshe joined for duty.

On the 14th February, whilst the 3rd Division was resting, the Germans attacked again in the salient, and succeeded in capturing the " Bluff " by blowing up a system of mines under our trenches. The " Bluff " was a feature of some tactical importance in the neighbourhood. The 76th Brigade was detailed to recapture it, and accordingly their rest was cut short, and they returned to Reninghelst to prepare for the counter-attack about the end of the month, the 8th Brigade remaining at Eperlecques.

On February 29th the 8th Brigade had orders to move up to support the attack of the 76th Brigade, which was fixed for the early morning of March 2nd, 1916. Accordingly the battalion entrained for Poperinghe, arriving in the evening of March 1st. That evening the 7th had the pleasure of meeting the 1st and 6th K.S.L.I, which were also billeted in Poperinghe. The men were close billeted, and all units were " standing by." The 76th Brigade attacked next morning without any preliminary bombardment and completely surprised the Germans. The attack was entirely successful, all the lost trenches being recovered and a small sector gained. The casualties during the attack itself were slight.

At 5 p.m. on March 2nd the battalion started from Ouderdom in a blinding snowstorm for the trenches, a distance of nine or ten miles, arriving at the dug-outs in Gordon Terrace at the " Bluff " about 2 a.m. Five minutes before the battalion marched off a despatch rider from Brigade Head-quarters dashed up bearing a bulky package marked " Urgent." Sheltering behind his horse, the C.O. broke the seals and with a somewhat tired smile handed to the Adjutant ten pages of correspondence relating to the loss of a packing-case, between Codford and Bournemouth, sixteen months before. The enemy bombardment on March 3rd and 4th, after the attack, was very severe and accounted for the heavy casualties (50 per cent) suffered by the 76th Brigade. Our friends the 10th R.W. Fusiliers, lost their C.O., Second in Command and Adjutant, besides a number of other officers. On March 4th the battalion took over the left sector of the newly captured " Bluff " trenches from the 7th Border Regiment. The trenches were so battered as to be hardly recognized as trenches, and most of the dug-outs were " crumped in." In addition, the weather was very severe, the ground being several inches in snow, and there was no dressing station. The mud was so deep in places that men had to be pulled out with ropes; others were stuck up to their waists for eighteen hours. Many wounded were suffocated in the mud.

The battalion was kept busy burying dead and consolidating the line until relieved by the 1st R. Scots Fusiliers on the night of March 7th/8th, when they returned to their old camp at Reninghelst. Casualties for the four days amounted to 3 killed, 11 wounded and 146 to the field ambulance. On March 10th Captain W. de B. Wood, the Adjutant, was evacuated to the Field Ambulance, and Captain D. D. Bowie took over the Adjutancy.

On March 11th the battalion returned to the old sector at Spoil Bank south of the canal. On the following day the weather, which had been intensely cold with blizzards of snow since March 2nd, changed and became warm and sunny.

On March 13th, 1916, Br.-General J. D. McLachlan was invalided home and Br.-General E. G. Williams, (Devon Regt.), succeeded to command of the 8th Brigade.

The battalion was relieved by the 1st North'd Fus. on March 14th, A and B Companies went to Voormezeele as Brigade Reserve and Head-quarters, C and D Companies back to Reninghelst. Whilst going round the trenches here, an inspecting officer had occasion to commend a platoon sergeant whom he found sitting on the fire-step unrolling and laying out neatly in pairs a consignment of socks newly arrived from home. " Careful sort of fellow that," remarked the staff officer, " sees they are sound before he issues them, eh?" " Well," replied the C.O. doubtfully, " the fact is one of the men found a pound note rolled up in the pair issued to him from the last consignment."

On March 19th the battalion was detailed in reserve to the 9th Brigade for an attack on the Mound at St. Eloi. On March 21st 2nd Lieut. C. V. Townsend, who had trained and organized the battalion snipers, of whom he was in charge, with great devotion and ability, was killed whilst on patrol. On March 26th we blew up several mines in front of the Mound and the 9th Brigade launched their attack, which was only partly successful, the 1st North'd Fus. reaching their objective, but the 4th R.S. Fusiliers being hung up. On March 27th the 8th Brigade was withdrawn, leaving the 8th E. Yorks and the 7th K.S.L.I. in the line, under the orders of the G.O.C. 76th Brigade.

The battalion was relieved on the night of April 3rd/4th by the 27th Regiment of Canadian Infantry, leaving the machine gunners and Lewis guns, under 2nd Lieut. E. H. Robinson, still in the line. On April 5th this officer was holding one of the craters with a Lewis gun, and although two of the team were killed, and he himself and another of the gunners wounded, he refused to leave the crater. 2nd Lieut. Robinson remained with the two uninjured members of the team working the gun after the infantry had retired, and until the gun itself was destroyed by shell fire. The Lewis gunners were relieved on the night of April 11th/12th, and the few remaining rejoined the battalion at Berthen. 2nd Lieut. Rumfitt was appointed Machine-gun Officer in succession to 2nd Lieut. Robinson.

On April 5th the battalion (less machine gunners) marched from Reninghelst, five miles south, to Berthen for rest, and was billeted in farms about the village. The following massage was read on parade :—

"Wire from G.O.C. 76th Brigade to G.O.C. 8th "Brigade, dated April 5th, 1916.

"I wish to bring to your notice the good work done "by the 7th K.S.L.I. and 8th E. Yorks during the time "they were under my command and hope that you will "inform the commanding officers how grateful I am "for their co-operation and continued cheerfulness under "trying conditions. Although the 7th K.S.L.I. had been "for a long period in the trenches, they were anxious to "send one of their companies to relieve the troops in the

" broken portion of the line on the right, which offer
" was much appreciated by all concerned."

On night of April 22nd/23rd the battalion relieved the
6th Durham L.I. (151st Brigade, 50th Division) in dug-
outs in Ridge Wood, just east of Dickebusch Lake,
moving up next night into the trenches at St. Eloi.
On the 30th the battalion was relieved by the 8th E.
Yorks and returned, as Brigade Reserve, to Ridge Wood.
During the month Major G. S. Rangecroft was sent to
the Field Ambulance, Captain F. Johnston was appointed
second in command and Lieut. Hughes-Hallett took over
command of C Company. 2nd Lieut. J. A. E. Upton
joined on April 10th. On May 5th the battalion was
relieved by the 1st R.S. Fusiliers and moved into camp
at La Clytte, finding large working parties each night for
the trenches. On the 8th the battalion relieved the 8th
E. Yorks in the trenches at Bois Carré, and remained in
this sector until the 28th, when they went into Corps
Reserve, returning to billets near Berthen. During this
tour 2nd Lieut. B. L. Bolt was killed and 2nd Lieut.
E. G. Rumfitt, Machine-gun Officer, was wounded.

On June 3rd Lieut. C. S. Gideon, the popular and hard-
working medical officer, left the battalion to take charge
of an ambulance train, and Lieut. Reeve joined as medical
officer. On June 5th 2nd Lieut. A. L. C. Spiers joined for
duty. The first number of the 7th K.S.L.I. regimental
paper " The Dud " was produced during this period of
rest, and reflects the spirit of fun and good comradeship
which always prevailed in this battalion. Four numbers
in all were produced in the course of about fifteen months,
the main features being a witty editorial by Lieut. Dell,
who produced the first number, and excellent caricatures
by Major Johnston. Early in the month news was received
that some trenches had been lost in Sanctuary Wood, and
the battalion was placed under orders to move at short
notice. These orders came whilst the battalion sports
were in progress on June 10th, and by 7 p.m. the battalion

was *en route* for Reninghelst. On the 11th the battalion relieved the Canadians in their old sector (the " U " trenches) at St. Eloi, where a good deal of work had been done improving the dug-outs in Spoil Bank. The sector was still fairly quiet, though one shell in D Company's trench caused 19 casualties (7 killed, including Sgt. Hatfield, and 12 wounded). The battalion was relieved by the 2nd Royal Scots on the 16th and proceeded to Scottish Wood, where they were relieved on the 20th by the 31st Canadians, and returned to camp at Reninghelst. A draft of 73 other ranks, the first of the " Derby " men, awaited the battalion in camp. On the 22nd the battalion entrained at Poperinghe for St. Omer, and from there marched to Boisdinghem, where the men were billeted in farms. During the month Captain F. N. Marcy left the battalion for the work of training reinforcements at home, and Lieut. J. G. Hopcraft went to the 8th Brigade as Brigade Transport Officer; 2nd Lieut. Deedes was appointed Battalion Transport Officer in his place. The battalion felt the loss of these two officers keenly. Lieut. Caesar rejoined from England and 2nd Lieuts. Dell and Baker from courses, and 2nd Lieuts. W. S. Charman and R. G. Byrt joined on first appointment. 2nd Lieut. Coe left for the Field Ambulance.

BATTLES OF THE SOMME, 1916

On July 1st the battalion, 33 officers and 905 other ranks strong, started on its journey south to the Somme. Captain Rigby rejoined from the base on the 4th, and 2nd Lieuts. W. O. Ford and O. R. Lloyd joined. Proceeding by easy stages, by night, the battalion marched through Nizernes, Fienvilliers, Flesselles, Cardonette and Corbie, arriving on July 7th at the ruins of Carnoy, about six miles east of Albert, where the battalion bivouacked. The next few days were spent in reconnoitring carefully the ground recaptured from the Germans during the first stage of the Battle of the Somme, and over which the 8th Brigade was detailed to attack. All officers were patrolling every night, and on the 12th 2nd Lieut. H. C. Tweedale was wounded in a bomb accident.

THE BATTLE OF BAZENTIN RIDGE

The attack took place at 3.30 a.m. on July 14th. The 7th K.S.L.I. and 8th East Yorks were the assaulting battalions, the 1st R. Scots Fusiliers in support, and 2nd Royal Scots in reserve. The 7th K.S.L.I. were on the left with the 13th King's Liverpools, 9th Brigade, on their left. The night assembly and deployment of the assaulting battalions went without a hitch, and by 11 p.m. on the 13th the battalion was in position in No Man's Land waiting for the dawn. The objective of the attack was the enemy front trench, and support line, running through Bazentin le Grand, a distance of about 1,500 yards. Owing to the undulation of the ground the enemy trenches were not visible. At 3.20 there was a brief preliminary bombardment, lasting for five minutes, which was mostly very short, and caused a number of casualties amongst our own men. Unfortunately the attack ran into exceptionally strong, and quite uncut, wire about 600 yards from the enemy front trench. Not a man of the first wave succeeded in getting through this wire, of which there were two rows, each ten to twenty yards deep. The succeeding waves of the attack closed on the first and the enemy had an easy target. After vain attempts to penetrate the wire, the remnants of the attacking force fell back to the shelter of a sunken road about 200 yards from the enemy trenches. Meanwhile Colonel Negus, with Ptes. Arrowsmith and Morgan, lying wounded in the wire, were captured by the Germans, and carried by them to a dressing station in their support line. About 11 a.m. the remains of the battalion, under the senior officer, Captain W. L. Lloyd, attacked again and, assisted by bombing parties from the flanks, succeeded in cutting their way through the wire, reaching the enemy trenches in time to join with the bombing parties in clearing them, and in rescuing the Colonel.

THE KING'S SHROPSHIRE LIGHT INFANTRY

The survivors of the battalion, consisting of 6 officers and about 135 other ranks, consolidated and held the new line, beating off five counter-attacks, until July 20th, when they were relieved by the 1st R.W. Fusiliers. Amongst numerous congratulatory messages received was a personal letter to the Colonel from the G.O.C. 3rd Division, General Haldane, who referred to " the " grand work of your battalion on the 14th, and your " gallant leading of them." The casualties in this action were as follows:—

Officers killed:—

Captain E. W. Rigby	Commanding D Company	
„ E. L. Wright	Commanding A Company	
„ G. F. Sylvester	Commanding B Company	
Lieut. C. P. Caesar	B Company	
2nd Lieut. L. M. Dell	Pioneer Officer	
„ C. E. Green	D Company	
„ C. O'C. McSwiny	D Company	
„ W. L. Davies	B Company	

Officers wounded:—

Lt.-Colonel Negus	Commanding Battalion
Major F. Johnston	Second in Command
Captain Hughes-Hallett	C Company
2nd Lieut. A. W. Johns	Bombing Officer
„ H. S. Hopcraft	Lewis-Gun Officer
„ O. R. Lloyd	A Company
„ W. O. Ford	C Company

Other ranks killed 163, wounded 294. This action practically annihilated what was left of the original battalion, within twelve months of their landing in France.

On July 15th Major R. E. M. Heathcote, 2nd Royal Scots, took over command of the battalion. The following extract from Buchan's *History of the War*, LXII, § 4, describes the action:—

THE SEVENTH BATTALION. AUGUST, 1916

" The 3rd Division attacked with two Brigades (8th
" and 9th), each consisted of two battalions of ' new '
" army and two of ' old.' The Divisional Commander
" entrusted the assault to the ' new ' battalions, and the
" Divisional front assaulting line consisted of four new
" army battalions, 13th R.W.F., 13th King's, 7th K.S.L.I.
" and 8th E. Yorks. The experiment proved the worth
" of the new troops, for a little after midday their work
" was done, their part of the German second line was
" taken and 662 unwounded men, 36 officers, 4 howitzers,
" 4 field guns and 14 machine guns were in their hands."

On July 21st the battalion proceeded to Montauban,
where 2nd Lieuts. R. P. Allday and G. F. D. Artaud,
and a draft of 130 other ranks, joined for duty. On the
23rd one detachment of the battalion proceeded to
Delville Wood and the remainder to Bernafay Wood,
digging a communication trench, during which 2nd
Lieut. R. P. Allday was wounded. On July 26th the
battalion was relieved by the 2nd H.L.I., and proceeded
to Happy Valley, near Bray, where it bivouacked until
the following day, when it moved into billets round
Meaulte, a small village two and a half miles due south
of Albert, for rest. The battalion remained at Meaulte
till August 18th, during which period the following
officers joined the battalion :—
2nd Lieuts. F. S. Corke, D. G. Tully, G. H. P. Jones,
F. H. Matthews. 2nd Lieuts. H. C. Trumpler and R. G.
Byrt rejoined. Captain and Adjutant D. D. Bowie was
sent to the Field Ambulance on August 1st, being succeeded in the Adjutancy by Captain A. C. Hetherington,
and on August 4th 2nd Lieuts. E. H. Waite and A. C.
Dyer were struck off the strength.
On August 7th Major-General Haldane left to command the VI Corps and was succeeded in command of
the 3rd Division by Major-General Deverell. On August
18th the battalion was placed under the orders of the
76th Brigade (Br.-General Kentish) and ordered to

support the 13th R.W. Fusiliers in an attack near Maltz-horn Farm, south-east of Montauban, and on the following day the battalion was detailed to take Lonely Trench, which was done with only 38 casualties, Lonely Trench being subsequently renamed Shropshire Trench. A terriffic enemy bombardment followed on August 20th. 2nd Lieut. J. A. E. Upton, acting Adjutant, died of wounds received on the 18th, and 2nd Lieuts. R. O. Huyshe and G. H. Richmond were wounded. On August 22nd the battalion was relieved and moved by train from Méricourt to Fienvillers and subsequently into billets at Beaumetz. On the 31st the battalion moved again to Philosophe. During the latter part of August, the following officers joined the battalion: Captain H. E. Keeble, 2nd Lieuts. S. L. Cannon, E. Geard, G. Hughes, A. H. S. Southwell, T. Tappenden and A. Thursfield, and R.Q.M.S. G. Clarke left to take up a commission.

On September 9th the battalion, with a strength of 28 officers and 690 other ranks, moved to Mazingarbe a village half-way between Lens and Bethune. Here Lieut. E. H. Robinson rejoined, and 2nd Lieuts. J. McEvoy, F. G. H. Salusbury and S. F. Leleu joined on first appointment.

On the 21st the battalion moved back to Reclinghem for rest. Reclinghem is a pleasant village about fourteen miles south of St. Omer, somewhat remote but surrounded by excellent country for training. The village being very small, two companies were billeted in the adjoining hamlet of Vincly. Training proceeded as usual during the period of rest. On October 4th Lt.-Colonel Heathcote, commanding the battalion, was sent to the Field Ambulance, and Lt.-Colonel K. H. L. Arnott of the East Lancs. took over command. On October 5th the battalion had orders to move and marched ten miles south to Crépy. On October 7th the march south was continued, the battalion entraining at St. Pol at 4 a.m. on the 8th, and detraining at 11 a.m. at Acheux, a small town about eight miles north-west of Albert. Here Major Smithard, second in command, reformed the bugle band. From Acheux the battalion marched to Mailly, arriving about 4 p.m. At Mailly the battalion was accommodated in huts, the strength being 37 officers and 907 other ranks. The 3rd Division was now concentrated and preparing to take its part in the Battle of the Ancre, the concluding stage of the ever-memorable fighting on the Somme. On October 10th Lieut. Robinson was sent to the Field Ambulance, and on the 15th, 2nd Lieut. A. A. Boucher, attached to the 8th Trench Mortar Battery, was severely wounded, dying on the following day. On October 18th the battalion moved back a couple of miles into camp at Bus. On the 22nd Captain Bowie rejoined and took over the adjutancy again from Lieut. Hetherington. On October 28th the battalion took over the trenches in the Serre sector from the 1st Gordons, and on the following day Lieut. W. A. N Baker was wounded. The battalion was relieved by the 8th E. Yorks on November 1st and proceeded to billets in Courcelles. On November 4th the battalion marched to Louvencourt and remained there, preparing for the attack on Serre, until the 12th.

THE BATTLE OF THE ANCRE, 1916

The attack was planned for 5.45 on the morning of Monday the 13th. Our artillery commenced a heavy bombardment, devoted to the destruction of the enemy wire and front line on the 11th, and kept it up more or less continuously throughout Sunday the 12th. The 8th Brigade was charged with the capture of the stronghold of Serre, one of the chain of heavily fortified villages— Gommecourt, Serre, Beaumont Hamel and Thiepval— which had checked our advance on July 1st. The 2nd Royal Scots on the right, and the 1st Royal Scots Fusiliers on the left, formed the assaulting line. The 8th East Yorks were in support of the Royal Scots and the 7th K.S.L.I. in support of the Royal Scots Fusiliers on the left. Thick fog was spread over the ground and at zero hour (5.45) the morning was black as the darkest midnight. In the pitch darkness, and through deep mud, it was difficult for the best-trained soldiers to keep direction, and the troops all along the 3rd Divisional front lost touch. The heavy state of the ground on the 8th Brigade front made it impossible for the tanks to operate, and they were withdrawn from the attack. About 8 a.m., as it began to get light, a thick fog made conditions no better, and at eleven, when the fog began to clear, it was found that all units had lost direction and were hopelessly mixed. To the southward the 51st (Highland Territorial) Division, and the Naval Division, had met with better fortune. Further south still, on the extreme right of the attack, the 39th Division captured St. Pierre Divion, and advanced a mile beyond the village. Later in the day Beaucourt and Beaumont Hamel were taken, and by the evening of the 14th we were in position well down the eastward slopes of the Thiepval ridge. The German counter-attack of the 15th failed everywhere along the five-mile front of battle and all new positions on the right were held.

Although on the left of the line the attack of the 8th Brigade on Serre had failed, the enemy first line had everywhere been penetrated in the first assault, but only a small part of the ground gained in the Serre sector could be held. The appalling conditions of the country in front of the 8th Brigade accounted for their failure. So deep was the mud in places that ration parties took over four hours to cover 1,000 yards of the ground. The following casualties occurred during this action. Killed : 2nd Lieuts. A. Price and A. H. S. Southwell. Wounded : Captain and Adjutant D. D. Bowie, Capt. V. E. Powell and 2nd Lieuts. E. Geard, C. B. H. Phipps, F. G. Salusbury, T. Tappenden, W. F. Woolf and R. G. Byrt. Amongst other ranks 214 men were reported killed, wounded and missing. Lieut. A. C. Hetherington took over the adjutancy again on November 14th, when the battalion was relieved by the 13th King's

Liverpools and marched to Bus, a distance of some seven
miles, arriving in the early morning of the 15th. The same
evening the battalion marched back to the trenches for
one night, being relieved on the 16th by the 2nd Royal
Scots. The battalion was back in the trenches on the
21st. and continued carrying out alternate tours of duty
with the Royal Scots in the Serre sector until the end of
December. During the month of November a draft of
107 other ranks was received. On December 7th Captain
W. L. Lloyd and 2nd Lieut. J. McEvoy were sent to the
Field Ambulance. The battalion was relieved in the
trenches on Christmas Eve, 1916, and celebrated Christmas Day in the hutted camp at Bus on the 27th. Major
Smithard presided, Colonel Arnott being on leave, and
the 3rd Divisional Band attended. On December 28th
and 29th 2nd Lieuts. H. Bush, G. H. P. Jones and A. B.
M. Thursfield were sent to the Field Ambulance. 2nd
Lieuts. W. E. Dallow and G. L. Davis joined for duty
during the last week of the year. During December the
weather was very bad, the camp at Bus was not well
situated and the huts (Adrian huts without floor boards
or doors) were very cold and cheerless. The condition
of the trenches was very bad and the country round a sea
of mud, rivalling the Ypres salient.

The battalion was under establishment and very short
of officers, making conditions particularly trying for all
ranks. The spirit of the men remained, however, as it
had always been under the worst conditions, supremely
optimistic and cheerful. It is perhaps worth while
mentioning that whilst at Louvencourt, in November,
a fire broke out in the neighbourhood of the Quartermaster's stores. It was a small fire soon extinguished.
Unfortunately, however, the locality of the outbreak
was somewhere in the lines between the 7th K.S.L.I. and
a neighbouring regiment. Round the identification of the
exact spot where the fire started raged a conflagration far
fiercer than the flames that did the damage. Some day
perhaps, should finality ever be reached, the minutes,

memoranda, summaries of evidence, files and documents
of this famous episode may be published in a series of
separate volumes.

The battalion remained in the Serre sector until
January 7th, 1917, when they left camp at Bus for Beau-
val, continuing the march on the 9th to Franqueville. On
January 5th Lieut. Tweedale rejoined the battalion from
England. The billets at Franqueville were good, the
Battalion Head-quarters being accommodated in the
Château of Houdencourt. Training was carried out
vigorously and continued until the 27th, when the battalion had orders to move to Beauval, proceeding subsequently via Bouquemaison and Ecoivres to Monchy-
Breton, where they arrived January 31st. During the
month Captain W. L. Lloyd rejoined and took over
command of D Company again. Lieut. Topham and
2nd Lieut. Bush rejoined from the Field Ambulance and
2nd Lieuts. Dibben and Wilmot joined on first appointment. The strength of the battalion during this month
of training averaged 32 officers and 900 other ranks. The
battalion remained at Monchy-Breton, in the St. Pol
area, carrying on training until February 8th, when they
marched via Maizieres and Sars-les-Bois to Denier, where
progressive training was continued until the 27th, when
the battalion moved again via Wanquentin into Arras.
Just outside the town the battalion lost 2 men, killed by
a shell bursting on the road. At this time the weather
was very cold, and the roads being covered with a thin
sheet of ice made the marches somewhat trying, especially for the transport. The bugle band, however, en-
livened the way and very few men fell out. During the
month of February 2nd Lieuts. S. L. Cannon and H. C.
Trumpler were transferred to the R.F.C., and Sgt. R. S.
Galliers, signalling sergeant since November, 1914, left
to take up a commission. The following officers joined
during the month : 2nd Lieuts. D. Fownes, R. C. L.
Roberts, T. H. Mattey, S. Dillon, R. O. Simon, J. Wilkinson, O. D. Wiles, A. R. Robertson and D. W. Williams.

The battalion strength was now made up to 39 officers and 953 other ranks.

In Arras the battalion relieved the 2nd Suffolks (76th Brigade) and was employed in working on the fortification of the caves and tunnelling systems. The town was shelled intermittently, but casualties were few. The caves and tunnelling system of Arras were, in their way, one of the wonders of the war. They were adapted from natural caves and made habitable with electric lighting and light railways by the R.E. Whole battalions could be accommodated in these caves, and some of the tunnels extended up to three miles in length, right up to the trenches, so that reliefs could be carried out underground. The Brigade was now in preparation for an impending attack on Tilloy. On the 21st the Brigade moved back to Liencourt for training in open warfare, and practice attacks were held daily until the 30th, when the battalion returned to Arras, and on the 31st took over a section of the trenches opposite Tilloy village from the 4th Royal Fusiliers. During the month of March Captain Keeble and 2nd Lieut. Simon were struck off the strength and 2nd Lieut. A. L. C. Spiers was sent to the Field Ambulance. Major Smithard left on March 25th for a Senior Officer's course in England. Captain Bowie rejoined on March 14th, taking over the Adjutancy again, and 2nd Lieuts. F. W. E. Blackford and O. F. St. John joined on first appointment. The following battle casualties occurred during the month : Wounded, Lieut. H. C. Tweedale, 2nd Lieuts. G. Hughes and S. F. Leleu. 2nd Lieut. Leleu died of his wounds a month later. Other ranks, killed 6, wounded 6.

On April 3rd the battalion had orders to capture a prisoner for identification purposes, several previous attempts having failed. The ground was thick with snow, and there was a three-quarter full moon. 2nd Lieut. A. Robertson, Sgt. Palmer, bombing sergeant, and 20 men were selected for the raid, and dressed in sheets and ladies' night-dresses, purchased in Arras, entered the enemy trenches at 3.45 a.m. In a quarter of an hour they returned with their prisoner, without suffering any casualties, but having accounted for several of the enemy. The prisoner proved to be a Gefreiter of the 38th Fusilier Regiment belonging to a Division recently returned from the Russian front. The information extracted from this prisoner proved of considerable value. On the 4th a gas attack was launched from our trenches. Eight hundred drums of gas were exploded by electrical power at dawn, over a front of 1,000 yards, with deadly effect. A heavy reciprocal bombardment followed, destroying the battalion cookers. On the same night the battalion was relieved and moved into underground tunnels. On Easter Monday, April 9th, the battalion was assembled in Blenheim Cave at 6 a.m., preparatory to the attack on Tilloy.

THE BATTLES OF ARRAS, 1917

The Battles of Arras began with a combined attack by the 1st and 3rd Armies on a fifteen-mile front from Croisilles to Givenchy. The 3rd Division were on the VI Corps right flank with the 12th Division on their left and the 14 Division (VII Corps) on their right. The preliminary artillery bombardment on the 8th Brigade front lasted for one hundred and twenty hours, the last twenty-four hours of which was continuous night and day. The preparatory organisation was most elaborate, the first instructions being issued by the 8th Brigade Commander on March 21st. A German agent in possession of bacteriological germs for spreading glanders was discovered in our lines shortly before the battle opened. The 1st and 3rd Armies were set the task of breaking through the Hindenburg line, running from Arras to Cambrai. The VI Corps, with the VII on their right, and the XVII on their left, had the River Scarpe as their objective. The VI Corps attacked with three Divisions (3rd, 12th and 15th) in the line and a Division in reserve. The 3rd Division were on the right, the 12th in the centre and the 15th on the left. The 9th Brigade had as its objective the German first line, the 76th Brigade the German second line and the 8th Brigade the German third system of trenches. The 8th Brigade was thus kept for the final assault, and the 7th K.S.L.I. was to capture the enemy third line and to secure the high ground immediately south of Fenchy Chapel, known as Chapel Hill. The 2nd Royal Scots and 7th K.S.L.I. were detailed as the assaulting battalions of the Brigade, the 8th East Yorks being in support, and the 1st R.S. Fusiliers in reserve.

FIRST BATTLE OF THE SCARPE, 1917

At 8.50 a.m. on April 9th the 8th Brigade advanced to the attack on the German third line. A strong west wind was blowing and heavy snow falling. On reaching Tilloy in the German second line it was found that the village had not been cleared. Captain Thursfield, commanding the left-front company, accordingly decided to move round the northern flank of the village and capture the Bois des Bœufs. On seeing this movement, parties of the enemy were sent from Tilloy to assist the garrison in Bois des Bœufs. These parties were attacked with bombs, cut off, and 3 officers and 90 men captured. The 7th K.S.L.I. then cleared the Bois des Bœufs, capturing a further 36 prisoners. The advance was then continued towards the German third line, but was hung up about 2.30 p.m. by intense rifle and machine-gun fire from the flanks. In addition, very strong wire, entirely untouched by the bombardment, was found in front of the position. A further bombardment to cut this wire was ordered at 5.30, the infantry attack to be resumed at 7 p.m. Unfortunately the bombardment failed in its purpose and the subsequent infantry attack was unsuccessful. The 12th Division on the left had been hung up early in the afternoon, and misleading reports as to their position exposed our left flank again to very heavy enfilade machine-gun fire. News was received that another bombardment of

237

the position was to be made, and a third infantry attack to follow on the morning of the 10th. In the meantime the 7th K.S.L.I. dug themselves in about 600 yards from the enemy, being on the left flank of the Brigade. The assault at 12 noon on the 10th was completely successful, and the enemy's third line (Fenchy-Wancourt) was taken. Congratulatory messages were received from the C.-in-C. and G.O.C. 8th Brigade, dated 10th and 11th. The 7th K.S.L.I. held their sector of the enemy line until relieved by the 1st Border Regiment on the night of April 13th/14th. The 7th K.S.L.I. had advanced over 5,000 yards, captured one 5·9 gun, a battery of 4·2 howitzers, a machine gun and 156 prisoners, including 4 officers. During this engagement the battalion suffered the following casualties: Killed: 2nd Lieut. W. E. Dallow (9.4.17); wounded: 2nd Lieuts. D. Fownes, S. C. Hopkins, T. H. Mattey, A. Robertson, O. F. St. John, F. Wilmot and G. L. Davis. Other ranks, killed 22, wounded 131, missing 5. The battalion returned to billets in Arras, and carried on their training on Arras race-course.

SECOND BATTLE OF THE SCARPE, 1917

On April 23rd, St. George's Day, the battle was resumed, and the battalion returned to the trenches, round Tilloy, the 8th Brigade being in reserve to the 15th Division, now carrying on the offensive on the 3rd Divisional front. On the 25th the battalion moved to fresh trenches, east and south-east of Monchy, beyond the old German third line. On the 27th the battalion moved back to support trenches in the old German third line. During the month the following casualties, in addition to those incurred in operations, April 9th–April 14th, referred to above, were suffered by the battalion. Officers wounded: 2nd Lieuts. W. H. Bryant and G. Clapham. On April 23rd, Lt.-Colonel K. H. L. Arnott was slightly wounded, and though remaining on duty was obliged to hand over command temporarily to Major J. L. Likeman (Gloucester Regiment, attached K.S.L.I.) a week later. On

April 28th 2nd Lieut. W. H. Dibben (attached 8th Brigade) was killed in the Brigade Head-quarters dug-out. The following officers joined during the month: 2nd Lieuts. V. G. Ursell, C. V. Eastham; Majors J. L. Likeman, Gloucester Regiment, and G. A. Delmé-Murray. Lieuts. A. C. Hetherington and A. W. Johns, and 2nd Lieut. F. Tucker rejoined.

THIRD BATTLE OF THE SCARPE, 1917

On May 2nd the third stage of the battle commenced with a general attack by the 1st and 3rd Armies from the line Fresnoy–Fontaine on the German line Drocourt–Quéant. The 8th Brigade was detailed to attack the Bois des Vert and the 7th K.S.L.I., after suffering severe casualties from a heavy barrage of gas shells on the way up, advanced from the assembly in support of the 2nd Royal Scots at 4.45 a.m. on the 2nd. Unfortunately the attack was checked by machine-gun fire from Infantry Hill, and the battalion dug themselves in about 8 a.m. During the advance three enemy machine guns were captured by the 7th K.S.L.I. No further advance in this sector was possible, and the battalion was employed consolidating the ground gained until relieved by the 1/13th London Regiment on May 7th. The following casualties occurred on May 3rd, 4th and 5th. Officers: killed, 2nd Lieut. V. G. Ursell (3.5.17), 2nd Lieut. C. V. Eastham (3.5.17); wounded, 2nd Lieuts. W. S. Charman (gas), J. Wilkinson (gas), A. W. Johns (slight): other ranks, 7 killed, 34 wounded, 57 missing. The battalion proceeded back to the trenches on May 10th, relieving the 2nd Suffolks at Monchy, where they remained till relieved by the 2nd S.W.B. on the 14th. Casualties during this tour, other than those referred to above, amounted to, other ranks: killed 11, wounded 29; and 2nd Lieuts. R. C. L. Roberts and F. G. Pecker wounded. On May 15th the battalion proceeded in motor lorries to Berneville for rest. The battalion remained at Berneville until the 17th, when they marched via Gouy-en-Artois to

Villers-sur-Simon, where they were billeted. Training, somewhat hampered by wet weather, was carried on by companies. Company and battalion sports were held, also a boxing competition. The battalion was worthily represented in the Brigade boxing competition, held at Izel-les-Hameau. During the month the following officers joined for duty : 2nd Lieuts. E. C. Gates, L. Clarke, J. H. Bury (2nd Monmouths) ; 2nd Lieuts. A. J. Topham, V. E. Powell, W. F. Woolf and F. W. E. Blackford rejoined from the Field Ambulance.

On June 1st the battalion moved back, in motor omnibuses, to Arras, and relieved the 1st Inniskilling Fusiliers in the reserve trenches the same night. On the 6th the battalion moved up to the front-line trenches in relief of the 8th East Yorks, remaining till relieved by the 2nd Suffolk Regiment on the night of the 12th/13th. During this tour of duty the battalion was constantly at work improving the front line. Enemy aircraft were very active, but casualties for the tour were light, amounting to : other ranks, 6 killed, 17 wounded. The battalion returned to billets in Arras. On June 17th the 7th K.S.L.I. was ordered to take over the Monchy defences from the 8th K.O.R.L. (76th Brigade). Eight officers remained behind with the details in Arras. The 76th Brigade made a very successful attack, capturing the mound on Infantry Hill. On June 30th the battalion was relieved and proceeded in buses to Berlencourt, moving on to Lignereuil on the following day. Here training proceeded, and included firing by companies on the ranges at Denier.

On June 28th the 3rd Division was transferred from the VI Corps to the IV Corps (commanded by General Woollcombe in General Byng's 3rd Army), and the battalion proceeded by rail to Gomiecourt. On the 30th the battalion marched via Bapaume to Frémicourt. During the month the following officers joined the battalion : Captain R. A. K. Wilson, 2nd Lieuts. A. E. Collis, K. B. Watkins, W. S. Crewe, D. Nicholson, J. H. Skidmore and G. F. Jones (formerly Sgt. Jones of B

Company). The following rejoined: Major F. Johnston, taking over second in command, Captain E. H. Robinson, 2nd Lieuts. S. Dillon and A. J. Topham. Lt.-Colonel K. H. L. Arnott rejoined from sick leave on June 15th and took over command again from Major Likeman, who left to command the 2nd Suffolks. Two drafts, totalling 158 other ranks, were received. Certain officers left the battalion on courses, making the total strength on June 30th, officers 39, other ranks 755. Casualties for the month, in addition to those already recorded: other ranks, killed 4, wounded 21.

On July 2nd the battalion relieved the 1/6th Gloucesters (144th Brigade) in the reserve-line trenches by Frémicourt. The 2nd Royal Scots, the 8th E. Yorks and the 1st R. S. Fusiliers were all in the first line. On the 11th the battalion was relieved by the 2nd Suffolks, and proceeded into camp.

Training was carried on in camp, and the officers reconnoitred the Beaumetz-Morchies defence line. On July 16th the battalion was inspected by Lt.-General C. L. Woollcombe, commanding the IV Corps. On the 18th the battalion relieved the 8th K.O.R.L. and the 13th King's (76th Brigade) in the support and reserve lines. The battalion was relieved on the night of 26th/27th after a singularly quiet tour by the 2nd Royal Scots, and proceeded back to camp at Velu, where training was continued until the end of the month. During July, Major R. G. Smithard and 2nd Lieuts. G. F. D. Artaud, G. Hughes and R. P. Allday rejoined the battalion. Major Smithard left during the month on appointment as second in command of the 1st R.S. Fusiliers. 2nd Lieuts. S. Dillon and F. D. Jewson left, the latter to the Field Ambulance. Drafts amounting to 133 other ranks were received. Casualties, other ranks, 1 killed and 1 wounded. Strength: Officers 40, other ranks 856.

The battalion remained at Velu until August 4th, when they relieved the 2nd R. Scots, being relieved in their turn on the night of August 11th/12th. During the relief a 7th K.S.L.I. patrol encountered a strong enemy patrol on the Bapaume-Cambrai road. Ten of the enemy were killed and a number wounded: our casualties were, killed: 2nd Lieut. G. Hughes and 1 other rank; wounded, 4 other ranks, 1 other rank missing, believed killed. The battalion returned to the line on the 20th, and on 26th D Company machine gunners brought down an enemy aeroplane. On August 28th the battalion was relieved and returned to Lebucquiere. During the month Lieut. H. Bush and 2nd Lieuts. Robertson, H. Boardley and A. J. Norris joined, and 2nd Lieut. K. B. Watkins was struck off the strength. Drafts amounting to 115 were received. Casualties, other than those referred to above, other ranks, 1 killed, 3 wounded.

Training was continued at Lebucquiere during the first week in September, the battalion moving to Ypres (8 miles S.E. of Bapaume) on the 4th. On September 8th Lt.-Colonel Negus, who had been badly wounded at Bazentin in July, 1916, rejoined. Unfortunately, being unfit for general service, his rejoining orders were cancelled, and he left the battalion on the 17th, being appointed shortly afterwards to command the 9th British West Indian Regiment.

THE BATTLES OF YPRES, 1917

The battalion was hard at work practising for their part in the advance to be made by the 3rd Division from Ypres on September 26th. During this period the work going on was inspected by Br.-General Holmes, commanding 8th Brigade, and Major-General Deverell, commanding the Division. On the 18th, the 3rd Division having been transferred from IV Corps (3rd Army) to V Corps (5th Army), the battalion marched to Bapaume and entrained for Watou, moving to camp at Brandhoek three days later. On the 25th the battalion moved up in the light railway from Toronto Camp into Ypres, preparatory to the attack by the 3rd Division on Zonnebeke,

timed for the following day. Strength of the battalion:
Officers 44, other ranks 957.

BATTLE OF POLYGON WOOD

The 8th Brigade attacked with the 2nd Royal Scots on
the right, and the 8th East Yorks on the left of the assault,
the 1st R.S.F. in support of the Royal Scots on the right,
and the 7th K.S.L.I. in support of the 8th East Yorks on
the left. The attack commenced at 5.30 a.m. on the 26th.
The 2nd Royal Scots had their right on the Ypres–
Roulers Railway, the 8th East Yorks were advancing on
a compass bearing. The objective was the enemy first-
line, support and reserve trenches on a frontage of
1,000 yards. Twenty officers only, in accordance with
the latest instructions, were taken into action.

The 8th E. Yorks captured the German front line,
and the 7th K.S.L.I., passing through the E. Yorks,
assaulted and carried the German second line, capturing
70 prisoners, 8 machine guns and one 77-mm. gun. A
strong counter-attack by the enemy at 6.30 p.m. forced
a retirement of some 200 yards of the troops on our right
and left. The battalion, retaining its ground, swung out
defensive flanks and maintained touch. Total gain,
approximately, 2,500 yards. The line was consolidated
and held until the 28th, when the Brigade was relieved
by the 9th Brigade. The 7th K.S.L.I. proceeded to Ypres,
and on October 1st returned to Toronto Camp. On
October 3rd the G.O.C. 3rd Division congratulated the
battalion on parade on its gallant conduct on September
26th. Strength: Officers 34, other ranks 670. During
September 2nd Lieut. C. B. O. Walker rejoined, and on
September 29th 2nd Lieuts. G. H. P. Jones, W. F.
Woolf and R. G. F. Vickery. Whilst at rest at Ypres, in
September, the battalion reached the last round of the
Brigade football tournament, being defeated in the final
(after a replay) by the 1st R.S. Fusiliers, by 2 goals to 1.
Casualties, September 26th–30th: Officers killed, Lieut.
A. L. C. Spiers, Lieut. G. F. D. Artaud, Captain V. E.

Powell, Captain A. J. T. Topham, 2nd Lieut. H. Boardley and Captain J. P. Pegum, R.A.M.C. (attached), wounded 5; other ranks killed 36, wounded 237, missing 27.*

Early in October the 3rd Division was transferred back to the 3rd Army and proceeded south to the Renescure area, near St. Omer. The 7th K.S.L.I. was accommodated in a hutted camp at Le Transloy, where training, somewhat handicapped by persistent bad weather, was continued. On October 10th the 3rd Division relieved the 62nd in the trenches of the new area Noreuil–Bullecourt, the 9th and 76th Brigades being in the line and the 8th Brigade in reserve at Favreuil. On October 30th the 8th Brigade relieved the 9th Brigade in the Bullecourt (right) sector of the line, the 7th K.S.L.I. relieving the 4th Royal Fusiliers. During the month the following officers joined the battalion: Major W. J. Brooke and Major C. E. Jenkins (Shropshire Yeomanry), and drafts amounting to 53 other ranks were received. The following officers left during October: Major F. Johnston to a course at the Senior Officers' School at Aldershot, Captain R. A. K. Wilson to the 3rd Army School as an instructor, Lieut. C. B. O. Walker on transfer to the R.F.C., Lieut. A. Fox invalided to England.

The new sector of the line proved to be a quiet one, and the battalion was relieved in the trenches by the 2nd Royal Scots on November 5th, without having suffered any casualties. The battalion marched to billets in Vaulx–Vraucourt. The battalion continued doing five days in the line and five days out with the Royal Scots until the end of the month. During November the following officers joined: 2nd Lieuts. R. Price, A. L. Margetts, T. A. Roberts, C. J. Wheeler, T. Morgans, and 2nd Lieut. F. W. E. Blackford rejoined. A draft of 14 other ranks was received. Lieut. R. P. Allday left the battalion on transfer to the Royal Flying Corps, and the Rev. P. E. Lee, greatly to the regret of all ranks, to take up the

* Lieut. L. Clarke died of wounds on October 4th, 1917.

appointment of S.C.F. 14th Division. Casualties for the month of November : wounded, 2nd Lieuts. R. Price and G. F. Jones; killed, 3 other ranks, wounded 9. Strength at the end of the month, officers 32, other ranks 734.

On December 1st C.S.M. Thornton was killed by shell-fire in his billet at Vaulx. The battalion relieved the 2nd Royal Scots in the same sector on December 4th, remaining in the line until the 11th, when the 8th Brigade was relieved by the 9th and went into reserve. The 7th K.S.L.I. marched to camp at Mory. On the 16th, the 18th Brigade, 6th Division, relieved the 8th Brigade in Divisional Reserve at Mory and the 7th K.S.L.I. marched to Blaireville for rest. The 16th Brigade, including the 1st K.S.L.I., relieved the 9th Brigade in Divisional Reserve. On December 22nd the 7th K.S.L.I. relieved the 8th Bedfords (16th Brigade) in the trenches where Christmas Day was spent, being relieved by the 1st R.S. Fusiliers on the 26th. Instead of proceeding to camp, however, the battalion took over the new trenches at Noreuil. These trenches had no cover, the snow was six inches deep, the weather intensely cold, and there were many casualties. On the evening of the 29th the battalion was relieved and marched to Dysart Camp, proceeding on the following day to camp at Hamelin-court, where they remained till the end of the month. The following officers rejoined during the month : 2nd Lieut. A. Robertson and Lieut. E. Geard. Captain A. W. Johns was transferred to England. Major Jenkins was posted as second in command to a battalion of the S.W.B. and Major Brooke as second in command to 21st Middlesex Regiment. Lieut. J. H. Bury was invalided. On December 23rd Lt.-Colonel K. H. L. Arnott was wounded, and Major E. H. Robinson took over temporary command. Drafts amounting to 35 other ranks were received. Casualties: other ranks killed, 3; wounded, 7. During the very severe weather in the latter part of the month 118 other ranks were evacuated to the Field Ambulance.

THE KING'S SHROPSHIRE LIGHT INFANTRY

On January 1st, 1918, Major F. Johnston rejoined and took over command of the battalion from Major Smithard, at Armagh Camp, near Hamelincourt, with Captain D. D. Bowie as Adjutant, the strength being 29 officers, 684 other ranks. Training was carried on, the ground being covered with snow, and the weather bitterly cold.

The companies were commanded as follows: A Company Lieut. G. F. Jones, B Company 2nd Lieut. G. V. Jones, C Company Captain Tully, D Company Lieut. W. S. Charman. On January 8th the battalion was inspected by Lt.-General Sir J. A. L. Haldane, the VI Corps Commander, who expressed himself as very pleased with the appearance and general turn-out of the battalion, especially the transport. On January 27th the battalion proceeded back to the line, relieving the 15th Royal Scots (101st Infantry Brigade) in Tunnel Trench, in front of Croisilles, which was in a very bad condition. This sector running north-east and east of Croisilles had a tunnel running under the front-line trench, said to be thirteen miles long. This tunnel was impassable at this period, and attempts to explore it were defeated by the appalling stench from the decaying bodies there. On the night of 31st/1st the battalion was relieved in the front line by the 1st R.S. Fusiliers, moving back to the support line in the neighbourhood of Croisilles. During the month the following officers joined the battalion: Captains H. de C. Duggan and W. Edwards and Lieut. D. G. Phare, all from the R.A.S.C.; 2nd Lieuts. W. H. Benbow and G. H. Brazier; 2nd Lieut. R. O. Simon was evacuated to the Field Ambulance, and subsequently to England. Drafts amounting to 90 other ranks were received. Casualties: other ranks, killed 2, wounded 1. On January 23rd, 1918, the decision, occasioned by the dearth of man-power, to reduce the strength of Infantry Brigades to three battalions was communicated privately to commanding officers. The 8th East Yorks was the battalion for disbandment in the 8th Brigade, and on February 10th they were broken up, much to the regret of all.

The battalion moved up to the relief of the 1st R.S. Fusiliers in the front line on February 3rd.

At daybreak on the 8th the enemy attempted a raid on No. 12 Post, held by the 7th K.S.L.I., but was driven off by rifle and Lewis-gun fire. 2nd Lieut. J. H. Skidmore, in charge of the post, and 5 other ranks were wounded. On the following day the battalion was relieved and returned to the support line, going up to the front line again on the 12th. Alternate reliefs with the 1st R. Scots Fusiliers between the front and support line continued throughout the month. On the 25th an enemy party attempted to surround a wiring party from the 7th, but was easily beaten off; about two hours later the enemy attempted a bombing raid on Post 13, but did not succeed in reaching our line. During the month the battalion received large reinforcements from the 5th K.S.L.I., which had been disbanded, due to the shortage of manpower. The following officers of the 5th joined the 7th for duty: Captain F. R. Burlton, 2nd Lieuts. A. H. Donaldson, D. L. Price, S. J. Goodchild, T. Fisher, E. E. V. Evans, A. H. Simpson, H. E. Randall, J. Wild and A. W. Lindsay. The following also joined: the Rev. P. Sellers, 2nd Lieuts. W. S. Herbert and J. Whitney. Drafts amounting to 207 other ranks, including 154 from the 5th K.S.L.I., were received during February. Casualties: Other ranks, in addition to those referred to above, 3 killed, 4 wounded; 2nd Lieuts. G. H. Brazier, C. J. Wheeler and T. A. Roberts were invalided. Owing to the severe weather and poor trenches the battalion had a large number of casualties through sickness during the months of January and February. Strength, March 1st: Officers 44, other ranks 789.

On March 1st the 8th Brigade was relieved by the 101st Brigade, 34th Division, and moved into reserve. The 7th K.S.L.I., on being relieved by the 16th Royal Scots, marched to Carlisle lines, Mercatel, three and a half miles south of Arras. The battalion was no sooner settled in than orders were received to return to the line, and on the night of the 2nd/3rd the 7th relieved their old friends the 13th King's (9th Brigade) in the trenches at Wancourt, ten miles north-east of Bapaume. The sector remained quiet until the battalion was relieved, by the 2nd Royal Scots, on March 6th. The battalion returned to Mercatel, moving up to the support line again on the 10th. News having been received of an impending offensive by the Germans on the VI Corps front, all units of the 8th Brigade in the line stood to from dusk to dawn, and patrolling became very active.

THE FIRST BATTLES OF THE SOMME, 1918

The offensive began on the 21st, and at eight o'clock in the morning the 7th K.S.L.I. was ordered to move up and occupy our reserve trenches in the Hindenburg line west of Heninel. By eight o'clock the battalion was in position, having suffered considerably from gas and high-explosive shells on the way up. Captains Burlton and Bowie were wounded and 2nd Lieut. J. Wild gassed, and about 80 other ranks casualties. By the end of the day the German attack had pressed back the Corps' front on the right, and the Division on our right had fallen back. The 3rd Division accordingly withdrew on the night of March 22nd to the partially prepared reserve line. 2nd Lieut. Wiles was appointed Adjutant in place of Captain Bowie. All three Brigades were placed in the front line, the 8th on the extreme right and the 7th K.S.L.I. on the left of the Brigade. The new trenches occupied by the battalion were only two feet deep, and the men at once set about improving them.

FIRST BATTLE OF BAPAUME

The enemy renewed his attack on the morning of the 24th, and at 4.30, after a lively bombardment, attempted to rush our trenches, but he was driven off. About four o'clock in the afternoon another attempt was made, under cover of a smoke screen, but was again repulsed. 2nd Lieuts. Vickery and Morgan were wounded in beating off these attacks. The 25th and 26th were spent in re-adjusting the Divisional front. The 8th Brigade was now holding the right of the line. The 7th K.S.L.I. was left with two companies in the front-line trenches, and two companies in support. The battalion sector, west of Henin, was in a shocking state, the trenches affording but little cover and having no wire in front. On the 27th a violent enemy bombardment took place, the front line being reduced to chaos, Lieut. W. F. Woolf and 2nd Lieut. D. L. Price being killed.

FIRST BATTLE OF ARRAS, 1918

On the 28th the attack was resumed with great violence. The first attack at 5.15 a.m. was beaten off, but a second, with largely reinforced numbers, at 7.15 a.m., succeeded in entering our trenches at the juncture of the two front companies B and C. After fierce fighting the enemy commenced to bomb outwards along our first line, and C Company on the right, having exhausted all its bombs, was obliged to fall back, with some twenty-five survivors, to the reserve line. In the meantime the 13th King's, on the left, had been forced back, but in spite of this the left company (B) K.S.L.I. formed a block, and held the enemy for an hour and a half until surrounded. Some fifteen survivors fought their way back, with a small party of the 13th King's, to the reserve line. Meantime the right support company (A) held on until twelve (noon), when their right flank became completely exposed. In order to avoid being surrounded, the company withdrew 300 yards to a sunken road, and the left support company (D) withdrew into line with the right. Unfortunately no counter-attack by the reserve battalion of the Brigade, the 2nd R. Scots, was possible, since the 9th Brigade front was reported to be broken, and a further withdrawal from the reserve line, which was everywhere intact on the 8th Brigade front, seemed imminent. At 5 p.m. the 3rd Division ordered a withdrawal from the reserve line to the " Green " line in rear.

The 5th Canadian Infantry Brigade relieved the devastated 8th Brigade on the night of March 29th/30th, the 22nd Canadian Regiment relieving the remnants of the 7th K.S.L.I., which proceeded to Bellacourt, where they arrived at 3 a.m. and proceeded to billets. At 5 a.m. orders to move at 2 p.m. were received, and the survivors of the battalion marched off at 2 p.m. to Sus-St. Leger, a distance of twelve miles. The rain poured incessantly and a bitterly cold head wind assailed men already drenched to the skin. The Colonel's diary tells us " the men marched magnificently and arrived at 7 p.m., all tails up." The battalion proceeded to billets and spent Sunday, March 31st, cleaning kit in the best of spirits. At 8 a.m. on the following day the 7th K.S.L.I. was on the march again.

During the month of March, 1918, the following officers joined the battalion: Lieut. and Qr.-Master A. C. Browse, East Yorks Regiment, and 2nd Lieut. R. C. Morgan. The following rejoined: 2nd Lieuts. T. A. Roberts (from hospital), A. J. Norris, A. H. Donaldson, R. G. F. Vickery and E. E. V. Evans. The following officers were struck off the strength : Lieut. and Qr.-Master W. T. Calthorpe, who had served with the battalion continuously since July, 1915, Lieut. A. C. Hetherington to a six months' tour of duty in England, and Captain D. G. Tully, Lieut. W. S. Herbert and 2nd Lieuts. H. E. Randall, E. C. Gates and D. W. Williams to courses. Drafts amounting to 292 other ranks were received. The battalion suffered the following casualties : Officers killed, Captain G. F. Jones and Lieut. D. G. Phare ; wounded, Captain and Adjutant D. D. Bowie, Captains F. R. Burlton, W. Edwards (died of wounds, 28.3.18), H. de C. Duggan, 2nd Lieuts. J. Wild, R. G. F. Vickery, R. C. Morgan, E. C. Gates, C. J. Wheeler ; invalided, 2nd Lieut. J. Whitney ; wounded and missing, 2nd Lieuts. A. J. Norris and S. J. Goodchild. (Norris and Goodchild reported killed 28.3.18.)

Total casualties for period March 21st–28th : Killed, 7 officers, 47 other ranks; wounded, 9 officers, 174 other ranks; missing, 3 officers, 157 other ranks. On April 1st the 3rd Division having been transferred from VI Corps (3rd Army) to I Corps (1st Army), the battalion started at 8 a.m. and marched to billets in Raimbert. The 3rd Division were placed in Corps Reserve, and on April 3rd the battalion continued the march north, via Drouvin, Fouquereiul, Houchin, to billets in the village of Vaudricourt. Br.-General L. A. E. Price-Davies assumed command of the 8th Brigade vice Br.-General Tanner, appointed to command the South African Infantry Brigade. A message from General Byng, commanding the 3rd Army, congratulating the 3rd Division on their endurance and determination during the severe fighting of the last fortnight in March, was circulated to all units, and also an extract from *The Times* of April 2nd, 1918, referring to the 3rd " Iron " Division.

THE BATTLES OF THE LYS

On April 9th a heavy attack was delivered against the 1st Army from La Bassée canal, south of Givenchy, to Bois Grenier, and the centre of our line had been pressed back. The 8th Brigade was warned to hold itself in readiness to move. On the morning of the 11th the 8th Brigade was transferred to the XI Corps and the 7th K.S.L.I. marched to Oblenghem the same night, taking over a position on the east side of La Bassée canal, running through Long Cornet, from the 1st Seaforths and 2nd Welch. Early in the morning of the following day the battalion moved up to the reserve line relieving the reserve battalion of the 154th Brigade, later moving up again into the front-line trench, the final relief being complete at about seven in the morning of the 12th. Strong patrols were sent out, which reported signs of an impending attack on our front. Meantime at dawn a heavy attack on the 152nd Brigade on our left had succeeded in driving in the flank, the Brigadier and his staff being captured, and the left of the 1st R. Scots Fusiliers being thus left exposed. Whilst these operations were in progress the 3rd Division was re-transferred from XI to I Corps. The 7th K.S.L.I. was holding the Le Hamel Switch between the La Bassée Canal and the Canal de la Lawe with the 8th K.O.R.L. in the same sector on their left. At 3 p.m. Captain Nicholson and D Company, under orders of the G.O.C. 166th Brigade, moved forward to protect the left flank of the 166th Brigade, and to hold the Pont Tournant–Locon road. At seven in the evening of April 12th D Company was heavily attacked, but held its ground, inflicting severe casualties on the enemy and maintaining its hold on the Pont Tournant. The G.O.C. 8th Brigade reported that " the handling and conduct of this company of the " 7th K.S.L.I., under Captain Nicholson, was most " creditable throughout the day." At 11.45 p.m. the whole of the 7th K.S.L.I. front was heavily attacked, but the enemy was driven off with considerable loss, leaving a machine gun in our hands. Captain E. H. Robinson was wounded. At 5 p.m. on the 13th the battalion was again attacked, but, the line having been reinforced by six Lewis guns and teams from the Tank Corps, the enemy was driven off with ease and severe casualties inflicted on him. 2nd Lieut. T. Morgans was killed during this attack. The remainder of the 13th and 14th were spent in consolidating the defences and wiring, and on the night of the 14th/15th the battalion was relieved by the 2nd Suffolks and 1st Gordons.

Locon and the surrounding farms were not much damaged and, on relief, the battalion was able to hand over, as trench stores, and none the worse : 1 cow, 1 calf, 6 tame rabbits, 1 dog, 1 cat, several chickens, a goat and 2 kids born (let us hope not prematurely) on the morning of the 14th ! The Divisional General reported that the conduct of the 8th Brigade during the difficult operations of the 12th April was most praiseworthy, the officers and men having fought with great tenacity against vastly superior numbers. On the 15th April the battalion moved to billets at Oblinghem in Divisional Reserve.

The battalion was back in the trenches on the 21st, relieving the 4th R. Fusiliers in the line east of the Canal De la Lawe, being relieved in its turn, after a quiet tour, by the 6th Sherwood Foresters on April 24th. The battalion proceeded to billets near Fouquereil and later to Vendin, a most unhealthy spot, full of gas. On the 30th the battalion moved once more to the trenches, relieving the 4th Royal Fusiliers in the line at Sevlinghe.

During the month the following officers rejoined: Captain D. G. Tully, Captain E. H. Robinson, and 2nd Lieut. G. H. Brazier. The following officers also joined: Lieut. F. S. Phillips, 2nd Lieuts. J. McCowan, F. H. Davies, G. Maxwell, M. T. O. Jones, J. R. Richards, H. Williams, L. R. Lewis, W. L. Prosser, E. T. Price, H. Butters, F. H. Weyman, T. J. Hughes, and A. L. Haines, and Captains R. W. St. J. W. Richards and A. B. M. Thursfield, and 2nd Lieut. R. C. L. Roberts rejoined.

The following left the battalion during the month: Captain E. H. Robinson and 2nd Lieut. E. C. Gates to England. To the Field Ambulance: 2nd Lieuts. R. G. F. Vickery, Donaldson, Whitney, Blackford (gassed), Weyman, Lewis and Geard. R.S.M. W. Hopkinson, C.S.M. H. Baron and C.S.M. R. Hilton left for Rouen for training duties at home. Reinforcements amounting to 235 other ranks were received. Casualties for the month, other than those referred to above, amounted to: Officers wounded 2; other ranks, killed 18, wounded 58.*

The strength of the battalion on May 1st, 1918, was 41 officers and 986 other ranks. The 8th Brigade remained at Bethune and the 7th K.S.L.I., in Brigade Reserve, was billeted at Locon. The battalion relieved the 2nd Royal Scots in the front line on the night of 4th/5th. At 3 a.m. on the 6th D Company carried out a successful

---

* 2nd Lieut. G. V. Jones died of wounds, in German hands, on April 24th, 1918.

little minor operation, advancing the right of the battalion sector about 500 yards. 2nd Lieut. Hughes and 16 other ranks were wounded during this advance. The battalion was relieved on the 8th by the 8th K.O.R.L. (76th Brigade), and the 8th Brigade was placed in Divisional Reserve. On the 9th the battalion had orders to be ready to move at half an hour's notice, and to " stand to " from 6 p.m. to 8 a.m. daily. On the 11th the 7th K.S.L.I. relieved the 1st Northumberland Fusiliers (9th Brigade), and on the 18th Lt.-Colonel Arnott rejoined and took over command from Lt.-Colonel Johnston. Early in the morning of the 20th the enemy put over a heavy bombardment with mustard gas shells which lasted for over two hours. Nine officers and 248 other ranks were gassed, although every precaution was taken during the gas shelling, helmets being adjusted, and the trenches sprinkled with chloride of lime after the bombardment. It appears that the heavy casualties throughout the Division were due rather to abnormal conditions—namely a very hot sun and no wind, which brought the fumes out of the ground and the men's clothing. The three battalions of the Brigade in the line had over 700 casualties from the gas on this occasion. The battalion was relieved on the evening of the same day, and proceeded to billets at Chocques. On 28th the battalion was warned that the 8th Brigade would relieve the 9th Brigade on the night of 30th/31st. The G.O.C. 8th Brigade, Br.-General B. J. Fisher, inspected the battalion on the 29th. The battalion marched from Chocques to relieve the 1st Northumberland Fusiliers, in support, on the evening of the 30th. The enemy put down harassing fire on the back areas at dusk, and during the hours of relief Lt.-Colonel K. H. L. Arnott and Lieut. G. H. P. Jones were killed, and Major F. Johnston and Captain and Adjutant D. D. Bowie were wounded. Both the latter died of their wounds on the following day. In Colonel Arnott and Major Johnston the battalion lost two of the finest officers that had ever served with it.

Major R. G. Smithard assumed command of the battalion. During the month of May the following officers rejoined the battalion : Lt.-Colonel K. H. L. Arnott (May 17th), Captain D. D. Bowie (May 14th), Lieuts. F. G. H. Salusbury, H. G. H. Monck, 2nd Lieuts. T. J. Hughes and F. W. E. Blackford. The following also joined: 2nd Lieuts. T. O. Morgans, T. L. Hopkins, G. Evans, T. Dowells, T. H. Jones, A. H. Day and G. B. Green. The following officers left the battalion during May: 2nd Lieuts. J. R. Richards, G. Maxwell, T. Roberts and F. H. Weyman, all to the Field Ambulance. 2nd Lieuts. F. A. Cooke, A. L. Margetts, W. H. Benbow, T. A. Roberts, G. H. Brazier and R. Deedes to courses, or other duties. Drafts amounting to 251 other ranks were received. Casualties: Officers killed, 5 (2nd Lieut. H. E. Randall died of wounds, May 20th); wounded 10 (including the following officers gassed on the 20th: Captains Thursfield and Nicholson, Lieuts. Blackford and F. S. Phillips, 2nd Lieuts. F. H. Davies, H. Butters, M. T. O. Jones, E. T. Price and A. L. Haines). Other ranks: killed 2, wounded 41, gassed 248.

On June 1st the battalion was in the support-line trenches at Locon, where, on the 3rd, Major L. T. V. Barnes (R. Warwick R.) joined for duty as second in command to Lt.-Colonel Smithard. On the 11th the battalion moved up to the relief of the 1st R.S. Fusiliers in the front line. During the relief 2nd Lieut. G. B. Green (R. W. Fus.) attached, was killed. The centre and left of the Divisional front was advanced some 500 yards over a frontage of about 3,000 yards by a very successful attack by the 9th and 76th Brigades on June 14th. On the 17th 2nd Lieut. J. McCowan was killed in action. The battalion moved back to the support line on the 20th. The battalion was relieved on the 27th and proceeded to rest in the sandpits near Gosnay. On the night of the 28th Major L. T. V. Barnes was killed, and Lt.-Colonel Smithard wounded. Captain H. S. Collins assumed temporary command of the battalion. The battalion remained at the Sandpits for the rest of the month. During June the following officers joined: 2nd Lieuts. S. Graham, Hurdidge, Edwards, H. Amey, G. F. Brundrett and I. P. Davies. Captain H. S. Collins joined from 2nd K.S.L.I., and 2nd Lieut. Fisher rejoined from the Field Ambulance. Reinforcements amounting to 40 other ranks were received. Casualties, other than those reported above, other ranks 31. The first few days of July were spent in the Sandpits near Gosnay in Brigade Reserve. On the night of the 4th/5th the battalion moved up to the forward zone, Locon section, in relief of the 1st R.S.F., and on the 11th relieved the 1st R.S.F. in the battle zone. The three battalions of the Brigade thus followed each other in regular rotation of reliefs from reserve in the Sandpits to forward zone, from forward zone to battle zone, and from battle zone back to Sandpits.

On the 8th Captain H. S. Collins was admitted to hospital, and Captain R. W. Richards took over temporary command with Captain D. G. Tully as second in command. On July 28th 2nd Lieut. H. Williams (Pembroke Yeo.), attached, was killed in action in the forward zone, Locon section. During the month the following officers rejoined : Lt.-Colonel R. G. Smithard (July 29th) from leave ; 2nd Lieuts. G. F. Brundrett, I. P. Davies and W. L. Prosser from courses ; 2nd Lieuts. M. T. O. Jones, F. A. Cooke, T. A. Roberts and Captain D. G. Tully from hospital, and Lieut. A. C. Hetherington from England. The following officers joined on first appointment : 2nd Lieuts. W. E. Piper, T. E. Bird, C. Raybould, A. C. Brashaw, J. H. Millington, J. E. Jordan and F. Mitchem. The following officers left the battalion for hospital during the month : Captains H. S. Collins, D. G. Tully and E. M. Dealtry, Lieut. H. G. H. Monck, 2nd Lieuts. S. Graham, M. T. O. Jones and A. H. Day. Reinforcements amounting to 148 other ranks were received. Casualties : other ranks, 5 killed, 15 wounded.

The battalion spent the first few days of August in the Locon section. On the 4th news of the relief of the 3rd Division by the 19th Division was received. The 56th Infantry Brigade relieved the 8th, and it was a welcome surprise for all when the 4th K.S.L.I. took over from the 7th on the night of August 6th/7th. On relief the battalion proceeded in motor buses to Dieval (via Bruay, Divian and Ourton), where they were accommodated under canvas in a very good camp. The strength of the battalion at this time was 48 officers and 880 other ranks. On August 2nd Captain J. G. Hopcraft, who had been transport officer of the battalion from its formation, and since June, 1916, 8th Brigade transport officer, left the 8th Brigade to take up the appointment of Staff Captain 15th Brigade. At Dieval intensive training was carried out during the morning, and games in the afternoon. Unfortunately the rest was not to last long. On the 13th the 3rd Division, which was in G.H.Q. Reserve, was transferred from 5th to 3rd Army, and was ordered to the VI Corps area, coming into 3rd Army Reserve. On the 12th the battalion moved by march route to Labeuvriere and thence by train to Saulty. On the 19th the battalion moved by night march to Monchy and bivouacked in the caves there, preparatory to the attack on Courcelles. The objective of the 8th Brigade attack was the Bapaume–Arras railway, east of Courcelles, on a frontage of some 1,800 yards. The 99th Brigade, 2nd Division, was to capture the enemy first line and then let the 8th Brigade through to continne the advance and capture the railway. The 1st R.S. Fusiliers were on the right and 7th K.S.L.I. on the left of the attack with the 2nd R. Scots in support and the 8th K.O.R.L. (76th Brigade) in reserve. The attack was to attempt a break through, it being hoped that, having secured the railway crossings, twenty-four whippet tanks could clear the way for the 2nd Cavalry Brigade. The 9th Infantry Brigade was operating on the right, and the 76th Brigade, less 8th K.O.R.L., was in reserve. The infantry attack of the

3rd Division was thus on a four-battalion frontage, and was supported by tanks, twelve tanks being allotted to each Brigade. The greatest care was taken to conceal the concentration of troops before the attack, and much was hoped for from the element of surprise.

BATTLE OF ALBERT 1918

The attack of August 21st was a general advance by the VI Corps in conjunction with the IV Corps, consisting of the 5th and 37th Divisions, which was operating on its right. The 7th K.S.L.I., as one of the two leading battalions of the 8th Brigade, had the railway line Bapaume–Arras as their objective, with orders to reach and hold the railway at all costs. The attack, timed for 4.55 on the morning of the 21st, was entirely successful. By 7.30 the battalion, in spite of the heavy mist, which made the work of keeping touch very difficult, had reached the railway embankment, which was strongly held by the enemy. The final assault was made with the bayonet, the enemy being driven out with great slaughter. Four German officers and many men were made prisoners. The objective reached, the battalion proceeded to consolidate the line and to throw out outposts 150 yards east of the railway. At daybreak on the 22nd a strong enemy counter-attack was launched, but only in a few cases did it succeed in reaching the line of the embankment, from which the enemy was everywhere driven back again. A second counter-attack, made in the evening, was again repulsed.

On the morning of the 23rd, at four o'clock the 7th K.S.L.I. continued the advance, reaching their second objective, inflicting severe loss on the enemy, and capturing 70 prisoners. At 11 a.m. the 2nd Division passed through, continuing the advance, and at the same time the 76th Brigade established itself in Gommie-court. On the 24th the 3rd Division, having again covered itself with glory, was withdrawn into Corps Reserve. The Division had captured 52 officers and 1,574 prisoners, 11 field guns, 2 howitzers, 227 machine guns and innumerable stores. Of these the 7th K.S.L.I. had captured 5 officers and 150 other ranks prisoners, 2 field guns, 37 machine guns and 6 trench mortars. A number of congratulatory messages was received. During the operations August 19th–24th the battalion lost 2nd Lieut. W. H. Benbow and 2nd Lieut. I. P. Davies (Cheshire Regt.), attached, killed, 8 officers wounded, 232 other ranks killed and wounded. The battalion was withdrawn to the neighbourhood of Moyenneville to reorganize and clean up. On the 29th they marched to Boiry St. Martin, where they remained till the end of the month. During August the following officers rejoined : Captain Dealtry, 2nd Lieuts. A. Day and M. T. O. Jones from hospital ; Lieut. Salusbury and 2nd Lieuts. A. H. Simpson and A. W. Lindsay from courses. The following officers joined on first appointment ; 2nd Lieuts. W. P. Branch, J. T. Johnson, P. Cookham, W. B. T. James, J. Bentley, A. R. Pitchford, A. James, A. E. Allnutt and C. Morley. The following left the battalion during the month : Captain A. Robertson, on transfer to R.F.C., 2nd Lieut. W. L. Prosser to base, 2nd Lieuts. A. C. Brashaw, R. C. L. Roberts and E. E. V. Evans to Field Ambulance. Reinforcements amounting to 301 other ranks were received. Casualties, other than those referred to above : wounded, 13 other ranks.

SECOND BATTLE OF BAPAUME

September opened with a big general advance by the VI Corps, in conjunction with the XVII Corps on its left. The attack on the 3rd Division front was entrusted to the 8th Brigade, which moved forward to the attack, through the 76th and 7th Brigades, at 5.30 a.m. on September 2nd. The 7th K.S.L.I. were on the right, 2nd Royal Scots in the centre and 1st R.S. Fusiliers on the left. The 62nd Division was on the right. Four " mark IV " tanks were alloted to the battalion area, and eight

259

whippet tanks, to operate clear of the battalion right flank. The objective of the 8th Brigade was the high ground about Lagnicourt, a very strongly defended enemy position. The 7th K.S.L.I. made a most gallant advance, reaching its objective some time before the rest of the Brigade. Owing to the failure of the Division on the right to progress, and the check experienced by the Royal Scots and Scots Fusiliers east of the railway on the left, the 7th was unable to maintain its position. The failure of the tanks, due to mechanical trouble, also retarded the advance. The 7th K.S.L.I. made a continuous advance of 4,000 yards, "a stiff test at the present standard of individual training." By nightfall the line, including most of the ground gained during the day, was consolidated. During the night the 8th Brigade was relieved by the 2nd and 3rd Guards Brigades which, encountering little enemy opposition, were able to capture Lagnicourt on the following day (September 3rd). The 7th K.S.L.I. in its first attack suffered severely, and when the high ground was gained the fighting strength was returned as 4 officers and 201 other ranks. The battalion captured 3 77-mm. guns, 32 machine guns, 8 trench mortars, 3 anti-tank rifles and 235 prisoners. A number of congratulatory messages was received.

On the 3rd the battalion withdrew and bivouacked near the railway by Hamelincourt. Total casualties during the advance on September 2nd : 2nd Lieut. J. Middleton killed, 2nd Lieuts. T. Dowells, J. T. Johnson, C. Morley and W. T. B. James wounded ; other ranks, killed 34, wounded 195, wounded and missing 2, missing 6, gassed 8. Total casualties 248.

On September 6th the 3rd Division went into VI Corps Reserve, and the battalion marched to trenches north of Adinfer Wood, moving on the 11th to Gommiecourt. On the 15th the battalion marched to trenches at Beugny for the relief by 8th Brigade of the 6th Brigade (2nd Division) in the trenches north-west of Havrincourt. On the 16th the battalion relieved the 17th Royal Fusiliers in Brigade support on the Hermies-Demicourt road. On the 17th the enemy attacked the R. Scots in the right sector, but was driven back, B Company being detailed to assist the R. Scots. On this day 2nd Lieut. A. R. Pitchford was reported " missing, believed killed," subsequently reported killed in action 17.9.18. On the 20th the battalion relieved the Royal Scots in the right sector.

BATTLE OF THE CANAL DU NORD

At 5.20 on the morning of the 27th the 8th Brigade attacked again. The 7th K.S.L.I. on the right, the Royal Scots on the left, the R.S. Fusiliers in support. The objective varied from 900 yards on the right to 2,000 yards on the left. The 76th Brigade was to pass through, after the first attack, to capture Flesquieres, being followed in turn by the 62nd Division directed on Marcoing. The 9th Brigade were attacking on the right of the battalion, and the 3rd Guards Brigade on the left. The attack, in spite of a heavy bombardment with gas shells by the enemy, starting about 3.30 and lasting till four, was a complete success. The 7th K.S.L.I. attacked at 5.20 a.m., three companies in the line, with magnificent dash in spite of severe opposition. A Company on the right had a particularly stiff fight to gain their objective, losing their commander, a platoon officer and 34 other ranks. The centre company pushing on slightly in advance of their objective, captured a German battalion commander and 150 of his men. In addition, the 7th K.S.L.I. captured 52 machine guns, 4 trench mortars, 3 anti-tank rifles and 350 prisoners, including 6 officers. A number of congratulatory messages was received.

During this attack 2nd Lieuts. H. Amey and A. Allnutt were killed. The following officers were wounded : Captain R. Deedes, 2nd Lieuts. S. Graham and J. P. Marriott. Casualties : other ranks, killed 37, wounded 127. On the 29th the battalion moved to trenches east of Doignies, and on the 30th, to trenches in the

Premy support line. During September the following officers rejoined: Major E. H. Robinson, Lieut. H. Bush and 2nd Lieuts. F. A. Cooke, O. D. Wiles and C. Raybould, from courses. From hospital, 2nd Lieuts. G. H. Brazier, A. C. Brashaw, S. Graham, R. V. N. Wiggins. The following joined on first appointment : 2nd Lieuts. S. Walton, A. B. Owen, R. D. Mullin, E. T. Moore and J. P. Marriott. The following officers left the battalion during the month: 2nd Lieuts. C. Raybould, C. James, A. W. Hurdidge, E. T. Moore and J. Bentley to courses. Major R. W. St. J. W. Richards, 2nd Lieuts. W. E. Piper and R. V. N. Wiggins, to hospital, and 2nd Lieut. R. D. Mullin for duty with the B.W.I. Regiment at the base. Reinforcements amounting to 265 were received. Casualties, other than those referred to above, other ranks, killed 6, wounded 20.

On October 1st the VI Corps continued its advance with two Divisions in line. The 3rd Division was on the right, the 2nd on the left, and the New Zealand Division on the VI Corps right. On the 3rd Division front the first assault was to be made by the 76th Brigade. The 8th Brigade was to pass through the 76th Brigade, when the latter had gained their objective, and continue the advance, clearing up the village of Seranvillers. The battalion was in the trenches east of Flesquieres, north of the Havrincourt–Marcoing railway, and was somewhat below establishment, having a strength of 34 officers and 651 other ranks. The attack of the 76th Brigade on October 1st proceeded well and by 5 p.m. they had captured Rumilly, and the 7th K.S.L.I. moved forward at nightfall, through the 76th Brigade, to establish a new line. During the advance Major Robinson was wounded. At dawn on the 2nd strong parties of the K.S.L.I. and Royal Scots Fusiliers were pushed forward to secure tactical points if possible, to assist the further advance, but with orders that, in the event of strong enemy resistance being encountered, the ground gained was to be consolidated and anything in the nature of a general action avoided. Strong opposition was encountered and the patrols withdrew.

On October 3rd Lt.-Colonel N. H. M. Burne took over command of the battalion, and Major P. D. Holt, joining on the 6th, was appointed second in command. On the night of 6th/7th the 76th Brigade came forward again to relieve the 8th Brigade, and the 7th K.S.L.I. moved back to the Havrincourt-Hermies area. The following four days were spent in rest at Hermies. On October 13th the battalion marched to the support trenches of the Hindenburg line in the Ribecourt–Marcoing area, where training was carried on. On October 17th a general situation report as follows was issued to all units: " Ostend reported occupied by " Allies. Belgians report line runs east of Henlebeke–" east of Pitthem, east of Elghem, 1,000 yards east of " Swevezeele–Ighteghem–Ghistelles. Fourth Army re-" port line to run Avdigny–east of La Valle Malatre–" west of Maizinghiem–Le Quenelet Fm.–Le Cateau. " 1,800 prisoners reported. Fifth Army report outskirts " of Lille reached. Civilians from Lille state Lille " evacuated and Germans retiring to Tournai. Patrols " east of following line: Oignies–Libercourt–Camphin " on Carembault–Ghemy, Seclin–Templemais–Wattig-" nies Habourdin-le-marais–factory J.29.c.–Lompret. " Many civilians reported in Haubourdin and Loos (east " of Haubourdin)." Meanwhile the 2nd Army had crossed the River Lys, between Armentières and Menin, and were on the high ground at Paulbucq. The 3rd Army had captured Haussy, and the enemy were fast retiring on the Roulers–Dixmude line. On the 18th the 1st Army reported that the Canadians had crossed the Sensee river on the entire front between Mont Longlot and Courchelettes.

On October 20th the battalion marched to billets in Cattenieres, moving the following day to Quievy. On the 22nd the battalion marched with the 8th Brigade to Solesmes and was billeted in cellars for the night. At dawn the following day the 76th Brigade attacked on a front of 800 yards and reached the village of Vertain, an advance of 6,000 yards.

BATTLE OF THE SELLE

At 6 a.m. on the 23rd October the 8th Brigade attacked with the Royal Scots in the assaulting line, the R.S. Fusiliers in support, and 7th K.S.L.I. in reserve. The Royal Scots gained their objective, and the R.S. Fusiliers, continuing the advance, had won through to their objective by noon. At 2.30 p.m. the 7th K.S.L.I., passing through the R.S. Fusiliers, continued the advance and by 5 p.m. had captured the final objective of the Brigade attack. The position was consolidated and handed over intact, at 2 a.m. on the 24th, to the relieving unit of the 9th Brigade. The battalion returned to billets at Escarmain. The casualties during this advance were comparatively light. The following officers were wounded: Captain F. Mitchem, Lieuts. H. Bush and O. D. Wiles (slightly), 2nd Lieuts. J. E. Jordan, C. James, A. B. Owen,* R. V. N. Wiggins (gassed) and Lieut. S. E. Wilhoit (U.S.A. Army, attached). The 9th Infantry Brigade attacked on the 24th, and the 8th Brigade, with 7th K.S.L.I. as advanced guard, was to pass through them and carry on the advance. The attack, which had the village of Ruesnes and the Le Quesnoy–Valenciennes railway as objective, was only partially successful, and the two squadrons of the Oxfordshire Hussars, standing by in readiness, were not used, The railway line was reached eventually, and on the 28th Ruesnes. On 25th 2nd Lieut. P. Southall was wounded.

On the 26th the 8th Brigade relieved the 9th and took over outpost duties over the whole Corps front. The 7th K.S.L.I. established their outpost line and pushed forward observation posts which, without engaging the enemy, were able to send back valuable information concerning movements of enemy troops in Villers Pol.

* Died of wounds on October 26th, 1918.

On the 29th the 8th Brigade was relieved by the 6th Brigade (2nd Division) and the 7th K.S.L.I. returned to billets in Romeries after ten days' continuous marching, fighting and holding the line.

This was the last fighting the battalion was to do. Casualties, October 22nd–29th : Officers wounded 8 (includes 2 gassed) ; other ranks, killed 19, wounded 138. On October 30th the battalion marched to billets in Bevillers. The following officers rejoined during October : 2nd Lieuts. G. H. Brazier, C. James, J. Bentley, A. W. Hurdidge and S. Walton, all from courses. Major Richards, 2nd Lieut. Wiggins and Lieut. Lewis from hospital. The following joined on first appointment : 2nd Lieuts. A. Allwood, P. Southall, H. Martin, A. H. Whitfield, N. Wilson, A. Fox and H. Taylor. The following officers left during the month of October : Major Richards to 8th Brigade Head-quarters, Captain Dealtry to England, sick, Captain T. Fisher to course. 2nd Lieuts. W. E. Piper and G. M. A. Maxwell to hospital, and 2nd Lieuts. S. Walton and T. Cockburn to courses. The strength on November 1st was 36 officers, 737 other ranks.

The first day of this month was spent in billets at Bevillers resting and refitting, and the following two days in platoon training, bayonet fighting and musketry. On November 4th the battalion marched to Solesmes, 11 miles due east of Cambrai, and on the 10th moved to billets at Romeries, where orders were issued announcing the move of the Brigade on the following day by march route to Frasnoy, two miles north-east of Le Quesnoy. By eight on the following morning news had reached General Fisher, the Brigade Commander, that the Armistice had been signed, providing for the cessation of hostilities at 11 a.m., and, as the head of the column reached the starting-point, all troops were sent back to billets. On the following day all units of the 8th Brigade started work on repairing the roads in the Brigade area, and it is perhaps interesting to mention that the first lecture by the Divisional Education Officer on "Demobilization and Reconstruction" was given on November 14th. On the 16th the Brigade marched to Frasnoy and the 7th K.S.L.I. arrived at Le Grand Sart on the 17th, and on the 18th, at Neuf Mesnil between the Forêt de Mormal and Maubeuge. On the 20th the battalion reached Ferriere la Grande, one mile south-east of Maubeuge, where an exceptionally warm welcome from the inhabitants was received, a bouquet of flowers being presented to the Bugle-Major after retreat had been played. The march into Germany was continued through the month, the battalion being billeted successively at Bousignes, Thuin, Nalinnes, Biesmeree, Yvoir and Spontin. Up to the time of the Armistice the following officers rejoined from courses, 2nd Lieuts. P. T. Cookham and E. T. Moore. The following joined on first appointment: 2nd Lieuts. T. Cropley, V. Tyrrell, C. W. Dale and W. B. Grierson. At the end of November the strength of the battalion was 34 officers and 754 other ranks. During the month 2nd Lieuts. A. H. Whitfield and N. Wilson were transferred to the Tank Corps. There were no casualties.

The rest of the story is soon told. The battalion, starting from the Château at Spontin on December 4th, marched via Natoye, Sinsin, Hotton, Ereeze, Oster le Batty to Joubieval, the last halt in Belgium, which was reached on December 11th. On the following day, crossing the frontier at Beho, just after noon, they reached Maldingen in Germany. Thence via Manderfeld, Kronenburg, Blankenheimendorf and Sievernich to their destination at Golzheim, which they reached on December 20th. The battalion remained at Golzheim for the rest of the month. At Golzheim on December 23rd the following officers of the original cadre rejoined: Captain H. M. Pendlebury, Captain A. W. Johns and Lieut. R. J. Davies. On the 29th the first draft for demobilization (coal miners) left the battalion.

At Golzheim on February 28th, 1919, General Plumer

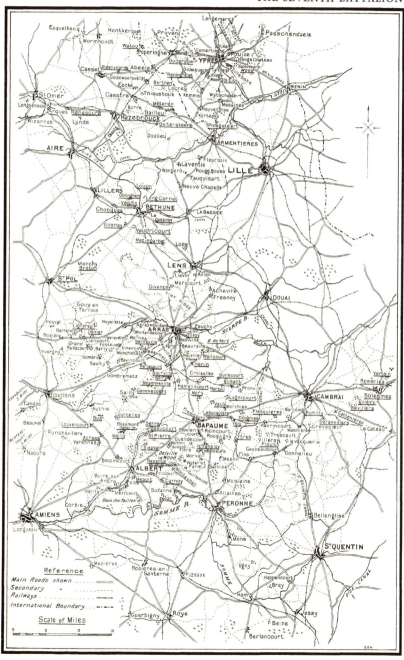

presented the Union colours to the battalion, then 33 officers and 579 other ranks strong. After that date the 7th K.S.L.I. rapidly faded away. On May 21st the cadre, consisting of Captain A. C. Hetherington, 2nd Lieut. S. Walton and 46 other ranks, returned with the colours to Aldershot. On June 4th 2nd Lieut. Walton and colour party were received by the Mayor of Shrewsbury and the colours deposited in St. Chad's Church. Three days later Captain Hetherington and the cadre returned to Shrewsbury, meeting with a great reception. Before leaving Germany farewell and congratulatory messages were exchanged between the 7th K.S.L.I., the 2nd Royal Scots, and the 1st Royal Scots Fusiliers.

On January 24th, 1920, a re-union dinner was held in Shrewsbury, at which Major-General C. J. Deverell, who commanded the 3rd Division from August, 1916, to the end of the War, was present. Later General Deverell, referring to the 7th K.S.L.I., wrote : " This was a battalion with a fine soldier-like spirit, upon whose gallantry, steadiness and cheerful willingness I was able to rely at all times and in all circumstances."

CHAPTER VII

THE EIGHTH BATTALION

THE battalion was raised at Shrewsbury and composed of men who voluntarily came forward to serve their country, and formed a unit in Kitchener's third army. After being assembled at Shrewsbury, about September 14th, 1,100 men, under command of Major L. A. Jackson, were sent first to Lewes and later to Seaford for organization and training.

Of the conditions under which this training was carried out nothing need be written, as the discomfort and hardships due to the lack of arms, equipment, blankets or clothing were common to all the newly formed battalions. It need only be said that all ranks carried out their duties cheerfully and willingly, displaying, from the commencement, that spirit of cheerfulness which remained with them throughout the war.

Colonel C. H. Stisted was first appointed to command the battalion with Major L. A. Jackson as senior major and Captain B. A. Jackson as adjutant. Later in the training period, in February, 1915, the 66th Infantry Brigade (of which the battalion formed a part, together with the 13th Manchesters, 12th Cheshires and 9th South Lancs) was moved to billets at Maidstone to work on the London defences. On March 8th Major J. Erskine, of the Manchester Regiment, was appointed to relieve Colonel Stisted in command.

The battalion shortly after returned to Seaford by route march, and later was moved, with the 66th Brigade, to Aldershot for Brigade and Divisional training; the 66th Brigade, together with the 65th and 67th Infantry Brigades, forming the 22nd Division. Finally, on September 5th, 1915, the battalion left Tweezledown Camp, and entrained at Aldershot for Southampton, *en route* to the front.

The senior officers at this time were Lt.-Colonel Erskine, commanding, Major L. A. Jackson, senior major ; Captain B. A. Jackson, adjutant ; Captain A. Profeit,

THE EIGHTH BATTALION. NOVEMBER, 1915

Major C. E. Pemberton, Captain E. C. Day and Captain R. D. Jackson, company commanders.

It is of interest to note that the average age of the officers proceeding to the front was only twenty-one years.

The battalion was sent first to Amiens and thence to Poulainville to billets, and on 11th September marched to Authie, and on the following day to Hebuterne to be attached to the 144th Brigade in the front line. On the 18th Captain A. Profeit was wounded by shrapnel, and on the same day the battalion moved out of the trenches and marched, via Authie and Poulainville, to the 22nd Division concentration area at Fouilloy and thence to Bayonvillers, arriving there on the 21st September. On the 29th September the battalion relieved the 9th East Lancs in the front line trenches at Foucaucourt. The battalion remained in this sector with the usual reliefs, suffering a few casualties, till October 21st, when it was relieved by French troops and marched to Proyart, and from that date to the 26th October via Fouilloy to Longeau, where it entrained for Marseilles.

On October 28th, 1915, B and D Companies, and Battalion Head-quarters, sailed in H.M.T. *Marathon*, and A and C Companies in the *Huntsend*, the strength of the battalion at this time being 29 officers and 1,003 other ranks.

No accommodation being available for horses or any transport, the battalion embarked with only what could be carried on the man. After an uneventful voyage the battalion disembarked at Salonika on the 6th and 7th November, 1915, and marched to bivouac about ten miles west of Salonika along the Monastir road to the River Galiko. This march was a very trying one, owing to the intense heat and the heavy weight to be carried. The Brigade gradually assembled at this camp and remained till the 20th, during which time training was carried out in the limited area allowed by the Greek troops. An amusing incident took place when a staff ride, a few miles into the hills, was interrupted by a Greek corporal and a file, who fired a shot over the party and turned it back. The situation seems to have been a bit strained at this period, and it was a comfort to know that the British Navy occupied the harbour. The weather broke about the middle of the month and there were heavy thunderstorms, the camp became a marsh, and cover had to be improvised with rushes from the river bed.

On the 20th November the battalion moved about three miles nearer the town on the Monastir road, and outposts were thrown out " for instruction purposes only." The weather now became really bad, with severe snowstorms and intense cold; fortunately a few tents were available, and stoves and blankets began to arrive, but by the end of the month 2 officers and 50 men had been admitted to hospital.

On the 12th and 13th December, the transport having arrived, the battalion marched via Kiordine to Naresh on the River Galiko, and with the French troops on our left entrenched a position across the railway to cover the retreating Serbian army, and our 10th Division. On the 16th and 17th December the Galiko was recrossed, and the battalion moved to a small Greek village called Gradobar, where orders were received to start making a road over the mountains. This work was vigorously carried out, and at the end of ten days a forward move was made over the rough track, one of the first wheeled vehicles to pass it being the medical cart which, after an adventurous day, negotiated the pass, though it ended up in a bog and had to be dug out.

At this period, although the Salonika winter was doing its best with rain, snow, wind and mud, the battalion still maintained that spirit of cheerfulness which was characteristic of it at all times and under all conditions. By the end of December the battalion was camped at Perriam and working on a support line to the Salonika defences which was generally known as the " Bird Cage."

During the whole of January and February, 1916, the

work on the defences was continued, the only incident of note occurring on January 7th, when hostile aeroplanes appeared, and two men of the battalion were wounded. German aeroplanes were also seen overhead during February.

On March 5th the battalion moved to Salonika and camped in the Besch Chinar Gardens, relieving the 1st K.O.Y.L.I., and taking over guard and garrison duties. Although these duties were by no means light, they afforded a pleasant change and an opportunity of cleaning up and seeing the sights. The spectacle of the guards being mounted and marched off, with the bugle band, caused much joy to the Greek gutter-snipes, who spent their days at the gate imitating the drill and calling out " shine Johnny " at intervals.

On the 27th March the enemy made an air raid on Salonika, and the battalion lost Pte. A. Higginson killed on guard duty.

On April 10th, 1916, the battalion was relieved by the 9th South Lancs and moved forward to the trenches in the front line. Before the relief was completed, Br.-General J. H. Poett paraded the battalion and praised them for the excellent work they had done. On the 17th the battalion left the trenches in the then front line, known afterwards as the " Bird Cage," and bivouacked for the night at Ambarkoj, forming part of a British advance detachment. On the following day an advance was made to Kukus, where the battalion bivouacked till the 20th, one company being sent on detachment to Dajandza. On the 20th a further advance was made to Irikli. While in bivouac here, German aeroplanes flew over and dropped bombs in the vicinity without causing any damage. We had no aeroplanes or anti-aircraft guns at this time, and the situation as regards the enemy seemed to be obscure. Until the end of April the battalion remained, though constantly moving, in the vicinity of Kukus, experiencing a great deal of discomfort from excessive heat varied by deluges of rain. The intervening months until November

271

can only be narrated from memory, no records remaining, but the battalion during this period appears to have been constantly on the march with light pack transport.

The climate and malaria took a heavy toll; three officers were evacuated to England in June, and no less than 8 officers and 322 other ranks were sick in hospital at the end of August.

In November, 1916, the battalion moved into what eventually became our front line of trenches, and took over a sector from the 12th Cheshire Regiment, just north of Ardzan, A and D Companies taking over the advanced posts known as Deux Ravins and Piton de Guetteurs.

On the 8th November a patrol of 2 officers and 40 men went out to reconnoitre the enemy's position just east of " the Nose." They were heavily fired on, but returned with useful information. Sgt. P. Davies was slightly wounded. On 23rd November Ptes. J. R. Remnant and I. Jones were killed by shell fire. On the night of the 26th and 27th a detachment of the battalion consisting of 9 officers and 275 other ranks, under the command of Captain E. C. Day, carried out a successful raid on the enemy's salient known as " the Nose." The raid was preceded by a heavy artillery preparation, the enemy's wire being successfully cut. The raiding parties entered the enemy's trenches at 9.15 p.m. and successfully cleared the trenches, killing all enemy encountered and capturing two of the 4th Regiment of the 9th Bulgarian Division. All dug-outs and defences were destroyed, and the raiding party withdrew in order. The following casualties occurred : Captain J. R. Hinmers, 2nd Lieuts. P. J. A. Bartlett, H. A. Sharp, H. S. Packman wounded ; 3 other ranks killed, one missing, believed killed ; 4 wounded. The operation was carried out under very heavy artillery, trench-mortar, machine-gun and rifle fire from the enemy.

An amusing incident occurred to one of the raiding parties, under the command of Captain Hinmers.

This officer, in jumping into an enemy trench, met a Bulgar, and forgetting to pull the pin out of his Mills' grenade, threw it at the Bulgar and, being a cricketer, with such precision that his opponent was knocked out and captured. Lieut. Lloyd did most excellent work as bombing officer, when, being left with only his sergeant, he bombed every enemy dug-out in the sector allotted to him.

At the latter end of this month the battalion was reinforced by drafts of 161 men from the 3rd Battalion, and during the month 6 officers and 185 other ranks were admitted to hospital.

During December the battalion moved into Brigade Reserve, but owing to sickness, as a result of the climate, 1 officer and 81 other ranks were admitted to hospital: Pte. W. F. Peate died in hospital from pneumonia, and Pte. T. Lloyd died from wounds.

Until the 23rd January, 1917, the battalion was in Brigade Reserve, generally working by night on digging trenches, and on the 23rd the battalion moved again into the front line relieving the 12th Argyll and Sutherland Highlanders.

At the end of the month the battalion moved into Brigade Reserve and suffered a few casualties from enemy shell fire. Two officers and 77 other ranks were admitted to hospital during February suffering from the prevalent malaria and dysentery, and Captain B. A. Jackson relinquished his appointment as Adjutant, and was succeeded by Lieut. G. Carr.

During the early part of February the battalion was in reserve and carrying out Brigade training, and on the 19th they once more moved into the front line in a new sector just west of Lake Doiran, covering what was known as the " Pip Ridge," the commanding position of the enemy's front.

During the month reinforcements were received, including Lieut. E. C. Faulkner, 2nd Lieuts. Fairer, Sheffield,

Woodhouse and Codling, with 150 other ranks. Captain B. A. Jackson was attached to the 66th Infantry Brigade for staff duties, and Captain J. R. Hinmers took over the duties of second in command. Routine work in the front-line trenches is all that can be recorded.

The battalion remained in the front line till the end of March without any particular incident, and was eventually relieved, on the 20th, by the 12th Cheshire Regiment.

There were 128 admissions into hospital during the month. Lt.-Colonel J. D. B. Erskine and Captain J. R. Hinmers were awarded the Croix de Guerre, and Sgt. W. A. Robinson the Médaille Militaire.

BATTLE OF DOIRAN, 1917

Considerable aerial and artillery activity was shown on both sides in the early part of April, and the battalion carried out further training, and worked on support trenches by night. On the 16th April the battalion was inspected by Major-General the Hon. F. Gordon, commanding the 22nd Division, and on the 20th they again relieved the 9th South Lancs in the same sector in the front line. The Divisional artillery now became very active on the enemy front-line trenches, cutting their wire. The battalion having received orders to capture and hold an advanced enemy position from Hill 380 to Doldzeli Ravine, B, C and D Companies were detailed as the attacking companies. B Company, commanded by Captain L. Profeit on the right, D Company, under Captain E. C. Day in the centre, and C Company, under Captain R. D. Jackson on the left, with a bombing party, under command of Lieut. Lloyd, worked forward up the Vladaja ravine. As soon as the attacking parties were clear of our front line, the enemy signalled the alarm and a heavy barrage fell on our front-line trenches. In spite of this, by 11.5 p.m. the enemy trenches were reported captured, and the new line was occupied and consolidated. About 10.15 there was a slight but noticeable lull in the enemy's barrage, which, however, increased again at 11.30. From reports received from the 11th Worcester Regiment, on the right, it appeared that B Company was encountering heavy resistance and that a company of the 11th Worcester Regiment was in difficulties. Two platoons were therefore sent up to support Captain Profeit, whose company had suffered considerably, Captain Profeit himself being killed. The enemy's position on Hill 380 was, however, again occupied and held. On the extreme left the enemy counter-attacked the left of Captain Jackson's company, but was repulsed. A few prisoners were taken, and on receipt of a report that there were many wounded of both sides lying in the open, the battalion medical officer, Captain Bowell, courageously went forward under heavy shell fire and succeeded in bringing in many of them.

During the following night the enemy again attempted to attack and regain the position on the Mamelon, but this attack was easily repulsed with heavy loss to the enemy, very few of them reaching our position.

Special mention should be made of the battalion signallers who, during this operation, established and maintained telephone communication under the most difficult circumstances on most exposed ground.

Our casualties in the attack were Captain L. Profeit and 12 men killed; Lieuts. Lloyd, Kaye, Cotton and Lanyon and 111 men wounded, and 2 missing.

On conclusion of the operation the following message was received: " The Corps Commander in forwarding " the following telegram from G.H.Q. conveys his warm- " est congratulations to the 66th Infantry Brigade.

" From Advanced G.H.Q. Lt.-General Commanding- " in-Chief wishes you to convey to the 22nd Division " his appreciation of the gallant and determined work " carried out by the 66th Infantry Brigade and the other " troops of that Division who have been responsible for " the capture, consolidation and holding against all " counter-attacks of the positions gained on the 24th " and 25th."

The following message was also received by the G.O.C. 66th Infantry Brigade from the Major-General Commanding the 22nd Division :—

" I wish again to express to you and your gallant troops " my sincere admiration on the first-rate work you are " all doing. Please try to inform the advanced troops " soon how rightly I value their noble and truly British " spirit displayed under severe conditions and their deter- " mined and successful resistance to the enemy's repeated " attempts to retake the captured positions."

After being relieved in the front line the battalion moved back into Corps Reserve.

During this month reinforcements consisting of 2nd Lieut. J. Swindell and 242 other ranks joined the battalion, and Captain B. A. Jackson was promoted Major and appointed second in command of the battalion.

After eleven days in reserve the battalion again took over a sector of the front line in the vicinity of Krastali village. On the night of 12th May a party of A Company engaged on wiring in front of our line met a Bulgar patrol about the strength of a platoon, which they drove off at the point of the bayonet. During this tour a good deal of patrol work was carried out and the enemy's artillery being fairly active the battalion suffered a few casualties from shell fire. 2nd Lieut. Ebden, with one N.C.O. and one man, endeavoured to enter the enemy village of Krastali by day. Leaving his two men outside the enemy wire, he succeeded in cutting through both lines of wire, when he ran into an enemy picket and was unfortunately wounded and captured.

From May 20th to 26th the battalion were in reserve, and on the latter date reoccupied the front line at Dold-zeli.

During this month 4 men were killed and 13 other ranks wounded, and 5 officers and 210 other ranks were admitted to hospital. 2nd Lieut. S. P. Pain and 390 other ranks reinforced the battalion from England.

Captain R. D. Jackson was awarded the Military Cross, and C.S.M. R. Wall, Sgt. F. Brown and L.-Corpl. C. Millin and Pte. R. Edevane were awarded the Military Medal after the operations of April 24th–27th. During the greater part of June the battalion was in reserve, moving forward into the front line on the 25th. The weather was exceedingly hot and there was a good deal of sickness, 137 other ranks being evacuated to hospital. Lt.-Colonel J. D. B. Erskine was awarded the rank of Brevet-Major in the June 3rd despatches.

The months of July and August, 1917, were without particular incident, the battalion occupying the front-line trenches, and going into reserve with almost monotonous regularity; the hospital evacuations were, as usual, very numerous.

In September, during a tour of the trenches, Sgt. Lewis, and 8 men of C Company, raided the enemy trenches and returned without casualties. A complimentary letter was received from the Major-General in command on the most creditable performance of the raiding party. Later in the month Sgt. Leighton, and 12 other ranks, again raided the enemy trenches in daylight; this raid being also successful, although 2 men were slightly wounded.

Up to the end of this year no particular incidents occurred and the battalion, when not in the front line, was continually working on trenches and communications, casualties occurring from time to time from enemy shell fire, which was generally active on both front line and reserve positions.

The early days of January, 1918, were, as usual during this period of the year, bitterly cold with much heavy snow, and the great winter enemy in Salonika, the Vardar wind, doing its best, often successfully, to bite through leather jerkins and every form of protection available. When the snow melted many of our roads were up to the horses' girths. The forces in Salonika had to contend, as regards climate, not only with severe cold and wet in the winter, but also in the summer, with the extreme heat of the East, and further with the malarial mosquito, whose activity almost defeated our expert medical men, who were often without adequate means to combat this devastating evil.

During the latter end of January the battalion was employed working on second-line defences, in reserve, but as often happened, they suffered as many losses in reserve as they did in the front line, owing to reserve battalions being always in occupation of ravines, well known by the enemy, and generally in close proximity to our own batteries. At this time the battalion lost 2 men killed, and 2nd Lieut. Hooper and one man wounded. During the month the battalion lost one officer and 74 other ranks evacuated to hospital. At the end of the month Sgt. Thackeray left for England, having been recommended for commissioned rank, and 36 men were sent to England suffering from chronic malaria. 2nd Lieut. Hart left the battalion to join the 16th Wing of the Royal Flying Corps.

The month of February passed without much to record, but the enemy in the front line were more active, both with their artillery and trench mortar, though the battalion suffered very few casualties. The weather was generally fine but very cold. Lieut. Cannon left the battalion to join the R.F.C., and Lieut. Bailey joined the battalion having been appointed Quartermaster.

During March the battalion moved into Corps Reserve, and thence to Army Reserve, carrying out intensive training chiefly in open warfare. The weather was still very cold, and there was a heavy fall of snow at the latter end of the month. During this month Lieuts. Wagner, Jehu and 2nd Lieut. Hooper were invalided to England, and L.-Corpl. A. H. Yeomans was awarded the Military Medal for gallant conduct in the field.

The battalion moved forward again during April towards the front line, working on communications and second-line defences, and on the 15th again occupied the sector covering the " Pip Ridge," taking over from the the 12th Cheshires. About this period the artillery duel appeared to become much more active, possibly owing to the exhaustion of man power on both sides. However, during the tour of the front line at the Horseshoe, in order to co-operate with operations on the flank, 2nd Lieut. Davis with a party of 15 men carried out a demonstration attack which was very successful in bringing down the enemy's protective barrage, and causing the enemy to be at a loss to know the correct points of attack. This party carried out its work excellently and without losses. During the month the battalion lost 5 men killed and 13 wounded.

The earlier part of May found the battalion chiefly occupied, while in Brigade Reserve, in carrying out anti-malarial schemes, canalising streams, and arranging for mosquito-proof bivouacs, also working on second-line defences. The latter part of the month they again re-occupied the Horseshoe sector in the front line, but beyond a few casualties there was nothing to record.

Major B. A. Jackson was promoted temporary Lt.-Colonel in command of the 9th King's Own Royal Lancasters, and Major W. H. Durst was appointed as Major and second in command.

During June the usual fortnightly routine work of front line and reserve trenches was carried out. During the month Captain J. B. Bettington with a strong patrol carried out a reconnaissance on the village of Krastali.

Lieut. N. R. Cosgrove and 2nd Lieut. A. C. Hill were posted to the battalion, and Lieut. F. S. Nalder rejoined from sick leave. Honours and awards in the orders for the month of June, 1918, were : Lt.-Colonel J. D. B. Erskine, the D.S.O. ; Lieut. H. E. Harris, the Military Cross.

The usual routine work was the programme for July, the only incident to record being a small raid carried out on 28th on the enemy's trenches by daylight with a party from B Company, which successfully entered the enemy's trenches, killing two of the enemy and retiring without loss.

On August 9th a very successful raid was carried out under the command of Lieut. T. W. Murphy on an enemy pill box near the town of Doiran. Moving out of our lines at dusk, the party entered the enemy trenches at their hour of relief, through a gap cut during the previous days by our artillery. They surprised the enemy night posts coming up, and six of the enemy were killed, valuable information being obtained concerning the enemy's defences.

Another raid took place on August 16th, a party of 8 men, under the command of Lieut. Richmond, raiding a portion of the enemy trenches. This raid was stoutly opposed and Lieut. Richmond, having shot two of the enemy, and the enemy trench having been well bombed, retired being threatened by enemy flanking parties. Lieut. Richmond and one man were wounded in this operation.

On the 18th August the battalion was relieved by the 1st York and Lancaster Regiment from another division, and moved during the following days to the vicinity of 12th Corps Head-quarters for training. The honours awarded during this month were 2nd Lieut. T. W. Murphy, Military Cross, for his gallant conduct during his raid, and Corpl. W. Wolley, the Military Medal.

From September 1st to 13th the battalion was carrying out training for operations, having received orders that it was to take part in a general attack on the enemy front, the point allotted to the Brigade being the Pip Ridge. During the days of the 14th to the 17th the battalion moved up towards the front line in preparation for its part in the attack.

BATTLE OF DOIRAN, 1918

The actual attack on the Pip Ridge during this fateful operation was carried out by the 66th Infantry Brigade. The ground was mountainous and, owing to the formation of the ridge, the attack had to be carried out on a platoon frontage of about 50 yards. The 12th Cheshires were the leading battalion, followed by the 9th South Lancashires; the 8th King's Shropshire Light Infantry being the third attacking battalion. The attack was preceded by an intense bombardment from our artillery. The advance through our lines to the forward place of assembly was carried out in perfect order, and just before dawn, on the morning of the 18th, the Brigade advanced to the attack. For a short time there was a peculiar silence, but just as our leading troops rushed the advance work, it was blown up, either by a land mine or the explosion of a bomb store, causing very heavy casualties. At the same moment an intense enemy barrage was concentrated on the attacking troops, and a heavy trench mortar bombardment, combined with cross fire from machine guns on the narrow frontage, almost annihilated our attacking party. A few scattered remnants actually penetrated the enemy main front line, but these were all killed, including the commanding officers of both the leading battalions. The 8th K.S.L.I. also suffered very severely, and having endeavoured to reorganize and break through at another point, and there being no organized unit remaining, Lt.-Colonel Erskine collected what men and officers he could gather from the remnants of the three battalions and reformed them under the shelter of Jackson's Ravine. For a time he commanded only 4 officers and 240 men, some of these having been wounded, but others afterwards came in. The approximate strength of the battalions was about 400, and during this attack the Brigade lost 37 officers and 800 other ranks, or about 65 per cent of its effective strength.

Later on in the same morning a further attempt was made, but this had to be abandoned, the enemy's hold of the ridge being unshaken. The consoling thought of those who took part in this forlorn hope may be that, owing to their determined effort, they were instrumental in holding the enemy's reserves, and thereby enabling our general attack to succeed at another point, forcing the enemy to retreat and evacuate his stronghold, and very shortly afterwards to sue for peace.

In this attack the battalion lost in killed, 2nd Lieut. H. A. Turner, R.S.M. C. G. Holden, C.S.M. R. Wall and 27 other ranks ; also, missing and believed killed, Captain F. S. Nalder (reported killed September 21st, 1918) and 15 other ranks. The wounded included Captain R. D. Jackson, Lieuts. G. L. Davis, N. R. Cosgrove, 2nd Lieuts. F. G. Mutton, T. W. Murphy, H. P. Watkins, E. Seymour and A. C. Hill. Other ranks wounded, 111.

Having held on to an advanced position during the day of the 18th, the remnants of the battalion were withdrawn to our front-line trenches, being relieved by parties of the 9th Border Regiment. During the latter days of this month the battalion was reorganizing behind the lines.

On the retreat of the enemy, the battalion advanced through the enemy lines into bivouac near Lake Doiran, and during the early part of October the battalion was engaged in carrying out salvage operations on the enemy's position at the Grande Couronne.

From October 11th to 20th the battalion marched with the Brigade to Stavros, and during this march was congratulated by the G.O.C. 66th Brigade on their march discipline. While at Stavros a Divisional parade was held, the Bishop of London addressing the Brigade, after which the Commander-in-Chief presented ribbons. The following received honours: Captain D. M. Boohan, R.A.M.C., attached 8th K.S.L.I., M.C.; C.S.M. G. W. Lloyd, D.C.M.; Corpl. J. D. Donald and Pte. W. Kearle, M.M.

On October 25th the battalion embarked on H.M. Destroyer *Fury* and proceeded to Dedeagatch, landing there on the 28th without incident, and going into camp in the vicinity of the town, where it remained awaiting the transport, which had proceeded by road, until the beginning of November.

Sketch Maps

ILLUSTRATING

OPERATIONS OF THE 8TH BATTALION

IN

FRANCE AND SALONICA

Reference

Main Roads shown...═══
Secondary "   "   ....
Railways   "   "   ..+++++

The following honours are recorded at this time:—
Captain R. D. Jackson, Bar to Military Cross.
Captain R. L. M. Lloyd, Bar to Military Cross.
Private P. Taylor, Military Medal.

At the beginning of November the battalion marched to Marhamli, and Lt.-Colonel Erskine left the battalion to take over temporary command of the 67th Infantry Brigade, Major Durst assuming command of the battalion.

From the middle of the month, hostilities with Turkey having ceased, the battalion marched via Dedeagatch, Drama and Cavalla, to Stavros, arriving there on 26th November. On the 29th, owing to the strength of the battalion having been reduced by casualties and sickness to an exceedingly low level, orders were received that it was to be amalgamated with the 2nd Regular Battalion. Certain officers and N.C.O.'s were transferred for base duties, but before leaving the 22nd Division the battalion was inspected by Major-General Duncan, the G.O.C. 66th Infantry Brigade, Lt.-Colonel Erskine, temporarily commanding the 67th Brigade, being in attendance. The Major-General in addressing the battalion before its departure spoke most highly of its services in the Division, and in particular said that the battalion was well known in his Division and also in the Salonika Army not only for its smartness, but for its splendid discipline.

As a record of the battalion, this concludes its history except that it should be stated that after a somewhat trying journey and march to join the 2nd Battalion, the party marched into its destination with such smartness as to earn for itself the congratulations of the General Staff of the Division, which were forwarded through the 22nd Divisional Head-quarters.

The most pleasant recollection that all who have served in the 8th K.S.L.I. will have is that of the strong spirit of comradeship and *esprit de corps* amongst all ranks, a spirit which enabled the battalion to carry through smiling to the end and win honour for itself and the regiment.

CHAPTER VIII
THE TENTH BATTALION

IN February, 1917, Sir Archibald Murray, Commander-in-Chief of the Egyptian Expeditionary Force, decided upon the amalgamation of the Yeomanry Regiments (mostly dismounted due to scarcity of horses) into a Division for service as infantry. Accordingly the 74th (Yeomanry) Division came into existence. On March 1st, 1917, the Shropshire Yeomanry arrived at Helmieh Camp, near Cairo, from Sherika, and were joined there on the following day by the Cheshire Yeomanry from Alamein; the two regiments were then amalgamated and became the 10th Battalion K.S.L.I.

The 10th K.S.L.I., together with the 24th and 25th R.W. Fusiliers and the 24th Welch Regiment, formed the 231st Infantry Brigade in the 74th Division, and was commanded by Lt.-Colonel H. Heywood-Lonsdale, with Lieut. J. E. Tomkinson as Adjutant.

The first three weeks of March were spent in re-organizing and equipping, followed by strenuous training in infantry work. On the 24th the battalion moved to Kantara, where training was continued until April 2nd when the Brigade moved north-east to take part in the second attack on Gaza.

SECOND BATTLE OF GAZA

The 74th Division was concentrated in reserve in the neighbourhood of Dier el Belah, at which place the battalion arrived, via Khan Yunus, on April 14th. The attack, which took place on the following day, was only partially successful, and on the 19th the battalion moved forward and entrenched itself in a position 2,000 yards south-east of Mansura Ridge. During the advance 2 other ranks were killed, and Captain Jones was wounded. On April 20th, the enemy having been strongly reinforced, the attack was broken off, and the K.S.L.I. remained in the trenches until relieved on April 28th by the 229th Brigade.

THE TENTH BATTALION. JULY, 1917

The battalion remained in camp, west of the junction of Wadi* Ghuzze and Wadi El Main, in support, until May 19th, employed in digging trenches and making strong points. On the 19th a move was made to reserve trenches on the south slope of Mansura Ridge, the battalion taking over from the 1/10th London Regiment, 162nd Brigade. On the 24th the battalion relieved the 24th R.W.F. in the front-line trenches north of the ridge. The battalion continued in this sector until July 9th. Although an uneventful period, the great heat, the "Khamsin" (a hot wind loaded with fine particles of sand), the dust, insects and other discomforts serve to make it memorable. Added to this there was a lack of vegetables, which in course of time caused a prevalence of septic sores amongst the men. Worst of all there was a serious shortage of water. Mansura Ridge consists of a long line of hills lying south-east of Gaza, prolonged westward to the sea. The trenches here had been dug hastily, and working parties were constantly employed at night in improving them and putting out wire. The tour of duty, interchanged with the 24th R.W.F., was seven days in the line and seven days in support.

The battalion held about 1,500 yards of line, situated nearly 3,000 yards from the Turks, who were very inactive. Although the battalion had patrols out nightly there were no encounters with the enemy, and the only incident recorded is one enemy sniper taken prisoner. The ridge was shelled occasionally but, although the battalions on the right and left were caught, the K.S.L.I. fortunately escaped. Casualties from sickness, considering the circumstances, were light, though Captain Swire was invalided with bad septic sores, and there was a slight epidemic of diphtheria.

On July 9th the 74th Division was withdrawn for rest, and the battalion marched to "Regent's Park" on the seashore about five miles south-west of Gaza, and half a mile north of the mouth of the Wadi Ghuzze. On June

* Wadi is Arabic for water-course, or river bed.

28th, 1917, General Sir Edmund Allenby succeeded Sir Archibald Murray in command of the E.E. Force, and during July the period of rest at " Regent's Park " became one of strenuous training of every description. On July 14th the battalion was inspected by Lt.-General Sir Philip Chetwode, Bt., who expressed himself as very pleased with the general turn out and bearing of the men. Competitions and sports of all kind relieved the hard work, and with sea bathing and better food the health of the men improved wonderfully, although the septic sores were not eliminated entirely. During July Captain J. E. Tomkinson left the battalion for duty at Head-quarters 74th Division, and Lieut. H. Aldersey was appointed adjutant. Lieut. A. T. Neilson, the very efficient transport officer, was invalided, and Lieut. T. Luce succeeded him as transport officer.

On August 3rd the battalion marched to camp at Khan Yunus, a good camp in a fig grove some three miles from the seashore. The march of about ten miles over sand dunes was somewhat trying. Training continued and included Brigade night operations under Lt.-Colonel Lord Kensington, who was temporarily commanding the 231st Infantry Brigade, in the absence of Br.-General Bowker. As time wore on training both by day and night became more strenuous, until it grew apparent to all that the time for another offensive was drawing near. During August Captain Booth, R.A.M.C., replaced Captain Scott as medical officer, and Lieut. A. R. Macklin joined for duty. 2nd Lieut. R. H. Jones was appointed bombing officer and 2nd Lieut. G. M. P. Mudduck scout officer. On August 27th the battalion moved to Sheikh Shabasi on the seashore about seven miles south of " Regent's Park," where they rested for nine days.

On September 5th the battalion marched south to a bad camp, about ten miles south of Deir el Belah and east of the fig grove at Khan Yunus, known as the " Dust Bin," which described it well. Here it remained training under Br.-General Heathcote, who had succeeded to command of the 231st Infantry Brigade, until the 20th, when it returned, much to the relief of all ranks, to " Regent's Park." Whilst at " Regent's Park " the battalion found large working parties every night for digging trenches and making strong points in the front line before Gaza for the 54th Division, as well as making roads and battery positions by day. Meanwhile training was carried on with bombers and range practice, and Lieut. Muddock, with Sgt. T. Price and Corpl. Brodie, brought the battalion scouts and snipers to a high standard of efficiency.

About October 5th it became known that the battalion would take part in the advance on Beersheba in the coming offensive, and officers were sent to reconnoitre the position. On the 6th the battalion moved south to Sheikh Nakhrur, where they remained till the 25th. Here the battalion won the Brigade competition for turn out in marching order, and were second to the Norfolks in the Divisional competition. On October 25th the whole 231st Brigade moved to Abu Sitta.

THIRD BATTLE OF GAZA

On October 30th the 74th Division was concentrated at Khasif, and that night the 10th K.S.L.I. crossed the Wadi Saba. On the 31st the 231st Brigade attacked at 11.30 p.m., the battalion being in reserve. The Brigade reached its objective, and the 10th K.S.L.I., advancing by " Hawke " Wadi, reached a position east of Saba on November 1st, having suffered only three casualties. Here news was received that Beersheba had fallen. The weather was intensely hot and there was again a grave shortage of water. On November 2nd the battalion, acting as advanced guard to the Brigade, moved north to Wadi Nimir, continuing the march on the following day towards Sheria, the next objective. On the evening of November 3rd a " Khamsin " started and blew for thirty-six hours, adding greatly to the discomfort of the troops. The water allowance was reduced to one-half gallon per man every twenty-four hours. On November 4th the battalion bivouacked west of the Beersheba-Gaza road, and that evening took over the outpost line of the 1/7th Cheshires, 53rd Division. The 10th K.S.L.I. held this line without water or rations for twenty-four hours, and in an exhausted condition set out to rejoin the Brigade at midnight on November 5th/6th. On November 6th the 229th and 231st Brigades attacked the defences of Sheria, the 10th K.S.L.I. being in reserve. The attack was successful and by dawn on the 7th Sheria was taken. Casualties in the battalion were light, amounting to 4 other ranks killed and 3 wounded. Meantime the rapidity of the attack on Sheria had forced a withdrawal of the enemy's right, and Gaza was in our hands. On November 7th the cavalry took the stage, pursuing the retreating enemy, and forcing the Turks back from Huj Gaza and Hareira. On November 9th the battalion marched to Irgeig, and on the 11th joined the remainder of the Brigade at Karm, after a trying march in heat and dust with the "Khamsin" in force again.

The battalion remained at Karm until November 17th, when they marched to Shellal and thence by stages north to "Junction Station," due west of Jerusalem, where they arrived on the 27th. The enemy was now engaged in a desperate attempt to save Jerusalem and was facing west on a line Hebron–Beit Jibrin–El Kubeibe. The march north along the sea coast from Shellal to "Junction Station," though trying at some stages, had been on the whole through pleasant country. The hard road, after months on soft sand, was very trying to the men's feet. A goodly supply of oranges along the route proved very acceptable. At 7 a.m. on the 28th the battalion marched from "Junction Station" north-east to Latrun. The road is continuously up hill, and streams of lorries going up to the front added to the difficulties of the march. Latrun was reached just after midday. At 7 p.m. the battalion continued its march up hill along the Latrun–Enab–Jerusalem road. At 11.45 p.m. the battalion halted for an hour on the rise above Enab at an altitude of 2,500 feet, where the cold by contrast seemed intense. At 12.45 a.m. on the 29th the march was resumed over a rough mountain track very steep in parts. Just before dawn the battalion reached Beit Annan, having marched twenty-six miles under most trying conditions since the previous morning. At 8.30 a.m. the 10th K.S.L.I. relieved the 8th Mounted Brigade in the outpost line on the ridge Beit Dukku–Khan Juena. The country in which the battalion was now operating is very difficult. Very steep hills rise from deep and narrow valleys to varying heights up to 2,000 feet. To descend into the wadis, even in daylight on foot, was very difficult, and transport mules could only be got down in the few cases where tracks existed.

At 4 p.m. on the 29th orders were received to send two companies forward to occupy the village of Et Tireh, where the 25th R.W.F. was to meet the 10th K.S.L.I., and prolong our advanced line to the left flank. Major Glazebrook, in command of numbers 2 and 4 companies, marched off after dark and occupied Et Tireh, without encountering much opposition. Owing to the nature of the country, and lack of maps, the 25th R.W.F. did not reach Et Tireh until two in the morning of the 30th. The village of Et Tireh lies in a hollow, and is commanded by one hill on the north, another on the north-east, and on the south by a ridge running south-west and already strongly occupied by the Turks. As soon as day dawned Major Glazebrook seized the hill (Sheikh Hassan) to the north-east, and the 25th R.W.F. occupied the hill to the north. At midday the Turks began a strong counter-attack and number 1 company 10th K.S.L.I., under Major Kynaston, advanced to assist Major Glazebrook's force. The counter-attack succeeded in driving our troops from the hills surrounding the village, and by 2 p.m. Et Tireh, commanded from north, north-east and south, and under heavy shell fire to which our guns made no reply, became untenable. Lt.-Colonel Heywood-

u

Lonsdale accordingly sent orders to retire. With great skill Major Glazebrook succeeded in extricating his small force and bringing in all his wounded. The following officers were killed: Lieuts. J. M. P. Muddock, V. C. Hares, and C. E. Henningsen. The following were wounded : Major Kynaston, Lieuts. Hallows and Eason. Casualties amongst other ranks, 19 killed and 74 wounded. The 10th K.S.L.I. reformed on the original outpost line, and remained there until relieved by the Leinsters on the night of December 4th/5th.

CAPTURE OF JERUSALEM

At 6 p.m. on December 5th the battalion marched to Beit Izza and took over a section of outpost line. On the 7th the 10th K.S.L.I. advanced and occupied unopposed the village of El Anaziyea. The successful attack on Jerusalem by the XX Corps took place on the 9th, the battalion standing-to in Brigade Reserve. The 10th K.S.L.I. remained at Beit Izza until the 22nd, the weather being atrocious with torrents of rain and bitterly cold. The battalion was relieved on December 22nd by the 12th Norfolks, and marched, via Wadi Marua, to the junction of Wadis Selman and Zeit, where they spent Christmas Day. On the 26th the 10th K.S.L.I. went into reserve to the 10th Division at Tahta, the weather being all this time exceptionally wet and cold. On the 27th the 229th Brigade drove the enemy from Zeitoun Ridge, and the 10th K.S.L.I., placed in reserve to the 229th Brigade, moved up and occupied the ridge. On the 28th the Brigade continued its advance and cleared Beit Ania, the battalion, following up the advance, occupied the village, remaining in billets there until the end of January, 1918.

At this period, in order to enable the victorious advance to proceed, a great deal of road-making had to be done, and the 10th K.S.L.I. were thus occupied throughout January. Beit Ania was a dirty village nearly 3,000 feet up, and consequently very cold. Rain and snow delayed

290

work on the roads, but, despite all, good progress was made on " Offa's Dyke," as the road on which the K.S.L.I. was working was named. During the stay at Beit Ania considerable reinforcements were received, also much-needed clothing and boots. On February 1st, owing to a case of typhus in the village, the battalion moved out of billets to bivouac. On the 17th the 10th K.S.L.I. moved forward to support the 181st Brigade in the attack on Jericho.

CAPTURE OF JERICHO

On February 19th, 1918, the battle opened and the battalion moved into bivouac at Mukhmas, and at dawn next day, still in reserve, occupied a position just west or Ras el Tawal. At dusk on the 20th the 10th K.S.L.I. relieved the 21st London Regiment on the high ground on the right of the 181st Brigade front. Patrols were pushed forward during the night of 20th/21st along the ridge south-east of Kurunthal, which village was found to have been evacuated by the Turks. By dawn on the 21st the enemy was in full retreat and Kurunthal and Jericho were occupied by the British troops; that night the battalion withdrew to Ras el Tawal without having suffered any casualties.

The 10th K.S.L.I. now returned to road-making, and remained on the Nablus road until March 2nd. On the resumption of the advance northwards the battalion moved to Wadi Stour on March 2nd, and came again under shell fire, but without any casualties until the 7th, when Major P. K. Glazebrook was killed and 3 other ranks wounded. Major Glazebrook, who had just been awarded the D.S.O. for his fine handling of the situation at Et Tireh the previous November, was a great loss to the battalion, being an officer who inspired all ranks with the greatest confidence. The battalion moved from the camp by Wadi Stour on the night of the 7th/8th to position for the attack on Selwad. There was a considerable amount of shelling during the move, and the battalion lost 2 other ranks killed, also several of the camels.

THE KING'S SHROPSHIRE LIGHT INFANTRY

ACTIONS OF TEL AZUR

The attack on Selwad was to take place on March 9th. On the night of the 8th/9th the battalion, excellently guided by their scouts, deployed to their position without a hitch, in spite of the darkness and rain, and the heavy, broken country. After a brief halt at 3.30 a.m. the battalion, advancing on a compass bearing, attacked and captured Selwad post by 5.15 a.m. Continuing the advance the 10th K.S.L.I. cleared Selwad village, capturing 5 officers and 23 other ranks. The battalion then pushed on towards Burj el Lisaneh, but was hung up by a deep wadi. Up till now the casualties had been comparatively light, about a dozen killed and wounded, but the position in which the battalion now found itself was very exposed. Neither the Brigade on the right nor left of the advance had been able to reach its objective. Tel Azur did not fall until the evening of the 9th, and Burj Badawil was in the hands of the Turks until midday of the 9th. With both flanks in the air the 10th K.S.L.I. spent an unpleasant day. Orders were received to attack Burj el Lisaneh again on March 10th.

At 2 a.m. on the 10th the battalion advanced, and over very steep and difficult ground scaled the slopes of Burj el Lisaneh. By 6 a.m. the summit was reached and the enemy driven from his position. The Turks immediately organized a strong counter-attack and some severe fighting followed, the left flank of the position being almost turned. Here Pte. Harold Whitfield single-handed charged and captured a Lewis gun, which was harassing his company at short range. He bayoneted, or shot, the whole gun team, and turning the gun on the enemy drove them back with heavy casualties, thereby completely restoring the whole situation in his part of the line. Later he organized and led a bombing attack on the enemy, who had established themselves in an advanced position close to our line, and from which they were enfilading his company. He drove the enemy back with great loss, and by establishing his party in their position saved many lives, and materially assisted in the defeat of the counter-attack. For these acts of bravery and absolute disregard of personal safety Pte. Whitfield was awarded the V.C. Two other determined counter-attacks followed but were beaten off, not one yard of the captured ground being yielded. An enemy officer and two other prisoners were taken during the day. The price was heavy. Capt. H. Aldersey, who had but lately relinquished the Adjutancy and taken over command of his company, which he loved so well, was killed. He was a fine regimental officer and a great loss. Ten other ranks were killed that day, and 2nd Lieut. W. E. Hallowes, 2nd Lieut. W. F. Pratt and 29 other ranks wounded.

The stalwart resistance met, and the heavy losses incurred by the enemy during his counter-attacks, had forced a retirement, and the Turks fell back on Sinjil and Amurieh. Accordingly at 3 a.m. on March 11th the battalion moved forward some two miles to the high ground north-west of Turmus Aya, being relieved at nightfall by the 24th R.W.F. Casualties for the day, 9 other ranks wounded. The battalion returned to bivouac on the Nablus road. The work of Lieut. Curtis and the battalion scouts in leading the battalion with unfailing accuracy over unknown and extremely difficult country, on compass bearings, in the darkness, was of inestimable value during this fighting. Special praise is also due to Captain Brooks for the manner in which he led the attack over the precipitous hills and deep wadis. The capture and gallant defence of Burj el Lisaneh formed a fitting climax to the work of the 10th K.S.L.I. in Palestine, for on April 29th the battalion struck camp at Kantara and entrained for Alexandria, whence they embarked on H.M.T. *Omrah* for France. The assistance of the 74th Division was now required in frustrating the Germans' last desperate bid for victory on the Western Front.

The 10th K.S.L.I. disembarked at Marseilles on May 7th, 1918, and on the 9th entrained for the front.

Arriving at Noyelles on the 12th, the battalion marched to Canchy, where it remained till May 22nd. On the 25th a move was made to Lattre St. Quentin, where, on June 20th, Lt.-Colonel Heywood-Lonsdale handed over command of the battalion to Lt.-Colonel Howell-Evans from the 24th R.W.F. (Denbigh Yeomanry). All ranks felt deep regret at parting from their commanding officer, who had led them since the formation of the 10th K.S.L.I. in March, 1917, and whose relations with many covered a very much longer period. On June 25th the batta ion moved to Aire (eight miles south-west of Hazebrouck), and on July 10th the training period came to an end and the 10th K.S.L.I. took over the trenches at St. Floris (south of La Lys Canal) from the 11th Suffolks, 61st Division.

The battalion was now in a fairly quiet sector of the line. Since March the Germans had advanced from Radinghem, Bois Grenier and Armentières some twenty miles to the eastern boundaries of the Fôret de Nieppe. The trenches were bad, the front line being disconnected and having no communication trenches, which made movement in the daytime impossible. The country was flat and planted with wheat, and the cottage gardens full of vegetables. The men had seen no fresh vegetables for two years, and realized that even war has its compensations. The battalion remained in these trenches, and at rest in La Haye, throughout July. On July 12th 2nd Lieut. R. G. Shackles and 2nd Lieut. J. J. Paterson joined the battalion from England. The former, wasting no time, organized a very successful daylight raid on July 27th, and getting into the German trenches with a party of 2 N.C.O.'s and 11 other ranks attacked a machine-gun post. Having killed two of the enemy, he returned with four prisoners and the machine-gun. For this feat he was awarded the M.C. On the 29th the enemy attempted a raid. The 10th K.S.L.I. withheld fire until the enemy was right up to their trench line, when they let go and annihilated the raiding party. Unfortunately Sgt. T. V. Price, the best shot in the battalion, was killed in this affray. During July Major C. W. Tomkinson left the battalion to take over the duties of Corps Agricultural Officer, and 2nd Lieuts. Jones and Betts were sent to the Field Ambulance. 2nd Lieuts. McEwan, Daniels and Nickson joined on first appointment. On July 13th 2nd Lieut. Madge was appointed Adjutant. Casualties for the month: wounded, 16 other ranks.

The battalion remained in the trenches at St. Floris until relieved by the 10th Buffs on August 4th. On the 3rd August 2nd Lieut. Curtis took out a patrol of scouts to destroy an enemy post, but, after cutting their way through a thick belt of wire, the patrol was hung up by a second even thicker belt within fifteen yards of the enemy trench. Whilst engaged on this belt the party was discovered, but managed to get back, losing Sgt. A. J. Brodey, the very efficient scout sergeant, killed, and having one man wounded. The battalion was at rest until August 21st, when they returned to the front-line trenches.

On August 22nd orders were received to move forward, at very short notice, in conformity with an advance of the Division north of the Lys Canal. The advance north of the canal was unfortunately hung up, and, without any information of the position on the left flank, the 10th K.S.L.I. proceeded into what proved to be for them a trap. Advancing through high standing corn the battalion continued until within a few hundred yards of the concealed enemy, who met them with a devastating fire from carefully prepared positions. He then followed up his advantage with a determined counter-attack and severe hand-to-hand fighting took place. The battalion was eventually forced back to its starting-point. The enemy made no attempt to press home the counter-attack. Casualties: Officers killed, Captain O. Cawley, Lieuts. O. S. Jenkins (R.W. Fus., attached) and F. C. Plowden ; wounded, Lieuts. Roden, Grimes and Nickson ; taken prisoner, Lieuts. Carless and McEwan. Casualties, other ranks killed, wounded and captured 171.

On August 24th the 229th Brigade came into the line, and the 10th K.S.L.I. was relieved and rested till the 29th, when the 74th Division was transferred to the 4th Army, and moved south to the Somme. Entraining at Aire on August 29th the battalion proceeded on a twenty-two hour journey to Méricourt, twelve miles north-east of Amiens, from whence they marched to Ribemont, one and a half miles north of Méricourt, where they remained till the end of the month.

On September 2nd the 74th Division attacked south of Moislains, and the 10th K.S.L.I. marched to Clery-sur-Somme, five miles south-east of Méricourt, in reserve. On the 3rd the battalion advanced north-east to Boucheauvesnes, in support of the 229th Brigade, where a 5·9 shell, landing in C Company's lines, killed 8 and wounded 7 other ranks. On September 6th the battalion moved to trenches at Templeux, preparatory to an attack on the following day. At 6.30 a.m. on the 7th the 10th K.S.L.I. passed through the 230th Brigade outpost line at Longavesnes and attacked Villers Faucon, which they surrounded and cleared of the enemy by midday. The 24th Welch continued the advance on the following day, and the battalion withdrew to Longavesnes to rest. Here it remained until the 17th September.

BATTLE OF EPÉHY

A general advance with the 12th, 18th and 74th Divisions began on the 18th September. The attack was timed for 5.30 a.m., and the 10th K.S.L.I., in support of the 16th Devons, passed through and reached their objective by midday. A considerable number of prisoners was taken and one 7·7-cm. gun. 2nd Lieut. W. McK. Millar was killed and Captain S. M. Marshall, Captain T. M. Brooks and 2nd Lieut. W. E. Hallowes were wounded. The advance was continued on the following day, when 2nd Lieut. R. G. Shackles was killed. September 20th was spent in consolidating the line and preparing for a fresh attack on the Hindenburg line at Gillemont Farm. The advance on the 21st was successfully carried out, except that the leading battalions of the Brigade failed to clear a strong post known as the " Quadrilateral." The 10th K.S.L.I. set about the task of clearing this point, and met with severe opposition, supported by heavy enemy shelling, which caused many casualties. By midnight on the 21st the " Quadrilateral " was still intact. About 1 a.m. on the 22nd the 10th K.S.L.I. rallied, and advancing under cover of our guns made a determined effort to get into the " Quadrilateral." After desperate fighting a footing was established, and the " Quadrilateral " was won. Upwards of 100 German dead were counted, and 200 prisoners and 30 machine guns were captured. 2nd Lieut. J. J. Paterson was killed, and Lieut. N. B. Brooks and 2nd Lieuts. J. M. McIntyre and R. S. Dove were wounded. The battalion was relieved on the night of the 22nd and returned to support trenches, moving into reserve on the 24th. Total casualties for the operations, September 18th–22nd : Officers killed 3, wounded 7. Other ranks, killed 41, wounded 168. On the 25th September the 74th Division left the 4th Army to return north, and the battalion marched to Peronne to entrain for Villers Bretoneux. The following marched out of action on the 24th :—

Head-quarters : Lt.-Colonel H. J. Howell-Evans, Captain F. G. Madge, 2nd Lieut. P. B. Whittier, 2nd Lieut. S. B. Cornes, 43 other ranks ; A Company, Lieut. T. S. Luce, 67 other ranks ; B Company, Lieut. E. W. Coe, 2nd Lieut. J. H. Hepworth, 62 other ranks ; C Company, 2nd Lieut. C. Wood, 39 other ranks ; D Company, 2nd Lieut. E. T. Williams, 68 other ranks.

The following is an extract from a letter from Major-General E. Girdwood, commanding 74th Division, to Lt.-Colonel H. Heywood-Lonsdale " Your old battalion " did one of the finest bits of work of the whole show. " After fighting from 5.40 a.m. (on September 21st)

" until night, having heavy casualties, I had to call upon
" them to take a certain strong post before daylight
" They went in at 12.30 a.m. (September 22nd), killed
" over 100 Boches, took 200 prisoners and 30 machine
" guns. . . . They are all heroes." The following
telegram was received by the O.C. 10th K.S.L.I. from
G.O.C. 74th Division, dated September 22nd, 1918 :—

" Please convey my hearty congratulations to you and
" all ranks 10th K.S.L.I. on magnificent work done last
" night. . . . For tired troops to have gained such signal
" success under the most trying conditions reflects the
" greatest credit upon the battalion and Brigade. . . .
" Corps Commander wishes me also to convey his con-
" gratulations and thanks to you and all concerned. . . .
" B.G.C. will take an early opportunity of expressing
" his own appreciation."

On September 28th General Rawlinson, Commanding
4th Army, addressed a communication to the G.O.C.
74th Yeomanry Division, in which he expressed his regret
at losing the Division from his command. He referred
to the prominent part taken by the Division in the successful advance of the 4th Army and wrote : " Brought to
" this country from a hot climate, where they took part in
" a very different method of warfare, the 74th Division
" has quickly adapted itself to the altered conditions and
" has fought with a determination and courage which
" is beyond praise."

On September 28th the battalion arrived at Chocques
and from there marched to La Vallée, where they
remained till the end of the month. Whilst at La Vallée
a draft of 2 officers and 102 other ranks was received.

On October 3rd the battalion took over trenches east
of Herlies where, on the 4th, Captain G. W. Sparrow was
killed and 2nd Lieut. Blair wounded. On September
9th C Company attempted a raid on La Haie, which was
unsuccessful, due to a number of men of one platoon
being cut off, about 20 being captured. Considerable

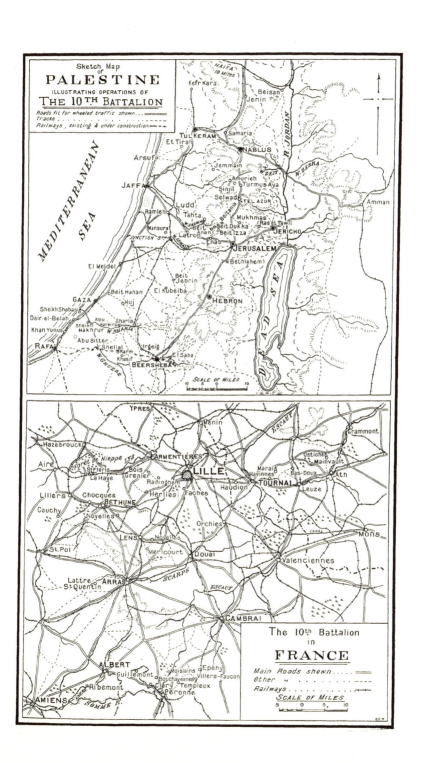

Sketch Map
of
PALESTINE
ILLUSTRATING OPERATIONS OF
THE 10TH BATTALION

Roads fit for wheeled traffic shown.....
Tracks ....
Railways, existing & under construction.----

The 10th Battalion
in
FRANCE

Main Roads shown......
Other   "   ......
Railways ....

SCALE OF MILES

casualties, however, were inflicted on the enemy and some prisoners were taken. During the raid Lieut. Moss was wounded and 25 other ranks. The platoon surrounded consisted mostly of a new draft. The battalion was relieved on October 10th and withdrew to Herlies. The 74th Division now began a steady advance on the retreating Germans. On the 17th the battalion reached Faches and received an enthusiastic welcome from the inhabitants, the 10th K.S.L.I. being the first Allied troops to enter the village since 1914. The battalion proceeded eastwards through Lesquin and Merchin to Haudion in Belgium, arriving there on October 20th. The battalion returned to the trenches at Marquain on the 30th where, on November 2nd, 2nd Lieut. T. Dodds was wounded during a raid on the enemy trenches.

On November the 9th the battalion drove the retreating enemy out of Tournai. The 10th K.S.L.I. were first across the river, and thus captured, for the second time, a town the name of which the regiment has borne upon its colours for a hundred and thirty years. The following communication was received by the G.O.C. 74th Division on September 9th: " The glorious British " Army has just liberated the Town of Tournai, it has " also released from slavery a population to whom liberty " is the most precious possession. Our gratitude has no " limit and I cannot find words to express the joy we have " experienced. Will you please convey to the officers, " N.C.O.'s and men under your command our heartfelt " thankfulness and everlasting gratitude?

" Believe me, Yours sincerely,
" DIERICK,
" Burgomaster of Tournai."

At nightfall on November 9th the battalion moved to Marais, and on the 10th to Basdoux, thence via Ostiches to Mainvault, which was reached on the 17th. News of the signing of the Armistice arrived whilst at Ostiches, and was received by the men with little apparent enthusiasm. It is interesting to compare the effect this piece of news produced amongst those at home and those on the battlefields. To the soldier it seems to have been unreal, and far less exhilarating than news of seven days' leave.

On November 18th the battalion arrived at Havinnes, where it remained until December 15th, moving on the 17th to Gramont. On January 26th, 1919, the battalion represented the Brigade in a parade before the King of the Belgians in Brussels. The cadre of the battalion returned to Shrewsbury on June 21st, 1919.

CHAPTER IX

THE DEPOT

THE following account is contributed by Colonel A. H. Doyle :—

In 1913, having reached the retiring age, I was fortunate enough on mobilization to be recalled to command the depot at Shrewsbury and the 53rd Area. Accordingly, on August 6th, 1914, I arrived at barracks at 5.30 p.m. and took over command. On mobilization the depot was automatically divorced from the 3rd Battalion and became a separate unit, with strength as laid down in *War Establishments*.

The depot was officered as under :—

O.C. Depot and 53rd Area, and competent military authority Shropshire, Herefordshire and Radnorshire—Colonel A. Doyle.

Second in command: Major Buchanan.

Quartermasters: Until August, 1917, Captain Wilson; afterwards, Captain Shearwood.

Recruiting officers: Major Cotton, Captain Willoughby Cotton, Captain Jackson and Lieut. Breffit.

Sgt.-Major Evans was appointed Sergeant-Major, and Quartermaster-Sgt. Hildrich was the Quartermaster-Sergeant.

The Army Reserve came pouring in, and it was pleasant to see again the faces of men I had served with. They were rapidly equipped and dispatched to the 1st Battalion. On August 11th the 3rd Battalion left for Pembroke Dock, 1,320 strong, under Major H. M. Smith. On the 10th orders to form the 5th Battalion arrived, and the depot became a perfect hive of industry, men swarming to enlist. The buildings were utterly inadequate, and part of the Guildhall and the next house were taken over as recruiting offices. The attestation of a man takes some time, and if ever such a mobilization occurs again it is to be hoped that the men may take the oath of allegiance in batches, and then have the right of soldiers, the proper attestation to take place when there is more leisure.

The supply of attestation papers was soon exhausted. The War Office was written to, and telegraphed to, and replied that there were no supplies available, and that they were to be *written* out—not very helpful. A copy was sent down to a local printer, who printed 2,000 copies in about sixteen hours at a very moderate rate. The Government contractor, a week later, wrote that unheard-of penalties could be inflicted for this breach of the regulations, but no notice was taken. War Office inspectors were exceedingly complimentary at the way this difficulty had been met.

The 5th Battalion was sent off to Blackdown by companies, the last company leaving August 27th.

From the time of enlistment drill and training were carried on; besides our own instructors we had the loan of some police and prison warders. Metropolitan police 5, Shropshire police 5, Shrewsbury warders 2, Hereford warders 2, Royal Marine instructor 1. These were of the greatest value, and when they were withdrawn we all agreed we never wished to meet with better comrades. The keenness of the men to learn was wonderful. At the end of the first week an experienced drill instructor said to me that in peace time he should have thought the squads had been a month or six weeks on the square.

The formation of the 6th Battalion began towards the end of August; companies were formed at Bridgnorth, Ludlow, Oswestry, Whitchurch, Wellington and Oakengates. They left for Blackdown September 10th. The formation of the 8th Battalion began September 1st, curiously enough before the 7th, and they were hurried off on September 14th, under Captain Jackson, to Lewes. The depot, in peace time, is supposed to accommodate 248 men, but in September, 1914, as many as 1,500 were sleeping there. A few structural alterations were admirably carried out by the acting Pioneer-Sergeant, such as an extra door to the men's mess-room, as dinners were in four or five reliefs, and wooden steps were erected to facilitate communications between offices. The War Office also erected tin huts for two companies in the recreation field.

Drafts were sent off daily, but the shortage of kit caused some delay. Permission was therefore asked to buy certain articles locally, but was refused. The congestion at the depot was so great, however, that it became necessary to disregard this order; and the list of articles purchased privately was a long one—6,000 shirts, 4,700 pairs of drawers, 6,200 pairs of boots, 1,500 great coats, 4,000 jerseys, 7,800 pairs of socks, and many other articles. Until the letter from Lord Kitchener to O.C. Depots, holding them responsible that everything was supplied, arrived, there was a somewhat uneasy feeling that the O.C. Depot might have to pay for most of these things himself; but after the Secretary of State's intervention all accounts were passed at once. We were again highly commended by War Office inspectors for having anticipated matters.

September 19th, 1914, the depot was fortunate enough to secure the services of Colonel E. V. D. Pearse, from retired list South Staffords, an officer with an unequalled knowledge of the King's Regulations whose assistance was invaluable. He was appointed Adjutant, and worked indefatigably in that capacity till posted to Records, Farnborough, February, 1918.

On September 14th the formation of the 7th Battalion began, and it left for Codford, Wilts, under Lieut. Linton, September 26th. The 9th Battalion was formed November 1st, and 950 men were sent to Pembroke Dock early in November. Major G. L. Buchanan left to join the 3rd Battalion, and was relieved on November 1st by Captain Luke.

In November, 1914, two hundred Royal Artillery were attached, but with no officer or N.C.O. Since their dress was rather peculiar, owing to delay in the issue of uniform, they were inclined to invite ridicule from some

303

of the other troops of the garrison, and information was received that on their last night they meant to take vengeance for the slights they had received. On the afternoon of that day they were paraded, and I congratulated them on their good behaviour, of which I told them I should inform their future commanding officers, and I begged them to keep it up; and the night in town passed off quietly.

In the spring of 1915 part of the recreation field was dug up and turned into a kitchen garden. This was admirably looked after by Captain Luke, and in the autumn of 1915 supplied the men in barracks with vegetables for a month, and in 1916 and 1917 for six weeks, a great saving to the mess books.

In June, 1916, two harvest companies were attached, and encamped on the race-course. In December a Substitution Company was formed to take men fit for service abroad and substitute men who had served abroad, and who though unfit to go back were fit to do the jobs of the "indispensables." In February, 1917, No. 423 Agricultural Company was formed under command of Captain Sir Beville Stanier, with Lieut. Charlton to assist him. In September Major Anderson took over command of this company.

The O.C. Depot was also O.C. Troops, Shrewsbury, the garrison of which at times amounted to about 3,000 men. The depot policed the garrison, and the conduct of all ranks was excellent.

As time went on the depot became the gathering ground of men discharged from hospital, who were waiting till fit enough to rejoin their battalions abroad. We had many sad cases, but they were on the whole extraordinarily cheerful, and one heard many a good story, which they enjoyed telling possibly "with advantage," the pleasantest touch of all being their pride and confidence in their officers. These men were entertained generally once a week, both by private persons and public bodies, notably the Pengwerne Boat Club; on these occasions beer, not exceeding three glasses, was allowed, and there never was the smallest unpleasantness. Our Medical Officer, Colonel Cureton, looked after these men in a way which excited our most lively admiration, and though on one or two occasions on the point of breaking down from over work, he was able to continue to the end of the war.

In 1916 the service for the first seven Divisions was held in the Albert Hall; tickets were sent to me to distribute and a good many wounded officers and men were able to go. A very pleasant recollection was the meeting of an officer of the 7th Battalion in the train on his way back to France, who got two extra days' leave to attend it. A wonderful service; the singing of " O little mighty force," and Lord Balfour's reading of the lesson " Now let us praise famous men," will not easily be forgotten. One story I heard in barracks from an officer, now alas dead, is, I think, worthy of record, as it illustrates the spirit of the Shropshire lads who went out from there. In the early part of the war the 1st Battalion were in trenches and there had been an attack, in which they had suffered severely. As there was a lull, a man (I wish I knew his name) thought he would have a smoke, and made his preparations, but not getting on very well, called out across two dead comrades, to a living one further down the trench: " I say, Bill, this 'ere Belgian tobacco and French matches will be the *death* of me some day."

All this time recruiting for the Army was going on increasingly. Major Cotton and his assistant recruiting officers worked at very high pressure, for the first three months, often from nine in the morning till after midnight. A great many posters were sent down by the War Office, and some were printed locally, a number being very good; among the best was one by Lieut. Breffitt, who illustrated Harold Begbie's poem. I believe some other regiments afterwards took this poster, but as he said to me " they can't get away from the bugles on the caps." Three or four times a week there were recruiting meetings which

x   305 had to be attended in different parts of the area, and the recruiting offices had to be visited, which, in Hereford-shire and Radnorshire, frequently entailed long days and nights of travelling. It is to be regretted that the exact number of men enlisted for the whole war cannot be stated, as towards the end of the war recruiting was in the hands of the Ministry of National Service, now defunct. Neither the depot, nor Record Office, nor the regional officers of pensions can help me; and the latest return is from August, 1914, to February 26th, 1917, inclusive.

	Shropshire.	Herefordshire.	Radnorshire.
Men enlisted	12,679	5,471	721
Mobilized from groups	6,527	2,957	481
„ „ classes	1,636	619	264
Grand total	20,860	9,847	1,466
Population	246,307	113,088	22,590
Percentage	8·46	7·99	6·48

Total enlistments 31,373
Total population 381,985
Percentage 8·08

One rather amusing incident occurred to me one morn-ing. A man came up to the recruiting office and demanded his day's pay, but was found not to be registered, so could not receive it. On enquiry why he was not registered, he hesitated for some time, but at last said to me, "Well, sir, I don't want it generally known, but as from *one gentle-man to another*, I was in Portland Prison." He had been, I believe, a valet convicted of theft.

When compulsory service was introduced and the tribunals were started, they performed their somewhat thankless duties with care, impartiality and sympathy. There were a few weak ones, but these were generally in the most out-of-the-way country districts, so that the net

THE DEPOT. FEBRUARY, 1917

result was not so much affected, and the appeal tribunal
was able to adjudicate when any glaring case of a
supposed indispensable was brought forward. There
were happily very few cases of conscientious objectors. There was one gentleman with three great sons,
who all came under this category. He claimed to be
descended from Thomas Plantagenet, Earl of Norfolk,
eldest son of Edward I by his second wife Margaret,
daughter of Philip III, King of France. Thinking it
might possibly do some good, I wrote him a chaffing letter,
saying that my wife, as a Howard, was also descended
from this gentleman, and that she felt sure, that when
blows were going and every man in England was wanted,
their common ancestor would turn in his grave at the
behaviour of his descendants. It was quite a private
letter and no rank was signed, as it was not impossible
that a very insolent letter might be received back. A
very civil answer was returned, but of such a character
as to suggest that future correspondence on the subject
would be a waste of time.

In 1917 the recruiting staff had grown so large that it
became necessary to take over the Raven Hotel as a recruiting office; and there were several cases of disappointed
travellers being turned away.

The work of Competent Military Authority in addition
to the recruiting took up a good deal of time. In this we
were most fortunate in having the whole-hearted assistance of the County and Borough Chief Constables and
police generally, and there never was the smallest friction
on any point whatever.

The first question to be considered was the regulation
of the liquor traffic, and this was interfered with as little
as possible, except that " treating " was prohibited in the
area. It appeared that ten or twelve men or youths used
to go out together, and one man would stand drinks at
the first public-house, another at the next, and so on,
till all had paid their round, and everyone would return
having drunk ten or twelve glasses of beer. This was a

307

very grave abuse, and it was quite time it was stopped. In 1915 a card was sent to me to enter my protest against the issue of rum to men in the trenches, quoting the opinions of many Generals on the danger and disadvantage of the rum ration. I replied that at one time or another I had dined with several of the Generals thus mentioned, with some on service, and with none had the precept been followed by practice. With one prominent General, who I believe was a great opponent of the issue of rum, I dined in South Africa, and he drank whisky and sparklet at dinner, and had one or two glasses of port afterwards. After that to object to a man's tot of rum seemed to me inconsistent.

There were a good many scares of spies, and reports of lights in the sky, to be investigated. After going carefully into the matter with the Chief Constable concerned, we came to the conclusion that the reports arose chiefly from cars travelling at night, and going up a steep incline, when naturally the lights were projected upwards. On one occasion a gentleman, living in the Severn Valley, reported that on one of the highest hills in Shropshire, above his house, there was a lonely farm, and that every night between 10 and 10.30 a light was hoisted on to a flagstaff; that the inhabitants were mysterious, and that if we could visit it we ought to bring an armed party. Major Cotton and I went down, armed to the teeth, climbed the hill, and got close under the house by 10 p.m. About 10.10 a particularly bright star, I believe Sirius, appeared above the house, and our friend exclaimed, " There, there, what did I tell you? " There was no flagstaff near the house at all that we could see.

On another occasion a trustworthy gentleman made a report to Chester which was referred to me. He explained that there was a light on one or other of the highest hills in his neighbourhood every night, but never on the same hill twice consecutively. He believed the purpose was to establish communication between submarines in the North Sea and those in the Irish Channel.

He used to bicycle night after night to try and surprise them, but always failed to do so as the centre light was surrounded by a cordon of lesser lights, which on his approach used to wave and give the alarm, and by the time he arrived everything had disappeared. I pointed out that if this was correct it meant the employment of a very large number of agents, and agents of a very high class, as otherwise someone would have given the show away. However, he still stuck to it, and also to his suspicions of certain country houses within a radius of thirty miles of his residence. His evidence regarding one house was so circumstantial that accompanied by the Chief Constable of the County we raided it one day; great care was taken that nothing should be injured, the police producing keys to open doors, drawers and cupboards in the most surprising way. The place was supposed to be filled with explosives, but was as bare as Mother Hubbard's cupboard, and after this I begged my keen and excellent friend to curb his imagination a little, and we had fewer scares in future.

On another occasion in 1915 a mysterious motor-car was reported to be travelling about Herefordshire with two foreigners. The number of the car having been obtained, it was ordered to be detained wherever found. It fortunately turned up at Shrewsbury, and on going down to the police-station the two foreigners proved to be Prince Antoine Bibesco, of the Roumanian Legation, and his brother.

In 1916 a mysterious foreigner was reported to be living in a lonely farm on the Longmynd, between Church Stretton and Bishop's Castle. He was supposed to be there to facilitate the landing of German aeroplanes, and one day we visited his house in the early morning. He said he was an Englishman, and had made a study of longevity, and was living there for that reason, as he had discovered there was one per cent more ozone in the air on the Longmynd than anywhere else in England. His appearance certainly bore out his story. He appeared to be no more than sixty, whereas he had been born at Glasgow in 1840, and was in fact seventy-six.

In 1917 the Assistant Provost-Marshal visited barracks and reported that a certain hotel in Llandrindod Wells was pro-German, that the hall porter was a German, and that they were very rude to soldiers. He begged me not to put it out of bounds to soldiers, which was what they wanted, but to close it entirely. It sounded a curious story and I declined to act till the complaint was put in writing; after some delay this was done. I went down to Llandrindod Wells and was most courteously received, and found that the hall porter was not a German. The evidence of officers and their wives was taken, in which they all stated that they had received every attention; it was a lesson to me never to act on verbal complaints.

Shrewsbury was visited at least once by Zepps, but no damage was done in the town. In February, 1917, I was ordered to select some positions for anti-aircraft defences, after the worst blizzard for years—the Brown Cleet a sheet of ice, and Harley Hill as bad; the car on one occasion turned completely round and descended the hill backwards. The idea never materialized.

In 1917 nine Sein Feiners came to the guard-room *en route* for Herefordshire. The Chief Constable, owing to the fact that Irish were employed in the munition works at Hereford, asked me to keep them away from that place, and to fix their place of residence at Ross and Leominster. But orders came from Chester that the military were not to interfere, and that it was to be left to the police. The Chief Constable forwarded a protest stating that he was powerless to make the men live at any particular place, but that the C.M.A. could do so, and could give orders they were not to move more than so many miles away. The order was, however, persisted in, and Captain Stanhope, the Chief Constable, being most helpful, we did manage between us to keep them away from Hereford, which was what was wanted, but it seemed a most futile way of dealing with the matter. The recommendation for the licensing

310

of arms and ammunition also came under the C.M.A., but these recommendations being on printed forms this work did not take up much time.

In conclusion, I think I may say that the depot did its duty, and was happy in having no history. We were exceedingly fortunate in our relations with the civil population. Everyone, from the Lords-Lieutenant downwards, clergy, county and borough chief constables, mayors, magistrates, police, schoolmasters, medical officers, railway employees, tradesmen, licensed victuallers, all seemed to combine to do everything they could to help the soldiers. Though there were thousands of more important commands held during the war, there could not have been a pleasanter one. The one sad remembrance is the thought of those magnificent fellows

> " The first proud mass of English manhood,
> A very sea of life,"

who passed out of that barrack gate, never more to return.

On the 31st January, 1917, Colonel A. H. Doyle relinquished command of the depot, being succeeded by Major A. T. C. Rundle. Captain T. H. Luke relieved Colonel E. V. D. Pearse as Adjutant, the latter having been appointed to the R.F.C. Record Office at Farnborough.

In June, 1918, the depot was selected as a reception depot for absentees under the Military Service Act, arrested in Ireland. These self-styled conscientious objectors consisted mostly of Jews from Leeds, communists from Glasgow and members of the Irish rebel army. The gymnasium and other buildings were utilized for their custody. Upwards of seventy were tried by court martial in two months.

Armistice Day was celebrated on the 12th November, 1918, when a parade of all troops was held. The National Anthems of Great Britain and the Allies were played and cheers given for the King, the Navy and Army.

THE KING'S SHROPSHIRE LIGHT INFANTRY

A special order was published on the 28th November, 1918, complimenting the troops on their behaviour in the town, the Chief Constable having reported that only fifteen cases of a civil nature had occurred since the outbreak of war; a remarkable record, considering the large numbers that had been at the depot.

Our prisoners of war from Germany began to arrive at the depot early in December, 1918, from the prisoners of war reception depot at Ripon. The majority showed obvious signs of the hardships they had undergone, looking ill and worn and depressed, in spite of their pleasure at being home again.

On the 3rd January, 1919, the depot started demobilizing, and the following month commenced to form the *post bellum* army.

In April the cadre of the 1st Battalion arrived and was received in the Market Square by the Mayor (Sir Samuel Morris) and Corporation. Later the cadres 6th, 7th and 8th Battalions arrived, ending with the 2nd Battalion in July, each in turn being received by the Mayor and Corporation, and afforded a heartfelt welcome.

CHAPTER X

THE RESERVE BATTALIONS

ONE result of the Haldane reorganization of our military forces was the transference of the old constitutional force the Militia—a Home Service force—into the Special Reserve, a force liable for service overseas and having the function, on mobilization, of training and supplying drafts to units in the fighting line.

On enlistment each recruit received six months' training at the depot, and was consequently well fitted in every respect when he joined his battalion for the annual monthly training.

In June, 1914, the 3rd K.S.L.I. carried out their annual training at Conway, at the termination of which every officer and man was passed "fit for active service." The battalion was up to its full establishment in non-commissioned officers and men, but short of six 2nd Lieutenants.

On August 4th, 1914, war with Germany having been declared, the calling-up notices were immediately despatched, and arrangements made for the complete mobilization of the battalion.

It would perhaps not be out of place to record that owing to the good recruiting work carried out by Major R. J. Bridgford, D.S.O., during the period he was in command of the depot, the 3rd Battalion on the day of its mobilization was able to parade at its full establishment.

The men of the Special Reserve (3rd K.S.L.I.) were of a solid, well set-up, type, drawn chiefly from the agricultural and labouring classes, but with a fair percentage of town men. Their behaviour at all times was exemplary, as the following extracts from letters will show:—

From Colonel R. J. Bridgford, Commanding the 2nd Battalion, K.S.L.I.

" I can certainly say while commanding the 2nd K.S.L.I.
" that the drafts we got from the 3rd K.S.L.I. were

" excellent. We received many hundreds of men from
" the 3rd K.S.L.I. actually during the Second Battle of
" Ypres, and we could not have wished for better men,
" and no men ever did better under the most tremendous
" difficulties. If I had to go through it all again, I would
" rather have the men I received from the 3rd Battalion
" than any I afterwards saw from any other regiment,
" and I saw a good many."

Letter from Officer Commanding Leinster Regiment,
4th August, 1917.

" I thought you would like to hear news of a draft of
" 108 men of the Shropshire L.I. who came to this
" battalion on the 29th July. On July 31st, as you know,
" the push had started. I was very loath indeed to take
" these men straight into battle, but, being very much
" under strength, I had no alternative. We came out
" after six days' continuous fighting, having suffered
" very heavy casualties. It was a terrible ordeal to put
" young and inexperienced men through. They were
" plunged into it barely twenty-four hours after their
" arrival.
" I have been out here since 1915 with this battalion.
" We thought we had been through hell on the Somme,
" at Guillemont, but the Somme was an entertainment
" in comparison.
" I had a very soft spot in my heart for this draft and
" kept a fatherly eye on them, and I can only say that I
" think they behaved magnificently; most of them were
" mere boys of nineteen, but they stuck it like old blooded
" troops.
" The King's Shropshire L.I. may well be proud of
" them and we are very proud to have them. We are
" just going in again for a second go.

" Yours sincerely,

" (Signed) G. A. M. Buckley."

In addition to the above, letters in the highest terms of praise were constantly being received from the O.C. 3rd Echelon at Rouen, regarding the drafts sent from the 3rd Battalion K.S.L.I. and the way in which they were equipped and trained.

On August 9th, 1914, the battalion was mobilized at the depot, Shrewsbury, and was joined by the surplus Army Reservists of the King's Shropshire L.I. who were not needed for immediate service, their number being approximately 800. On mobilization the following officers were posted for duty to the 1st Battalion stationed at Tipperary:—

> Lieut. J. A. S. Mitchell
>   ,,   F. L. Hulton-Harrop
>   ,,   C. E. Parker

The battalion, under the command of Lt.-Colonel T. Dickin, numbering 1,502, proceeded in three special trains to its war station at Pembroke Dock.

Great interest was taken in the departure of the battalion by the inhabitants of Shrewsbury, and the streets were crowded as the troops marched to the railway station, headed by the Shrewsbury Borough Band, and they were cheered with much enthusiasm from Copthorne to Castle Gates. The streets of Frankwell, Mardol and Pride Hill were lined with women and children to bid God-speed to their soldier men. Thus, to the strains of "It's a long, long way to Tipperary," did the 3rd K.S.L.I. leave their county town of Shrewsbury—1,500 of as finely set-up men as ever wore uniform.

As an example of zeal displayed, it may be recorded that a gentleman (who had previously served in the army) was promised a commission in the battalion in the morning, fitted himself out during the day with borrowed uniform, and marched out with his new battalion the same day.

The officers who accompanied the battalion were, in addition to the commanding officer:—

THE KING'S SHROPSHIRE LIGHT INFANTRY

Major H. M. Smith, D.S.O.,
„ Hon. F. H. S. Weld Forester

Captain C. R. B. Wingfield	Lieut. I. Rivers Bulkeley
„ F. G. P. Philips	„ J. R. Pound
„ W. J. Brooke	„ R. S. Whitmore
„ E. C. L. van Cutsem	„ F. C. Bird
„ D. H. Leslie	„ S. H. Starey

Adjutant: Captain A. P. Bowen
Quartermaster: Captain A. R. Woodland
Regimental Sgt.-Major T. Avery

On arrival at Pembroke Dock the battalion was first encamped near Llanion Barracks, adjacent to the 3rd Battalion South Wales Borderers, the Brigade Staff at Pembroke Dock being Br.-General B. G. Stavert; Staff officers, Captain A. T. C. Rundle, K.S.L.I., and Lieut. J. G. Bosvile, the troops at Pembroke Dock being under the command of Brig.-General C. P. Triscott. The first move of the battalion from Llanion was to Imble Lane Camp, adjoining Bush House, the residence of the Honorary Colonel of the battalion—Colonel Sir T. C. Meyrick, Bart.—detachments being stationed at Pennar Barracks, Golden Hill and Pembroke Green Camps.

After mobilization, recruits joined steadily in such large numbers that the utmost difficulty was experienced in fitting out the men with clothing and other necessaries. The first men to join were the enthusiastic volunteers— also retired N.C.O.'s and men who had completed their period of service with the colours, and in the Army Reserve, and joined in response to the appeal issued by Lord Kitchener. These men came forward in large numbers, and having learned the use of the Lee-Enfield rifle were ready for overseas drafts in quite a short time. After the first rush the physique of the recruits deteriorated somewhat, but the healthy life, regular food and exercise soon brought the men up to standard. The "Derby" scheme did not bring many men to the 3rd K.S.L.I.

By the latter part of 1915 the best men (physically) were recruited, and this may be accounted for by the fact that, on the outbreak of war, the farmers released those men whose services they could most easily spare. After the 1915 harvest was over, the farm hands and ploughmen, who had completed their year's engagement with their masters, became available and voluntarily enlisted in large numbers.

About this time many " men " who had enlisted under the age of seventeen were released, some of whom had already been wounded and completed a tour of service in France and Belgium. On conscription coming into force, men of superior education, drawn from all kinds of trades and professions, came into the battalion; they were not physically of so high a standard as the " farmer's boy," but training very quickly improved them in all ways.

In years previous to mobilization, 1914, the 1st Battalion was quartered at Pembroke Dock. In those days the officers and men had made hosts of friends, and consequently, when the 3rd Battalion came to be quartered there, it was received with open arms by all classes, for the 1st Battalion had been very popular and left a splendid name behind them.

Again, the Honorary Colonel of the 3rd Battalion, Sir T. C. Meyrick, Bart., who in previous years had commanded the battalion, was the owner of the estate at Pembroke Dock upon which the battalion was encamped for about three years. He presented a hut to the Y.M.C.A., with a proviso that it should be erected in the Shropshire camp, an act which was much appreciated by the men. Colonel F. Meyrick, his son, lived at Bush, and both he and Mrs. Meyrick showed the battalion every kindness.

In the early days of the war the difficulty of clothing and equipping the recruits, arriving daily in large numbers, was very great. The Army Clothing and Ordnance Department could not meet the demand, consequently a great deal of clothing, etc., had to be purchased locally, some of which can still be seen in the districts to this day (1923). It was well that the battalion had mobilized with many spare Army Reservists, because certain articles of clothing, such as boots, jackets and trousers, could be, and were, taken from them to complete the recruits. All such difficulties were, however, eventually overcome, and although the discomforts were many, they were cheerfully borne by all.

Recruits on arrival were inspected and, from the first day, were divided up and trained for the special work for which they seemed best fitted. For instance, men who were accustomed to control other men were set apart for training as N.C.O.'s, those with a mechanical turn of mind for the Machine Gun Corps; telegraphists were trained as signallers, but the large majority were trained for infantry duties.

From August 9th, 1914, to the 8th September, small drafts of men were sent to the 1st Battalion to replace unfit men, and it was not until the 15th September that the first draft of any size proceeded overseas. When this draft paraded the excitement was intense. The 3rd Battalion S.W. Borderers, in an adjoining camp, had dispatched a draft ten days earlier, and the K.S.L.I. thought the war would be over before they could get out! However, when the day came 100 Special Reservists, under the command of Lieut. F. L. Hulton-Harrop, left Imble Camp with 1,500 sorrowing men left behind. These men, however, did not forget to cheer, and wish their more fortunate comrades good luck and a safe return. Soon these drafts became the usual order of weekly affairs, until in one memorable and depressing period, early in 1915, the call for men was so great that no less than 1,300 men were sent overseas in a fortnight.

Each man proceeding overseas was presented with an enamel mug and supplied with a pair of socks, comforter or scarf, which had been knitted by many kind friends in Shropshire and Pembroke Dock, and presented to the

318

battalion. The thanks of officers and men are hereby recorded for these kind expressions of goodwill.

On November 17th, 1914, the Head-quarters of the battalion, with 800 men, proceeded to Colinton Barracks, Edinburgh, for duty, those remaining at Pennar Barracks, Pembroke Dock, being under the command of Major C. R. B. Wingfield, who was joined by Major G. L. Buchanan, Reserve of Officers, from the depot. Both at Pembroke Dock and Edinburgh the battalion was engaged in preparing drafts for the battalions of the Shropshire L.I. serving overseas.

In March, 1915, after a short stay at King's Park and Gillespie Schools, Edinburgh, the Head-quarters of the battalion returned to Pembroke Dock and was accommodated in hutments at Bush Camp, with detachments at Golden Hill, Pembroke Green, and in the barracks at Pennar.

The draft-finding services of the battalion continued, and weekly drafts, at the rate of 300–400 per month, were sent overseas to replace casualties in the 1st, 2nd, 5th, 6th and 7th Battalions, besides sending a nucleus of N.C.O.'s and men to form the 9th Battalion, men to form garrison battalions, and fifty men per month to the Machine Gun Corps at Grantham, the latter being specially selected men.

As the war progressed the training varied from time to time and many changes were experienced. On the outbreak of war the training was on somewhat similar lines to that which obtained during the South African War, 1899–1902, except that the training for " rapid " fire was worked up to a high pitch, and the advances and retirements were carried out in short rushes. The first change of importance was the emphasis laid upon the fitness of the soldier for long marches in full marching order, and the consequent necessity for good-fitting boots and frequent foot inspection. This was followed by constant practice in accurate bomb-throwing, in which undoubtedly the " cricketer " excelled, followed again by bomb-throwing in connection with trench work, relieving of trenches, revolver shooting for officers, and bayonet fighting over trenches.

There is no doubt the institution of the Boy Scouts played a helpful part in the war. It instilled discipline, taught self-reliance and gave a smattering of training, which in the hands of a good N.C.O. took only a short time to produce a man fit for the firing line. In the 3rd K.S.L.I. nearly all ex-Boy Scouts went to the N.C.O.'s training class, and, all credit to them, they deserved the trust placed in them.

The constant fluctuation of the strength of the battalion was a source of trouble to the Quartermaster, particularly as regards the catering for the men's comfort. At the outbreak of war the battalion consisted of 1,600 men, in addition to officers; in 1915 it rose to upwards of 110 officers and 3,300 men, while in March, 1918, the number dwindled to 356 all ranks, principally officers and N.C.O.'s. It was a great relief to the Quartermaster's department when an officer was appointed in charge of messing duties, a change which worked most satisfactorily.

On February 17th, 1917, to the great regret of all ranks, Lt.-Colonel T. Dickin left the 3rd Battalion K.S.L.I., with which he had served since 1889. He proceeded to France to the command of a Labour battalion. His successor was Major the Hon. F. H. S. Weld Forester, formerly second in command.

In December, 1917, the battalion was suddenly moved to Ireland to replace an Irish battalion at Crosshaven Hutments, Queenstown Harbour. The hutments being too small to accommodate the battalion, Fort Carlisle near by was also occupied. The majority of the officers lived at the Crosshaven Hotel.

After a very brief stay at Queenstown, the battalion was sent to Fermoy and occupied the New Barracks, while the overflow was accommodated at Kilworth Camp (service companies) and the Old Barracks. The strenuous work of draft finding was still continued, heavy calls being made for officers and men, many of whom had to be sent overseas without their customary period of short leave.

The battalion was inspected by Field-Marshal Sir J. French just before he was appointed Viceroy of Ireland, who said how pleased he was to inspect the regiment again, and informed them that everything in the battalion was progressing satisfactorily.

During its stay at Fermoy the " lighter side " was not neglected. The battalion was fortunate in possessing two officers, Lieuts. Nalder and Goldsmith, who gave excellent theatrical performances and ran a company, which was much appreciated by everyone. The King's Liverpool Regiment also sent their theatrical company to cheer up their old comrades.

The work in a Special Reserve Battalion was mostly carried out at high pressure, and it must be recorded that the way in which all ranks worked harmoniously together for the good of the regiment undoubtedly accounted for the high efficiency obtained, which was so freely spoken of by Inspecting Officers. In addition to this the splendid reputation gained by the battalion from the different townspeople, and in the station where they were carrying out their duties, was specially gratifying.

During the war no less than 546 officers and 16,107 men were sent overseas to the various seats of war, including Salonika and Egypt. In addition men were sent to other units outside the county regiment, such as Garrison battalions, Labour battalions, Machine Gun Corps and other infantry units.

The following warrant officers and N.C.O.'s of the Permanent Establishment were granted commissions during the war:—

Quartermaster-Sergeant A. M. Watson	Quartermaster
Sergeant-Major T. Avery	2nd Lieutenant
Colour-Sergeant S. G. Beaumont	,,
,, O. Underhill	,,

Sergeant H. E. Steer ____ 2nd Lieutenant
Company Sergeant-Major J. Higginson ____ „
„ ____ „ ____ F. Tucker ____ „
„ ____ „ ____ W. V. Tucker ____ „

The following served as Adjutants to the battalion :—
Captain A. P. Bowen.
Lieut, T. Lloyd.
Captain T. D. Perkin.

The following served as Quartermasters :—
Major A. R. Woodland to September, 1918.
Lieut. J. Dunn.

The following were attached as Medical Officers :—
J. T. Dow. ____ J. Bradley Hughes.
R. Williams. ____ J. Wilkinson.

Draft-conducting Officers :—
Colonel Hon. R. H. Bertie. ____ Major G. R. Stephens.

The following officers of the battalion were killed in action or died of wounds, etc :—

Lieut. R. C. Adams-Posner ____ A.-Captain O. R. Lloyd
„ ____ T. Avery ____ Lieut. M. I. Machell
„ ____ J. S. H. Beamish ____ Captain C. J. Maclaverty
„ ____ A. C. P. Biddle-Cope ____ Lieut. D. F. Maclean
„ ____ F. C. Bird ____ Captain J. A. S. Mitchell
„ ____ C. R. Blackett ____ Lieut. G. J.A. S. O'Fflahertie
Captain W. J. Brooke ____ „ ____ T. Onslow
Lieut. H. H. Buckley ____ „ ____ A. B. Owen
„ ____ W. B. Burns ____ Captain F. L. Platt
„ ____ S. L. Cannon ____ Lieut. C. E. Postles
„ ____ J. V. Church ____ Captain J. R. Pound
„ ____ F. R. Currie ____ A.-Captain V. E. Powell
„ ____ G. H. Davies ____ Lieut. R. G. Pugh
„ ____ A. O. Egerton ____ „ ____ R. G. Shackles
A.-Captain A. Fox ____ „ ____ H. S. Sherwood
Lieut. S. J. Goodchild ____ „ ____ D. C. Hair

THE RESERVE BATTALIONS

Lieut. C. P. Hazard
„ D. G. Hazard
„ G. C. D. Hill
T.-Captain E. G. James
Lieut. C. W. Jeffreys
„ E. G. M. King
„ J. A. Lee
„ J. D. G. Lewis
„ G. K. Lloyd

Captain B. H. Sparrow
Lieut. C. Steward
Captain J. K. Symonds-
Taylor
A.-Captain R. G. Thomson
„ A. J. T. Topham
Lieut. G. R. Venables
„ I. P. Williams
„ W. F. Woolf

A large number of casualties also occurred to N.C.O.'s and men of the 3rd Battalion in common with those of other units, and it is pleasing to record that the names of the fallen are perpetuated in the parish churches of Pembroke Dock and Pembroke by a carved screen in the former and a stained glass window in the latter, erected to those who were stationed at the Golden Hill and Green Camps, and who lost their lives at the front.

The 9th (Reserve) Battalion K.S.L.I. was formed November 1st, 1914, and was stationed at Pembroke Dock, later moving, under command of Colonel J. M. Ransom (I.A. retired), to Prees Heath, near Whitchurch, in Shropshire. The 9th Battalion remained at Prees Heath throughout the war, training drafts and sending out reinforcements of officers to the service battalions of the K.S.L.I. Although designated, at a later period, the 49th Training Reserve Battalion, when the personnel became mixed with officers and men of other regiments, the spirit and traditions of the K.S.L.I. were always preserved.

The reserve battalions of the Territorial Army consisted of the 2/4th and 3/4th, which later became the 4th Reserve Territorial Force Battalion.

The 2/4th was formed at Shrewsbury in October, 1914, under command of Lt.-Colonel E. L. Cunliffe. The 2/4th K.S.L.I. served successively at Shrewsbury, Barry Dock, Cardiff, Sittingbourne, the Isle of Man, Bedford and Aldeborough until becoming, in December, 1916, the 50th Provisional Battalion.

THE KING'S SHROPSHIRE LIGHT INFANTRY

The 3/4th K.S.L.I. was formed in May, 1915, under command of Lt.-Colonel J. H. Cooke at Shrewsbury. Lt.-Colonel R. H. T. Symonds-Taylor succeeded to command of the battalion in November, 1915. The battalion was stationed at Oswestry, Tenby and Swansea. Whilst at Swansea in 1917 the 2nd Battalion Herefordshire Regiment was amalgamated with the 3/4th K.S.L.I.

On 25th August, 1916, the 3/4 K.S.L.I. became known as the 4th (Reserve) Battalion, and was disbanded whilst under command of Lt.-Colonel J. Fane at Pembroke Dock after the Armistice.

CHAPTER XI

ACTIVITIES AT HOME

THE V.A.D. movement in Shropshire, with which in this short report is included the activities of the St. John's Ambulance Association and the British Red Cross Society, was organized by the County Director, Colonel Cureton, in 1910. At the outbreak of war there were in being in the county 24 women's and 5 men's detachments.

Owing to the energy of Colonel Cureton, and the prescience of the commandants, these detachments were in a highly efficient state. On January 1, 1915, when Colonel Cureton's services were required by the W.O., the following hospitals had already been opened and occupied.

HOSPITAL	COMMANDANT
Cynfield, Shrewsbury	Mrs. Bather
Baschurch	Miss Hunt
Attingham Park	Mrs. Van Bergen
Oakley Manor	Miss Hughes
Essex House, Church Stretton	Miss Urry
Quarry Place	Mrs. Derriman
Sharrington	Hon. Mrs. Heywood-Lonsdale

Seven others were ready for occupation :

HOSPITAL	COMMANDANT
Broughall Cottage	Mrs. Lambert
Broadway House, Church Stoke	Miss Montford
Hatton Grange, Shifnal	Lady Mabel Kenyon Slaney
Trimpley Hall, Ellesmere	Mrs. Mainwaring
Market Drayton Cottage Hospital	Hon. Mrs. Heathcote
Leintwardine	Mrs. Jebb

On Colonel Cureton's resignation, Lord Powis, President of the Shropshire Territorial Force Association, asked Mr. William Swire of Longden Manor, Shrewsbury, to take over the duties of County Director. Fortunately Mr. Swire accepted, and although the work grew to be almost beyond the power of one man, he kept to his post for the duration of the war. Mr. Swire's extraordinary powers of organization, his tact and inexhaustible patience made the voluntary work in Shropshire an unparalleled success. During the next years the following hospitals were opened :—

HOSPITAL	COMMANDANT
Ardmillan, Oswestry	Mrs. Ridley Thomas
Earlsdale, Pontesford	Mrs. Jameson and Miss Ellison
Cheswardine	Mrs. Donaldson Hudson
Hildern, Shifnal	Mrs. Reid-Walker
Hodnet Hall	Mrs Heber Percy
Longford Hall	The Hon. Mrs. Leeke
Pellwall Hall	Mr. Munro Walker
Pentrepant Hall	Mrs. Montgomery
Peplow Hall	Lady Stanier
Seven Sisters, Ellesmere	Mrs. Mainwaring
Oteley, Ellesmere	Mrs. Mainwaring
Cloverley, Market Drayton	The Hon. Mrs. Blezard
Westholme, Market Drayton	The Hon. Mrs. Heathcote
The Lodge, Ludlow	Mrs. Kennedy
Walcot, Lydbury North	Miss Garnett Botfield
Aston Hall, Aston-on-Clun	Miss Garnett Botfield
Wellington College	Mr. Bailey, Mrs. Bayliss
Worfield, Bridgnorth	Mrs. H. Corbett
St. George's, Pontesbury	Mrs. Seddon

The civil hospitals which gave beds were :—

HOSPITAL	MATRON
Royal Salop Infirmary, Shrewsbury	Miss Garside
Eye, Ear and Throat Hospital, Shrewsbury	Miss Gill

HOSPITAL	MATRON
Lady Forester Hospital	Miss M. Smith
Lady Forester Hospital, Broseley	Miss C. Morris
Cottage Hospital, Oswestry	Mrs. Mason
Cottage Hospital, Whitchurch	Miss E. Middlemist
Cottage Hospital, Wellington	Miss Darrell
The Infirmary, Bridgnorth	Miss H. M. Bailie

In May, 1916, the War Office took over the buildings belonging to the Atcham Board of Guardians at Berrington, and a Central War Hospital was founded in these buildings which administered Shropshire, Hereford, Radnor, etc. A certain number of the hospitals in Shropshire received cases direct from the ambulance trains from Dover and Southampton, a compliment to their high standard of medical skill, nursing and equipment.

Sir William Gray gave Hawkstone Park as an officers' hospital in 1915, and it was constantly and appreciatively used.

It is interesting to give the names of the detachments and their commandants in January, 1915.

WOMEN'S DETACHMENTS

2.	Shrewsbury	Miss Hughes	St. John's
4.	Madeley	Miss Foley Evans	,,
6.	Ironbridge	Mrs. White	,,
8.	Shrewsbury	Mrs. Derriman	Red Cross
10.	Meole Brace	Mrs. Bather	,,
14.	Baschurch	Miss Hunt	,,
16.	Wem	Mrs. Stapleton Cotton	,,
18.	Shifnal	Lady M. Kenyon Slaney	,,
20.	Bolas	Mrs. W. Dugdale	St. John's
22.	High Ercall	Miss Brooks	Red Cross
24.	Oswestry	Lady Lloyd	,,
26.	Whitchurch	Mrs. Lambert	,,
28.	Bridgnorth	Mrs. Wood	,,
30.	Ludlow	Miss Marston	,,
32.	Shrewsbury	Miss Strange	,,

327

34.	Church Stretton	Miss Urry	St. John's
36.	Ellesmere	Mrs. Mainwaring	Red Cross
38.	Whittington	Mrs. Ridley Thomas	,,
40.	Gobowen	Mrs. Montgomery	,,
42.	Worfield	Mrs. H. Corbett	St. John's
44.	Bishop's Castle	Miss Garnett Botfield	Red Cross
46.	Market Drayton	Hon. Mrs. Heathcote	St. John's
48.	Leintwardine	Mrs. Jebb	Red Cross
50.	Broseley	Miss H. Potts	St. John

Since January 1, 1915, the following detachments were formed —

52.	Westbury	Mrs. Gray	Red Cross
54.	Pontesbury	Mrs. Jameson	St. John's
56.	Hanwood	Mrs. Chitty	,,
58.	Wellington	Mrs. Bayliss	,,
60.	Shifnal	Mrs. Reid Walker	Red Cross
	Reserve Shropshire.	Mrs. R. Sandford	

MEN'S DETACHMENTS

Shrewsbury	Dr. Woodwad Riley	St. John's
Baschurch	Mr. W. Lewis	Red Cross
Whitchurch	General P. T. Baston	,,
Oswestry	Dr. A. Lewis	,,
Bridgnorth	Major W. Westcott	

Of course, the men's detachments became very much smaller as the members were required for the Volunteer Force, service overseas, etc., but the Shrewsbury detachment St. John's Ambulance Brigade, under Ambulance Officer Percy Allen, kept up its numbers well, and had upwards of sixty members.

The V.A.D. members working in the county were beyond all praise. Although very many would have preferred serving abroad, the girls and women stuck fast to their posts, and did all the hospital drudgery as well as the interesting nursing with great courage and patience. In 1919 when Shropshire gave its great " Welcome Home " to Shropshire troops who had served abroad, it was unanimously decided to ask the nursing detachments to walk in the procession and receive the praise that was their due.

The honours awarded by the King were :—

COMMANDER OF THE ORDER OF THE BRITISH EMPIRE

William Swire, Esq.

OFFICER OF THE ORDER OF THE BRITISH EMPIRE

Mrs. Bather	Mrs. Urwick
Mrs. Mainwaring	Mrs. van Bergen

ROYAL RED CROSS

Miss Garside	Miss Agnes Hunt

MEMBER OF THE ORDER OF THE BRITISH EMPIRE

Miss C. Kendall	Mrs. Barnett
Mrs. Lambert	Mrs. Herber Percy
Miss Marston	Mrs. Ridley Thomas

W. H. Novis, Esq.

ASSOCIATE ROYAL RED CROSS

Sister Anne Farmer	Miss C. E. Hughes
Sister Lily Griffiths	Miss Morris
Lady Headlam	Miss Murray
Sister M. Smith	

A hostel was started by V.A.D. members in Shrewsbury in 1916. No. 3 Council House Court was rented and most ably managed by Lady Norman, who served for two years. Naturally the financial difficulties became very great as the years wore on. Mr. Bridgeman, the then Home Secretary, came forward and offered to raise a collection all over the county. This produced £2,785. The Farmers' Red Cross sales were excellent mediums for collecting money, and Sir Beville Stanier had a system of Red Cross collecting-boxes which raised large sums. Church collections, theatrical, and various entertainments all did useful work and the County Fund kept going until the end of the war. The work of Mr. Swire's staff, in his central office, was very fine, and among many devoted servers the names of Mr. Novis and Mrs. Rowan Robinson (now Mrs. Mavrocordato) stand out prominently.

One of the most difficult questions was that of transporting the patients from trains to hospitals, and in the early days of the war this transportation was undertaken by Shrewsbury tradesmen and their commercial cars, and by private cars from friends near. Later, however, many ambulances were given. Mr. and Mrs. Logan of Overley gave a 36 h.p. Panhard, Lt.-Colonel and Mrs. Donaldson Hudson a 30 h.p. Hotchkiss and Miss Hallowes a 40 h.p. Napier. The people of Shrewsbury gave a Ford "two cot" car, and Mr. R. E. Jones of Oakley Grange gave a "four-stretcher" Ford. Mr. and Mrs. Heber Percy and the parishioners of Hodnet gave a 36 h.p. Renault ambulance which was used at Berrington. Major and Mrs. Mainwaring ran a "four stretcher" car to Ellesmere. Oswestry gave two ambulances. Broughall and Market Drayton each had an ambulance, and Mr. Hall of Hales Hall lent his private car whenever necessary.

The private cars of Major Browne, Mr. M'Corquodale, Mr. Bibby and Mr. Phillipps always came when wanted, as did the cars of the Salop Steam Laundry, the Co-operative Stores, Messrs. Maddox, Messrs. Blower and numerous others.

The Voluntary Aid Organization was a great institution, and bands of women worked at the Ladies' Club, Shrewsbury, where the garments made by work parties throughout the county were collected and packed.

Mrs. Donaldson Hudson, Mrs. van Bergen and Mrs. Urwick were some of the outstanding workers in this department. There were Red Cross work-rooms in every village and town, and swabs, bandages and garments of all kinds were supplied in tens of thousands. The head depot in Shrewsbury, in which about 150 ladies worked, was most ably managed by Lady Stanier, Miss Neilson, Mrs. Blower, Miss Stevenson, Mrs. Hallowes, Miss Evans, Miss Lloyd Oswell, Miss Wright and Mrs. Clark.

ACTIVITIES AT HOME

Wounded men coming in on ambulance trains, and men passing through Shrewsbury to hospitals, were all given food, thanks to the energies of Mr. Hughes, Mrs. Davis, Mrs. Urwick and a band of women workers.

Foremost amongst the voluntary funds started in Shropshire and Herefordshire for the counties' fighting men must be mentioned :—

THE KING'S SHROPSHIRE LIGHT INFANTRY PRISONERS OF WAR FUND

(Registered under War Charities Act, 1916), which was organized as follows :—

PATRONS

The Earl of Powis, Lord-Lieutenant of Shropshire
Sir John Cotterell, Bart, Lord-Lieutenant of Herefordshire

PRESIDENT

Mrs. Reade

VICE-PRESIDENTS

Captain Sir Beville Stanier, Bart., M.P.
Colonel A. Doyle, Colonel C. K. Wood,
Major A. T. Rundle

COMMITTEE

Mrs. Doyle	Mayor of Shrewsbury
Mrs. Higginson	,, ,, Hereford
Mrs. Horace Smith	,, ,, Leominster
Mrs. Urwick, O.B.E	,, ,, Ludlow
Colonel O. R. Middleton	,, ,, Oswestry
Lt.-Colonel Symonds-Taylor	,, ,, Bishop's Castle
Captain MacAlister, M.B.E.	,, ,, Bridgnorth
Mr. T. B. Butcher	,, ,, Wenlock
Mr. Dickin	
Mr. Edge	
Mr. How	
Mr. W. H. Smith	

331

THE KING'S SHROPSHIRE LIGHT INFANTRY

This fund was started in June, 1915, at the suggestion of the commanding officers of the various battalions of the K.S.L.I., by Mrs. Luard, M.B.E., whose husband, Lt.-Colonel E. B. Luard, D.S.O., was in command of the 1st Battalion, then serving in the Ypres salient.

For the first few months parcels could be sent by relatives and friends of the men, and only extras, such as bread, clothing and tobacco, were supplied by the Fund.

In December, 1916, the War Office put forth a new scheme, as it had been found that parcels, purporting to be sent to prisoners of war by their friends, were in some cases being sent by German spies in this country to Germany, and a copy of an important chart was found concealed in a tin of lard! Also it was found that many of the private parcels never reached their destination owing to bad packing.

As a result of this scheme instructions were issued by the Government that only authorized Committees with registered packers should dispatch parcels, and full instructions were sent from time to time as to the most useful contents.

In January, 1917, therefore, Mrs. Luard with the most able assistance of Mr. T. B. Butcher of 7 Castle Street, Shrewsbury, who had undertaken the packing from the formation of the Fund, organized a staff of packers who began work at Mr. Butcher's own house, but in July,

1918, St Alkmund's Rooms had to be taken on a lease. Starting with four packers the staff had increased by January, 1918, to fourteen, and by November 11th, 1918, it had risen to 112, all of whom, together with a number of ladies who assisted in the clerical work done at Hereford, gave their services as voluntary workers. It is impossible to estimate the debt owed by the prisoners of war and the organizers of the fund to Mr. and Mrs. Butcher, and their daughter, who undertook the heavy task of keeping all lists and changes of address as forwarded by the Hon. Secretary.

On January 1st, 1918, thirty-four men were receiving parcels, on March 1st, ninety-six, and on Armistice Day over nine hundred men were having parcels dispatched to them. This rapid increase in numbers threw very heavy work on the whole staff, and the parcels could not have been dispatched had not Mr. Butcher and his helpers worked every day and all day, and one cannot say enough in praise of their splendid enthusiasm and devotion.

Three parcels a fortnight went to each man, costing, to begin with, 6/- each, but owing to the increase in prices this had risen to 10/- each in 1918. Each food parcel contained two tins of meat or of fish, oatmeal or other dry grain, jam or syrup, margarine or dripping, chocolate, soups, tea or cocoa, sugar, condensed milk, soap, salt, pepper, etc., and tinned vegetables, cake or some other extra was added when possible. Tobacco and cigarettes were included in the parcels, and bread specially prepared was sent from Berne and arrived in three to five days in a fresh and wholesome condition. Postcards were sent in each parcel addressed to the donor of the parcel, and a high percentage of these cards was received back signed by the recipient. Books were also sent occasionally, and any special request from a man, such as for a mouth-organ, or paints and brushes with which to paint scenes for a play, was always granted and the required article supplied.

Clothing was issued by the Government twice a year

to each man, and in addition to helping from the beginning in packing the food parcels, Mrs. Urwick, O.B.E., undertook to pack and dispatch the clothing, when it grew too large to be dealt with by the depot staff, which, however, with the T.F. Staff gave every assistance in its power.

In the earlier years of the war, when only a few men had to be dealt with, individual gifts of money from friends amply supplied the need, but the regiment suffered so heavily in the March fighting in 1918, that it became evident that a much larger fund would be required to supply the necessary parcels to the K.S.L.I. prisoners of war. Meetings were called at Shrewsbury and Hereford, and a magnificent response was the result. Almost every town and village in the two counties answered the appeal. A special fund was started by the *Wellington Journal* and the *Hereford Times*, and the following figures will give some idea of the amazing rapidity with which the fund grew. In 1915 the receipts amounted to £27 2s. 6d.; in 1916, £158 12s.; in 1917, £1,025 1s. 3d., and in 1918, £25,888 15s. 5d.

Mrs Luard acted as Hon. Secretary and Treasurer during the whole period, receiving every possible assistance from the late Captain Sir Beville Stanier, Bart., M.P., the secretary of the T.F. Association, who very kindly undertook to act as Hon. Secretary with regard to any men who might become prisoners of war from the T.F. He was also largely responsible for the collection of funds in Shropshire. In recognition of the splendid work done by Mrs. Luard in connection with this fund she was awarded the M.B.E.

The expenses connected with the administration of the fund were extremely small, as the entire work was done by voluntary helpers, and in 1918 when over 13,000 parcels were dispatched from Shrewsbury, the office expenses amounted to under £150.

Nine hundred and seventy-three men were dealt with between June, 1915, and November, 1918; of these twenty died in captivity, of the rest all except sixty-five were repatriated. In addition to the prisoners of war in Germany, men of the 8th Battalion were interned in Serbia, and some few 2nd Battalion men were in prisons in Asia Minor.

The Christmas parcels were actually packed when the Armistice was declared, and these parcels were sent as a welcome home to each man on his arrival in this country. This proved a happy inspiration, as the men were delighted that their families should see a sample of the parcels they had received in captivity, and one man, in acknowledging his parcel, said the contents were quite a revelation to his people.

Many of the men taken prisoner in the last months of the war were never taken to Germany, but were kept at work behind the lines, and of these very few got any parcels. But even these unlucky ones wrote that the hope and expectation of getting parcels helped to keep them alive.

The following extracts taken from among hundreds of letters received by the Hon. Secretary, after the men returned from captivity, speak for themselves :—

" All the parcels from you rank amongst the best, and " thanks to Mr. Butcher and the careful packing, without " a single exception they have all arrived here in most " perfect condition, which is more than can be said of " a good many parcels which the others get."

" When you sent those books you could hardly have " done anything better for us; I was longing for a book " to read."

" I must say if it had not been for the parcels which " I received while in Germany I should not be here to " write this. The first three months of my captivity we " were kept behind the German lines, carrying shells and " burying dead. During that time three-parts of the " men died from starvation and exposure. But with my

" usual luck I managed to scrape through, though it was
" by eating various things, which if I mentioned them
" would put you off your food."

TOTAL RECEIPTS AND EXPENDITURE FOR 1915–1918

Receipts

	£	s.	d.
June to December, 1915	27	2	6
January to December, 1916	158	12	0
January to December, 1917	1,025	1	3
January, 1918, to January 25th, 1919	25,888	15	5
	27,099	11	2

Expenditure

	£	s.	d.
June to December, 1915	9	19	10
January to December, 1916	46	4	2
January to December, 1917	655	8	10
January, 1918, to January 25th, 1919	12,167	2	3
Balance in hand, January 25th, 1919	14,220	16	1
	27,099	11	2

The cost of the parcels was nearly £3,000 a month at
the moment of the Armistice, therefore the very considerable surplus in hand would not have been more than
enough to ensure a constant supply of necessities for the
men for three or four months, but it became necessary
after the return of the prisoners of war to call meetings
of subscribers at Shrewsbury and Hereford to decide
in what way this sum could be most usefully employed.
It was unanimously agreed at both meetings to devote
the money in Shropshire and Herefordshire to assist ex-
service men of the two counties, and particularly of the
county regiment, on their return to civilian life. Two-
thirds were allotted to Shropshire, and one-third to Herefordshire, and local committees were formed at once to
deal with this money.

As regards Herefordshire a fund called the Herefordshire Imperial Service Fund was started in February, 1919, with £6,339 6s. 3d. handed over from the Prisoners of War Fund. The Imperial Service Fund activities were closed down at a meeting of the General Committee, held in the Town Hall, Hereford, in November, 1921, when the balance of £16 7s. 1d. was formally handed over to Lt.-Colonel H. E. P. Pateshall, D.S.O., commanding the Hereford Regiment, to be used in any cases of special need which might come to his notice. Mrs. Luard, chairman of the sub-committee of the Herefordshire Imperial Service Fund, announced that in the two and a half years of its existence the Fund had dealt with 1,441 applications and made 849 grants and loans to ex-service men, their widows or orphans, who belonged to Herefordshire or had served in the Herefordshire Regiment.

On 15th March, 1919, £11,666 13s. 4d. was handed over from the K.S.L.I. Prisoners of War Fund to form, the nucleus of the Shropshire Soldiers' Assistance Fund. Other sums to the amount of £4,607 17s. 10d. accrued from subscriptions and investments, making a total of £16,274 11s. 2d. for distribution. The following composed the Committee which administered the fund :—

President : The Rt. Hon. the Earl of Powis

Chairman : Colonel the Lord Harlech, C.B.

Mr. Davies
O.C. Depôt K.S.L.I.
O.C. 4th Battn. K.S.L.I.
Capt. Sir Beville Stanier, Bart., M.P.
Br.-Gen. H. C. Cholomondley, C.B., C.B.E.
The Mayors of Shrewsbury, Bridgnorth, Oswestry, Ludlow, Much Wenlock, and Bishop's Castle
Mr. T. B. Butcher
Mrs. Luard, M.B.E.
Mr. W. Swire, C.B.E.
Colonel R. Leeke
Mr. J. Gallimore
Mr. W. Holloway

Hon. Sec. : Lt.-Colonel J. W. Mackeson

Asst. Hon. Sec. : Capt. D. A. McAlister, M.B.E.

z

The Fund was for the benefit of soldiers who had served in the K.S.L.I. in the Great War and their families; also for soldiers of other Corps and their families who, having served in the Great War, were resident on 15th March, 1919, in the County of Shropshire. The essential condition was that the applicant should have suffered directly in mind, body, or estate through the War.

The total number of applications received was 2,386, and in 1,885 cases grants from £5 to £100 were made.

The Fund was closed, all moneys having been distributed, at a meeting held on November 1st, 1924, at which high tribute was paid to the continuous care and personal attention given to the administration of the Fund by Lieut.-Colonel W. J. Mackeson and Mr. T. Butcher, and to the patience and tact of Capt. D. A. McAlister.

Mention should be made of the Comforts Fund of the 1st Battalion K.S.L.I., which was formed in September, 1914, for the purpose of sending out articles of warm clothing, tobacco, games and newspapers to the men of the 1st Battalion. Mrs. Luard, M.B.E., whose husband was in command of the battalion, undertook the collection of money and articles, and by keeping in constant touch with the officers of the 1st K.S.L.I., was able to send out just what was most needed at the time. £950 16s. 2d. was collected between 1914 and 1918, and over 11,000 woollen articles were received.

On August 5th, 1919, the county of Shropshire welcomed home those of her sons who survived the Great War after serving their King and country overseas.

The Earl of Powis, Lord-Lieutenant of the county, appealed for voluntary contributions to defray the expense, with the splendid result that nearly 8,000 officers, warrant officers and other ranks were entertained at luncheon in the Quarry at Shrewsbury, and were given light refreshment on the race-course, the place of assembly. The transport and assembling of the troops and all arrangements for their food were undertaken by the Shropshire Territorial Army Association.

Major-General Deverell, C.B., C.M.G., commanding the 53rd Welsh Infantry Division, ably assisted by the divisional staff, commanded and directed the processional march of the troops through the principal streets of Shrewsbury to the Quarry.

The route taken was via

1.	Monkmoor Street	7.	Chester Street
2.	Abbey Foregate	8.	Smithfield Road
3.	Wyle Cop	9.	Mardol
4.	High Street	10.	Shoplatch
5.	Pride Hill	11.	St. John's Hill
6.	Castle Street	12.	St. Chad's Terrace

The bands of the 2nd Battalion Cheshire Regiment, 2nd Battalion S.W.B., 1st K.S.L.I. and 1st R.W.F. took part in the procession. The band of the 10th K.S.L.I. (Shropshire and Cheshire Yeomanry) gave a selection of music in the Square.

Lord Harlech, representing the Lord-Lieutenant of the county (absent through illness), and Lt.-General Sir T. D'O. Snow, K.C.B., K.C.M.G., Commanding-in-Chief the Western Command, received the salute at the Clive statue in the Square. On arriving at the Quarry the troops proceeded to the various marquees in which an excellent luncheon was eaten. Lord Harlech and General Snow visited each marquee and welcomed the troops most cordially. The afternoon was spent in enjoying the various sports and entertainments most generously provided by the Mayor, Sir Samuel Morris, and Corporation of Shrewsbury. The weather was brilliant and the whole ceremony was most impressive, being witnessed by huge crowds of spectators from the town and all parts of the county.

APPENDIX I

Nominal roll of officers who were killed in action, or died of wounds or disease, in the Great War, 1914–1919. Reprinted from the official list, with certain additional names. [The figure preceding the names indicates the number of the battalion.]

1 Adams-Posner, RobertCecil, 2/Lt.
10 Aldersey, Hugh, Capt.
6 Allin, Harold Wyse, Lt.
7 Allnutt, Albert, 2/Lt. (Res. att. 7th Bn.)
7 Amey, Harold, 2/Lt.
   Arnott, Kenneth Hugh Lowden, D.S.O., M.C., T/Lt.-Col. (E. Lan. R. att. 7th)
7 Artaud, Gerald Frank Deveniere, Lt.
   Atchison, Charles Ernest, Major (A/Lt.-Col.), D.S.O.
4 Atherton, Walter, Lt.
5 Avery, Thomas, 2/Lt. (T/Capt.)

1 Bamford, Harold W., 2/Lt.
9 Barnes, John Robert Evans, 2/Lt. (att. 6th)
   Barnes, L. T. V., Major (R. War. R., att. 7th)
   Battye, Clinton Wynyard, Major (A/Lt.-Col.), D.S.O.
9 Bausor, Thomas Paul, 2/Lt. (T.M.B.)
2 Beacall, Hugh, Lt.
3 Beamish, John Spread Hamilton, Lt.
5 Beaumont, Samuel George, Capt.
5 Bellasis, Philip Joseph, Capt.

7 Benbow, Walter Harold, 2/Lt., M.M.
3 Biddle - Cope, Anthony Cyprian Prosper, 2/Lt. (att. 2nd Bn.)
3 Bird, Francis Clifford, 2/Lt.
3 Blackett, Charles Robert, 2/Lt. (att. 2nd)
1 Blake, George Victor, 2/Lt.
7 Boardley, Harold, Lt.
6 Boddington, Myles, T/Capt.
7 Bolt, Bertram Leslie, 2/Lt.
7 Boucher, Albert Adolph, 2/Lt. (att. 8th T.M.B.)
7 Bowie, David Drummond, T/Capt., M.C.
   Brandon, Brian Lloyd, 2/Lt. (Res. att. 1/7 Cheshire)
   Brooke, William John, Capt.
2 Bryant, Henry Grenville, Capt., D.S.O.
3 Buckley, Hubert Hyde, Lt. (att. 1st Bn.)
5 Bugden, Robert Gordon, Lt.
1 Burke, Thomas Edward, 2/Lt. (T/Capt.) (att. 5th)
10 Burkett, Harold, T/Capt.
3 Burns, Walter Bell, Lt. (att. 4th Glos.)
6 Burrough, Francis Thomas, T/Capt.
9 Butt, Robert Acton, 2/Lt. (att. 5th)

341

7 Caesar,Charles Patrick,T/Lt.
7 Cannon, Sidney Leslie, 2/Lt. (att. R.A.F.)
10 Cawley, Oswald, Capt.
5 Chapman, Joseph Robert, 2/Lt.
1 Charles, James Arthur Merriman, 2/Lt.
3 Church, John Victor, Lt. (att. 6th)
4 Clarke,Leonard,Lt.(att.7th)
5 Clarke, Robert Shuttleworth, Capt.
   Coakley, Charles Stewart, 2/Lt. (att. 1/4th Bn.)
1 Colville, Henry George Coulson, Capt. (att. H.Q., 16th Inf. Bde.)
   Cooke, Cecil Pybus, 2/Lt. (att. 5th Bn.)
   Corbet, John Hugh, 2/Lt. (att. R.F.C.)
6 Cox, Leonard Albert, 2/Lt.
4 Crabtree, J. H., 2/Lt. (att. 7th)
3 Currie, Frederic Rivers, Lt. (att. 1st)

7 Dallow,William Ewart,2/Lt.
1 Davenport, Francis Edward Alexander, 2/Lt.
3 Davies, George Herbert, Lt. (att. 1st Bn.)
   Davies, I.P., 2/Lt. (Cheshire Regt., att. 7th)
1 Davies, James Gordon, 2/Lt.
   Davies, James Parton, 2/Lt. (att. 7th Bn. Ches. R.)
7 Davies, Walter Llewelyn, 2/Lt.
7 Dell, Louis Michael, 2/Lt.

8 Dennett, Stephen Hepworth, 2/Lt. (att. R.F.C.)
7 Dibben, W. H., 2/Lt. (att. 8th Bde. H.Q.)
9 Dyer, Edward Arnold, Lt.
1 Dymock, Robert Townsend Vaughan, Lt.

1 Eakin, Robert Andrew,Capt.
7 Eastham, Clement Vincent, 2/Lt.
   Edwards, William, Capt. (R.A.S.C., att. 7th)
3 Egerton, Arthur Oswald, 2/Lt. (att. 5th)
5 Elliott, Robert Chambers Macdonald, 2/Lt.
5 Ellis, Basil Herbert, Lt.
1 Evans, Albert Ashley, 2/Lt.
6 Evans, Kenneth George Ogle, 2/Lt.

5 Faber, Walter Louis, T/Lt.
9 Fisher, Hubert Patrick, 2/Lt.
6 Fitzmaurice, John Herbert, 2/Lt.
1 Foulger, Maurice, 2/Lt.
3 Fox, Arthur, A/Capt., M.C. (att. 1st)
5 French, Charles John, T/Major (att. 255th Tunn. Co., R.E.)
5 French, Valentine Douglas, 2/Lt.
   Frost, Percy Causton, 2/Lt. (att. 10th.)

4 Gallimore, Hubert Thomas Keith, Lt.
6 Garnett, Ivan William, 2/Lt.
5 Gittins, Albert, T/Lt., M.C.

10 Glazebrook, Philip Kirkland, Major, D.S.O.
1 Goodale, Arthur William, 2/Lt.
3 Goodchild, Stewart John, 2/Lt. (att. 7th)
9 Green, Charles Ernest, 2/Lt. (att. 7th)
7 Green, G. B. (R.W.F.), 2/Lt.
6 Green, Richmond Edward Ormond Lyttleton, 2/Lt.
 Griffen, Harold Samuel, 2/Lt. (att. 5th)
 Gubbins, Richard Rolls, Bt.-Lt.-Col., D.S.O.

6 Hair, Donald Campbell, 2/Lt.
6 Hamer, John, 2/Lt.
6 Hannah, Edward Meale, 2/Lt., M.C.
4 Hannon, Thomas James, 2/Lt. (att. 6th)
6 Hares, Vincent Colin, T/Lt. (att. 10th)
2 Harper, Charles, 2/Lt.
 Harrop, James Allinson, 2/Lt. (att. 1st.)
 Harty, William, 2/Lt. (att. 4th)
6 Hawkins, William Percy, Lt.
1 Hazard, Charles Piper, 2/Lt.
3 Hazard, Douglas George, Lt.
10 Henningsen, Cecil Eric, Lt.
1 Herbert, Edmund Widdington, 2/Lt. (att.1/4thChes.R.)
1 Herdman, Arthur Widdrington, Lt.
 Hibbard, Richard, 2/Lt. (att. 4th)
1 Higgins, Percy Clynton, Capt. (att. Nig. R.)

6 Higginson, Tom Arthur, Capt.
2 Hill, Guy Charles Dunlop, 2/Lt.
1 Hitchcock, Cyril Augustus, 2/Lt.
5 Holder, Charles Vincent, 2/Lt.
2 Holman, Geoffrey, Lt.
 Hornby, Cyril Blurton, 2/Lt.
6 Howell, Norman Asquith, 2/Lt.
7 Hughes, George, 2/Lt.
5 Hunt, Francis Henry Walter, Capt.

1 Isaac, Frank Philip, 2/Lt.

 Jackson, Douglas William, T/Lt. (att. 1st Bn.)
1 Jackson-Taylor, John Curzon, 2/Lt.
1 James, Eric Gwynne, T/Capt and Adjt., D.S.O.
 Jeffreys, Charles Wilfred, 2/Lt. (att. 5th)
1 Jenings, George Pierce Creagh, Lt.
 Jenkins, Sidney Oswald, 2/Lt. (R.W.F., att. 10th)
1 Johnston, Alec, T/Lt.
7 Johnston, Frank, Capt., T/Major
7 Jones, George Frederick, 2/Lt., A/Capt., M.C.
7 Jones, George Harold Price, Lt.
4 Jones, Griffiths Vaughan, 2/Lt. (att. 7th)
 Jones, John William, 2/Lt. (att. Camel Cps.)

3 King, Edward Gordon Mac-
gregor, 2/Lt. (att. Glos.
Regt.)

2 Koch, Marcus Addison, 2/Lt.

5 Lawrence, Rudolph Russell,
2/Lt.

2 Leach, Francis James, Capt.

9 Lee, Eric Hanson, 2/Lt.
(att. 1st.)

3 Lee, John Arthur, 2/Lt.
(att. 5th)

Lee, Percy William, 2/Lt.
(att. 5th)

Leech, Robert Edward Holt,
2/Lt. (att. 4th)

7 Legg, William Norman,
T/Lt.

7 Leleu, Sydney Francis, 2/Lt.

1 Lewis, Archibald Ernest,
2/Lt.

3 Lewis, John Dunning
Gaunt, Lt. (att. 1st)

5 Llewellyn, John Herbert,
T/Capt.

9 Lloyd, Francis Oswald,
2/Lt. (att. 6th)

3 Lloyd, Gilbert Kingsley,
2/Lt. (att. 2nd)

2 Lloyd, Lewis John Bevenall,
Lt.

3 Lloyd, Owen Robert, 2/Lt.,
A/Capt., M.C. (att. 7th)

9 Lowry, John, 2/Lt. (att.
2nd)

1 Luard, Edward Bourryau,
T/Lt.-Col., D.S.O.

6 Lutener, Richard Arthur
Maurice, 2/Lt.

4 McAlister, Gordon Dun-
can, 2/Lt.

7 McCowan, J., 2/Lt.

3 Machell, Maurice Irving,
2/Lt. (att. 5th)

1 Maclaverty, Colin Johnston,
Capt.

Maclean, Dugald Fitzroy,
2/Lt. (att. 1/4th Glos. R.)

9 McMordie, James Wilson,
2/Lt. (att. 2nd Yorks L.I.)

9 McSwiny, Claude O'C.,
2/Lt. (att. 7th)

Marindin, Henry Eden
Allan, 2/Lt., M.C. (att. 4th)

1 Marriott, Richard Henry,
Lt., M.C.

9 Martin, William Henry,
2/Lt. (att. 6th)

1 Masefield, Robert, Major

Mealing, Maurice Edmund,
2/Lt. (att. R.F.C.)

7 Middleton, James, 2/Lt., M.C.

1 Miles, Robert Patric, Capt.
(att. R.I.R.)

Millar, William McKay,
2/Lt. (att. 10th)

3 Mitchell, Julian Alan Spencer, Capt.

Morgan, Joseph Anthony,
T/Lt. (att. R.F.C.)

7 Morgans, Thomas, 2/Lt.

4 Morley, Gordon Harper,
Lt.

5 Mould, Charles William,
T/Capt.

10 Muddock, Jasper Milton
Preston, 2/Lt.

1 Mylius, John Kingsford, Lt.

8 Nalder, Frank Shirley, Capt.

7 Newell, W. J., Lt.-Col.

7 Norris, Alfred James, 2/Lt.

6 O'Connor, Hubert Michael, Capt., M.C.
3 O'Fflahertie, Godwin Joseph Anthony Swifte, Lt. (att. 1st G.B. King's Liv.)
3 Onslow, Tom, 2/Lt. (att. 5th)
6 Ormiston, Robert Williams, 2/Lt.
3 Owen, Arthur Bankes, 2/Lt. (att. 7th)
9 Owen, Philip Charles, 2/Lt. (att. 5th)
   Owen, William Llewellyn, 2/Lt. (att. 1/4th Bn.)

5 Palmer, Charles, T/Capt.
5 Partridge, Ernest William, 2/Lt.
   Paterson, John Jamieson, 2/Lt. (att. 10th)
7 Pecker, Francis George, A/Capt.
   Phare, Dudley Gersholm, Lt. (R.A.S.C., att. 7th)
7 Pitchford, Arthur Reginald, 2/Lt.
3 Platt, Frank Lindsay, Capt. (att. 1st)
10 Plowden, Francis Charles, Lt.
3 Postles, Charles Ernest, 2/Lt. (att. 1st Ches. R.)
3 Pound, John Russell, Capt. (att. 2nd)
3 Powell, Victor Edmund, T/Lt. (A/Capt.) (att. 7th)
7 Price, Arthur, 2/Lt.
5 Price, David Leonard, 2/Lt. (att. 7th)
8 Profeit, Leopold, T/Capt.

3 Pugh, Ronald George, 2/Lt. (att. 7th N. Staffs)
   Pye, Colin, 2/Lt. (att. 1st)

7 Randall, Herbert Ernest, 2/Lt.
9 Ridout, Clarence Grosvenor, 2/Lt. (att. 1st)
7 Rigby, Edward William, T/Capt.
   Robinson, Geoffrey Francis, Capt. (att. 1/4th Ghurkas)
1 Rooper, Trevor Godolphin Hungerford, 2/Lt.
2 Rowan-Robinson, William James, Major

   Sampson, Tom Burton, T/Lt. (att. 6th)
1 Savory, Francis Richard Egerton, Capt.
   Shackles, Ronald Guy, 2/Lt., M.C. (att. 10th Bn.)
2 Shaw, William Easterby, Lt.
3 Sherwood, Hamilton Stanley, 2/Lt. (att. 1/4th Bn.)
9 Shields, William Francis Waugh, T/Lt. (att. 5th)
6 Sidebotham, John Frith, T/Lt.
7 Silvester, Geoffrey Francis, T/Capt.
5 Simpson, Victor James, 2/Lt.
2 Skinner, James Stuart, Capt.
5 Smith, Charles Cyril, 2/Lt.
6 Smith, Douglas George, T/Lt., M.C.
4 Smith, Norman Louis, Lt.
6 Smith, Roderic Franklyn, T/Capt., M.C.
7 Southwell, Arthur Horace Steadman, 2/Lt.

3 Sparrow, Brian Hanbury, Capt., M.C. (att. 7th N. Staffs)
4 Sparrow, George William, Capt. (att. 10th)
1 Spearman, John Vanstone, 2/Lt.
7 Spiers, Archibald Lionel Clive, T/Lt.
3 Steward, Charles, 2/Lt. (att. 2nd)
3 Symonds-Taylor, Frederick Kingsley, Capt. (att. 1st)

1 Taverner, Arthur Frederick, 2/Lt.
5 Taylor, Ronald Francis, 2/Lt.
3 Thomson, Reginald Gresham, Lt., A/Capt. (att. 1st)
2 Tippett, Alexander Arnold, 2/Lt.
3 Topham, Alfred James Tudor, 2/Lt., A/Capt. (att. 7th)
7 Townsend, Charles Victor, 2/Lt.
5 Turner, Henry Alfred, 2/Lt. (att. 8th)
Turner, Reginald, 2/Lt. (att. 6th)

9 Underhill, Cyril Scott, 2/Lt.
7 Upton, John Alberic Everard, 2/Lt.
8 Ursell, Victor George, 2/Lt. (att. 7th)

3 Venables, Gilbert Rowland, 2/Lt. (att. 2nd)

1 Verner, Frederick Charles, 2/Lt.
2 Vyvyan, Walter Drummond, Lt.

4 Wace, Henry Edward, Capt,
9 Walker, Eric Arthur, 2/Lt. (att. 6th)
5 Ward, Alfred Claude, T/ Capt. and Adjt.
5 Webb, Arthur Pelham, 2/Lt.
6 Welch, Harold Echalaz, Lt.-Col., D.S.O. and Bar
Wellings, Henry William, 2/Lt. (att. M.G.C., 17th Bn.)
White, Arthur Ingram, 2/Lt. (att. 4th)
1 Whitmore, Roger Searle, Capt., M.C.
1 Wildig, G., Lt.
2 Wilkinson, Clement Arthur, Major
Williams, Hugh, 2/Lt. (Pemb. Yeo., att. 7th)
3 Williams, Ivor Phillips, 2/Lt. (att. 4th Bn. S. Wales Bdrs.)
1 Wilson, Harold Algar, 2/Lt., T/Capt.
1 Woodland, Richard William, Lt.
3 Woolf, Walter Francis, Lt. (att. 7th)
7 Wright, Edmund Lancelot, 2/Lt.

5 Yeomans, Walter Joseph George, 2/Lt.

APPENDIX II

Nominal roll of warrant officers, N.C.O.'s and men killed in action, or died of wounds or disease, in the Great War, 1914–1919. Reprinted from the official list.

FIRST BATTALION

Acton, F., 7257, Pte.
Aldcroft, A., 10351, Pte.
Allen, J. D., 30001, Pte.
Allen, W., 43583, Pte.
Allen, W. J., 17177, Pte.
Allerton, J. W., 8057, Pte.
Allport, T. A., 43269, Pte.
Amison, J., 27032, L/Cpl.
Andrews, W. C., 7465, Pte.
Ankers, W., 21473, Pte.
Apperley, W., 7546, Pte.
Archard, C. E., 9761, Pte.
Archer, H., 5564, Pte.
Armitt, J., 43463, Pte.
Arndell, C. H., 16873, Pte.
Arrowsmith, T. A., 6343, Pte.
Ashall, T., 43461, Pte.
Ashby, T., 7349, Pte.
Ashley, H., 23852, Pte.
Aspinall, J., 7666, Pte.
Aston, F., 26731, Pte.
Atewell, R. J., 27355, Pte.
Atherton, J., 7057, Pte.
Avery, H. V., 8296, Sgt.
Aylward, H. T., 9113, Pte.

Bacon, F., 31257, Pte.
Badcock, W. H., 8432, Sgt.
Bailey, H., 27034, Pte.
Bailey, J. A., 10046, Cpl.
Baines, W., 7460, Pte.
Baistow, J. H., 15598, Pte.
Baker, C. A., 205837, Pte.
Baker, J., 10182, Pte.
Baker, T., 7695, C.S.M.

Baker, W., 17257, Pte.
Baker, W. H., 8240, Pte.
Ball, F., 31283, Pte.
Ball, H., 38457, Cpl.
Barber, A. J., 9046, Pte.
Barber, J., 8272, Pte.
Barfield, A., 7428, Pte.
Barker, G. E., 9455, Sgt.
Barker, H., 8291, Sgt.
Barker, J., 205823, Pte.
Barnett, H., 15882, Pte.
Barnett, J., 204485, Pte.
Baron, J. H., 10346, Pte.
Bartlett, V. P., 10281, Pte.
Barton, E., 7380, Cpl.
Barton, H., 7401, Pte.
Bason, A. H., 18420, Pte.
Bateman, J., 27018, Pte.
Bates, H. P., 10209, Pte.
Batho, G., 7826, Cpl.
Batin, G., 22841, Pte.
Batson, J. D., 8676, Pte.
Bebb, D. E., 8471, Pte.
Bebbington, A., 7084, Pte.
Beddow, C., 10375, Pte.
Beddow, M., 7667, Pte.
Beddows, W., 5501, Cpl.
Beech, H., 19236, Pte.
Beech, W., 15058, Pte.
Bell, G., 27013, Pte.
Benbow, J. W., 12520, L/Cpl.
Bennett, G. H., 26772, Pte.
Bennett, J. R., 7365, Pte.
Bennett, S., 10224, Pte.
Bennett, T. L., 10320, Pte.

347

Bennett, W. H., 10225, Pte.
Benning, E. J., 8611, L/Cpl.
Bentham, A., 7150, Pte.
Berry, B., 19110, Pte.
Best, W., 7673, L/Cpl.
Bevan, A., 7336, Pte.
Bevan, C. E., 7537, Cpl.
Bevan, J. H., 230450, Pte.
Biggs, N., 3959, Pte.
Biggs, T., 5320, Sgt.
Bird, H. G., 27369, Pte.
Bisson, J. H., 26738, Pte.
Blades, E., 32239, Pte.
Blakemore, E., 17596, Pte.
Blakeway, J. E., 9622, Pte.
Blocksidge, G. W., 9345, L/Cpl.
Bloom, A., 17635, Pte.
Bloomfield, G., 26048, Pte.
Boden, C., 19188, Pte.
Boothby, R., 7511, Pte.
Boston, C., 11237, Pte.
Botfield, F., 27149, Pte.
Botwood, H., 17969, Pte.
Boucher, W., 7146, Pte.
Boulton, H., 12816, Pte.
Bowen, E. A., 13151, Pte.
Bowen, S. J., 10285, Pte.
Bowers, F. J., 12449, Pte.
Bowers, F. W., 18945, Pte.
Bracegirdle, W., 24336, Pte.
Bradburn, J., 20330, Pte.
Braddick, S., 10427, Pte.
Bradley, H., 204486, Pte.
Bradley, I. T., 17093, Pte.
Bradley, J., 8107, Pte.
Bradshaw, J., 43236, Pte.
Brampton, F. M., 20016, Pte.
Brand, H., 20133, Cpl.
Bray, L., 13935, Cpl.
Bray, T. C., 10085, Pte.

Brazier, E., 12872, Pte.
Brazier, W. T., 5322, Sgt.
Breese, A. S., 204326, Pte.
Breeze, A., 10164, Pte.
Breeze, W. D., 10266, Pte.
Brick, J., 34387, Pte.
Brickley, T., 6599, Sgt.
Bridger, J., 8341, Pte.
Bridges, A., 5544, Pte.
Briggs, A., 6680, Pte.
Brine, W. R., 27832, Pte.
Brittain, J., 7191, Pte.
Bromley, B., 18245, Pte.
Brookes, F. G., 11353, Pte.
Brookes, G. V., 20939, Pte.
Brooks, W., 28149, Pte.
Broome, H., 18828, Pte.
Brown, A. G., 10429, Pte.
Brown, G., 24643, Pte.
Brown, G. A., 8925, Pte.
Brown, J., 22393, Pte.
Brown, T., 7994, Pte.
Brown, W., 7767, Pte.
Brundle, A. G., 27147, Pte.
Bryan, A., 27144, Pte.
Bubb, A. J., 17232, Pte.
Buckley, H. E., 17319, Pte.
Buckley, W., 27023, Pte.
Budd, C., 8246, Pte.
Bunce, T., 6246, Pte.
Burd, N., 7505, Pte.
Burgess, A., 6171, Pte.
Burke, M., 7112, Pte.
Burns, S., 7585, Pte.
Burton, J., 16008, Pte.
Butcher, H. R., 19567, Pte.
Butler, E. W., 18994, Pte.

Cadden, H., 10162, L/Cpl.
Cale, J., 17401, Pte.

APPENDIX II

Campbell, H., 27844, Pte.
Candlin, E. S., 10105, L/Cpl.
Carroll, T., 9493, Cpl.
Carswell, J., 16485, Pte.
Carter, B. J., 10205, Pte.
Carter, G. L., 25711, Pte.
Carter, J., 6100, L/Cpl.
Cartmel, W., 26776, Pte.
Cartwright, A., 9747, Cpl.
Cartwright, A., 10284, Pte.
Cartwright, C., 10870, Pte.
Cartwright, H., 21212, Pte.
Cartwright, L., 18408, Pte.
Catterall, F., 26779, Pte.
Chadney, E., 7806, Pte.
Chadwick, E., 18848, Pte.
Challinor, F. C., 204407, Pte.
Challoner, A., 27184, Pte.
Chant, T. E., 10261, Pte.
Chantry, C. J., 9330, L/Sgt.
Checkland, A., 26777, Pte.
Cheetham, H., 15991, Pte.
Cheetham, W., 17446, Cpl.
Chesters, F., 17942, Pte.
Chetwood, J. E., 24963, Pte.
Chetwood, J. T., 24196, Pte.
Clark, J., 15024, Pte.
Clark, T., 17571, Pte.
Clarke, A., 5025, Pte.
Clarke, A., 9888, Pte.
Clarke, C., 7431, Pte.
Clay, I., 204446, Cpl.
Coburn, L. D., 30010, Pte.
Cofax, J., 26266, Pte.
Coleman, J. W., 205838, Pte.
Colley, D., 18149, Pte.
Collins, A. G., 19365, Pte.
Collins, W. A., 7362, Pte.
Conway, P., 27044, Pte.
Cook, E. A., 25713, Pte.

Cooper, J. E., 22484, Pte.
Cording, A., 19301, L/Cpl.
Corke, A., 23524, Pte.
Corn, C. W., 201347, Pte.
Cornes, C. E., 15526, L/Cpl.
Cornfield, J., 10386, Pte.
Cotterill, G. T., 10379, Pte.
Cotton, A., 10452, Pte.
Cotton, H. T., 5675, Pte.
Coxall, J. 7682, Cpl.
Crane, J., 6067, Cpl.
Cresswell, G., 7475, Pte.
Crompton, F., 7614, Pte.
Crompton, J., 19444, Pte.
Crump, J., 10464, Pte.
Cumberlin, A. E., 10032, Pte.

Dakin, C. B., 18214, Pte.
Dalley, E., 7082, Pte.
Dance, C. H., 7924, Pte.
Davenport, H. B., 5889, Pte.
Davenport, T., 19329, Pte.
Davies, A., 8122, Pte.
Davies, D., 10398, Pte.
Davies, E., 6299, Cpl.
Davies, E. J., 7480, Sgt.
Davies, F., 16100, Pte.
Davies, F. C., 6578, Pte.
Davies, G., 10298, Pte.
Davies, H., 7503, L/Cpl.
Davies, H., 10192, Pte.
Davies, J., 10793, Sgt.
Davies, J., 17425, Pte.
Davies, J., 5553, Pte.
Davies, R. J., 17205, Pte.
Davies, R. H., 19092, Pte.
Davies, T., 10022, Pte.
Davies, W., 10141, Pte.
Davies, W., 14715, Pte.
Davies, W., 23752, Pte.

Davis, J., 10407, Pte.
Dawes, L., 18281, Pte.
Dawes, R., 10393, Pte.
Deakin, F. E., 25038, Pte.
Dean, H. A., 204309, Pte.
Dew, H. T., 19517, Pte.
Didlick, G., 9283, Sgt.
Didluck, J. A., 8271, Pte.
Dixon, F. P., 26221, Pte.
Dodd, W. A., 24383, Pte.
Dodd, W. G., 18257, Pte.
Donaldson, F. T., 27181, Pte.
Doswell, H., 204176, Pte.
Downes, S., 14998, Pte.
Downes, W. C., 7433, Pte.
Downing, L., 21375, Pte.
Downs, R., 38479, Pte.
Draper, H., 8166, Pte.
Drinkwater, T., 7415, Pte.
Driver, F., 26748, Pte.
Drury, D., 14564, Pte.
Drury, G., 24114, Pte.
Duerden, W. H., 32603, Pte.
Dunn, G., 16793, Pte.
Dunning, W. H., 24432, Pte.
Dutton, J., 19441, Pte.
Dyke, A., 21223, Pte.
Dykes, E. J., 26039, Pte.
Dyter, W. H., 8066, Pte.

Edge, H. T., 8797, Pte.
Edgerton, C., 7842, Pte.
Edmett, G., 8317, L/Cpl.
Edmondson, A., 26851, Pte.
Edmunds, H. E., 6867, Cpl.
Edwards, E., 27336, L/Sgt.
Edwards, F. R., 20952, Pte.
Edwards, G., 5188, Pte.
Edwards, J. A., 10265, Pte.
Edwards, J., 19790, Pte.

Edwards, J. W., 18567, Pte.
Edwards, J., 23821, Pte.
Edwards, P., 7794, Pte.
Edwards, P., 6771, Pte.
Edwards, R., 10047, Pte.
Edwards, T., 17585, Pte.
Edwards, T. J., 18308, Pte.
Elcock, W., 23879, Pte.
Ellis, F., 5883, Pte.
Ellis, J., 26850, Pte.
Ellis, J. M., 26849, Pte.
Elphick, J. F., 12840, Pte.
Emery, C. T., 205200, Pte.
Evans, A. E., 12369, Pte.
Evans, C. A., 26752, Pte.
Evans, D., 20242, Pte.
Evans, F. G., 204347, Pte.
Evans, G. H., 7890, L/Cpl.
Evans, H., 25716, Pte.
Evans, H. E., 21347, L/Cpl.
Evans, H. R., 5640, Pte.
Evans, S. G., 18367, Pte.
Evans, T., 8480, Pte.
Evans, T., 18032, Pte.
Evans, T. C., 10258, L/Cpl.
Ewell, B., 14997, Pte.

Fairey, W. G., 17671, L/Cpl.
Farlow, J. E., 12077, Pte.
Farnsworth, R. H., 13700, Pte.
Fell, J., 38492, Pte.
Fearnall, W., 6222, Pte.
Featherstone, J., 8215, Pte.
Feltus, A., 16422, Pte.
Ferrington, J. H., 17600, Pte.
Fielding, F., 204490, Pte.
Fisher, C., 7641, Pte.
Fisher, I., 9560, Pte.
Fisher, J. R., 20142, Pte.
Fitzhenry, J., 9956, Pte.

APPENDIX II

Fitzmaurice, J. M., 13856, Pte.
Fletcher, A., 18816, Pte.
Fletcher, A., 7572, Cpl.
Fletcher, J., 7420, Pte.
Fletcher, J., 4915, Pte.
Foster, T., 20132, Pte.
Foulkes, A., 10191, Pte.
Foulkes, G., 203604, Pte.
Fowler, J., 10075, Pte.
Fox, A., 19219, Pte.
France, J., 7519, Pte.
Francis, A. A., 17461, Pte.
Francis, T., 10495, Pte.
Freer, J., 7733, Pte.
Frost, A., 25483, Pte.
Furber, T., 12221, Pte.

Gardener, W., 22021, Pte.
Garratt, W., 204491, Pte.
Garside, W., 7297, Pte.
Gaston, G., 38493, Pte.
Gaunt, J., 27418, Pte.
Gawthorpe, F. C., 20163, Pte.
Gibbins, H., 7399, Pte.
Gibbons, J., 20131, Pte.
Gibbs, A. E., 8685, Pte.
Glover, G., 10058, Sgt.
Glynn, W., 7334, Pte.
Godsall, A., 7823, L/Cpl.
Godsall, G. H., 10419, Pte.
Goodall, H. T., 18275, Pte.
Goodwin, F. R., 17674, Pte.
Gordon, L., 7499, Pte.
Gorman, T., 7110, Pte.
Goulden, J., 204457, Pte.
Grady, J., 200193, Pte.
Grady, W., 10135, Pte.
Graham, A., 26757, Pte.
Grainger, J., 33442, Pte.
Gray, A. E., 27420, Pte.

Greaves, E., 9699, Pte.
Green, C., 30018, Pte.
Green, E., 26756, Pte.
Green, F., 10322, Pte.
Green, J. H., 6488, Pte.
Greenough, R., 6501, L/Cpl.
Griffiths, A., 17252, Pte.
Griffiths, C. S., 19247, L/Cpl.
Griffiths, J., 21242, Pte.
Griffiths, R. W., 6891, Pte.
Griggs, J. W., 8792, Pte.
Griggs, W. G., 8816, L/Sgt.
Grogan, E., 6458, Pte.
Groom, A., 18754, Pte.
Grout, L., 9189, Pte.
Grundy, B., 43387, Pte.
Gwilliam, A., 8083, Pte.
Gwilliam, C. H., 10362, Pte.
Gwilliam, S., 8292, Pte.
Gwilt, E., 9850, Pte.
Gwilt, T., 9586, Pte.
Gwyther, J. N., 9840, Pte.

Hadcocks, J., 7637, Pte.
Haddon, D., 18321, Pte.
Haines, G. W., 10268, Pte.
Hale, R., 26796, Pte.
Hall, G. W., 7168, Cpl.
Hall, R., 7615, Pte.
Hall, W. H., 15966, Pte.
Halton, H., 18196, Pte.
Hampson, A. J., 27748, Cpl.
Hampson, S., 17395, Pte.
Hancox, A. A., 8959, Sgt.
Hancox, S., 17776, Pte.
Hanmer, J., 11194, L/Cpl.
Harding, A. E., 7956, L/Cpl.
Harding, E., 13264, Pte.
Harding, J., 26800, Pte.
Harding, L., 8092, Pte.

FIRST BATTALION—(continued)

Harding, T. W., 25718, Pte.
Hardman, F., 7278, Pte.
Harpin, F. L., 10481, L/Sgt.
Harris, E., 19266, Pte.
Harris, F., 38478, Pte.
Harris, J. A., 19587, Pte.
Harris, J. E., 9873, Cpl.
Harrison, C., 10240, Pte.
Harrison, J., 15987, Pte.
Harriss, G. H., 8407, Pte.
Harrop, H., 7390, Cpl.
Hart, F. C., 8892, Sgt.
Haste, A., 19336, Pte.
Hawe, T., 26797, Pte.
Hawkins, W. H., 7179, Pte.
Haydock, T., 19386, Pte.
Hayes, T. F., 32491, Pte.
Hayward, S., 10352, Pte.
Heath, W., 204053, Pte.
Hewer, H. J., 24771, Pte.
Hickman, H., 15003, Pte.
Hiesley, T., 6466, Pte.
Higginbottom, H., 43227, Pte.
Higgins, F., 19879, Pte.
Higgins, H., 5111, Cpl.
Higgins, L. T., 31433, Pte.
Hill, E., 7936, Pte.
Hill, J., 11556, Pte.
Hill, P., 22461, Pte.
Hilton, G. H., 18637, Pte.
Hobbs, S. O., 24424, Pte.
Hodgekiss, E., 17138, Pte.
Hodges, F. W., 27162, Pte.
Hodson, W., 27161, Pte.
Hoggins, E., 7180, Pte.
Holbrook, W., 21246, Pte.
Holloway, E., 22374, Pte.
Holloway, E. J., 18917, Pte.
Holloway, R., 27422, Pte.
Holroyd, S., 26201, Pte.

Holt, J. J., 7731, L/Cpl.
Homer, A., 11370, Pte.
Hope, G., 19088, Pte.
Hopkins, F. J., 10367, Pte.
Hordern, J., 7311, L/Sgt.
Horler, H. J., 27423, Pte.
Hough, S. J., 14454, Pte.
Howard, J. C., 10008, L/Cpl.
Howarth, S., 204508, Pte.
Howels, G., 9808, Pte.
Hudman, E., 17455, Pte.
Hudson, J., 9774, Pte.
Hughes, E., 204180, Pte.
Hughes, W. R., 18879, Pte.
Hulse, W., 7599, Pte.
Humberstone, J. T., 8875, Pte.
Humphreys, A. J., 8267, Sgt.
Hunt, B., 6636, Pte.
Hunter, W., 25074, Pte.
Hurdley, G., 10036, L/Cpl.
Hyde, A., 10094, L/Cpl.

Ingham, F. S., 32147, Pte.
Ingham, J., 16050, Pte.
Inglebach, C., 34929, Pte.
Instone, R. H., 7878, Pte.
Irving, J., 26760, Pte.
Ivins, V. O., 20942, Pte.

Jackson, C., 24379, Pte.
Jackson, G., 7962, Sgt.
Jackson, G. L., 8794, Pte.
Jackson, H., 26806, Pte.
Jackson, J., 5868, Pte.
Jackson, S., 7632, Sgt.
Jacobsen, N., 35021, Pte.
James, C. R., 26807, Pte.
James, F., 25720, Pte.
James, H., 10107, Pte.
James, W., 27451, Pte.

APPENDIX II

James, W. A., 9029, Cpl.
Jamieson, H. F. F., 6419, Pte.
Jays, W. A., 10194, Pte.
Jeffries, J., 23855, Pte.
Johnson, C. W., 7367, L/Sgt.
Johnson, F., 22116, Pte.
Johnson, G. H., 12437, Pte.
Johnson, J., 26193, Pte.
Johnson, T. W., 10344, Pte.
Jones, A., 9951, Pte.
Jones, A., 7246, Pte.
Jones, E., 34858, Pte.
Jones, E. F., 31373, Pte.
Jones, H., 27063, Pte.
Jones, H., 31540, Pte.
Jones, H. T., 33087, Pte.
Jones, J. H., 21256, Pte.
Jones, J., 26821, Pte.
Jones, R., 18172, Pte.
Jones, T., 6296, L/Cpl.
Jones, T. S., 18134, Pte.
Jones, T. W., 10165, L/Cpl.
Jones, W. L., 21257, Pte.
Jones, W., 7876, Pte.
Jones, W., 17939, Pte.
Jordan, F. E., 12273, Pte.
Jowett, W., 15932, Pte.

Kay, R., 11368, Pte.
Kearns, T., 5471, Pte.
Kelly, E., 7398, Sgt.
Kelly, T., 7300, Pte.
Kennedy, A., 15078, Pte.
Kennett, H., 201203, Pte.
Kenyon, J., 25721, Pte.
Kershaw, C., 28159, Pte.
Kick, M., 7311, Sgt.
Kilvert, H., 18960, Pte.
Kinnaird, E. A., 29896, Pte.
Kirby, J., 7425, Pte.

Kirkbride, A., 7642, L/Cpl.
Kitsull, G. H., 21266, Pte.
Knight, T., 6532, Pte.
Knowles, S. W., 18443, Pte.
Kyte, T. C., 10425, Pte.

Lace, W. G., 26337, Pte.
Lagden, A. C., 27471, Pte.
Lamb, G., 27026, Pte.
Lamport, T., 8610, Pte.
Lane, J., 10227, Pte.
Lang, G., 6278, L/Cpl.
Langan, J., 7097, Pte.
Langford, T., 10463, Pte.
Laval, H. J. E., 28713, Pte.
Lavelle, M., 15075, Pte.
Law, P., 32463, L/Cpl.
Law, T., 16692, Pte.
Law, W., 21272, Pte.
Lawrence, J., 8365, L/Cpl.
Lawrence, S., 7121, Pte.
Lawton, T., 17645, Pte.
Lea, H., 7566, Pte.
Leake, W., 21274, Pte.
Leaver, J., 26813, Pte.
Leay, A., 27137, Pte.
Lees, R. D., 24863, Pte.
Leighton, T., 18216, Pte.
Lewis, A. J., 10030, Bugler.
Lewis, B., 18991, Pte.
Lewis, E., 38476, Pte.
Lewis, G., 10317, Pte.
Lewis, I., 10016, Pte.
Lewis, J., 25890, Pte.
Lewis, J. H., 6432, Pte.
Lewis, W., 11006, Pte.
Lewis, R., 10203, Sgt.
Lewis, T. H., 27474, Pte.
Leworthy, E., 27570, Pte.
Lincoln, E., 17189, L/Cpl.

FIRST BATTALION—(*continued*)

Lloyd, M., 27475, Pte.
Lloyd, F., 28670, Pte.
Lloyd, E., 7051, Pte.
Lloyd, H., 11127, L/Cpl.
Lloyd, H. C., 9900, Pte.
Lloyd, R. J., 9718, L/Sgt.
Lloyd, T., 9893, Pte.
Lloyd, W. H., 27469, Pte.
Lomax, H., 43474, Pte.
Loose, C. H., 16926, Pte.
Lovelace, H., 23153, Pte.
Lowe, E., 10197, Pte.
Lucas, G., 22206, Pte.
Luscott, A., 19127, Pte.

MacLarty, A., 9402, Bugler.
Maddox, F., 5830, Pte.
Maddox, W., 19825, Pte.
Mainwaring, R., 43350, Pte.
Malone, T., 43280, Pte.
Malsom, G., 10023, Pte.
Malyn, C. H., 27490, Pte.
Mann, A. H., 9213, Cpl.
Mantle, A. E., 16788, Pte.
Mapp, W., 6731, Pte.
Marshall, S. G., 7462, Sgt.
Marsland, C., 10590, Pte.
Martin, J. H., 8000, Pte.
Martin, R., 27164, Pte.
Mason, P., 26823, Pte.
Massey, J., 6084, Pte.
Masters, D., 14065, Pte.
Mather, A., 7400, Pte.
Matthews, F., 10290, Pte.
Matthews, G., 9925, Pte.
May, W. J., 20252, Pte.
Maycock, J., 24546, Pte.
Mayo, C. V., 6561, Pte.
McAvan, F., 10151, Cpl.
McCawley, F., 8782, Pte.

McMaster, W., 7623, Cpl.
McMullin, T. E., 28676, Pte.
McNulty, J., 7116, Pte.
Mellon, T., 27048, Pte.
Mellor, J., 7522, Pte.
Mellor, W., 9986, Pte.
Meredith, C., 7561, Pte.
Meredith, J. W., 10431, Pte.
Merredy, S. R., 8216, Pte.
Merrett, J. H., 27251, Pte.
Merrifield, W., 10395, Pte.
Merrill, S., 27483, Pte.
Metcalfe, M., 18220, Pte.
Milburn, J., 9533, Pte.
Millichamp, G., 25054, Pte.
Millichope, R. H., 19186, Pte.
Millman, J., 204389, Pte.
Minton, W., 5189, L/Cpl.
Mitchell, J., 12164, Pte.
Mitton, G., 17309, Pte.
Monger, C., 27253, Pte.
Monnington, A., 23888, Pte.
Mooney, J., 5746, Pte.
Moore, J., 5609, L/Cpl.
Moore, T., 7720, Sgt.
Moran, J., 7453, Pte.
Morgan, A., 19860, Pte.
Morgan, G. F., 14340, Pte.
Morgan, H., 10515, Pte.
Morley, L. J., 22456, Pte.
Morris, A., 17384, Pte.
Morris, A. E., 7884, C.S.M.
Morris, F., 26519, Pte.
Morris, J., 18339, Pte.
Morris, J. J., 17038, Pte.
Morris, J. W., 10235, Sgt.
Morris, P., 18712, Pte.
Morris, S., 13952, Pte.
Morris, W., 8042, Pte.
Morris, W. E., 12970, L/Cpl.

FIRST BATTALION—*(continued)*

Moseley, W., 7735, Pte.
Munslow, G. L., 43422, Pte.
Musson, R., 27750, Pte.
Myerscough, T., 7584, Pte.

Nagington, F., 8123, Pte.
Nash, F. H. J., 27256, Pte.
Neate, F., 10811, Pte.
Needham, H., 204470, Pte.
Neild, J., 16023, Pte.
Neill, S., 18190, Pte.
Nevin, C. R., 28252, Pte.
Nicholas, G., 7384, Pte.
Nicklin, L. A., 27131, Pte.
Nightingale, T., 10200, Pte.
Nock, B., 7186, Pte.
Nock, E., 19868, Pte.
Nock, J. E., 10444, Pte.
Norris, W. A., 203578, Pte.
Norry, W. J., 21289, Pte.
Nott, S. F., 10345, Pte.
Nugent, E. R., 16989, Pte.
Nugent, E., 15542, Pte.

Oakes, B., 13280, L/Cpl.
Oakley, A., 7791, Pte.
O'Brien, H., 28086, Pte.
O'Connor, E., 6980, Pte.
O'Hara, J. W., 7687, Pte.
Oliver, J., 27061, Pte.
Oram, A. H., 27498, Pte.
Osborne, B., 17086, Pte.
Osborne, R., 10340, Pte.
Owen, C., 7630, Pte.
Owen, J., 24065, Pte.
Owen, J., 16335, Pte.
Owens, A. V., 204499, Pte.

Pace, H., 7516, Pte.
Page, FitzC. S., 10187, L/Sgt.

Page, W., 7390, Pte.
Pagett, A., 20186, Pte.
Palmer, W. H., 16643, Pte.
Parfitt, A. P., 27505, Pte.
Parker, H., 15995, Pte.
Parker, W., 7979, Pte.
Parkin, H., 27501, Pte.
Parks, J. W. A., 10332, Pte.
Parr, E., 7723, L/Cpl.
Parton, A., 9784, Pte.
Payne, J., 17217, Pte.
Peach, J., 9132, L/Cpl.
Pearce, T., 11437, Pte.
Pearson, J. C., 7732, Pte.
Peate, E., 10673, L/Cpl.
Peate, J., 22666, Pte.
Peddar, J., 15266, Pte.
Peer, J. J., 8926, Pte.
Pendry, R. H., 27134, Pte.
Penn, J., 27262, Pte.
Penny, F., 21298, Pte.
Penson, C., 17659, Pte.
Perks, S. T., 21295, Pte.
Perrin, L., 35009, Pte.
Perry, A., 27007, Pte.
Phillips, J. H., 9390, Pte.
Phillips, J. C. O., 10331, L/Cpl.
Phœnix, S., 26825, Pte.
Pickford, J., 22340, Pte.
Pickford, S., 7622, Pte.
Pickles, E. H., 19158, Pte.
Pilkington, E., 204463, Pte.
Pilling, J., 29113, Pte.
Pinches, E., 17819, Pte.
Piper, J., 19240, Pte.
Pitt, G., 9392, Pte.
Pitt, T., 7864, Pte.
Plant, T., 19079, Pte.
Plevin, F. A., 6584, Pte.
Pole, W. J., 27340, Cpl.

FIRST BATTALION—(continued)

Poole, W., 7027, Pte.
Pooler, J., 10371, Pte.
Porter, R., 43393, Pte.
Porter, R., 10220, Pte.
Poulton, J., 23766, Pte.
Powell, A., 10377, Sgt.
Powell, C., 23864, Pte.
Powell, J., 10234, Pte.
Powell, S. C., 28559, Pte.
Powles, H., 23884, Pte.
Pratt, L., 8411, Pte.
Preece, A., 10206, Pte.
Preece, A. H., 10172, Pte.
Preece, F. G., 6703, Pte.
Prenter, J., 6693, Pte.
Price, A. T., 10438, Pte.
Price, A. E., 10316, Pte.
Price, C. J., 9858, Pte.
Price, G., 6129, Pte.
Price, G., 7443, Pte.
Price, H., 7438, Pte.
Price, H., 7664, Pte.
Price, H., 17549, Pte.
Price, J. W., 25315, Pte.
Price, R., 15081, Pte.
Price, T., 6635, Pte.
Price, T. R., 10231, Pte.
Price, W., 9654, Pte.
Pritchard, F., 9952, Pte.
Pritchard, J., 7308, Pte.
Probert, H., 8170, Pte.
Prouten, H., 9716, L/Cpl.
Pryce, G., 7675, Pte.
Pugh, F., 8473, Pte.
Pymble, F. J., 16543, L/Cpl.

Ratcliffe, J., 205827, Pte.
Ray, F., 17661, Pte.
Redford, J. R., 5777, C.S.M.
Reese, F. J., 7859, Pte.

Reeves, J. R., 43496, Pte.
Reynolds, J., 17254, Pte.
Reynolds, W., 10325, L/Cpl.
Richards, E., 19351, Pte.
Richards, E., 34251, Pte.
Richards, H. S., 7883, L/Cpl.
Richards, T., 10079, Pte.
Rigby, C., 9479, Sgt.
Rigby, D., 10057, L/Cpl.
Riley, A., 7097, Pte.
Rippard, R. J., 7295, Pte.
Roberts, A. H., 25031, Pte.
Roberts, D., 10450, Pte.
Roberts, E. C., 18306, Pte.
Roberts, J., 7039, Pte.
Roberts, J., 17000, Pte.
Roberts, J. H., 15067, Pte.
Roberts, R., 10490, Pte.
Roberts, T., 8349, Pte.
Roberts, W., 31443, Pte.
Robinson, G., 7151, Pte.
Robinson, T., 8063, L/Cpl.
Rogers, B., 6938, Pte.
Rogers, R., 8389, Pte.
Roper, J., 13278, Pte.
Rotherham, H., 22912, Pte.
Rothwell, H., 7606, Sgt.
Rouse, G., 10812, Pte.
Rouse, T., 10813, Pte.
Rowlands, D., 20210, Pte.
Rowlands, G., 10399, Pte.
Rowlands, J., 7657, Pte.
Rowson, G., 17014, Pte.
Rudge, R., 21506, Pte.
Ruff, W. H., 17218, Pte.
Russell, T., 19397, Pte.
Ryall, E. H. B., 36650, Pte.
Ryder, T. E., 6595, Pte.

Sallis, A. V., 30045, Pte.

APPENDIX II

Salman, F., 14960, Pte.
Salmon, C. S., 22412, Pte.
Sambrook, C., 21316, Pte.
Samuels, T., 6669, Pte.
Sanders, F. C., 8889, Sgt.
Savage, T., 14025, Pte.
Sawkins, W., 11163, Pte.
Sawyer, C. W., 20772, Pte.
Scudamore, J. N., 25000, Pte.
Seabourne, W. J., 11244, Pte.
Sellman, W. R., 17365, Pte.
Semmens, A. F. W., 30111, Pte.
Seville, W., 7410, Cpl.
Sharratt, G. H., 19396, Pte.
Shaw, C., 21524, Pte.
Sheldon, C. E., 33564, Pte.
Shellam, C. J., 6533, Pte.
Shepherd, C., 22406, Cpl.
Sherry, W., 10170, Pioneer.
Shingler, J. E., 12543, Pte.
Shorrocks, J. B., 27065, Pte.
Shortt, C., 19793, Pte.
Shuker, E. C. E., 18240, Pte.
Shuker, H., 18239, Pte.
Simmill, J. T., 9815, Pte.
Simmonds, P., 25262, Pte.
Simmonds, T., 6747, Pte.
Simon, J. H., 11643, L/Cpl.
Skeen, L. A., 205846, Pte.
Skerratt, J. R., 18008, Pte.
Smith, A., 19742, Pte.
Smith, A., 19743, Pte.
Smith, A. R., 26246, Pte.
Smith, C. H., 18728, Pte.
Smith, E., 8054, Pte.
Smith, E. H., 7167, Pte.
Smith, F., 18260, Pte.
Smith, F., 204502, Pte.
Smith, F. E., 5887, Pte.
Smith, H., 10244, Pte.

Smith, J., 7432, Pte.
Smith, J., 43512, Pte.
Smith, R. G., 7964, Pte.
Smith, S., 4280, Pte.
Smith, T., 26858, Pte.
Smith, T. A., 9874, Cpl.
Smith, W., 23703, Pte.
Spencer, C., 7235, Pte.
Spencer, J., 6691, Pte.
Spencer, W. H., 7553, Pte.
Stack, A. H., 31946, Pte.
Stainton, G., 33532, Pte.
Staley, A., 7485, Pte.
Stedman, T. A., 19239, Pte.
Stevens, W., 27565, Sgt.
Stock, E., 20973, Pte.
Stockton, W., 21311, Pte.
Stow, R., 7548, Pte.
Street, F., 7344, Pte.
Stubbs, W., 23021, Pte.
Sullivan, C., 10409, Pte.
Summerill, H., 30046, Pte.
Surr, S., 7294, Pte.
Swift, W. H., 27529, Pte.
Swindles, E., 27523, Pte.
Swinnerton, H., 6220, Pte.
Symonds, G., 9313, Sgt.

Talbot, A., 17486, Pte.
Tanner, O. B., 27341, Cpl.
Tanswell, H. H., 9897, Pte.
Tart, W., 9837, L/Cpl.
Taylor, R., 28711, Pte.
Taylor, S. A., 6724, Pte.
Taylor, T., 7914, Pte.
Taylor, T. H., 10315, Pte.
Taylor, W., 27015, Pte.
Teague, A. W. T., 10039, Pte.
Terry, R., 38454, Pte.
Thomas, A., 21411, Pte.

THE KING'S SHROPSHIRE LIGHT INFANTRY

Thomas, E., 7227, Pte.
Thomas, H., 7758, Cpl.
Thomas, J. E., 9921, Pte.
Thomas, M. R., 7084, Pte.
Thomas, R. W., 17430, Pte.
Thomas, W., 10070, Pte.
Thomas, W., 25727, Pte.
Thomas, W. E., 7585, Pte.
Thomas, W. F., 27536, Pte.
Thomason, H., 23820, Pte.
Thompson, M., 17743, Pte.
Thompson, R., 5046, Cpl.
Thompson, T. H., 27947, Pte.
Tingle, W. R., 10204, Pte.
Tipton, W. T., 25025, Pte.
Titley, C. L., 14994, L/Cpl.
Titley, G., 23626, Pte.
Titheridge, J. F. C., 25489, Cpl.
Tombs, W. O., 19714, Pte.
Tomlinson, H. V., 8047, Pte.
Tomlinson, J., 25010, Pte.
Tonkin, F., 27535, Pte.
Trafford, W., 7970, Pte.
Tringham, T. W., 7249, Pte.
Tunstall, J. R., 18137, Pte.
Turner, G. J., 25053, Pte.
Turner, J. H., 18001, Pte.
Twiddy, S., 20147, L/Cpl.
Twigger, N., 7680, L/Cpl.

Upton, H. H., 8378, L/Sgt.

Vaughan, R., 6250, Pte.
Venables, J., 10369, Pte.
Venables, W., 7854, Pte.
Vernall, T., 9073, L/Cpl.
Viney, P. C., 27754, L/Cpl.

Wainwright, G. H., 28719, Pte.
Waldron, W. J., 9604, Pte.

Walford, J. C., 9910, Pte.
Walkden, T., 17744, L/Cpl.
Walker, F., 27195, Pte.
Walker, G., 14152, Pte.
Walker, G. F., 38446, Pte.
Walker, H., 35881, Pte.
Walker, J., 7389, Pte.
Walley, G., 16094, Pte.
Walmsley, O., 28010, Pte.
Walsh, J., 15597, Pte.
Walsh, J. H., 26865, Pte.
Walsham, H., 19818, Pte.
Walton, M., 26871, Pte.
Ward, G., 6692, Pte.
Waterhouse, T., 7408, Pte.
Waters, C. D., 26868, Pte.
Watkins, D. G., 14537, L/Cpl.
Watkins, J. W., 27557, Pte.
Watkins, W., 17017, Pte.
Watkins, W. A., 34911, Pte.
Watson, J., 16776, Pte.
Watson, J. A., 9003, Pte.
Watts, H. S., 27598, Pte.
Weale, A. S., 25603, Pte.
Weaver, F. H., 27180, Pte.
Weaver, V. J., 38498, Pte.
Weaver, W. H., 6497, Pte.
Webb, C. F., 8814, Pte.
Webb, R., 23673, Pte.
Webley, J., 10092, Pte.
Wellings, T. J., 11659, Pte.
Wellington, J., 8301, Sgt.
Wells, S., 26838, Pte.
Wells, W. D., 7841, Sgt.
Weston, T., 5882, Pte.
Whinfield, C., 24260, Pte.
White, B., 9719, Pte.
Whitefoot, W., 18362, Pte.
Whitefoot, W. R., 10134, L/Cpl.
Whitfield, C. H., 10145, Pte.

APPENDIX II

Whitney, A., 7328, L/Cpl.
Wickham, M., 9234, Pte.
Wigley, T. H., 21329, Pte.
Wignal, M., 7652, Pte.
Wilcox, H., 23572, Pte.
Wilde, W. H., 21337, Pte.
Wilkes, S. J., 6621, Pte.
Wilkes, W. S., 6113, Pte.
Wilkinson, J., 7617, Pte.
Williams, A., 7952, Pte.
Williams, C., 23609, L/Cpl.
Williams, E., 25419, Pte.
Williams, G., 6333, Pte.
Williams, G., 26864, Pte.
Williams, G. J., 4977, C.Q.M.S.
Williams, H., 230488, Pte.
Williams, J., 27192, Pte.
Williams, J. E., 8188, Pte.
Williams, J. I., 202121, Pte.
Williams, J., 6275, Pte.
Williams, P. C., 10238, Pte.
Williams, W. H., 7980, Pte.
Williams, W., 8072, L/Cpl.
Williams, W., 26845, Pte.
Williams, W., 8263, Sgt.
Wilson, E., 9780, Pte.
Wilson, J., 43518, Pte.
Wilson, W. H., 9017, Sgt.
Wiltshire, W., 20329, Pte.

Windsor, E., 204509, Pte.
Winn, J. S., 8724, Pte.
Winterbottom, J., 204450, Pte.
Wintle, R., 205847, Pte.
Wood, C., 18682, Pte.
Wood, E., 205832, Pte.
Wood, H., 26354, Pte.
Wood, W., 6574, Pte.
Wood, W. J., 7371, Pte.
Woodcock, H., 20177, Pte.
Workman, A.W., 205169, L/Cpl.
Worrall, E., 21343, Pte.
Wright, E., 33851, Pte.
Wright, H., 11488, Pte.
Wright, T., 25901, Pte.
Wright, W. J., 8901, L/Cpl.
Wrigley, J., 204475, Pte.
Wyer, E. B., 16871, Pte.
Wylde, J., 8055, Cpl.
Wyles, R., 204460, Pte.

Yapp, H., 21345, Pte.
Yates, W. E., 17367, Pte.
Yelland, F., 6245, Pte.
Yeomans, G. H., 18189, Pte.
Young, C. W., 6076, Bugler.
Young, G., 9852, L/Cpl.
Young, J. T., 5681, L/Cpl.
Young, W. H., 8458, Pte.

SECOND BATTALION

Aldred, W., 7378, Pte.
Allen, G., 9297, L/Cpl.
Allsopp, F. J., 6646, C.S.M.
Arrowsmith, A., 6054, Pte.
Arthurs, F. S., 8433, Pte.
Ashton, E., 6758, Pte.
Axten, J. F., 9245, Pte.

Baikie, S. J. C., 6304, R.S.M.
Baker, W., 9715, Pte.
Baldwin, H., 9446, Pte.
Bamber, W., 13806, Pte.
Barnett, A. E., 6652, Pte.
Beasley, E. W., 8810, Pte.
Beech, J., 7922, Pte.

THE KING'S SHROPSHIRE LIGHT INFANTRY

Bell, H., 6834, Pte.
Bell, W., 8824, Pte.
Bennett, J., 7364, Pte.
Bentley, A., 8701, Pte.
Bethell, J., 24799, Pte.
Bevan, G., 7384, Pte.
Bibby, J., 6727, Pte.
Biddulph, F., 6057, Pte.
Bignell, E. R., 17234, Pte.
Bisbrown, W., 16724, L/Cpl.
Blackmore, H., 14909, Pte.
Blake, P., 16405, Pte.
Bond, J., 5318, Pte.
Bookes, F., 16214, Pte.
Bray, W., 5994, Pte.
Bright, J., 6776, Pte.
Bromfield, W., 5247, Sgt.
Brooks, H., 6427, Pte.
Brough, J., 5984, Pte.
Brown, D., 8381, Pte.
Burgess, F. A., 9236, Pte.
Burgess, J., 7193, Pte.
Burrell, E. G., 8822, L/Cpl.
Burton, F. C., 7100, Pte.
Butcher, A., 10010, Pte.

Caffull, W., 9867, Pte.
Callf, R. F., 9167, Cpl.
Camp, W. H., 7836, Pte.
Carlton, A. F., 8550, Pte.
Carthew, J., 9081, Pte.
Cartwright, E., 16928, Pte.
Casewell, W. J., 6286, Pte.
Chapman, B. W., 8600, L/Cpl.
Charles, H., 6055, Pte.
Clarke, W., 9422, Pte.
Clarke, W. C., 5927, Pte.
Cliff, P., 11208, Pte.
Clueit, N., 16387, Pte.
Collier, F., 7618, Pte.

Collingwood, T., 6295, Pte.
Collins, G., 22042, Pte.
Coney, W. H., 8985, Pte.
Cooper, R. H., 6699, Pte.
Cooper, T., 6713, Pte.
Cornwell, J. R., 6774, Pte.
Cracknell, A., 31784, Pte.
Crawford, D., 6467, Pte.
Crompton, R. McC., 16704, Pte.
Cronshaw, R., 6586, Pte.
Crook, D., 6082, L/Cpl.
Cunnington, T., 15055, Pte.

Dale, A. J., 9127, Pte.
Daly, B., 8145, Cpl.
Davies, A., 9146, Pte.
Davies, E., 6387, Pte.
Davies, S., 8070, Pte.
Davies, T., 9816, L/Cpl.
Davies, T. J., 6513, Pte.
Davis, C., 8996, Pte.
Davis, S., 9539, Pte.
Dearling, A., 8877, Pte.
Dickinson, C. T., 6877, Sgt.
Dixon, G., 6689, Pte.
Dockerty, W., 6079, Pte.
Douglas, W., 7008, Pte.
Dugmore, W. H., 8598, Sgt.
Dwyer, W., 45648, Pte.
Dyas, G., 9302, Pte.
Dyke, G. E., 24193, Pte.
Dyter, A., 8089, Pte.

Ebrey, T. H., 9441, L/Cpl.
Edmondson, R. H., 31682, Pte.
Edwards, T., 15017, Pte.
Edwards, W. A., 8441, Pte.
Ellis, J. W., 8766, Pte.
Ellis, W., 7577, L/Cpl.
Ellison, H., 10493, Pte.

APPENDIX II

SECOND BATTALION—(*continued*)

Evans, J. H., 9068, Sgt.
Evans, T. H., 7269, Pte.
Evans, W. E., 6490, L/Cpl.
Evans, W. H., 7851, Pte.
Evans, W., 9738, Pte.

Field, H., 8579, Pte.
Field, W. H., 7497, Pte.
Finn, J., 14410, Pte.
Follis, S., 6091, Pte.
Fox, A. W., 8311, Pte.
Foxall, R. E., 6813, Pte.
Foxall, T., 8027, C.S.M.
Fraser, W., 8585, Pte.
Frost, T. B., 6507, Pte.
Fulcher, A. E., 8956, Pte.

Gardner, E., 9561, Pte.
Gilbert, W., 10004, Pte.
Glassey, W., 16203, Pte.
Goodall, J., 7192, Pte.
Gray, J., 6746, Pte.
Gray, T., 6386, Pte.
Greatwich, J., 6821, Pte.
Griffiths, A. D., 6504, Pte.
Griffiths, C. S., 7483, Pte.

Hague, T., 6264, Pte.
Hale, W. G., 7626, Pte.
Hall, E. G., 9161, Pte.
Halliday, J., 8199, Pte.
Halliwell, G., 16250, Pte.
Hamer, A. H., 7201, Pte.
Hampson, James, 15990, Pte.
Hancocks, H., 15940, Pte.
Hancox, C., 5081, Sgt.
Handley, M., 8694, Pte.
Hanners, R. A., 9420, Pte.
Hanson, F., 9139, Pte.
Harris, J., 7324, Pte.

Harris, J., 8305, Pte.
Harris, S., 16796, Pte.
Harris, T., 16456, Pte.
Harvey, W., 6130, Pte.
Haycocks, J., 10706, Pte.
Haylock, G., 8315, Pte.
Hayward, M., 4319, Pte.
Hedges, W., 6408, Pte.
Hepworth, E., 6696, Pte.
Herriman, J., 5827, Pte.
Heywood, G., 9500, Pte.
Higgins, A. G., 11909, L/Cpl.
Hill, J. W., 8085, Pte.
Hill, T., 7703, Pte.
Hill, W. E., 8350, Pte.
Hill, W. E., 10373, Pte.
Hines, W., 6591, Pte.
Hinksman, G. J. F., 8686, Pte.
Hodgetts, G. H., 7413, Cpl.
Hodson, T., 6866, Pte.
Holland, W., 6565, Pte.
Holt, J., 6410, Pte.
Hopkins, W., 6097, Pte.
Hostler, H. G., 9192, L/Cpl.
Howells, J., 7179, Pte.
Huband, G., 5984, Cpl.
Hulston, G., 9683, Pte.
Humphries, A. E., 6371, Pte.
Hunter, F. T., 8648, Pte.

I'Anson, E., 8856, Pte.
Iveson, C., 6134, Pte.

Jarman, J., 9775, Pte.
Jarrett, J., 7414, Pte.
Jarvis, I. J., 6138, L/Cpl.
Jarvis, W., 6160, Pte.
Jeffs, W., 6437, L/Cpl.
Jenkins, J., 14570, L/Cpl.
Jenner, C. W., 8744, Pte.

THE KING'S SHROPSHIRE LIGHT INFANTRY

SECOND BATTALION—(continued)

Johnson, H., 16467, Pte.
Johnson, H. W., 9565, Pte.
Jones, A. G., 6900, Pte.
Jones, C., 9080, Sgt.
Jones, D., 9724, Pte.
Jones, E., 9431, Pte.
Jones, E., 6600, Pte.
Jones, F., 11004, Pte.
Jones, G., 5631, Pte.
Jones, H., 8054, Pte.
Jones, H., 6351, Pte.
Jones, H., 7466, Pte.
Jones, H., 8482, Pte.
Jones, J., 6828, Pte.
Jones, J., 9318, Pte.
Jones, S. H. W., 11157, Pte.
Jones, W., 11299, Pte.
Jones, W., 6650, Pte.
Jordan, T., 7834, L/Cpl.
Jordan, T., 4924, Pte.

Kay, J., 16676, Pte.
Kennard, W. F., 31713, Pte.
Kenyon, W., 16220, Pte.
Kerridge, H., 6514, Pte.
Killeen, J., 7169, Pte.
Kingsbury, J., 7260, Pte.
Kitchen, L. C. B., 9537, Pte.
Kite, G. W., 9235, Pte.
Knowles, J. H., 15993, Pte.

Law, H. A., 6438, L/Cpl.
Lawless, J., 6739, Cpl.
Lawrence, G., 8710, Pte.
Leach, J. A., 16217, Pte.
Leavens, R. C. W., 9492, Pte.
Lester, E., 6898, Bugler
Levitt, A., 35565, Pte.
Lewis, A. P., 9786, Pte.
Lewis, D., 8474, Cpl.

Lewis, J., 9655, Pte.
Lilwall, T., 6203, Pte.
Lloyd, G., 16164, Pte.
Long, R., 9609, Pte.
Longworth, J. T., 7021, Pte.
Loose, A. E., 6154, Pte.
Lucas, G., 7290, Pte.

Manns, F., 8299, Pte.
Manuel, J. A., 6644, Pte.
Marmont, E., 9777, Pte.
Martin, H. J., 16423, Pte.
Mason, T., 6201, Pte.
Massey, H., 6982, Pte.
Massey, J., 6628, Pte.
Mauger, H. T., 8515, Pte.
McAvan, W., 9024, Pte.
McGuire, T., 6103, Pte.
McLarty, D. M., 6909, C.S.M.
Meaney, J., 9267, Pte.
Meredith, G., 5719, Pte.
Meredith, W. A., 9305, Bgl.
Miller, J., 8906, Pte.
Millington, H., 6667, Pte.
Minshall, W., 11186, Pte.
Mitchell, A., 9333, Pte.
Moore, J. H., 6402, Pte.
Morgan, J., 7104, Pte.
Morrey, A., 6781, Cpl.
Morris, A. E., 9635, Pte.
Morris, F. C., 9329, Cpl.
Morris, J., 7292, Pte.
Morris, J., 7997, Pte.
Morris, R., 16680, Pte.
Munday, W., 15054, Pte.
Myerscough, G., 6513, Pte.

Nightingale, H., 6501, Pte.
Noble, J. L., 8895, Sgt.
North, H., 6396, Pte.

APPENDIX II

Ould, A. H., 8514, L/Cpl.
Owen, F., 5588, Pte.
Owen, F., 8882, Pte.
Owen, G., 15052, Pte.
Owen, T., 9693, Pte.

Palin, F., 9814, Pte.
Palmer, F. H. C., 31841, Pte.
Patten, G., 16022, Pte.
Peters, O., 6958, Pte.
Peters, W. J., 31848, Pte.
Pheasant, J., 24111, Pte.
Phillips, T. H., 8564, Pte.
Phillipson, J., 5931, Pte.
Phillpotts, A., 6899, Pte.
Plant, J. E., 7371, Pte.
Podd, C. T., 8552, Pte.
Porter, C. D., 8187, Sgt.
Povey, W., 6869, Pte.
Powell, A., 8118, Pte.
Prater, J. T., 24703, Pte.
Preece, H., 9011, Pte.
Preece, T., 16949, Pte.
Price, C., 6440, Pte.
Price, R. H., 9039, Pte.
Pritchard, J., 6568, Pte.
Pritchard, J., 8983, Pte.
Pulling, H. T., 7580, Cpl.

Radborn, J., 7787, Pte.
Ralph, J., 16739, Pte.
Randles, F., 9722, Pte.
Reakes, W. G., 7445, Pte.
Redwood, F. C., 9148, Pte.
Reeves, H. T., 9052, Cpl.
Reynolds, E., 9576, Pte.
Reynolds, T., 8878, ——
Rhodes, L., 6425, Pte.
Ricketts, A., 6487, Pte.
Ridgley, A., 8091, Pte.

Ridgway, J., 6793, Pte.
Riley, A. E., 8609, Pte.
Riley, W., 9678, Pte.
Robinson, J., 9515, Pte.
Rogers, A., 10181, Pte.
Rollings, T., 6620, Pte.
Roscoe, F. H., 16708, Pte.
Rosser, G., 7607, Pte.
Roster, T., 6838, Pte.
Rostron, J., 16403, Pte.
Russell, V., 9817, Pte.

Sankey, B., 6809, Pte.
Saunders, F., 6896, Pte.
Scudamore, T. A., 23531, Pte.
Selby, J., 6662, Pte.
Seymour, J., 6694, Pte.
Shellam, A. E., 6534, Pte.
Shepherd, S., 6096, Pte.
Shorland, J., 25932, Pte.
Shrubsole, H. A. V., 8902, Pte.
Simcox, A. E., 6909, Pte.
Simmons, W., 8351, Cpl.
Simonds, A. T., 6528, Pte.
Simpson, T. B., 7682, Pte.
Smith, G., 8692, Pte.
Smith, H., 5364, Sgt.
Smith, J., 9627, Pte.
Smith, T., 5932, Pte.
Smith, W., 6502, Pte.
Smith, W., 6529, Pte.
Speake, A., 9226, Pte.
Spear, H., 5420, Sgt.
Spooner, J., 6242, Pte.
Stargatt, M., 9149, Pte.
Steers, G. J., 9265, Pte.
Stephan, F., 24064, Pte.
Stevens, P., 6204, Pte.
Stevenson, F., 16419, Pte.
Street, S., 16813, Pte.

THE KING'S SHROPSHIRE LIGHT INFANTRY

Tanner, H. J., 34664, Pte.
Taylor, H., 5393, Pte.
Terry, A. E., 8491, Cpl.
Thomas, W., 9796, Cpl.
Thompson, G., 9638, Pte.
Tilbee, W., 9240, Pte.
Till, J., 16108, Pte.
Travers, T., 7242, Pte.
Treliving, A., 7810, Pte.
Trevor, A., 6663, Pte.
Trow, T. W., 7035, Pte.
Turnbull, F., 32828, Pte.
Turner, J. W., 10542, Pte.

Venning, E. M., 9646, Cpl.

Wait, J., 6845, Pte.
Walker, H. F., 6554, Pte.
Wall, B., 5979, Pte.

Walsh, D., 15802, Pte.
Watkins, G., 9589, Cpl.
Wells, S. A., 10654, Pte.
West, J. G., 31756, Pte.
White, W. J., 6521, Pte.
Widdicks, A. V., 9190, Pte.
Wilkinson, C. W., 31754, Pte.
Williams, A. E., 9228, Pte.
Williams, E., 6155, Pte.
Williams, M., 7991, Pte.
Williams, W. H., 6579, L/Cpl.
Wilson, F., 9136, Pte.
Worrall, F. G., 8496, L/Cpl.
Wright, J., 6862, Pte.
Wycherley, F., 6076, Pte.
Wynn, T., 10453, Pte.
Wynne, T., 9752, Pte.

Young, B., 20642, Pte.

THIRD BATTALION

Bowness, W. E., 15282, Pte.
Burke, P., 18655, Pte.
Cure, W. H., 7493, Pte.
Evans, A. G., 19805, Pte.
Evans, T. H., 44204, Pte.
Good, W. T., 24492, Pte.
Grundy, T., 16411, Pte.
Jenkins, E. J., 8036, Pte.
Jenkins, T., 43793, Pte.
Johnson, M., 7721, Pte.
Kenny, T., 6987, Pte.
Knapper, A., 44101, Pte.
Lloyd, A., 11931, Pte.
Matthews, J., 33228, Pte.
McCullock, W., 21591, Pte.
McLean, J., 17514, Sgt.
Mellor, A., 8338, L/Cpl.

Morgan, D., 12413, Pte.
Openshaw, W., 23913, Pte.
Powles, J. T., 22052, Pte.
Pritchard, W., 44138, Pte.
Smith, F., 22083, Pte.
Sullivan, E., 11290, Pte.
Summers, A., 44016, Pte.
Taylor, T., 33276, Pte.
Thomas, H. G., 9300, Pte.
Turk, J., 20842, Pte.
Turner, G., 18501, Pte.
Walker, S., 12485, Sgt.
Watson, W., 32369, Pte.
Wells, G., 16071, Pte.
Willison, C., 23900, Pte.
Winter, R., 17608, Sgt.
Winterbottom, E., 7490, Pte.
Wright, G., 7785, Pte.

APPENDIX II

FOURTH BATTALION

Adams, L. H., 200110, Sgt.
Aldersey, J., 35712, Pte.
Allen, F., 11618, Pte.
Andrews, F., 200416, Pte.
Ashton, S., 31464, Pte.
Asterley, C., 200961, Pte.
Atkinson, R., 35718, Pte.

Baguley, S. W., 28373, Pte.
Bailey, F., 200358, Pte.
Bain, W. W., 201861, Pte.
Baker, H. F., 28396, Pte.
Band, C., 35719, Pte.
Barker, W., 35722, Pte.
Barnett, J., 200540, Pte.
Baron, W., 35723, Pte.
Beard, M., 200202, Pte.
Beech, F., 201040, Pte.
Bennett, W. H., 201097, Pte.
Berry, H., 28278, Pte.
Bibby, R., 27987, Pte.
Bickers, E., 16406, Pte.
Bingham, E., 200220, Pte.
Bishop, C., 201281, Pte.
Boden, W. J., 201379, Pte.
Bounds, O., 201460, Pte.
Bracegirdle, R., 43053, Pte.
Bradeley, G., 200321, Pte.
Bradley, E., 16484, Pte.
Bradley, J., 200495, Pte.
Brazier, W. E., 203588, Pte.
Breeze, C. J., 1379, Pte.
Brereton, J. H., 22273, Pte.
Briggs, S. J., 200092, L/Sgt.
Briggs, W., 200710, L/Cpl.
Brisco, R., 200782, Pte.
Broadhurst, A., 43049, Pte.
Brooks, C., 29211, Sgt.
Brooks, T., 36482, Pte.
Brown, C. E., 31636, Pte.

Brown, G., 200909, Pte.
Brown, W., 18476, Cpl.
Brown, W. A., 35734, Pte.
Brunt, G., 17693, Pte.

Carline, J., 200163, Pte.
Carter, T., 43041, Pte.
Challenor, F., 11462, Pte.
Chetwood, A., 201398, Pte.
Clague, W. J., 31486, Pte.
Clapinson, H., 201471, Pte.
Clayton, W. A., 6238, Pte.
Cole, F., 28608, Pte.
Connolly, W., 35751, Pte.
Cooke, E. R., 28391, Pte.
Cooke, H., 19249, Pte.
Corbett, G., 34394, Pte.
Corbett, G. A., 200076, Pte.
Corfield, E. G., 24080, Pte.
Craven, H., 13643, Pte.
Cross, V. W., 22159, Pte.
Cullis, A., 200185, Pte.
Cullis, L. J., 200417, Pte.

Dainty, T., 201258, Pte.
Darricott, G., 200336, Pte.
Davies, B. L., 27853, Pte.
Davies, C., 15922, Sgt.
Davies, C. H., 201126, Pte.
Davies, E. R., 16823, Pte.
Davies, E., 18288, L/Cpl.
Davies, F. W., 35895, Pte,
Davies, G., 201301, Pte.
Davies, J., 26788, Pte.
Davies, T. H., 201130, Pte.
Davies, W. P., 200073, Sgt.
David, E., 204095, Pte.
Dawson, A., 205124, Pte.
Dawson, S. J., 31490, Pte.
Dennis, T., 14366, Pte.

365

FOURTH BATTALION—*(continued)*

Denyer, A., 26101, Pte.
Driffill, H., 35767, Pte.
Dudley, W., 200733, Pte.
Dungey, H. W. T., 28622, Pte.
Dunkerley, H., 28213, Pte.
Dyke, A. G., 31641, Pte.
Dykes, R., 24523, Pte.

Easthope, R. J. H., 201518, Pte.
Edwards, G. A., 9961, Sgt.
Egglestone, F. W., 29243, Pte.
Elcock, S. T., 201447, Pte.
Ellery, W., 28115, Pte.
Elsby, A., 34569, Pte.
Emery, H., 200276, Pte.
Evangelista, A., 28722, Pte.
Evans, A., 10851, Pte.
Evans, B. P., 31508, Pte.
Evans, H., 31503, Pte.
Evans, M. E., 36503, Pte.
Evans, W., 200661, Pte.

Faragher, W., 33491, Pte.
Fellows, A., 200682, Pte.
Ferguson, T., 28300, Pte.
Fieldhouse, T. R., 201263, Pte.
Fletcher, T., 31526, Pte.
Follows, H., 35780, Pte.
Franklin, H. R., 204097,
    A/L/Cpl.
Freeman, C., 200205, Cpl.
Freeman, J., 200302, Sgt.
Furber, W., 26900, Pte.

Gamage, E. J., 31511, Pte.
Gemmell, A. H., 35783, Pte.
Godwin, T., 201254, Pte.
Goodman, T., 34705, Pte.
Goodson, S. R., 28289, Pte.
Goodwin, G., 200084, Sgt.

Green, W., 200303, Pte.
Gregory, P., 43050, Pte.
Grice, O., 200099, Sgt.
Griffiths, J. L., 200452, Pte.
Griffiths, W., 200498, L/Cpl.
Groves, J. S., 200747, Pte.
Guntripp, T. E., 31522, Pte.
Gwatkin, W. T., 25604, Pte.

Haines, S., 200749, Pte.
Hall, A. E., 35788, Pte.
Hall, F. G., 205186, Cpl.
Hall, S., 204822, Pte.
Hall, W. T., 200783, Pte.
Hamer, G., 200748, Pte.
Hanson, A. C., 200551, Pte.
Harley, J., 200257, Bugler.
Harries, P. A. V., 21952, Pte.
Harris, T., 29242, Pte.
Harrison, T. A., 35794, Pte.
Hart, E., 20850, Pte.
Harvey, A. J., 29217, Pte.
Haseley, F., 200191, L/Cpl.
Haywood, W. J., 14427, Pte.
Head, E., 200291, Pte.
Head, J. E. E., 200738, Pte.
Healey, A. V., 200097, L/Sgt.
Healey, J., 200522, Cpl.
Hewitt, C. A., 200617, Pte.
Hibbert, H., 204177, Pte.
Higginson, A., 200314, Pte.
Higham, T., 35801, Pte.
Hilton, W., 35804, Pte.
Hobin, W., 200737, Pte.
Hobson, J., 31513, Pte.
Hockenhull, E., 33597, Pte.
Hodson, J., 200329, Pte.
Hope, H., 35807, Pte.
Hoskison, H., 28291, Pte.
Howe, T. J., 31531, Pte.

APPENDIX II

Howell, G. O., 31521, Pte.
Howells, J., 200954, Pte.
Hughes, A., 35811, Pte.
Hughes, J., 200505, L/Cpl.
Hughes, J. M., 25848, Pte.
Hughes, M., 201370, Pte.
Hughes, M., 31518, Pte.
Humphreys, J. H., 200482, L/Cpl.
Husband, J., 200809, Pte.

Jackson, W., 200369, Pte.
James, A., 32742, Pte.
James, G., 27891, Pte.
Johnson, W. H., 9567, Cpl.
Jones, A. J., 17123, L/Cpl.
Jones, A. W., 200400, Pte.
Jones, A., 201499, Pte.
Jones, B., 201357, Bugler.
Jones, C. E., 35817, Cpl.
Jones, E., 201042, Pte.
Jones, H. D., 201178, Pte.
Jones, J., 31608, Pte.
Jones, J. R., 200588, Pte.
Jones, M. W., 201277, Pte.
Jones, N., 200184, Pte.
Jones, P., 200622, Pte.
Jones, P., 201373, Pte.
Jones, S. O., 200208, Cpl.
Jones, T. H., 200533, Cpl.
Jones, W. E., 202810, Sgt.
Joyce, A., 200180, Pte.

Kaler, F., 31541, Pte.
Kelly, W., 25374, Pte.

Lane, E., 35827, Pte.
Lane, P., 201112, Pte.
Latter, J., 27088, Pte.
Lees, P., 201317, Pte.

Lester, E., 43056, Pte.
Lewis, A., 200915, Pte.
Lewis, J., 201495, L/Cpl.
Lewis, T., 200363, Sgt.
Light, J. J., 204107, Pte.
Lloyd, G., 200599, Cpl.
Lloyd, S. S., 31631, Pte.
Lloyd, T. M., 201441, Pte.
Lowe, J., 35898, Pte.
Lowe, L., 21277, Pte.

Makin, H., 7506, Pte.
Maley, J., 200169, Pte.
Mansell, W., 200195, Pte.
Mansell, W. G., 201226, L/Cpl.
Marriott, T., 28297, Pte.
Martin, A., 201076, Pte.
Mason, G., 19687, Pte.
Mason, W., 36543, L/Cpl.
Maughan, J., 31989, Pte.
Maund, F., 200531, Pte.
McCullock, A., 29111, Pte.
McKay, T., 35833, Pte.
McKeown, P., 36546, Pte.
Meredith, H. J., 31552, Pte.
Meyer, M. S. D., 29166, Pte.
Millward, J., 201247, Pte.
Mitchell, J., 35840, Pte.
Moore, T., 35841, Pte.
Moreton, P. C., 14702, Pte.
Morgan, J. E., 200635, L/Cpl.
Morris, C., 200532, Pte.
Mullard, W. J., 200200, L/Cpl.
Myers, M. B., 29235, Pte.
Myles, J., 28495, Pte.

Newnes, G., 200665, Pte.
Nicholas, B., 200081, Sgt.
Nock, A., 200433, Pte.
Norman, G., 35844, Pte.
Norris, J., 34606, Pte.

367

FOURTH BATTALION—(continued)

Oakley, W., 200309, Pte.
O'Neill, E., 36415, Pte.
Onions, H., 11240, Pte.
Orme, A., 35846, Pte.
Orrell, P., 35847, Pte.
Owen, G. E., 203722, Pte.
Owen, J., 201333, Pte.
Owen, T. C., 200264, Pte.
Owen, W. H., 29163, L/Cpl.

Paddock, W. H., 200677, Pte.
Paine, O. J., 28395, Pte.
Parker, W. F., 35850, Pte.
Parry, H. L., 31556, Pte.
Parry, R., 35852, Pte.
Parsons, M., 31569, Pte.
Pearce, A., 200233, Pte.
Pearson, G. R. D., 200333, Sgt.
Pennock, J. A., 31565, Pte.
Percy, T. F., 36420, Pte.
Perry, F. A., 200275, Pte.
Picken, W., 21383, Pte.
Pickford, R., 26998, Pte.
Pidcock, H., 31614, Pte.
Pinfold, W. J., 28381, Pte.
Plant, G., 200253, Sgt.
Plant, J., 201007, Pte.
Player, G. A., 201508, Pte.
Potter, W. J., 200569, Pte.
Powell, G., 200868, Pte.
Pratt, V. D., 28380, Pte.
Price, J., 201418, Pte.
Price, J., 201428, Pte.
Price, S., 200390, Pte.
Prince, F. A., 201077, Pte.
Prodger, A. E., 200618, Pte.
Pryce, W., 200821, Pte.
Pugh, A. T., 18618, Pte.
Pugh, G. H., 200932, Pte.
Pugh, H., 7698, Pte.

Pugh, W. W., 201327, Pte.
Purdy, T., 9467, Sgt.
Purslow, E., 200822, Pte.

Quayle, R., 31617, Pte.

Redpath, W., 31378, Pte.
Rider, B., 11895, Pte.
Ridgway, F., 18602, Sgt.
Rigby, S., 200374, Pte.
Riley, W., 36431, Pte.
Roberts, C. J., 36436, L/Cpl.
Roberts, G., 201116, Pte.
Roberts, G. H., 34453, Pte.
Roberts, W., 10037, Pte.
Rogers, F. W., 200789, Pte.
Rogers, J., 200146, Pte.
Rogers, T. E., 6540, Pte.
Rogers, W., 200775, Pte.
Rowlands, D. T., 26036, Pte.
Rowley, J., 2493, Pte.
Rudd, A., 1421, Pte.
Ryder, W. H., 4483, Pte.

Sanders, F. W., 28529, Pte.
Sanderson, W. T., 24934, Pte.
Sandham, A., 28530, Pte.
Sawyer, J. J., 34248, Pte.
Scarratt, G. H., 201311, Pte.
Scutt, H. V. G., 35336, Pte.
Seamark, G. A., 28525, Pte.
Self, G. D., 200536, Pte.
Shaw, W. H., 200857, Sgt.
Shellard, W., 204119, Pte.
Shipp, W. E., 205138, Sgt.
Skelton, T., 201012, Pte.
Small, J. W., 200034, Sgt.-
    Major.
Small, J., 24425, Pte.
Smallman, H., 200690, Pte.

APPENDIX II

FOURTH BATTALION—(continued)

Smith, F. D., 28284, Pte.
Smith, J. G., 200771, Pte.
Smith, P. E., 200995, Pte.
Smith, S. A., 28384, Pte.
Smith, W. H., 28207, Pte.
Spain, H., 27669, Pte.
Spencer, J., 34579, Pte.
Stacey, W., 8180, L/Cpl.
Standfield, A. J., 15123, Pte.
Steele, A. B., 31277, Cpl.
Steele, L., 14451, Pte.
Stephenson, J. F., 35870, L/Cpl.
Steventon, J., 200640, L/Sgt.
Stinchcombe, A. H., 200105, Cpl.
Stott, W., 35871, Pte.
Street, A. H., 28369, Cpl.
Stuart, D., 35872, Pte.
Sumner, J., 34553, Pte.
Suthern, T., 200885, Pte.
Symonds, H. W., 34452, Pte.

Taylor, A. F., 200997, Pte.
Taylor, F., 35874, Pte.
Taylor, J. G., 26122, Pte.
Taylor, R., 8583, Sgt.
Tew, L., 201316, Pte.
Thomas, M. L., 14265, Pte.
Thorn, P. D., 34882, Pte.
Tingle, H. J., 25830, Pte.
Tipton, E. E., 200266, Pte.
Tomlinson, L. R., 12566, Pte.
Townson, C., 28214, Pte.
Tudor, H., 718, Sgt.

Vaughan, S., 200077, L/Cpl.
Vaughan, T., 11751, Pte.

Vaughan, W. A., 200151, L/Cpl.

Walker, A., 1839, Pte.
Walker, J. A., 23949, Pte.
Ward, G. E. A., 34033, Pte.
Ward, H., 1300, Pte.
Wardle, J., 26480, Pte.
Wardle, T., 201132, Pte.
Watkins, D., 25137, Pte.
Weir, J. W., 28287, Pte.
Wenlock, J. A., 201388, Pte.
White, G., 201298, Pte.
White, J. W., 28546, Pte.
Wilkins, E., 27559, Pte.
Wilkins, W. H., 28388, Pte.
Wilkinson, J., 31449, Pte.
Wilkinson, P., 24251, Cpl.
Williams, A. J., 200487, Pte.
Williams, R. L., 31591, Pte.
Williams, S., 17081, Pte.
Wilson, E., 201393, Pte.
Wilson, S., 43864, Pte.
Wilson, W. G., 35888, Pte.
Windibank, F. A., 205140, Pte.
Wise, C., 35889, Pte.
Woodward, H., 28305, Pte.
Woodyer, J., 31607, Pte.
Woosnam, S. J., 201467, Pte.
Worthington, F., 31633, Pte.
Wright, F. J., 17398, Pte.
Wycherley, R. H., 200094, L/Cpl.

Yates, A., 36460, Pte.
Yeomans, E., 200658, Pte.
Young, H., 36461, L/Cpl.

THE KING'S SHROPSHIRE LIGHT INFANTRY

4TH RESERVE BATTALION

Brown, J. L., 45149, Pte.
Clare, W. H., 45146, Pte.
Collins, W. R., 45071, Pte.
Davidson, S. J., 2165, Pte.
Davies, F. N., 45169, Pte.
Eaton, A. C. P., 45226, Pte.
Evans, T., 44346, Pte.

Hill, T. M., 44385, Pte.
Huxley, H., 45094, Pte.
Jones, F., 44317, Pte.
O'Brien, J., 45534, Pte.
Rowe, W., 209080, Pte.
Ward, J. H., 201529, Cpl.

2/4TH BATTALION

Banks, F., 21100, Pte.
Barnett, H., 20950, L/Cpl.
Davies, T. W., 21075, Pte.
Fiswick, W., 20662, Pte.
Hepworth, H., 4882, Pte.

Hyam, A., 20886, Pte.
Plimmer, J., 20793, Pte.
Thornes, R., 20688, Pte.
Vaughan, C., 2743, Pte.
Ward, W. H., 2211, Sgt.

3/4TH BATTALLION

Davies, A. H., 4232, Pte.

FIFTH BATTALION

Abbot, H., 16814, Pte.
Abram, R., 17737, Pte.
Adderley, F. S., 17222, Pte.
Addis, J. A., 11292, Sgt.
Addison, A. C., 20892, Pte.
Addyman, H., 6738, Pte.
Aldred, W. G., 20821, Pte.
Alldred, E., 20877, Pte.
Allman, H., 18850, L/Cpl.
Allsopp, E., 20065, Pte.
Allsopp, G., 11046, Pte.
Almond, W., 32149, Pte.
Amos, A. T., 8528, Pte.
Amos, H., 18227, L/Cpl.
Anderson, W. J., 8849, Cpl.

Andrews, H., 12106, Pte.
Andrews, J., 11619, Pte.
Andrews, S., 19324, Pte.
Ankers, F., 11116, Cpl.
Annum, B. J., 10763, Pte.
Apperley, F., 24071, Pte.
Arrowsmith, J. C., 16361, Pte.
Attwood, C., 10044, Cpl.
Attwood, H., 204085, Pte.
Austin, F., 17534, Pte.
Austin, P. E., 11054, Pte.
Aylwin, G., 26149, Pte.

Bache, R., 10595, Pte.
Bagley, W. J., 11120, Pte.

FIFTH BATTALION—*(continued)*

Bailey, E., 18127, Pte.
Baker, W., 10655, Sgt.
Baldwin, W., 17233, Pte.
Ball, A. E., 10498, L/Cpl.
Barber, R. A., 16967, Pte.
Barker, J., 17466, Pte.
Barnes, J., 14990, Pte.
Barnes, J., 16058, Pte.
Barnett, W., 11443, Pte.
Bartlam, T., 20652, Pte.
Bate, J. T., 11119, Pte.
Bates, J., 26170, Pte.
Bath, H., 13219, Pte.
Baugh, G., 18159, Pte.
Bayliss, R. J., 17427, Pte.
Beaty, J., 18325, Pte.
Bebbington, A., 14402, Pte.
Bebbington, H., 11461, Sgt.
Beck, A. H. G., 6701, Pte.
Beck, G., 20007, Pte.
Beckworth, S. F., 17794, Pte.
Beddoe, B., 11490, Pte.
Beddow, J., 200975, Pte.
Beech, F., 24078, Pte.
Beeston, H., 9714, C.S.M.
Belton, T. W., 16134, Cpl.
Benjamin, E. J., 204089, Pte.
Berger, H. E., 26173, Pte.
Bickley, H., 9789, Sgt.
Birch, A., 18126, Pte.
Blackburn, W., 20028, Pte.
Blair, W., 17877, Pte.
Blakemore, T., 10669, Pte.
Blandford, G.W., 11739, L/Cpl.
Bohen, J., 205016, Sgt.
Bonner, J., 26105, Pte.
Bostock, H., 24225, Pte.
Bowen, J. W., 18107, Pte.
Bowen, T. A., 7975, Pte.
Boycott, H., 17392, Pte.

Boyde, G., 20104, Pte.
Brace, L., 5337, Pte.
Bradley, A., 16685, Pte.
Bray, W., 8793, Pte.
Brayne, T., 17382, Pte.
Brewell, S., 26161, Pte.
Bridgewater, T., 11063, Pte.
Bright, S., 15603, Pte.
Brightwell, J. H., 20026, Pte.
Bromley, H. J., 10983, L/Sgt.
Brookfield, R., 11833, L/Cpl.
Brown, A., 15109, Pte.
Brown, F., 14689, Pte.
Brown, J. H., 23687, Pte.
Bruce, E., 15944, Pte.
Brunt, J., 11621, Pte.
Bryant, A. E., 26956, Pte.
Bryce, H., 16454, Pte.
Buckley, A., 11003, Pte.
Buckley, E., 10826, Pte.
Buckley, J., 6337, Pte.
Bullock, V. W., 20653, Pte.
Bullock, W., 11045, Sgt.
Burbridge, R. W., 4497, C.S.M.
Burgess, T., 19041, Pte.
Burke, M., 20046, Pte.
Burrows, F., 20092, Pte.
Butcher, E., 17878, Pte.
Butler, F. C., 20822, Pte.
Butler, J., 17296, Pte.

Cafferty, J., 10839, Pte.
Chadwick, R., 15005, Pte.
Chadwick, W., 10543, Pte.
Challoner, W., 6884, Sgt.
Charrington, H., 16105, Pte.
Cheetham, R., 7507, Pte.
Chilton, A., 10751, Pte.
Chittenden, C., 10488, L/Cpl.
Clark, W. G. F., 16168, Pte.

FIFTH BATTALION—*(continued)*

Clarke, A. E. J., 5905, Sgt.
Clarke, F. S., 18328, Pte.
Clarke, J. T., 8022, Pte.
Clarke, W. T., 10295, L/Sgt.
Clee, C. H., 16806, Pte.
Cleeton, E., 22370, Pte.
Clemett, H. W., 8588, Pte.
Clough, R., 16880, Pte.
Cockerill, F. W., 16098, Pte.
Cockshott, E., 26189, Pte.
Collins, E. G., 26982, Pte.
Conn, R., 33009, Pte.
Cook, F., 8715, L/Cpl.
Cook, S., 8988, Pte.
Cooper, J., 19085, Pte.
Cooper, J. H., 11690, Pte.
Cornes, W. E., 25510, Pte.
Cory, R. A., 20878, Pte.
Cotton, H., 16103, Pte.
Counsell, J., 16821, Pte.
Court, C. P., 11060, Pte.
Cowgill, C., 18297, Pte.
Cowles, T. H., 6610, Pte.
Cox, W. T., 8912, Sgt.
Craddock, G. W., 6623, Pte.
Craig, W. J., 10251, Pte.
Crawshaw, J., 16044, Pte.
Cripps, F. H., 16330, Pte.
Cripwell, J. E., 26220, Pte.
Cross, G., 16148, Pte.
Crump, A., 11429, Pte.
Cunnick, W. H., 15549, Cpl.
Cunningham, J., 26984, Pte.
Cureton, S. C., 17824, Pte.

Dale, H., 23928, Pte.
Darby, J., 18796, Pte.
Davenport, H., 15860, Pte.
Davies, A. J., 17765, Pte.
Davies, D. L., 7612, Pte.

Davies, E. J., 20157, Sgt.
Davies, G., 6765, Pte.
Davies, G., 15040, Pte.
Davies, H. E., 12726, Pte.
Davies, J. T., 10636, L/Cpl.
Davies, J., 10526, Pte.
Davies, R., 11308, Pte.
Davies, T. E., 16815, Pte.
Day, W. W., 14557, Pte.
Debney, G., 15011, Pte.
DeVulder, A., 20122, Pte.
Deykes, J., 10908, Pte.
Dickens, A., 20760, Pte.
Diss, A. R., 10950, Sgt.
Dodd, W. J., 11317, Pte.
Donovan, J., 20126, Pte.
Dorricott, T., 24428, Pte.
Douglass, G., 11487, Pte.
Downes, A., 16924, Pte.
Downes, R., 17666, Pte.
Downey, M. J., 11502, Pte.
Downing, A. E., 20775, Pte.
Dunn, A., 10589, Cpl.
Durkin, J., 9621, Pte.
Dyke, E., 23709, Pte.
Dyke, G., 17287, Pte.

Eastabrook, G. H., 11658, Pte.
Eaton, C. T., 18182, Pte.
Edwards, A. J., 18065, Pte.
Edwards, C., 22287, Pte.
Edwards, P., 16079, L/Sgt.
Edwards, S., 10823, L/Cpl.
Elcock, W., 9860, L/Cpl.
Elliott, T., 7235, Pte.
Evans, F., 11501, Pte.
Evans, G., 17543, Pte.
Evans, G., 24319, Pte.
Evans, H., 26110, Cpl.
Evans, H., 16666, L/Cpl.

APPENDIX II

Evans, J., 16514, Pte.
Evans, J. A., 11277, Pte.
Evans, T. G., 17377, Pte.
Evans, W., 6141, Pte.
Evans, W., 6352, Pte.
Evans, W. D., 22479, Pte.
Ewell, E., 17570, Pte.

Fairey, G., 26228, Pte.
Farlow, W., 8995, Pte.
Farman, T. H., 21623, Pte.
Felton, R., 24110, Pte.
Felton, W. H., 11307, Pte.
Fewtrell, E., 9087, Pte.
Fewtrell, W. W., 17611, Pte.
Fieldwick, T. E., 26181, Pte.
Finch, F. J., 17638, Pte.
Fletcher, W., 19073, Pte.
Ford, A. J., 20043, Pte.
Ford, R., 10713, Pte.
Ford, W. C., 16089, Pte.
Forrester, W. H., 10873, Pte.
Foster, T., 11623, Pte.
Foulds, I. W., 20158, Pte.
Fowler, A. J., 20776, Pte.
Fowler, F., 16263, Pte.
Fox, J., 18326, Pte.
France, H., 16496, Pte.
Francis, H., 17258, Pte.
Francis, R., 10747, Pte.
Fridd, T., 9185, L/Cpl.
Frith, E. G., 10922, L/Cpl.
Fryer, F. W., 8795, Cpl.
Fullen, A., 6993, Cpl.

Galliers, C., 22362, Pte.
Gardiner, W. J., 18704, Pte.
Gardner, P., 26247, Pte.
Garrity, P., 11532, L/Cpl.
Gater, P., 18695, Pte.

Gatward, C., 26243, Pte.
Gibbs, F., 6108, Sgt.
Gigg, B., 11274, Pte.
Gillett, A. J., 26224, Pte.
Gittins, H., 16114, Pte.
Gogerty, H., 17701, Pte.
Golding, J., 5486, Pte.
Goodwin, W., 11574, Sgt.
Gough, H., 14908, Pte.
Gower, G., 8627, Cpl.
Grady, A., 10087, Pte.
Grant, G. F., 26214, Pte.
Greaves, G., 17011, Pte.
Green, A., 17447, Pte.
Griffiths, E. J., 10836, Pte.
Griffiths, G., 18301, Pte.
Griffiths, H., 16853, Pte.
Griffiths, J., 5675, Pte.
Griffiths, J., 9823, Pte.
Griffiths, W. C., 9695, Pte.
Gull, H., 20813, Pte.
Guy, F. J., 11740, Pte.
Gwynne, H., 10545, Pte.

Hacking, J. W., 16953, Pte.
Hall, E. G. V., 204100, Pte.
Hall, J., 9519, Pte.
Hallett, F., 16346, Pte.
Hallmark, H. E., 17893, Pte.
Hamilton, A., 7521, Pte.
Hammond, G., 26164, Pte.
Hampson, H., 11081, L/Cpl.
Hancocks, F., 8854, L/Cpl.
Harding, W. E., 17303, Pte.
Harford, A. D., 11056, Pte.
Harris, S., 17750, Pte.
Harris, T., 15057, Pte.
Harris, W., 11542, Pte.
Harrison, N., 32204, Pte.
Harry, D., 17342, L/Cpl.

FIFTH BATTALION—(*continued*)

Hassall, S., 17894, Pte.
Hatfield, T., 17934, Pte.
Hay, J., 32255, Pte.
Haycock, W., 10965, Sgt.
Hayes, W. J., 20114, Pte.
Hayward, A., 19083, Pte.
Hazeldine, W., 16072, Pte.
Healey, F. J., 17227, Pte.
Healey, W. J., 6471, Pte.
Heath, J. W., 9728, Sgt.
Heath, W. H., 16741, Pte.
Heaton, R., 20212, Pte.
Henley, V. J. V., 11247, Pte.
Henshaw, G., 32176, Pte.
Hewitt, G., 11460, Pte.
Hewitt, T., 9304, Pte.
Higginbotham, J., 11270, Sgt.
Highfield, E. T., 12637, Pte.
Higley, F., 11591, Pte.
Hill, A. J., 10746, Pte.
Hill, A. W., 20202, Pte.
Hill, J. E., 11731, Pte.
Hill, W. G., 17717, Pte.
Hince, B. H., 11506, Pte.
Hindle, R., 22244, Pte.
Hindley, H., 16049, Pte.
Hoard, C. J. A., 17952, L/Cpl.
Hodges, W., 24978, Pte.
Holden, R., 32378, Pte.
Holder, L., 10871, Pte.
Holland, P., 9448, Pte.
Holley, H. J., 11227, L/Sgt.
Homewood, C. E., 26983, Pte.
Hopson, E., 10903, Pte.
Hormby, T., 16452, Pte.
Horner, L., 11537, L/Cpl.
Hotchkiss, S., 7230, Sgt.
Howarth, G. R., 17843, Pte.
Howells, J., 10817, Pte.
Howlett, W., 15907, Pte.

Huffadine, H., 8068, Pte.
Hughes, C. T., 13045, Pte.
Hughes, S., 10827, Pte.
Hughes, T. H., 17265, Pte.
Hynett, A., 8016, Pte.

Jackson, F., 16219, Pte.
Jackson, O. E., 11300, Pte.
Jaundrell, J., 18197, Pte.
Jayne, D., 6426, Pte.
Jelley, W., 20843, Pte.
Jennings, T. G., 6228, Pte.
John, F. W., 31159, Pte.
Johnson, A. F., 20879, Pte.
Johnson, S., 16042, Pte.
Johnson, W. J., 20155, L/Cpl.
Jones, A., 16826, Pte.
Jones, A. E., 10921, Pte.
Jones, C. E., 11285, Pte.
Jones, C. H., 17797, Pte.
Jones, D. T., 23899, Pte.
Jones, E., 11631, Pte.
Jones, E. W., 13911, L/Cpl.
Jones, F., 25226, Pte.
Jones, G., 9871, L/Cpl.
Jones, G., 16862, Pte.
Jones, H., 16732, Pte.
Jones, H., 18579, Pte.
Jones, J. F., 14648, Pte.
Jones, J. H., 17757, Pte.
Jones, J. P., 5969, Sgt.
Jones, L., 14963, Pte.
Jones, R. I., 9797, Pte.
Jones, W., 11746, Pte.
Jones, W. F., 10868, L/Cpl.
Judge, C. C., 17061, Pte.

Kearn, T., 7469, Pte.
Kearton, J. E., 16778, Pte.
Keddle, E., 12000, Pte.

APPENDIX II

Kenny, J., 18202, Pte.
Kilcoyne, P., 11356, L/Cpl.
King, A., 11495, L/Sgt.
King, R. W., 20168, Pte.
Knibb, H. B., 9360, Sgt.

Lakins, F. A., 18509, Pte.
Lamb, F., 17479, Pte.
Lamborn, R., 8469, Cpl.
Lander, H. W., 9202, Sgt.
Lane, W. B., 10539, L/Sgt.
Langdon, J., 16504, Pte.
Langford, G. L., 11434, Pte.
Larsen, T. B., 14938, Pte.
Latham, H., 13605, Sgt.
Latham, W., 20087, Pte.
Lawless, W., 11337, Pte.
Lawley, A. H., 11139, Cpl.
Lawley, J., 11508, Cpl.
Leach, J., 16025, Pte.
Laycock, J. A., 17343, Pte.
Leese, J., 11169, Pte.
Leonard, J., 16505, Pte.
Lewis, E., 11357, Pte.
Lewis, G. R., 11024, Pte.
Lewis, E., 7996, L/Cpl.
Lewis, O. H., 17267, Pte.
Lewis, T., 10610, Pte.
Lewtas, J., 16063, Pte.
Lindsay, A. J., 20765, Pte.
Lloyd, D. I., 17552, Pte.
Lloyd, J., 9905, Pte.
Lloyd, R., 6446, Pte.
Lloyd, R., 11417, Pte.
Long, J., 16956, Pte.
Longmate, A. G., 18314, Pte.
Longson, W., 16744, Pte.
Lowe, E., 11253, L/Cpl.
Lowe, R., 10484, Pte.
Lowe, T. J., 11565, Pte.

Loynton, W., 17220, Pte.
Lupton, T., 11371, Pte.

Mabbott, W. H., 17208, Pte.
Maddocks, J., 11637, Pte.
Maddox, W. R., 18110, Pte.
Major, C. H., 8629, L/Cpl.
Malkin, J., 10624, Pte.
Manders, H., 17052, Pte.
Mann, C. W., 20865, Pte.
Martin, J., 24084, Pte.
Martin, J., 14961, Pte.
Martin, W., 17293, Pte.
Mash, C. S., 20073, Pte.
Maund, J., 17709, Pte.
Meadmore, J. H., 11399, L/Cpl.
Meek, E. C., 9959, Pte.
Meen, H. B., 20890, Pte.
Meredith, F., 8050, Pte.
Meredith, W., 15117, Pte.
Merritt, H. J., 15184, L/Cpl.
Millichamp, G., 25387, Pte.
Mills, J. H., 18344, Pte.
Mitchell, E., 10803, Pte.
Mitchell, E., 26144, Pte.
Monks, R., 17526, Pte.
Monnery, W., 26156, Pte.
Morgan, A., 11255, Pte.
Morgan, J., 8053, Pte.
Morgan, J., 15889, Pte.
Morgan, J. H., 15927, Pte.
Morrey, S., 11197, Pte.
Morris, A., 19077, Pte.
Morris, C., 16987, Pte.
Morris, C., 17260, Pte.
Morris, E., 17283, Pte.
Morris, E., 19072, Pte.
Morris, L., 6342, Sgt.
Morris, T., 24202, Pte.
Moss, T., 16516, L/Sgt.

375

THE KING'S SHROPSHIRE LIGHT INFANTRY

Mottram, F., 7114, Pte.
Mullineaux, J., 16762, Pte.
Mullins, T., 6719, Sgt.
Murray, J. R., 6741, Pte.
Murton, A., 26249, Pte.

Neaves, J. W., 20870, Pte.
Needham, W. G., 18178, Pte.
Nevett, T. A., 13041, L/Cpl.
Neville, F. H., 26145, Pte.
Newitt, F., 10544, Pte.
Newman, L., 14238, L/Cpl.
Nicholls, C., 16078, Pte.
Noden, C., 17804, Pte.
Norton, P. J., 16783, Pte.
Nutt, H., 10741, Pte.
Nuttall, H., 11981, Pte.

O'Neill, W., 9755, Pte.
Onions, W., 11602, Cpl.
Onslow, W., 18869, Pte.
Osborne, J., 5416, Pte.
Owen, E., 11557, Pte.

Page, J. J., 17739, Pte.
Palmer, A., 16992, Pte.
Palmer, H., 18049, Pte.
Parr, W., 24382, Pte.
Parry, E., 18046, Pte.
Parry, T. F., 17243, Pte.
Parton, H., 10869, Pte.
Partridge, G. E., 13825, L/Cpl.
Payne, E. C., 17285, Pte.
Pearce, H., 11844, Pte.
Pearce, J., 11676, Pte.
Pearce, J. R., 11632, Pte.
Perks, W. S., 17917, Pte.
Peters, A., 23516, Pte.
Peterson, O. C., 12102, Pte.
Phillips, F., 26952, L/Sgt.

Phillips, J., 10979, Cpl.
Phillips, J. T., 11311, Pte.
Phillips, P., 6953, Pte.
Pitman, O., 20281, Pte.
Platt, H., 15104, Pte.
Ponting, E. J., 17065, Pte.
Poole, W. E., 10148, Pte.
Pope, S. W., 10620, Pte.
Potter, J., 20836, Pte.
Povey, S., 17631, Pte.
Powell, E., 14950, Pte.
Powell, J., 20242, Pte.
Powell, J., 17988, Pte.
Powis, H., 16517, Pte.
Preece, A., 11043, Pte.
Preece, J., 10215, Pte.
Preece, L., 6779, Pte.
Preston, W., 11122, Pte.
Price, A., 10933, Pte.
Price, T., 10791, Pte.
Prince, J., 15022, Pte.
Pritchard, A., 10800, Pte.
Pritchard, A., 12210, Pte.
Privett, J. F., 26970, Pte.
Probert, E., 15566, Pte.
Pugh, A. H., 11015, Pte.
Pugh, A., 8075, Pte.
Pugh, T. J., 17236, Pte.
Pugh, W., 19101, Pte.
Putnam, W. J., 20856, Pte.

Quick, J. E., 18376, Pte.

Ralphs, F., 11121, Pte.
Ramsbottom, J., 11575, Pte.
Ramsden, L., 16129, Pte.
Ratcliff, R., 10179, Pte.
Ravenhill, G., 11706, Pte.
Reach, C. W., 20849, Pte.
Reece, J., 18543, Pte.

APPENDIX II

Rees, T., 13762, Pte.
Reeves, J., 11180, Pte.
Reynolds, C., 21307, Pte.
Richards, J., 11204, Pte.
Richardson, E. B., 20787, Pte.
Rickard, J., 8073, Pte.
Ridehalgh, F. W., 32109, Pte.
Riley, C., 10847, Sgt.
Rindle, J., 11379, L/Sgt.
Rivers, L. H., 20883, Pte.
Roberts, G., 18302, Pte.
Roberts, J., 11035, Pte.
Roberts, O., 11496, Pte.
Roberts, T., 11034, Pte.
Robinson, A., 11796, Pte.
Robinson, J., 17494, Pte.
Robinson, W., 15783, Pte.
Roby, W., 20191, Pte.
Rogers, J., 10677, Sgt.
Rollinson, W. J., 20151, Pte.
Roper, R. H., 18330, Pte.
Rose, E. F., 20887, Pte.
Rossell, G., 20085, Pte.
Rowlands, A., 17827, Pte.
Rowlands, J., 18039, Pte.
Rowley, W. J., 17487, Pte.
Roylance, H., 21303, Pte.
Russell, A. W., 26195, Pte.
Ryan, C., 6483, Pte.
Rylands, T. H., 26488, Pte.

Sale, W., 24376, Pte.
Salter, W., 6944, L/Cpl.
Sambrook, T. H., 17646, Pte.
Sanderson, T., 22185, Pte.
Saunders, A., 10385, Pte.
Scholes, T., 17741, Pte.
Scothern, A., 16848, Pte.
Shaw, H., 18268, Pte.
Shenton, E., 6525, Pte.

Shergold, E., 8573, Sgt.
Shotton, F. J., 18315, Pte.
Sivier, W., 20082, Pte.
Skerratt, J., 18010, Pte.
Smale, L. C., 14767, Pte.
Smallwood, J. T., 11448, Pte.
Smith, E. F., 17276, Pte.
Smith, G., 11205, Pte.
Smith, G. J., 7013, Sgt.
Smith, S. J., 11072, Pte.
Smith, W. J., 6336, Pte.
Southerton, W. J., 24318, Pte.
Sowden, A., 10585, L/Cpl.
Spence, J., 27100, Pte.
Sperring, V. R., 11378, Pte.
Spragg, L. H., 17866, Pte.
Stacey, F. G., 17272, Pte.
Staffin, M., 26879, Pte.
Starling, J., 20835, Pte.
Steel, J. S. S., 20812, L/Cpl.
Stephens, A. H., 11168, Pte.
Stevenson, R., 17298, Pte.
Stocker, A., 16919, Pte.
Stockton, W., 23916, Pte.
Stokes, G., 10507, Pte.
Stones, W., 6683, Pte.
Stuart, C. A., 13043, Pte.
Stuart, J., 17844, Pte.
Sullivan, J. F., 8524, Pte.
Sumner, D., 16028, Pte.
Swindells, J., 205049, Pte.

Taylor, A. E., 18143, Pte.
Taylor, G. H., 26579, Pte.
Taylor, H., 16130, Pte.
Taylor, J., 23956, Pte.
Taylor, J. W., 26185, Pte.
Taylor, N., 16852, Pte.
Taylor, T., 6023, Pte.
Taylor, W., 11146, C.S.M.

THE KING'S SHROPSHIRE LIGHT INFANTRY

Taylor, W., 11516, Pte.
Taylor, W. L., 26134, Pte.
Teece, T., 12866, Pte.
Thelwall, S., 26454, Pte.
Thomas, E., 17922, Pte.
Thompson, R., 12763, Cpl.
Townsend, G., 10739, Pte.
Tregunna, F., 15088, Pte.
Tringham, J. C., 17060, Pte.
Tweed, A. V., 20838, Pte.
Tyler, E. E., 18073, Pte.
Tyler, H. T., 17951, Pte.
Tyrer, C., 6938, L/Cpl.
Tyrrell, F. G., 20766, Pte.

Underwood, W. G., 19838, L/Sgt.
Upton, F. G., 16030, Pte.

Vaughan, J. E., 10185, Pte.
Vaughan, R., 17435, Pte.
Vaughan, R. J. G., 15012, Pte.
Vickers, R., 17561, Pte.
Vine, G. E., 26245, Pte.
Voce, W., 7185, Pte.

Wackett, F. J., 17920, Pte.
Wakeley, C. W., 18282, L/Cpl.
Walker, R., 26212, Pte.
Wall, J., 16902, Pte.
Wall, S. B., 11959, Pte.
Waller, H., 10485, Pte.
Walters, F., 17660, Pte.
Warburton, J., 22457, Pte.
Ward, G., 15899, Pte.
Ward, H., 8584, Pte.
Ward, J., 16495, Pte.
Ward, W. J. P., 26148, Pte.
Waterton, C., 17727, L/Cpl.
Watkins, W. H., 16896, Pte.

Watson, A., 11599, L/Cpl.
Watson, E. E., 8683, Pte.
Weeks, G., 11293, Pte.
Wesley, H., 20831, Pte.
Westbury, T. A., 17307, Pte.
Weston, H. A., 16955, Pte.
Wharton, T. B., 18119, Pte.
Wheadon, A., 7437, Pte.
Wheatcroft, W., 13696, Sgt.
Wheeldon, J. A., 26188, Pte.
White, B. C., 26124, Pte.
White, F., 20279, L/Cpl.
Whitney, W., 7853, Cpl.
Whitworth, C., 16844, Pte.
Whitworth, W., 16843, Pte.
Wild, T., 14955, Pte.
Wilderspin, H. A., 20806, Pte.
Wilkinson, L. N., 16156, Pte.
Williams, A. G., 11622, Pte.
Williams, A., 17338, Sgt.
Williams, B., 9261, L/Cpl.
Williams, D., 6455, Pte.
Williams, D., 18247, Pte.
Williams, E., 9591, Pte.
Williams, E., 7296, Cpl.
Williams, F., 10611, L/Cpl.
Williams, G., 10009, Pte.
Williams, J., 11044, Cpl.
Williams, J., 10432, Pte.
Williams, J. H., 17380 Pte.
Williams, J. G., 11672, L/Cpl.
Williams, R. H., 10761, L/Cpl.
Williams, R. J., 19683, Pte.
Williams, S., 16136, Pte.
Williams, T. J., 17250, Pte.
Williams, T. R., 7006, Cpl.
Williams, T. W., 10732, L/Cpl.
Williams, W. E., 10995, L/Cpl.
Williams, W., 15264, Pte.
Williams, W. A., 33373, Pte.

378

APPENDIX II

FIFTH BATTALION—*(continued)*

Wilshaw, M. B., 15106, Pte.
Wilshire, H., 8593, Pte.
Wilton, J. A., 16683, Pte.
Wiltshire, A., 23568, Pte.
Wood, A., 5932, Sgt.
Wood, H., 18324, Pte.
Wood, J., 11055, Pte.
Woodhead, J., 9846, Pte.
Woodyatt, T., 10795, Pte.
Woolley, G., 16040, Pte.

Woolley, J. T., 18432, Pte.
Wootton, R., 16925, Pte.
Wortham, J., 8645, Pte.
Worthing, W., 17437, Pte.
Wright, W. A., 17950, Pte.
Wynn, G., 17385, Pte.

Yates, F., 10864, Sgt.
Yates, J., 17786, Sgt.
Yates, J., 16215, Pte.

SIXTH BATTALION

Abbott, W. W., 11388, Pte.
Adams, G., 25821, Pte.
Adamson, J., 15330, Sgt.
Aldridge, N. J., 19635, Pte.
Allen, C., 12453, Pte.
Alliston, W., 25462, Pte.
Allsop, A. S., 26431, Pte.
Archer, J. T. G., 35372, Pte.
Ashwood, A., 20994, Pte.
Austin, E., 11813, Pte.
Austin, W., 21420, Pte.

Badrock, W., 26897, Pte.
Baggott, W., 15606, Pte.
Bailey, F., 16399, Pte.
Bailey, J. T., 11792, Pte.
Bailey, L., 15440, Pte.
Baker, H., 26530, Pte.
Baker, W. C., 15547, Cpl.
Ball, C. A., 23509, Pte.
Ball, E., 15359, Pte.
Ball, H., 35379, Pte.
Ballard, T. W., 21482, Pte.
Banks, W., 13259, L/Cpl.
Barclay, H. C., 12751, Pte.
Barclay, T. H., 12267, Sgt.
Barker, W., 6885, Pte.

Barnett, A. A., 16780, L/Cpl.
Barnett, T., 24098, Pte.
Barrett, J. E., 13686, C.S.M.
Baugh, W., 26094, Pte.
Beadle, D., 20319, Pte.
Beaton, T. H., 12329, Pte.
Bebb, J. R., 26599, Pte.
Beedles, R., 7454, Pte.
Bengree, J., 33627, Pte.
Berry, J., 15309, Pte.
Bevan, K., 11286, Pte.
Bevan, S. C., 27986, Pte.
Bickley, J., 15225, Pte.
Biffen, A. S., 34027, Pte.
Birch, J. J., 12183, L/Sgt.
Blount, A., 12057, Pte.
Blount, E., 14415, Pte.
Bowe, D., 203807, Pte.
Bowen, S., 13155, Pte.
Breakwell, J., 12143, Pte.
Breese, J. S., 13380, Pte.
Breeze, E., 33080, Pte.
Breeze, W., 12944, Pte.
Brice, E., 35390, Pte.
Brocklehurst, G., 8093, Sgt.
Brookes, G. W., 12340, Pte.
Broomfield, J. R., 16508, Pte.

THE KING'S SHROPSHIRE LIGHT INFANTRY

Brothwood, E., 11849, Pte.
Brown, A., 12215, Pte.
Brown, A., 11358, Pte.
Brown, F., 12781, Cpl.
Brown, G. I., 11967, Pte.
Brown, J. S., 12082, Pte.
Brown, J., 26024, Pte.
Brown, W. G. P., 33481, Pte.
Buckley, G., 15798, Pte.
Bucknall, A. L., 26229, Pte.
Bunker, R. E., 9748, L/Sgt.
Burborough, P., 12001, Cpl.
Burden, A., 15447, Pte.
Burnett, E., 12174, Pte.
Butler, A., 11754, Pte.

Cadman, W. S., 21217, Pte.
Campbell, A., 35389, Pte.
Carroll, C., 21211, Pte.
Carter, W., 19401, L/Cpl.
Cartright, E., 19684, Pte.
Casey, M. P., 15659, Pte.
Cashion, E., 26054, Pte.
Caton, G., 15053, Pte.
Cattrall, E., 12778, L/Cpl.
Challinor, W. W. H., 19823, Pte.
Challoner, O. W., 19852, Pte.
Checkland, B., 26778, L/Cpl.
Chester, J. H., 24628, Pte.
Chidlow, W. A., 12909, L/Cpl.
Chilcott, J., 15804, Pte.
Christie, F., 13177, Pte.
Clarke, J., 26415, Sgt.
Clarkson, C., 11688, Pte.
Claybrook, A., 13199, Pte.
Cocker, W. H., 35384, Pte.
Cole, J. S., 202026, Pte.
Colebatch, A. E., 26891, Pte.
Colley, J. T., 12980, Cpl.

Collings, W. A., 7078, Pte.
Cook, J., 26459, Pte.
Cooke, H., 12527, Cpl.
Cooper, A. W., 26005, Pte.
Cooper, F., 12928, Pte.
Corbett, G., 15417, Pte.
Corbett, W., 14377, L/Cpl.
Corfield, G., 12448, Pte.
Corfield, J., 12456, Pte.
Corlett, J. E., 33518, Pte.
Crane, W. G., 21216, Pte.
Crofts, T., 35387, Pte.
Crowther, W., 32406, Pte.
Cureton, W., 16655, Pte.
Curtis, J., 26067, Pte.

Darby, E. A., 22420, Pte.
Darlington, A., 26899, Pte.
Davies, A., 11817, Pte.
Davies, A., 11894, L/Cpl.
Davies, E. E., 26271, L/Cpl.
Davies, E. G., 21423, L/Cpl.
Davies, F. R., 19821, Pte.
Davies, G., 11288, Pte.
Davies, H. J., 26896, Pte.
Davies, R., 12796, Pte.
Davies, R., 18166, L/Cpl.
Davies, S. E., 24712, Pte.
Davies, T., 201526, Pte.
Davies, W., 11342, L/Cpl.
Davis, H. J., 18751, Pte.
Dawes, R., 26959, Pte.
Dean, J., 33089, Pte.
Dell, P. J., 26109, Pte.
De Peare, P. A., 11123, L/Cpl.
Dixon, W., 11971, Sgt.
Dodd, A., 27856, Pte.
Dollin, T. W., 13307, Pte.
Downes, J., 33081, Pte.
Downs, S. J., 19521, L/Cpl.

APPENDIX II

SIXTH BATTALION—(continued)

Dudley, W., 26421, Pte.
Dytor, G. A., 22359, Pte.

Earl, M. J., 26255, Pte.
Eaton, J., 21555, Pte.
Eaton, W., 18535, Pte.
Edgerton, J., 33122, Pte.
Edmondson, R. T., 11842, Pte.
Edmunds, A. H., 33588, Pte.
Edsforth, W., 12126, Pte.
Edwards, A., 11890, Pte.
Edwards, E., 21227, Pte.
Edwards, G., 12725, Pte.
Edwards, J. S., 21228, Pte.
Edwards, J. H., 26291, Pte.
Edwards, R., 11865, Pte.
Edwards, R. J., 26542, Pte.
Edwards, T., 15344, Pte.
Edwards, W., 11703, Pte.
Edwards, W., 21394, Pte.
Ellis, H. B., 12768, L/Cpl.
Ellis, J. R., 17481, Pte
Espley, J., 21469, Pte.
Evans, A. T., 35399, Pte.
Evans, A., 26545, L/Cpl.
Evans, A. R., 12800, Pte.
Evans, A., 19602, Pte.
Evans, C. G., 26544, Pte.
Evans, D. G., 22840, Pte.
Evans, E. S., 15211, Pte.
Evans, F., 27860, Pte.
Evans, J., 26013, Pte.
Evans, J., 26547, Pte.
Evans, J. M., 21923, Pte.
Evans, T. J., 12238, Pte.
Evans, W., 19578, Pte.
Evans, W. R., 15411, Pte.
Evans, W. T., 13680, L/Sgt.

Farmer, G. E., 12317, L/Cpl.

Farrer, J., 12134, Pte.
Fellows, S., 14498, Pte.
Ferrington, T., 27090, Pte.
Fletcher, C. E., 35409, Pte.
Fletcher, E. J., 11918, Pte.
Fletcher, G., 12531, Pte.
Ford, F., 201202, Pte.
Forster, H., 15518, L/Cpl.
Foulkes, E., 21237, Pte.
Foulkes, J., 15131, Pte.
Fox, H. L., 19036, L/Cpl.
Foxall, H., 25407, Pte.
France, G. E., 26612, Pte.
Francis, B., 15717, Cpl.
Francis, J., 15805, Pte.
Francis, T., 15690, Pte.
French, E., 32221, Pte.

Gandy, W., 26273, Pte.
Gaskin, W., 202406, Pte.
Gilbank, E., 12282, Sgt.
Gollins, H., 7338, Sgt.
Gomery, C., 13917, C.S.M.
Gorely, R. B., 12737, Pte.
Gorrod, B. W., 20799, Pte.
Gough, A., 17655, Pte.
Gough, F., 21377, Pte.
Gough, W., 26550, Pte.
Gough, W. T., 16581, L/Cpl.
Gould, E., 18082, Pte.
Greatwich, F., 13192, Cpl.
Green, E., 35411, Pte.
Green, J., 33148, Pte.
Green, T. G., 28037, Pte.
Gregory, F. C., 26615, L/Cpl.
Greig, J., 26436, Pte.
Griffiths, A., 16576, Pte.
Griffiths, B., 12301, Pte.
Griffiths, J., 12528, Pte.
Griffiths, L. J., 20935, Pte.

Grimes, F., 12620, Pte.
Gutteridge, T. A., 12897, Pte.
Gwilliam, A., 12103, Pte.
Gwilliam, R. E., 19667, Pte.

Haines, H., 11704, Pte.
Hallowell, W., 22138, Pte.
Halls, W. W., 7549, Pte.
Hammond, J. W., 12794, Pte.
Hanley, W., 32793, Pte.
Harmer, T. J., 12518, Pte.
Harris, H. T., 8937, Pte.
Harris, J. H., 11555, Pte.
Harrison, W. J., 12069, Pte.
Hawkins, W., 15137, L/Cpl.
Haynes, J., 32926, Pte.
Hayward, C., 13140, Pte.
Heaford, W., 15141, L/Cpl.
Heath, T., 15507, Pte.
Heaton, T., 12435, Cpl.
Heeley, A., 18144, Pte.
Hendrick, A. C., 12744, L/Cpl.
Hicks, A., 11941, L/Cpl.
Higgins, T., 200920, Pte.
Hill, A. T. H., 25175, Pte.
Hill, L., 15548, L/Cpl.
Hind, A., 11609, Pte.
Hinton, C., 14373, Pte.
Hobbs, T., 26230, Pte.
Hodgson, T., 32388, Pte.
Hodkinson, F., 11847, Pte.
Holden, H., 16664, L/Cpl.
Holland, J., 13164, Pte.
Holland, W. A., 200509, Pte.
Hollinshead, P., 32928, Pte.
Homer, A., 33002, L/Cpl.
Horton, W., 11522, Pte.
Houghton, H. E., 12733, L/Cpl.
Howells, W. H., 22118, Pte.
Howes, G. C., 22260, Pte.

Hudson, W. T., 17703, Sgt.
Hughes, A. J., 26441, L/Cpl.
Hughes, H., 31962, Pte.
Hughes, W. E., 12519, Pte.
Humphreys, J., 27880, Pte.
Husbands, C. C., 25416, Pte.
Husbands, W. H., 21425, Pte.

Ikin, H. W., 24029, Pte.
Ingham, F., 12131, Cpl.
Izod, J., 25719, Pte.

Jacks, S., 12161, Pte.
James, H., 26526, Pte.
James, H., 18646, Pte.
James, T., 26471, Pte.
Jarvis, F., 18410, Pte.
Jarvis, W., 33062, Pte.
Jeynes, S., 25030, Pte.
Johnson, A., 28100, Pte.
Johnson, J., 11970, Pte.
Johnson, R., 19034, Pte.
Jones, A., 11519, Pte.
Jones, A., 12524, Pte.
Jones, C., 12099, Pte.
Jones, C., 201129, Pte.
Jones, C. H., 12021, L/Cpl.
Jones, D. W., 15119, Pte.
Jones, F., 33082, Pte.
Jones, G., 12209, Pte.
Jones, H., 33013, Pte.
Jones, J. H., 26527, Pte.
Jones, J. W., 12295, L/Cpl.
Jones, J. M., 35431, Pte.
Jones, J. T., 12339, Pte.
Jones, M., 11785, L/Cpl.
Jones, R., 12525, Pte.
Jones, R., 15348, Pte.
Jones, R. E., 15748, Cpl.
Jones, S., 26485, Pte.

APPENDIX II

Jones, T. W., 27894, Pte.
Jones, W., 12260, Pte.
Jordan, E., 26037, Pte.
Juckes, A. N., 26621, Pte.
Judson, T., 24915, Pte.

Kelly, T., 26443, Pte.
Knights, E. G., 20819, Pte.
Knowles, A., 35440, Pte.

Lanata, D., 35444, Pte.
Lane, T., 15422, Pte.
Lane, W., 15817, Pte.
Langford, G., 19231, Pte.
Langford, J. J., 19856, Pte.
Langford, J. W., 25404, Pte.
Langford, T. F., 35443, Pte.
Langley, C., 26560, Pte.
Lee, E. J., 15614, Pte.
Lees, G., 14936, Pte.
Lewis, C. J., 26528, Pte.
Lewis, D. E., 21404, Pte.
Lewis, G., 13191, L/Cpl.
Lewis, G. W., 15854, Pte.
Lewis, H., 6810, Pte.
Lewis, H. D., 20869, Pte.
Lewis, T. L., 26623, Pte.
Lewis, W. E., 12268, Pte.
Lewis, W. H., 15749, Pte.
Lloyd, J. B., 14269, L/Sgt.
Lloyd, J. E., 12247, Pte.
Lockley, E., 11908, C.S.M.
Locklin, R. H., 26019, Pte.
Lowe, V., 25488, Pte.
Lowndes, S., 19501, Pte.

Magee, J., 33513, Pte.
Maharry, R., 18203, Pte.
Mahon, J., 12579, Pte.
Maiden, A. H., 14710, Pte.

Major, F., 26275, Pte.
Malins, J., 9894, Pte.
Mann, F. J., 20762, Pte.
Manning, R. H., 20356, L/Sgt.
Mantle, J., 12517, Sgt.
Marcroft, G., 27914, Pte.
Marsden, A., 12119, Pte.
Marston, J., 26562, Pte.
Marston, W. D., 33626, Pte.
Martin, J. G. E., 20156, Pte.
Martin, W., 35454, Pte.
Matthias, P., 26517, Pte.
Mays, T., 20208, Pte.
McAvan, L., 15476, Cpl.
Meredith, J. E., 22381, Pte.
Millward, J., 26395, Pte.
Milman, S., 13144, Pte.
Mole, W. E., 33670, Pte.
Moody, F. H., 28073, Pte.
Moore, H., 18114, Pte.
Moore, J. R., 12628, Pte.
Moore, J. H., 27091, Pte.
Morgan, A. A., 21382, Pte.
Morgan, H., 12932, Pte.
Morgan, W., 7568, Pte.
Morrey, W., 24886, Pte.
Morris, T. J., 25493, Pte.
Morris, W., 12218, L/Cpl.
Morris, W. S., 12989, Pte.
Morris, W. E., 9770, Pte.
Mountford, J., 11776, Pte.

Naylor, E., 32379, Pte.
Nevett, H., 26567, Pte.
Newhall, H., 24263, Pte.
Nicholas, C. V., 11479, Pte.
Nicholls, W., 23614, Pte.
Nicholson, J., 26397, Cpl.
Nixon, W., 16596, Pte.
Norbury, S., 205109, L/Cpl.

THE KING'S SHROPSHIRE LIGHT INFANTRY

Norgrove, E., 13158, Pte.
Norton, R., 15720, Pte.

Oakes, G., 11452, Pte.
Oakley, R., 12990, Pte.
O'Brien, G., 13147, Cpl.
Ogden, C., 32138, Pte.
Okell, J., 26447, Pte.
Oliver, T. E., 11660, Pte.
Orwell, W., 10710, Pte.
Overton, S., 33126, Pte.
Owen, M., 31154, Pte.
Owen, R., 35463, Pte.
Owen, W. E., 15473, Pte.
Owen, W. H., 28084, Pte.
Oxenbury, W. A., 35465, Pte.

Paddock, W., 26569, Pte.
Paggett, H., 11492, Pte.
Parker, H., 15636, Pte.
Parkinson, G. H., 201676, Pte.
Partington, J., 35466, Pte.
Payne, A., 17305, Pte.
Peake, J., 12107, L/Cpl.
Penton, H. A. W., 13153, Pte.
Phillips, E. C., 11348, Pte.
Philpotts, E. A., 10131, L/Cpl.
Phipps, W., 6612, Pte.
Pinches, E., 8671, Pte.
Pleass, H., 28088, Pte.
Plested, C., 26128, Pte.
Podmore, G., 11875, Pte.
Pogson, W., 24555, Pte.
Pomfret, T., 11983, Pte.
Poole, H., 27922, Pte.
Powell, H., 12020, Pte.
Powell, J., 33502, Pte.
Powell, W., 17959, Pte.
Preece, H., 6517, Pte.
Price, A., 11861, Pte.

Price, A., 12306, Pte.
Price, H., 13197, Pte.
Price, J. W., 204112, Pte.
Price, M., 12204, Sgt.
Price, R. P., 12793, Pte.
Price, W., 12177, Pte.
Pritchard, A. L., 11804, Pte.
Prosser, E., 6196, Pte.
Pruce, A. E., 17362, Cpl.
Pugh, E. J., 24704, Pte.

Rawlings, T., 16584, Pte.
Rees, E., 15277, Pte.
Reeves, W., 9666, Cpl.
Reid, J. B., 13216, C.S.M.
Rich, S., 12685, Sgt.
Rigby, T., 11747, Pte.
Roberts, A., 202775, Pte.
Roberts, A., 12294, Pte.
Roberts, H., 6444, Pte.
Roberts, J., 26590, Pte.
Roberts, P., 11944, Pte.
Roberts, R. L., 19732, Pte.
Roberts, T., 19272, Pte.
Roberts, T. L., 12286, Pte.
Roberts, W., 21384, Pte.
Roberts, W. J., 24656, Pte.
Robins, T. H., 26576, Pte.
Robinson, J., 17566, Pte.
Rogers, R., 12251, Pte.
Rogers, S., 11580, Pte.
Rogers, T., 12207, Pte.
Rogers, T., 26281, Pte.
Rooke, H., 11951, Pte.
Rooks, J. H., 204115, Pte.
Rose, W., 10421, Pte.
Rowberry, T. W., 25199, Pte.
Rowe, B., 26632, Pte.
Rowlands, C., 15736, Pte.
Rowlands, J. T., 15582, Pte.

APPENDIX II

Ruscoe, E., 12433, L/Cpl.
Rushton, A. B.,12094, L/Cpl.

Sackett, R., 12730, Pte.
Sadler, S., 18981, Pte.
Salt, C. W., 22485, Pte.
Sankey, C., 34010, Pte.
Saunders, A. G., 22195, Pte.
Saunders, J., 6531, Pte.
Schoolden, J. D., 26398, Pte.
Scott, R., 12571, L/Sgt.
Shearwood, F., 26219, Pte.
Sheldon, G., 13141, L/Cpl.
Shingler, F. J., 15353, L/Cpl.
Shipway, E., 14779, Pte.
Shuck, W. H., 18017, Pte.
Simpson, W., 27941, Pte.
Sirman, F. J., 13180, Pte.
Skitt, J. W., 12206, Pte.
Smith, A. R., 12269, Sgt.
Smith, C., 27296, Pte.
Smith, E. P., 33480, Pte.
Smith, H. G., 11059, Pte.
Smith, J. B., 17051, L/Cpl.
Smith, J. H., 15772, Pte.
Smith, R., 20834, Pte.
Smith, T. H., 15294, Pte.
Smith, W., 7638, L/Cpl.
Smith, W. G., 21369, L/Cpl.
Solkow, A. P., 26892, Cpl.
Southall, G. H., 17651, Pte.
Southerton, W., 32923, Pte.
Southgate, J., 25300, Pte.
Spencer, J. E., 16530, L/Cpl.
Sprague, A. T., 15633, Sgt.
Standing, E., 12118, Cpl.
Stanley, W. H., 12951, L/Cpl.
Steele, J. H., 12760, Pte.
Stevenson, J., 16591, Pte.
Still, L. J., 13156, Pte.

Stocker, D., 13220, Pte.
Stoker, G., 26583, Pte.
Stokes, L. W., 28055, Pte.
Stone, R., 32922, Pte.
Sutton, W. E. G., 27293, Pte.
Swanwick, J., 21386, Pte.
Swift, H., 11911, Pte.
Synnock, J., 16318, Pte.

Tattersall, T., 9607, Pte.
Taylor, A. E., 23514, Pte.
Taylor, J., 16248, Pte.
Taylor, J., 12769, Pte.
Taylor, J., 15397, Pte.
Taylor, L., 15223, Pte.
Thomas, A. E., 12522, Pte.
Thomas, E., 19378, Pte.
Thomas, F., 8373, C.Q.M.S.
Thompson, A., 11956, Pte.
Thompson, J. S., 12262, Pte.
Thornton, J., 19849, Pte.
Timmis, C. J., 12964, Pte.
Timmis, F., 20924, Pte.
Timmins, R., 25696, Pte.
Tipton, B., 33153, Pte.
Tobin, J., 11748, Pte.
Tong, R., 201110, Pte.
Tonks, P., 11926, Pte.
Totterdell, W. J., 27300, Pte.
Townsend, T. E., 33625, Pte.
Trigg, C., 27301, Pte.
Turner, E., 22165, Pte.
Turner, R., 21412, Pte.

Underwood, A. J., 13159, Pte.

Vernalls, W. H., 32877, Pte.

Wakeham, S., 12039, Pte
Walker, E., 22089, Pte.

2 C

SIXTH BATTALION—*(continued)*

Walker, J., 11789, Pte.
Walker, T. W., 12758, L/Cpl.
Wall, A. V., 11752, Pte.
Ward, C. T., 17953, L/Cpl.
Ward, E., 19866, Pte.
Warwick, G., 12198, Pte.
Watkin, W., 11882, Pte.
Watkins, C., 7129, Pte.
Webb, F., 19016, Pte.
Webster, J. H., 27548, Pte.
West, F. G., 25192, Pte.
White, F., 15376, Pte.
Whitehead, W., 7749, Pte.
Whiteley, W., 26450, Pte.
Whiting, A., 11958, Pte.
Whittaker, R., 18863, Pte.
Whitworth, J., 12563, Pte.
Wicks, G., 27311, Pte.
Wilcox, C., 26582, Pte.
Wilkins, F. W., 15634, Pte.
Wilkinson, J., 26498, Pte.
Wilkinson, W., 15791, Pte.

Williams, A. E., 26839, L/Cpl.
Williams, A., 12975, Cpl.
Williams, C., 11859, Pte.
Williams, C., 14388, Pte.
Williams, C. L., 12490, Pte.
Williams, E. S., 12258, Sgt.
Williams, F. J., 12024, Pte.
Williams, H., 10833, Pte.
Williams, J., 10760, Pte.
Williams, P., 20916, Pte.
Wilshaw, J. A., 12076, Cpl.
Wilson, R., 26429, Pte.
Wood, F., 28596, Pte.
Wood, H., 16523, Pte.
Wood, W. G., 11816, Pte.
Woodhouse, R., 8920, Pte.
Woodhouse, T. H., 12736, Pte.
Wooding, J. H., 19739, Pte.
Worrall, A., 22250, Pte.

Yates, S., 17811, L/Cpl.
Young, A. E., 12749, Pte.

SEVENTH BATTALION

Acton, C. U., 17007, Pte.
Adams, J. E., 43646, Pte.
Addison, G. H., 22063, Pte.
Ainsley, J., 13740, Pte.
Alcock, A., 27702, Pte.
Allanson, E., 22149, Pte.
Allen, G., 21895, Pte.
Allen, J. S., 13019, Cpl.
Alvis, F. R. W., 200419, Pte.
Andrews, W. C., 22109, Pte.
Angell, W., 27763, Pte.
Anslow, F. C., 26951, Pte.
Arrowsmith, E. V., 27706, Pte.
Ashman, E. F., 27707, Pte.
Ashton, H., 18471, Pte.

Ashton, T., 205219, Pte.
Askey, S., 11401, L/Cpl.
Atkinson, A., 28354, Pte.
Austin, G., 14569, Pte.

Bailey, J., 23915, Pte.
Bailey, J. H., 230857, Pte.
Bailey, L., 14919, Pte.
Bailey, T., 18532, Pte.
Baker, D., 17104, L/Cpl.
Baker, W. H., 7339, Pte.
Baldry, H. W., 20048, L/Cpl.
Baldwin, R., 19363, Pte.
Ball, A., 26296, Pte.
Balmer, M., 38536, Pte.

APPENDIX II

Barber, E., 20025, Pte.
Barker, E. A., 17391, Pte.
Barlow, C., 36586, Pte.
Barlow, J. E., 26915, Pte.
Barnes, H., 22471, Pte.
Barton, T., 23982, Pte.
Bartram, W. R., 27810, Pte.
Bates, E., 29690, Pte.
Bates, G., 26197, Pte.
Baxter, A. E., 18628, Pte.
Bayley, G. H., 18821, Pte.
Baynham, H. C., 15852, Pte.
Beale, F., 27708, Pte.
Beasty, H., 26410, Pte.
Beattie, W., 21896, Pte.
Beaumont, G., 25196, Pte.
Beaven, J. H., 19135, Pte.
Beckett, W., 21205, Pte.
Beddoes, H., 16088, Pte.
Beech, R., 16291, Pte.
Beeston, F. W., 205077, Pte.
Bell, A., 27709, Pte.
Bell, R. J., 26770, Pte.
Bellows, R. H., 28513, Pte.
Bennett, J. C., 35496, Pte.
Bennett, W., 5468, C.S.M.
Bethell, T. H., 6871, Pte.
Bevan, B. T., 15281, Pte.
Bevan, R. D., 21904, Pte.
Bickell, R., 14714, Pte.
Billings, W. H., 18251, Pte.
Birch, A. H., 14480, Pte.
Birtles, A., 23977, Pte.
Blacker, E. J., 7586, Cpl.
Blackwell, A., 8933, Cpl.
Blaise, W., 18666, Pte.
Blears, C. T., 28437, Cpl.
Bleasdale, D., 18233, Pte.
Bleasdale, R., 7012, Pte.
Bloomfield, J. H., 15157, Pte.

Bloomfield, R., 15241, Cpl.
Bloor, F., 18899, Pte.
Blower, J., 9626, Pte.
Boden, A. H., 200133, Pte.
Boden, G. F., 14482, Cpl.
Boles, M., 33637, Pte.
Boliver, E. A., 16265, Pte.
Boliver, J., 27095, Pte.
Booker, A. E., 17688, Pte.
Booth, F. C., 36619, Pte.
Booth, G., 19163, Pte.
Bosley, W. C., 27218, Pte.
Botting, A., 14491, Pte.
Boulton, W., 18373, Pte.
Bourne, J., 26324, L/Cpl.
Bowden, F. G., 35382, Pte.
Bowden, H., 15758, Pte.
Bowen, C. J., 19669, Pte.
Bowen, C. W., 14740, L/Cpl.
Bowen, H., 22349, Pte.
Bowen, J., 7595, Pte.
Bowen, T., 18798, Pte.
Bowers, A. J., 23853, Pte.
Boycott, T., 18499, Pte.
Boylin, F. R., 7639, Pte.
Bracegirdle, F., 26294, Pte.
Bradbury, J. W., 44430, Sgt.
Bradley, W., 19649, Pte.
Brammer, H., 6621, Pte.
Bray, J., 19710, L/Cpl.
Brazenell, J., 22281, Pte.
Brazier, J. E., 13303, Pte.
Breeze, R., 26506, Pte.
Briars, M., 24356, Pte.
Brick, J. C., 14519, Pte.
Brick, L., 22011, Pte.
Bridges, C., 14201, Pte.
Britton, T. H., 19547, Pte.
Brooks, E. A., 15968, Pte.
Brooks, T., 13432, Pte.

387

SEVENTH BATTALION—(continued)

Broome, T., 24674, Pte.
Broster, P., 13868, Cpl.
Brown, A., 22141, Pte.
Brown, J. J., 26504, L/Cpl.
Brown, N. C., 26656, Pte.
Brown, T., 14820, Pte.
Brown, W. M., 26533, Cpl.
Brunt, A., 19783, Pte.
Bryant, G. B., 17629, Pte.
Bubb, F., 6431, Pte.
Buckley, S., 23978, Pte.
Bull, D., 13174, Pte.
Bull, J. S., 24976, Pte.
Bull, R. C., 35503, Pte.
Burd, J. A., 23615, Pte.
Burgoyne, W. L., 18690, L/Cpl.
Burke, J., 26372, Pte.
Burkitt, T., 14605, Pte.
Burns, H., 12391, Pte.
Burns, W. H., 14673, Pte.
Burrows, J. S., 22126, Pte.
Burrows, W., 20055, Pte.
Burt, F., 31646, Pte.
Burton, H. J., 13858, Pte.
Bushell, F., 9630, Pte.
Butcher, T. W., 15302, Pte.
Butterworth, H., 18849, Pte.
Button, H., 36630, Pte.

Cain, J. K., 38541, Pte.
Caldwell, P. P., 26301, Pte.
Cameron, H., 28330, L/Cpl.
Cantwell, W., 17558, Pte.
Capper, W., 23685, Pte.
Cardwell, J., 35256, Pte.
Carline, T., 15426, Pte.
Carpenter, P., 14628, Pte.
Carswell, E., 13919, Cpl.
Carter, L., 24100, Pte.
Cartwright, A., 16362, Pte.

Cartwright, F., 18853, L/Cpl.
Carwood, E., 38499, Pte.
Caseley, J. W., 18051, Pte.
Cawley, J., 6723, Pte.
Chadwick, J. R., 22388, Pte.
Chadwick, J. W., 7834, Pte.
Chandler, I. W., 15838, Pte.
Chapelhow, S. E., 34176, Pte.
Chetwynd, E., 38515, Pte.
Chidlow, A., 23721, Pte.
Childs, G., 21206, Pte.
Chilton, A. E., 21908, Pte.
Chipman, J. W., 18629, Pte.
Chorlton, A., 24340, Pte.
Christal, J., 20898, L/Cpl.
Churms, F. H., 16331, Cpl.
Clark, J., 43597, Pte.
Clarke, F., 22034, Pte.
Clarke, T. D., 22211, Pte.
Clarke, W., 43146, Pte.
Clear, D., 31101, Pte.
Cleaver, F., 21913, Pte.
Cleaves, G. E., 14958, Pte.
Clifford, A., 6546, Pte.
Clift, A., 19832, Pte.
Clinton, J., 22196, Pte.
Cocker, F., 35747, Pte.
Colburn, W., 17039, Pte.
Collins, C., 6762, Sgt.
Collins, J., 14479, Pte.
Collinson, P., 204853, Pte.
Connor, P., 32562, Pte.
Cook, T. R., 14640, L/Sgt.
Cooke, F., 10149, Pte.
Cooke, J. H., 19798, Pte.
Cooke, M. W., 14658, Pte.
Coombs, J., 26958, Pte.
Cooper, F., 14539, L/Cpl.
Cooper, J., 16305, Pte.
Cooper, J., 18177, Pte.

SEVENTH BATTALION—*(continued)*

Cooper, R. H., 42989, Pte.
Corbett, W. H., 17292, Pte.
Corbett, W. H., 19675, Pte.
Corfield, H., 23640, Pte.
Cornes, J., 14429, Pte.
Cotton, A. A., 27613, Pte.
Coulby, G. T. H., 36559, Pte.
Cox, T., 23630, Pte.
Cresswell, W., 26225, Pte.
Croft, H., 20630, Pte.
Cruise, W. H., 9336, Pte.
Curtis, J. H., 27215, Pte.
Cutt, J. A., 28435, Cpl.

Dakin, J., 26304, L/Cpl.
Dale, W. J., 25140, Pte.
Daniel, J. A., 19278, Pte.
Daniels, W., 26305, Pte.
Darrall, H. W., 23728, Pte.
Davies, A. H., 7669, Pte.
Davies, A., 13960, Pte.
Davies, C., 205128, L/Cpl.
Davies, D., 21915, Pte.
Davies, D. J., 38552, Pte.
Davies, D. R., 14400, Sgt.
Davies, E., 14729, Pte.
Davies, E., 201160, Pte.
Davies, E., 14531, Pte.
Davies, E., 35493, Pte.
Davies, F., 25274, Pte.
Davies, F. O., 14577, Pte.
Davies, G. I., 13407, Pte.
Davies, H. W., 23525, Pte.
Davies, J., 14974, Pte.
Davies, J. G. G., 33767, Pte.
Davies, J. H., 17627, Pte.
Davies, J., 14040, Pte.
Davies, J., 16515, Pte.
Davies, L., 16162, Pte.
Davies, P., 14354, Pte.

Davies, W., 24889, Pte.
Davies, W., 13388, Pte.
Davies, W., 28338, Pte.
Davies, W. E., 13016, Sgt.
Davies, W. H., 16000, L/Cpl.
Davies, W. H., 28963, Pte.
Davies, W. J., 13970, L/Cpl.
Davies, W. J., 26746, Pte.
Davies, W. J., 6487, Pte.
Davis, A., 24296, L/Cpl.
Davis, C. J., 19596, Pte.
Davison, J. L., 205001, Pte.
Daw, G., 25293, Pte.
Dawson, J., 25329, Pte.
Deakin, T., 14977, Pte.
Dean, T., 9940, Sgt.
Derrick, J., 7664, Pte.
Devall, W., 9682, Pte.
Dewhurst, J., 29701, Pte.
Dickinson, A. F., 27799, Pte.
Dickinson, G. G., 38551, Pte.
Donnelly, J. M., 35121, Pte.
Doriss, J., 38546, Pte.
Dovaston, J. W., 19723, Pte.
Dover, A. E., 25168, Pte.
Dowley, R. G., 16551, Pte.
Downes, J. H., 19574, Pte.
Ducat, B., 13648, Pte.
Duckett, J. O., 14189, Pte.
Duckworth, F., 32127, Pte.
Dudley, H., 24667, Pte.
Dunn, R. J., 207884, Pte.
Durbin, J., 15207, Pte.
Dyke, T., 12697, Pte.

Easthope, B. S., 14521, L/Cpl.
Eddleston, A., 13294, Pte.
Edgerton, I., 19530, Pte.
Edmunds, R., 13678, Pte.
Edwards, J. H., 5341, Sgt.

389

SEVENTH BATTALION—(continued)

Edwards, P. G., 19304, Pte.
Edwards, S., 22440, Pte.
Edwards, T. H., 35505, Pte.
Edwards, W. H., 23735, Pte.
Edwards, W. M., 11904, Pte.
Egan, A. L., 35179, Pte.
Elliott, H. B. R., 28629, Pte.
Elliott, H., 204096, Pte.
Ellis, E. A., 29705, Pte.
Ellis, T. P., 38556, Pte.
Ellis, T. R., 22382, Pte.
Evans, A. E., 6611, Cpl.
Evans, A., 16372, Pte.
Evans, D., 13861, Pte.
Evans, E. D., 14401, C.S.M.
Evans, E. T., 27010, Pte.
Evans, G., 10993, Pte.
Evans, H., 6332, Pte.
Evans, R., 15694, Pte.
Evans, T. D., 14872, Pte.
Evans, W., 14559, Pte.
Evans, W. A., 17847, Pte.
Evans, W. C., 17023, Pte.
Evison, A., 23527, Pte.

Fardoe, G., 13894, L/Cpl.
Farley, F., 13063, L/Cpl.
Farmer, G. S., 26661, Pte.
Farquharson, W. G., 19708, Pte.
Farr, C. A., 22216, Pte.
Farrall, E., 35407, Pte.
Feltus, H., 19730, Sgt.
Ferriday, L., 19535, Pte.
Fisher, R., 38558, Pte.
Fleet, E., 21235, Pte.
Fleet, H. J., 26381, Pte.
Fleetwood, A. J., 7492, Pte.
Fleming, H. J., 15412, Pte.
Fletcher, J., 7319, Pte.
Fletcher, J. F., 15352, Pte.

Fletcher, J., 14374, Pte.
Fletcher, S. M., 26329, Pte.
Fletcher, T., 19513, Pte.
Foote, J. W., 29706, Pte.
Ford, A. T., 22163, Pte.
Ford, W. E., 26666, Pte.
Forrester, W., 11536, Pte.
Fosker, A. J., 20798, Pte.
Foster, H. C., 27648, Pte.
Foster, W., 24166, Pte.
Foulkes, J., 23868, Pte.
Foulkes, T., 201335, Cpl.
Foulkes, T. G., 27226, Pte.
Fowles, F., 22301, Pte.
Fox, G. J., 24562, L/Cpl.
Frampton, A. E., 14507, Pte.
Francis, G., 17048, Pte.
Francis, J., 13403, Sgt.
Francis, T., 18035, Pte.
Francis, W. O., 18036, Pte.
Franklin, C., 22076, Cpl.
Furber, J., 22385, Pte.
Furber, W. H., 18312, Pte.

Gallacher, J., 40428, Pte.
Galley, A. E., 14196, Pte.
Gambriel, E., 10792, Pte.
Garbett, S. G., 22350, Pte.
Gardiner, J. W., 9973, L/Cpl.
Garner, J., 32158, Pte.
Garvey, P., 27802, Pte.
Gater, G. H., 13685, Pte.
Gaughan, J., 14403, Pte.
Geary, G., 24079, Pte.
Gill, J. J., 38566, Pte.
Gittens, E., 23712, Pte.
Gittens, W., 23714, Pte.
Gleeson, B., 14669, Pte.
Glossop, S., 15865, Pte.
Glover, F., 10819, Pte.

APPENDIX II

SEVENTH BATTALION—(*continued*)

Glynn, J., 16329, Pte.
Goodall, H., 20920, Pte.
Goodfellow, W., 7614, C.S.M.
Goodman, F., 204851, Pte.
Gore, T., 13596, Pte.
Gough, J., 201174, Cpl.
Gould, S., 24310, L/Cpl.
Grainger, G., 36560, Pte.
Grass, F. W., 14303, L/Cpl.
Grayson, G. W., 36621, Pte.
Greatwich, H., 18723, Pte.
Greeley, P., 7640, Pte.
Green, A., 22282, Pte.
Greenfield, G. R., 14273, Cpl.
Greening, L. H., 14836, Sgt.
Greenwood, W. E., 35786, Pte.
Gregory, E., 27244, Pte.
Gregory, J., 42991, Pte.
Grice, H., 19027, Pte.
Grice, J. T., 24911, Pte.
Griffiths, B., 14598, Pte.
Griffith, D., 26874, Pte.
Griffiths, E. T., 38568, Pte.
Griffiths, E., 18965, Pte.
Griffiths, E., 24177, Pte.
Griffiths, G. E., 34813, Pte.
Griffiths, H., 15367, Pte.
Griffiths, W. J., 20213, L/Cpl.
Grimes, H. E., 27678, Pte.
Grindley, F., 23668, Pte.
Grocott, H., 15289, Pte.
Guegan, F. C., 28638, Pte.
Guy, T., 13450, Pte.
Gwilliam, C., 22377, Pte.
Gwilliam, J., 13606, Pte.

Hadfield, C., 22463, Pte.
Haines, G. H., 22253, Pte.
Halford, J. R., 13602, Pte.
Hall, J., 11674, Pte.

Hall, W. R., 14881, Pte.
Hallam, S., 23980, Pte.
Hallett, G. C. D., 28642, Pte.
Hallwood, W., 43135, Pte.
Hamblett, H., 14183, Pte.
Hamer, R., 14322, Pte.
Hamlett, W. H., 16418, Pte.
Hancock, H., 14199, L/Cpl.
Hancock, W., 14263, Pte.
Hannant, C., 8307, Pte.
Harcourt, W., 32084, Pte.
Harding, G., 26908, Pte.
Harley, T., 9400, Pte.
Harp, S., 17354, Pte.
Harper, A., 14114, Pte.
Harper, F. G., 22433, Pte.
Harper, R. T., 18990, Pte.
Harris, A., 18352, Pte.
Harris, W., 18542, Pte.
Harrison, J. B. F., 35501, Pte.
Harrison, W. A., 26386, Pte.
Harrison, W. J., 28651, Pte.
Hatfield, P., 13018, Sgt.
Hatton, W., 12060, Pte.
Hawkins, C. T., 19550, Pte.
Hay, D., 9640, C.S.M.
Haynes, A., 10718, Pte.
Haynes, S. J., 23823, Cpl.
Hayward, E. V., 15740, Cpl.
Hayward, F., 26671, Pte.
Hayward, G., 13583, Pte.
Hazel, W. W., 16201, Pte.
Heakin, S., 26927, Pte.
Heal, T. J., 21959, Pte.
Hearth, T., 13779, Pte.
Hedges, B., 15836, Pte.
Hemmings, W., 7095, Pte.
Herbert, J., 19468, Pte.
Heyward, C., 43572, Pte.
Hicks, J., 19768, Pte.

Higgins, J. W., 24113, Pte.
Higgins, J., 18930, Pte.
Higgins, W., 22445, Pte.
Hill, E., 23880, Pte.
Hill, F., 11655, Pte.
Hill, L. H., 9354, Pte.
Hill, W., 43656, Pte.
Hill, W. E., 13325, Pte.
Hilton, W., 24615, Pte.
Hinchcliffe, W., 35506, Pte.
Hinksman, M. W., 17126, Pte.
Hinsley, A., 6252, L/Cpl.
Hodges, W. C., 6302, Pte.
Hodgson, A., 32561, Pte.
Hogg, G., 26333, Pte.
Holliday, C., 27775, Pte.
Hollis, R. G., 21948, Pte.
Holmes, J., 15757, Pte.
Holt, J., 19888, Pte.
Hooton, R., 29713, Pte.
Hopkins, T., 14913, Pte.
Hopson, J., 23511, Pte.
Hopwood, G., 15324, Pte.
Horn, A. E., 27662, Pte.
Hotchkiss, J., 13817, Pte.
Hough, W. R., 205199, Sgt.
Howard, W. J., 26016, Pte.
Howells, C. E., 19819, Pte.
Howells, H., 15415, Pte.
Howells, S., 24708, Pte.
Howells, T. J., 16264, Pte.
Howting, E., 27806, Pte.
Huffer, J., 23607, Pte.
Huggins, A. G., 8626, L/Cpl.
Hughés, A. E., 27243, Pte.
Hughes, F. R., 17010, Pte.
Hughes, H., 22355, Pte.
Hughes, J. B., 205053, Pte.
Hughes, T. R., 26880, Pte.
Hull, J., 13639, Pte.

Hull, R., 26992, Pte.
Humphrey, C. L., 21947, Pte.
Humphreys, J., 8716, Pte.
Humphreys, P., 26335, Pte.
Humphries, W. E., 14275, L/Cpl.
Hunter, J., 18597, Cpl.
Hyde, E., 23504, Pte.
Hyde, P. H., 13011, Sgt.

Ingleby, J., 13494, Pte.

Jacka, H., 28662, Pte.
Jackson, C., 20335, Pte.
James, E., 21975, Pte.
James, G. T., 24842, Pte.
James, J., 14315, Pte.
James, R., 35060, Pte.
James, R. H., 20992, L/Cpl.
James, W., 43263, Pte.
Jandrell, T., 23704, Pte.
Jarvis, C., 13484, Pte.
Jarvis, V., 27695, Pte.
Jeffery, F., 28656, Pte.
Jenkins, T. D. P., 21969, Pte.
Jinks, J. W., 15069, Pte.
Johnson, J., 26359, Pte.
Johnson, J. W., 25614, Pte.
Johnson, R. J., 27694, Pte.
Jones, A., 26978, Pte.
Jones, A., 33270, Pte.
Jones, A. W., 22124, Pte.
Jones, A., 23861, Pte.
Jones, A. G., 26674, Pte.
Jones, A., 26389, Pte.
Jones, A., 19855, Pte.
Jones, A. T., 11416, Pte.
Jones, B., 21970, Pte.
Jones, C., 9307, L/Cpl.
Jones, C., 13877, Pte.

APPENDIX II

Jones, C., 22028, Pte.
Jones, C. H., 15007, Pte.
Jones, D., 43309, Pte.
Jones, D., 21962, Pte.
Jones, E. O., 13900, Pte.
Jones, F., 13327, Pte.
Jones, F. A., 14515, Sgt.
Jones, F. T., 13745, Pte.
Jones, F., 26390, Pte.
Jones, G. F., 19737, Pte.
Jones, G. R., 22309, Pte.
Jones, G. J., 13788, Pte.
Jones, H., 22079, Pte.
Jones, H. C., 20944, Pte.
Jones, H. E., 35058, Pte.
Jones, H. J., 18320, Pte.
Jones, J., 11885, Pte.
Jones, J., 16268, Pte.
Jones, J., 33084, Pte.
Jones, J. H., 26314, Pte.
Jones, J., 17943, Pte.
Jones, J., 18843, Pte.
Jones, J. J., 13557, Pte.
Jones, J. W., 19023, Pte.
Jones, M., 21963, Pte.
Jones, O., 19763, Pte.
Jones, R. H., 29207, Pte.
Jones, T., 23764, Pte.
Jones, W. J., 201195, Bglr.
Jones, W., 13759, Pte.
Jones, W., 13965, Pte.
Jones, W., 27233, Pte.
Jones, W. F., 19633, Pte.
Jones, W. R., 38589, Pte.
Jones, W. R., 19553, Pte.
Jones, W. T., 25149, Pte.

Kearsley, F., 26994, Pte.
Keay, C., 19310, Pte.
Keay, J. J., 17049, Pte.

Keenan, J. A. C., 14783, L/Cpl.
Kelly, J. W., 22418, Pte.
Kelly, T., 6762, Pte.
Kempster, P., 38591, Pte.
Kenworthy, W., 13736, Pte.
Keogh, J. A., 28664, Pte.
Kerle, J. H., 27616, Pte.
Kershaw, H., 21976, Pte.
King, F. G., 24890, Pte.
King, G., 26391, Pte.
King, J. A., 24359, L/Cpl.
Kingsbury, W., 18713, Pte.
Kitching, A. W., 27636, Pte.
Kitson, J., 26643, Sgt.
Kniveton, G., 23962, Pte.
Kyte, F., 21977, Pte.

Lane, E. H., 13561, Pte.
Langford, J. J., 17970, Pte.
Langslow, J., 23891, Pte.
Langston, H., 40467, Pte.
Lapham, H. R., 27816, Pte.
Latcham, L., 21986, Pte.
Latham, J. T., 34861, Pte.
Lawson, A. G., 20587, Pte.
Layton, A. E., 10233, Pte.
Leach, R., 43608, Pte.
Leaver, V., 24083, Pte.
Lee, J. B., 26472, Pte.
Lees, J., 19420, Pte.
Levy, B., 26256, Pte.
Lewis, A., 5422, Pte.
Lewis, G. B., 13601, Pte.
Lewis, H., 43257, Pte.
Lewis, H., 16414, Pte.
Lewis, J., 16321, Pte.
Lewis, R., 200931, Pte.
Lewis, W., 24034, Pte.
Lewis, W. J., 14698, Sgt.

SEVENTH BATTALION—(continued)

Lighton, W. E., 24341, Pte.
Limb, W., 14499, L/Cpl.
Litherland, F. W., 205002, Pte.
Little, C. T., 16137, Pte.
Littledike, G., 204840, Pte.
Llewellyn, C. H., 15847, Pte.
Lloyd, G., 18785, Pte.
Lloyd, J., 12356, Pte.
Lloyd, S., 14226, Pte.
Lloyd, W., 7461, Pte.
Lockett, H. J., 18786, Pte.
Loder, E., 31543, Pte.
Long, A. V., 15774, Sgt.
Longworth, W., 17707, Pte.
Lovatt, J. A., 22043, Pte.
Lovatt, T., 24181, Pte.
Lovatt, W. J., 22284, Pte.
Low, R., 21645, Pte.
Lowe, A. H., 23767, Pte.
Lowe, G. B., 26339, Pte.
Lowe, J., 14923, Pte.
Lowe, R. C., 16269, Pte.
Lucas, H., 14372, Pte.
Lundy, J., 29749, Pte.
Lusty, F., 24060, Pte.
Lyndon, W. E., 21270, Pte.

Mabbutt, A., 10917, Pte.
Macbeth, J. H., 23142, Pte.
Macefield, A., 23725, Pte.
Machin, G. E., 7411, Pte.
MacKenzie, P., 24350, Pte.
Maclean, F., 27112, Pte.
Maddox, C., 26408, L/Cpl.
Mainwaring, A., 14741, Pte.
Makin, D., 21998, Pte.
Male, W., 14818, Pte.
Malt, V., 11648, Sgt.
Mander, W. G., 27236, Pte.
Manford, W., 14962, Cpl.

Martin, A. W., 19701, Pte.
Martin, B., 24091, Pte.
Martin, E., 12149, Pte.
Maskery, W., 16951, Cpl.
Masterson, J., 13812, Pte.
Mather, H. W., 18421, Pte.
Mather, J. E., 26645, Pte.
Matthews, A., 35226, Pte.
Matthews, A. J., 23535, L/Cpl.
Matthews, C., 29722, Pte.
Matthews, E. C., 25227, Pte.
Matthews, W., 13007, Pte.
Maude, G., 25304, Pte.
McDermott, W. F., 38606, Pte.
McWilliam, S., 21357, Pte.
Meacham, R. F., 19641, Pte.
Medlicott, L. J., 10691, Pte.
Metcalf, H. L., 16773, Pte.
Middelton, W. T., 19857, Pte.
Millard, P. T., 14578, Pte.
Miller, P., 8776, Pte.
Millin, C. R., 9376, Pte.
Mills, J. E., 16610, Pte.
Milner, A. B., 13404, Pte.
Milner, W., 24165, Pte.
Miner, P. W., 13873, L/Cpl.
Minshall, J., 10015, L/Cpl.
Minshull, W., 34556, Pte.
Mitchell, C., 38598, Pte.
Monks, G., 36602, Pte.
Morgan, C. H., 24092, Pte.
Morgan, E., 20355, Sgt.
Morgan, J. H., 11476, Pte.
Morgan, M., 13999, Pte.
Morgan, R., 38603, Pte.
Morgan, W., 8284, Sgt.
Morgan, W., 11561, L/Cpl.
Morgans, M., 13968, Pte.
Morris, D., 38423, Pte.

SEVENTH BATTALION—*(continued)*

Morris, E. O., 13888, C.S.M.
Morris, E. J., 14386, Pte.
Morris, H., 201789, Pte.
Morris, H., 14592, Pte.
Morris, J., 32177, Pte.
Morris, L., 35305, Pte.
Morris, R., 16075, L/Sgt.
Morris, R. E., 15782, Pte.
Morse, J., 23715, Cpl.
Mort, H., 38597, Pte.
Moss, D., 26315, Pte.
Moss, H. C., 38604, Pte.
Moulstone, T., 15672, Pte.
Moyle, A. C., 19787, Pte.
Mulhare, M., 14611, Pte.
Mullinder, G., 20308, Pte.
Murray, H., 22495, Pte.
Myatt, G., 27000, L/Cpl.

Neild, P., 38608, Pte.
Newell, J., 26363, Pte.
Newton, A., 28439, Cpl.
Nicholas, J., 14937, Pte.
Nicholls, J., 6590, L/Cpl.
Nicholson, C., 36590, Pte.
Ninnis, W. D., 6427, Pte.
Noakes, A., 20106, Pte.
Nobbs, A. G., 16295, Pte.
Norton, P., 19648, Pte.
Nottingham,W. M., 10273, Pte.

Oakes, B. W., 22219, L/Cpl.
Oakes, J., 10483, L/Cpl.
Oakley, A., 36656, Pte.
O'Boyle, C. A., 14910, Pte.
O'Brien, P., 7716, Pte.
O'Brien, W., 6081, Pte.
Ockey, M., 19801, Pte.
O'Leary, J., 6783, C.S.M.
Oliver, G., 16316, Pte.

Oliver, H., 15199, Pte.
Onions, E., 13718, Pte.
Orbell, A., 15896, Pte.
Osburn, H. E., 40454, Pte.
Ostick, A. J., 33496, Pte.
Owen, R., 200324, Pte.
Owen, W. R., 23865, Pte.
Owens, R. W., 13969, Pte.
Oxford, S., 20829, Pte.
Oxley, R. C., 26684, Pte.

Page, W., 13741, Pte.
Page, W. T., 14609, Pte.
Pagett, W. J., 24940, Pte.
Palmer, W., 16501, Pte.
Parker, W., 22031, Pte.
Parker, W. G., 35314, Pte.
Parker, W. H., 14426, Pte.
Parker, Z., 24057, L/Cpl.
Parkinson, T. G., 27726, Pte.
Parr, C. K., 31961, Sgt.
Parry, F., 16280, Pte.
Parry, J., 35337, Pte.
Parry, R. H., 31611, Cpl.
Parsons, A. J., 27640, Pte.
Parsons, G., 14424, L/Sgt.
Parton, N. L., 23887, Pte.
Payne, W. H., 16740, Pte.
Peacock, W. A., 13650, Pte.
Pearce, A., 15695, Cpl.
Pearce, E. A., 204111, Pte.
Pearce, H., 24750, Pte.
Peate, W., 16317, Pte.
Perry, A. E., 8367, Pte.
Pewtress, W., 22133, Cpl.
Phibben, F., 27786, Pte.
Phillips, H., 15192, Pte.
Phillips, H., 35318, Pte.
Phillips, W., 15869, Pte.
Phipps, C., 7597, Pte.

THE KING'S SHROPSHIRE LIGHT INFANTRY

Phipps, H. W., 27614, Pte.
Pickard, W., 38613, Pte.
Picken, F. H., 26685, Pte.
Pickering, J. E., 35115, Pte.
Pierce, O. G., 29733, Pte.
Pile, E. C., 27803, Pte.
Pitt, J., 17777, Pte.
Plimmer, C., 6025, Pte.
Poole, A., 23738, Pte.
Poole, G., 22059, Pte.
Poole, J. F., 22154, Pte.
Pope, A. G., 8200, Sgt.
Pope, C. J., 13743, Pte.
Pope, D., 23737, Pte.
Pope, F. G., 8201, Cpl.
Porter, V. G., 14383, Pte.
Potts, E. S., 24088, Pte.
Poulter, C., 11790, Pte.
Poulter, G. H., 19527, Pte.
Powell, F. G., 16430, Pte.
Powell, H. V., 35312, Pte.
Powell, W. T., 35310, Pte.
Powis, C. B., 42955, Pte.
Powis, T. A., 17118, Sgt.
Poyner, A., 15828, Pte.
Poynton, W. H., 23548, Pte.
Preece, P., 19606, Pte.
Price, F. G., 19722, Pte.
Price, H., 14593, Pte.
Price, H., 14750, Pte.
Price, H. E., 38614, Pte.
Price, J., 15437, Pte.
Price, J., 16894, Pte.
Price, J., 35495, Pte.
Price, J., 9806, Cpl.
Price, O., 32737, Pte.
Price, P. H., 32331, Pte.
Price, R., 20363, Pte.
Price, R. H., 16277, L/Cpl.
Price, W., 24322, Pte.

Pritchard, H., 14471, L/Cpl.
Pritchard, T. P., 14251, Cpl.
Probert, J., 14932, Pte.
Probert, L., 19729, Pte.
Probert, T. I., 11061, Pte.
Proctor, N., 202800, Pte.
Prunnell, J. W., 14287, L/Cpl.
Pryce, W. E., 17239, Pte.
Pugh, E. R., 16996, Pte.
Pugh, J. G., 24854, Pte.
Purcell, H., 22023, Pte.
Purvey, H., 27620, Pte.
Purvis, W. R., 32683, Pte.
Putt, T. E., 14614, Pte.

Quelch, T. H., 204846, Pte.
Quinn, J., 35320, Pte.

Ralphs, S., 16525, Pte.
Ralphs, S. C., 38620, Pte.
Randles, E. J., 22279, Pte.
Rawlings, T. G., 18244, Pte.
Rawlins, J. W., 36643, Pte.
Ray, A., 32403, Pte.
Ree, H., 14952, Pte.
Reed, C. H., 13780, Pte.
Reed, H., 14313, Cpl.
Rees, A. J., 19782, Pte.
Reeves, J. W., 22477, Pte.
Regan, J., 34800, Pte.
Renforth, W. R., 36588, Pte.
Reynolds, J. H., 13875, Pte.
Rhodes, C. A., 13006, Pte.
Rhodes, F., 18176, Pte.
Richards, H., 43006, Pte.
Richards, T., 14288, Pte.
Richards, W., 14175, Pte.
Richards, W., 14500, Pte.
Richards, W. G., 22123, Pte.

SEVENTH BATTALION—(*continued*)

Riches, L., 26345, Pte.
Rider, J. J., 33492, Pte.
Ridyard, J. J., 205853, Pte.
Rigby, J., 13913, Pte.
Riley, T., 38619, Pte.
Rimmer, J., 28352, Pte.
Rippin, W. J., 26633, Pte.
Robb, L., 16701, L/Cpl.
Roberts, A. S., 19735, Pte.
Roberts, A., 24756, Pte.
Roberts, C., 16182, Pte.
Roberts, D. J., 13941, L/Cpl.
Roberts, E., 23831, Pte.
Roberts, E. L., 23695, Pte.
Roberts, G., 17361, Pte.
Roberts, H., 31245, Pte.
Roberts, H. A., 14280, Pte.
Roberts, L., 19774, L/Cpl.
Roberts, T., 26365, Pte.
Roberts, T. E., 16693, Pte.
Roberts, W. H., 26346, Pte.
Roberts, W. G., 35322, Pte.
Robinson, S. H., 38618, Pte.
Robinson, W., 35324, L/Cpl.
Rogers, A., 22070, Pte.
Rogers, E., 13755, Pte.
Rogers, E., 26689, Pte.
Rogers, E. W., 8120, Cpl.
Rogerson, W., 23699, Pte.
Rose, E., 13726, Pte.
Rose, G., 22469, Pte.
Rose, J., 7615, Pte.
Rosser, D. R., 14807, Pte.
Rothwell, E., 14438, Pte.
Rowley, W. H., 24742, Pte.
Roxbury, T. H., 15608, Pte.
Ruscoe, J., 14603, Pte.
Russell, E., 14870, L/Cpl.
Ryan, D., 205048, L/Cpl.
Ryder, J. C., 22235, Pte.

Samuels, F., 35155, Pte.
Sandells, G., 22254, Pte.
Sansam, R., 12537, Pte.
Sargent, F. C., 26974, Pte.
Saunders, W., 18800, Pte.
Sayce, G. W., 26947, L/Cpl.
Sayer, A., 22157, Pte.
Scannell, M., 15771, Pte.
Scholes, A., 13924, Pte.
Scragg, L., 26317, L/Cpl.
Seaborne, E. C., 19618, Pte.
Seare, E., 14835, Pte.
Sedgley, H., 26367, Pte.
Sexton, J. W., 27729, Pte.
Seymour, J. F., 9564, Sgt.
Shelby, C., 35478, Pte.
Shenton, F. J., 12995, Cpl.
Shenton, W., 23874, Pte.
Shepherd, E., 25319, Pte.
Sheppard, A. H., 27604, Pte.
Sherry, G. H., 22252, Pte.
Shirley, C., 22168, Cpl.
Sidebottom, H. O., 34795, Pte.
Simons, E., 205082, C.Q.M.S.
Simpson, J. W., 13659, Pte.
Sims, T., 14436, Sgt.
Slawson, W. G., 6379, Pte.
Smith, A., 19326, Pte.
Smith, F., 25301, Pte.
Smith, F., 23769, Pte.
Smith, I. T., 22451, Pte.
Smith, J., 13813, Pte.
Smith, R. H. B., 14823, Pte.
Smith, S., 38627, Pte.
Smith, T., 19629, Pte.
Smith, T. D., 18781, Pte.
Smith, W., 14203, Pte.
Smith, W. F., 20802, Pte.
Smith, W. J., 14252, Pte.
Smout, E., 13855, Pte.

Smithyman, E. H., 27219, Pte.
Snelgrove, C., 35474, Pte.
Snowdon, E. W., 15984, Pte.
Sockett, J., 18300, Cpl.
Southway, A., 7647, Pte.
Speakes, G., 16559, Pte.
Spencer, E. J., 38500, Pte.
Spreadborough, A. G., 29121, Pte.
Sprittles, W., 15874, Pte.
Squire, A. H., 205075, L/Sgt.
Starkey, F., 18444, Pte.
Steadman, C., 14069, Pte.
Stearman, B. H. M., 204835, Pte.
Steele, T., 16322, Pte.
Stephens, J., 15834, L/Cpl.
Stephen, S. J., 14533, Pte.
Storr, B. W., 10663, Pte.
Stripp, H., 14418, L/Cpl.
Sutton, C., 19475, Pte.
Swanwick, A. J., 13026, Pte.
Sweeney, E., 24301, L/Cpl.
Swindells, F., 26319, Pte.
Symonds, J., 13571, L/Cpl.

Talbot, S., 19785, Pte.
Taylor, A., 23705, Pte.
Taylor, E. E., 19164, Pte.
Taylor, F., 9767, Sgt.
Taylor, H., 27731, Pte.
Taylor, J. E., 6514, Pte.
Taylor, J., 22877, Pte.
Taylor, S. F., 21362, Pte.
Taylor, W., 26986, Cpl.
Taylor, W., 16313, Pte.
Taylor, W., 22167, L/Cpl.
Terretta, J., 26695, Pte.
Tew, S., 12466, Sgt.
Thexton, R., 29742, Pte.

Thomas, A., 9572, L/Cpl.
Thomas, C., 16462, Cpl.
Thomas, E., 6194, L/Cpl.
Thomas, R., 12702, Pte.
Thomas, S., 11109, Pte.
Thomas, W., 13989, Pte.
Thomason, G., 26697, Pte.
Thompson, G., 29605, Pte.
Thompson, S., 25305, Pte.
Thornton, W. T., 8543, C.S.M.
Thwaite, C. L., 31997, Pte.
Titley, G. H., 35161, Pte.
Toft, A., 23846, Pte.
Tomkins, E. T., 23521, Pte.
Tomkinson, J., 16829, Pte.
Tomlins, P., 12440, Pte.
Tompkins, F., 16864, Pte.
Tootle, C., 18461, Pte.
Towert, W. S., 24400, Pte.
Towns, J., 14930, Pte.
Tranter, H., 35188, Pte.
Tranter, J., 28426, Pte.
Trelfa, J., 22156, Pte.
Tuckley, A. E., 14414, C.S.M.
Tudor, P., 25491, Pte.
Tunstall, G., 26321, Pte.
Turner, J., 25188, Pte.
Turner, W., 27732, Pte.
Twiss, T. W., 18087, Pte.

Unsworth, J., 20263, Pte.

Vallender, G., 15775, Pte.
Vanner, T., 27649, L/Cpl.
Vater, J., 14045, Pte.
Vaughan, T., 23650, Pte.
Vaughan, W., 14104, L/Cpl.
Venables, C., 12038, Pte.
Venables, C., 13912, Cpl.

APPENDIX II

Wade, G. M., 19544, Pte.
Waites, J., 25082, Pte.
Walford, F., 26257, Pte.
Walkden, L., 29747, Pte.
Walker, R., 38648, Pte.
Wallis, J. E., 13021, Pte.
Wallwork, S., 16328, Sgt.
Walmsley, T. B., 11994, L/Cpl.
Walters, D. J., 14336, Pte.
Walton, C. B., 36599, Pte.
Ward, G., 7512, Pte.
Ward, H. H., 15866, L/Cpl.
Wardrop, J., 14293, Sgt.
Waring, A. G., 35487, Pte.
Warren, G. J., 7488, Pte.
Watkins, G. A., 33583, Pte.
Watkins, R., 14176, Sgt.
Watkins, T., 25143, Pte.
Watts, A. J., 14254, Pte.
Watts, D., 13793, Cpl.
Weaver, W., 13533, Pte.
Webb, G. W., 20872, L/Cpl.
Wedge, G., 6672, Pte.
Weedon, F. T., 27652, Pte.
Weedon, H., 35486, Pte.
Weir, F., 24059, Pte.
Wellens, H., 6289, Pte.
Wellings, G., 26700, Pte.
Wellings, J., 26701, Pte.
Wells, G., 27817, Pte.
Wharton, J. E., 26352, Pte.
Whettall, L., 12075, Pte.
White, E. R., 27657, Pte.
White, G., 7665, Pte.
White, H. G., 27655, Pte.
White, T., 13769, Pte.
Whitehead, B., 13425, Pte.
Whitfield, C., 26407, L/Cpl.
Widdup, W., 15876, L/Cpl.
Wilcox, J. W., 22019, Pte.

Wilde, H., 201220, C.Q.M.S.
Wilde, J., 15753, Pte.
Wilkins, A., 204128, Pte.
Wilkinson, J., 14522, Pte.
Willett, G., 19760, Pte.
Williams, A. E., 11906, Pte.
Williams, A., 18022, L/Cpl.
Williams, B., 15809, Pte.
Williams, C., 16300, Pte.
Williams, C. R., 22357, Pte.
Williams, E., 35494, Pte.
Williams, E. J., 5947, Pte.
Williams, E. J., 14743, Sgt.
Williams, F., 10704, Pte.
Williams, F., 22286, Pte.
Williams, G., 14684, Pte.
Williams, G., 26409, Pte.
Williams, G. W., 26703, Pte.
Williams, H., 24018, Pte.
Williams, J., 17261, Pte.
Williams, N., 35133, Pte.
Williams, R. J., 14192, L/Cpl.
Williams, R. B., 22300, Pte.
Williams, T., 35491, Pte.
Williamson, H. G., 16273, Pte.
Willmott, H. J. C., 19094, Pte.
Wilson, E., 24691, L/Cpl.
Wilson, R. L., 26704, Pte.
Withington, W., 201458, Pte.
Wolstencroft, E., 23943, Pte.
Wood, A., 18740, L/Cpl.
Wood, F. S., 23322, Pte.
Wood, W. T., 200507, Pte.
Woods, J., 15326, Sgt.
Woodward, T., 24602, Pte.
Woollard, S., 35492, Pte.
Woolley, C. W., 16638, Pte.
Woolley, J. L., 38650, Pte.
Woolridge, E., 14833, Pte.
Wright, H., 16282, Pte.

THE KING'S SHROPSHIRE LIGHT INFANTRY

Wright, P., 22459, Pte.
Wyatt, T., 8977, Pte.
Wylde, J., 15167, Pte.

Wynne, A., 17916, Pte.
Yapp, F., 23634, Pte.
Youd, S., 43290, Pte.

EIGHTH BATTALION

Allman, J., 20682, Pte.
Anderson, C., 32609, Pte.
Anderson, T., 26763, Pte.
Austin, L. C., 16412, Pte.

Barber, C., 13389, Sgt.
Barnfield, J., 14209, Pte.
Beeston, C. E., 12683, L/Cpl.
Bentley, A., 16562, Pte.
Bevan, A. E., 14138, Pte.
Bright, A., 23772, Pte.
Bromley, J. A., 8994, Pte.
Brown, R. G., 31124, Pte.
Brown, W., 24132, Pte.
Bullough, H., 13237, Pte.
Burgess, S., 23905, Pte.
Butcher, J., 15329, Pte.

Cadwallader, L., 15959, Cpl.
Cantrill, R., 20686, Pte.
Carsley, F. H., 15731, L/Cpl.
Cassidy, J., 13742, Pte.
Cheadle, W., 12617, Pte.
Coar, J., 32299, Pte.
Colley, E., 16642, Pte.

Davies, C., 23789, Pte.
Davies, W. A., 13381, L/Cpl.
Devenport, F., 12597, Pte.
Doughty, G., 45761, L/Sgt.
Downes, A. C., 16908, Cpl.
Dyke, W., 12879, Pte.

Edwards, F., 23803, Pte.

Farrell, J., 13540, Pte.
Finch, J. J., 17002, Pte.
Fox, W., 25402, Pte.
Francis, R., 12399, Pte.
Furber, W. J., 23997, L/Cpl.

Gammond, T., 13570, Pte.
Gardiner, A. W., 12815, Pte.
Gough, A., 24047, Pte.
Greatrex, F. C., 12629, Pte.
Greenwood, V., 32228, Pte.
Griffiths, R. F., 16612, Pte.
Griffiths, R., 13440, Pte.
Griffiths, T., 12561, Pte.
Grimshaw, H., 32502, Pte.
Grubb, W., 25506, Pte.

Habberley, W. H., 16932, L/Cpl.
Halford, G., 13611, Pte.
Halford, L., 16646, Pte.
Hall, W., 12880, Pte.
Hallworth, A., 32512, Pte.
Hamer, W., 13094, Pte.
Handley, C., 32446, Pte.
Hartley, R., 32370, Pte.
Higginson, A., 15308, Pte.
Hilliard, P., 35608, Pte.
Hills, S. S., 16574, Pte.
Holden, C. G., 14404, R.S.M.
Hollinshead, G., 13334, Pte.
Hornby, F., 12831, Pte.
Howarth, L., 16621, Pte.
Hughes, D. J., 13926, Pte.

400

EIGHTH BATTALION—(*continued*)

Hughes, H., 24367, Pte.

Jennings, F., 25442, Pte.
Jones, A. E., 19001, Pte.
Jones, J., 14153, Pte.
Jones, J. G., 13478, Pte.
Jones, W., 35609, Pte.
Joshua, J. A., 19791, Pte.

Kelly, E. J., 12115, Pte.
Knapper, G. T., 20710, Pte.
Knowles, S., 16641, Pte.

Laskey, E. G., 14061, Pte.
Law, H., 32539, Pte.
Lewis, A., 24305, L/Cpl.
Lewis, J., 13422, Pte.
Lloyd, J., 23796, Pte.
Locklin, A. J., 12689, Pte.
Longworth, J. E., 13286, Cpl.
Lowe, E. R., 13608, Pte.

Maddox, E., 12681, Cpl.
Martin, J., 13827, Pte.
Mawdsley, J. H., 24622, Pte.
Meats, R. F., 20720, Pte.
Middlecote, G. A., 13473, Pte.
Mills, E., 15170, L/Cpl.
Moffatt, J., 32556, Pte.
Moore, G., 12662, Pte.
Morgan, W. H., 23542, Pte.
Morris, D. G., 15625, Pte.

Nicholls, R., 12868, Pte.

Oliver, W., 12818, L/Cpl.
Owen, G. T., 12679, Cpl.

Palmer, L. E., 16733, Pte.
Parfitt, W., 14055, Pte.

Parkinson, H., 45746, Pte.
Parry, D. J., 13791, Cpl.
Partridge, J. R., 25749, Pte.
Peach, H. E., 12843, Pte.
Peate, W. T., 12687, Pte.
Phillips, E., 9781, Pte.
Pinches, J., 16587, Pte.
Plane, E., 32120, Pte.
Pointon, H. F., 19661, Pte.
Powner, H., 12593, Cpl.
Pulfer, J. W., 17167, Pte.

Remnant, J. R., 14168, Pte.
Rhodes, R., 32371, Pte.
Roberts, E., 13716, Pte.
Royle, H., 23909, Pte.

Sampson, D. J., 14011, Pte.
Smart, G., 14094, Sgt.
Spark, J. H., 35574, Pte.
Speak, A., 32376, Pte.
Stockton, E., 12477, Pte.
Sweet, G., 13668, Pte.
Swift, E. E., 16897, L/Cpl.

Taylor, J., 32633, Pte.
Thomas, E. R., 25524, Pte.
Tipping, F. G., 45729, Pte.
Tolson, F., 45742, Pte.
Tranter, R. W., 12512, L/Sgt.
Tranter, W. H., 19551, Pte.

Veale, W., 12809, L/Cpl.

Wall, R., 8853, C.S.M.
Walton, H., 16885, L/Cpl.
Wane, T., 13115, L/Cpl.
Watkins, W., 14051, Pte.
Watson, W., 31112, Pte.

THE KING'S SHROPSHIRE LIGHT INFANTRY

Webb, W. C., 20677, Pte.
White, F., 16898, Pte.
Wilkins, A. V., 20660, Pte.
Williams, F. B., 32332, Pte.

Williams, G. A., 12713, L/Cpl.
Williams, H., 13991, Pte.
Williamson, G., 24397, Pte.
Workman, T., 21354, Pte.

NINTH BATTALION

Adams, T. H., 19851, Pte.
Alecock, A., 14348, Cpl.
Desborough, E. R., 22129, Pte.
Donnell, E. R., 12729, Pte.
Edmunds, W., 14828, Pte.
Graydon, J., 22387, Pte.
Humphrey, G., 22306, Pte.
Jackson, H., 17317, Pte.
Jones, J., 22025, Pte.

Jones, T. C., 19689, Pte.
Moore, A. E., 23027, Pte.
Murphy, J., 23256, Pte.
Pye, T. H., 22353, Pte.
Redman, J., 22742, Pte.
Trow, H., 19653, Pte.
Walters, J. T., 22422, Pte.
Whitby, J. R., 15227, Sgt.

TENTH BATTALION

Anderson, A. G., 27704, Pte.
Austin, G. F., 230137, Pte.
Austin, P., 230395, Pte.

Bailey, A., 29791, Pte.
Bailey, F., 203570, Pte.
Baird, H. S., 230535, Sgt.
Ball, E., 16810, Pte.
Barkley, W., 230467, Pte.
Barlow, G., 33499, Pte.
Barlow, J., 230938, Pte.
Battersby, J. W., 34057, Pte.
Bebb, J., 230151, Pte.
Bedell, F. L., 230497, Pte.
Beeby, T., 230245, Pte.
Bell, E. L., 34151, Pte.
Bell, H., 34203, Pte.
Bennett, W., 32610, Pte.
Bishop, W. H., 33247, Pte.
Blewitt, F., 230188, Pte.

Bolt, J., 21602, Pte.
Booth, F., 230547, Sgt.
Bostock, E., 230459, Pte.
Bower, S., 33749, Pte.
Bowers, S., 230674, Pte.
Brace, E. G., 230144, C.S.M.
Bracegirdle, J., 230548, Pte.
Bradshaw, W. H., 34201, Pte.
Bright, R. T., 230452, Pte.
Brodey, A. J. B., 230823, Sgt.
Brooks, J. J., 230437, Pte.
Brown, R., 230829, Pte.
Butcher, T. H., 230116, L/Cpl.

Chamberlain, H., 34043, Pte.
Chrimes, W., 30058, Pte.
Chubb, G. J., 207878, Pte.
Church, S. T., 8359, Sgt.
Cook, J., 29799, Pte.

APPENDIX II

Cooke, A., 230204, Sgt.
Cookson, V., 33284, Pte.
Coombes, A., 33027, Pte.
Cotton, J., 23661, Pte.
Davies, A. E., 230155, Pte.
Davies, A., 230121, Cpl.
Davies, J., 31949, Pte.
Davies, J. S., 34206, Pte.
Davis, G., 15347, Pte.
Dawson, H., 230648, Pte.
Dentith, W., 230808, Pte.
Diggle, H. V., 230356, Pte.
Doody, W., 31930, Pte.
Doogan, J., 230070, Cpl.
Dorrell, H. E., 230256, L/Cpl.
Dugdale, A. S., 230875, Pte.
Dunford, A. J., 230717, Pte.
Dutton, F. I., 230784, Pte.
Dutton, J., 230860, Cpl.

Eccleston, W., 32911, Pte.
Eden, W., 20076, Pte.
Edge, T. W., 230798, Pte.
Edkins, D., 34141, Pte.
Edwards, T., 230485, Pte.
Ellis, D. T., 230402, Pte.
Ellis, E. S., 230341, Pte.
Elston, W. B., 230006, C.Q.M.S.
Evans, F., 230126, Pte.
Everall, J., 230231, Pte.

Fairbrother, J. G., 31866, Pte.
Faulkner, S. R., 230304, Pte.
Fearnall, H., 230288, Cpl.
Foster, T. G., 230502, Pte.
Foxcroft, J., 33514, Pte.
Foxley, W., 34062, Pte.
Frank, T. L. I., 230233, Pte.

Galliers, C., 33246, Pte.
Gaskell, J., 230627, Pte.

Goff, W. E., 230873, L/Cpl.
Gower, V., 34137, Pte.
Green, J., 33291, Pte.
Greenhalgh, T., 25862, Pte.
Grenville, F., 231061, Pte.
Griffiths, C. E., 230572, Pte.
Griffiths, H., 230397, Pte.
Griffiths, J., 16560, Pte.
Griffiths, J., 29775, Pte.
Grindley, C. J., 230434, Pte.
Gudgeon, T. J., 34131, Pte.
Guest, A. T., 19314, Pte.

Hall, C. H., 230262, Pte.
Hardwicke, E. P., 231018, Pte.
Harley, T., 231019, Pte.
Harsley, L. W., 230716, L/Cpl.
Heynes, F. C., 230327, Pte.
Hill, O., 34054, Pte.
Himsworth, T., 31944, Pte.
Hines, J., 9653, L/Sgt.
Hinton, J., 230361, L/Cpl.
Holden, W. H., 230385, Pte.
Holder, L., 230824, Pte.
Hollins, W., 203609, Pte.
Hollowood, E., 231023, Pte.
Hollowood, H., 29788, Pte.
Howitt, A. E., 29822, Pte.
Humphries, G., 230342, Pte.

Jackson, F., 230752, Pte.
James, D. H., 29780, Pte.
Jarrett, F. H., 230346, Pte.
Jarvis, J. M., 230465, Pte.
Johns, H. G., 230315, Pte.
Johnson, W., 21688, Pte.
Jones, C., 231024, Pte.
Jones, E., 230820, Pte.
Jones, F. P., 230528, Cpl.
Jones, J. R., 230004, C.Q.M.S.

Jones, J. R., 29779, Pte.
Jones, M. H., 203574, Pte.
Jones, S. A., 230107, Pte.
Jones, W. B., 230456, L/Cpl.
Jones, W., 29761, Pte.

Kelly, H., 31947, Pte.
Kerry, J., 36722, Pte.
Knight, F. G., 230774, Pte.
Knott, J., 25869, Pte.

Langford, W., 230157, Pte.
Langley, E. C., 34183, Pte.
Latham, H. S., 30079, Pte.
Law, G., 33240, Pte.
Lawrence, F. C., 29286, Pte.
Lawrence, J. P., 17781, Pte.
Ledgard, J. W., 40446, Pte.
Leech, E., 22162, Pte.
Lewis, J. T., 230966, Pte.
Lewis, R. H., 25900, Pte.
Lloyd, E., 230732, Pte.
Lucas, C., 19837, Pte.

Maddock, C. E., 34045, Pte.
Martin, F. H., 12091, Pte.
Martin, R., 230745, Cpl.
Mason, H., 6238, Sgt.
Matthews, T., 225559, Pte.
McDonald, N. G. M., 34184, Pte.
MacKay, G., 21651, Pte.
Meakin, C., 230041, Sgt.
Miller, A. E., 34173, Pte.
Moores, G. A., 34041, Pte.
Morris, G., 34985, Pte.
Morris, H., 31897, Pte.
Morrison, T., 231029, Pte.
Moss, A. H., 225545, L/Cpl.
Moss, J. E., 8172, Pte.
Mullock, J., 230072, Sgt.

Nickson, J. A., 230734, C.Q.M.S.
Noble, L., 8023, Cpl.

Oliver, C. H., 33248, Pte.
Owen, E. H., 33256, Pte.

Parcell, H. E., 34091, Pte.
Parsons, W. W., 230038, Cpl.
Pattinson, S., 230908, Pte.
Pearce, B., 230657, Cpl.
Pearce, G., 203618, Pte.
Pearman, J., 31870, Pte.
Pearson, I. M., 28180, Pte.
Pengelly, E. L., 21689, Pte.
Perkins, N., 203613, Pte.
Phillips, E., 11258, Pte.
Philpott, J. A., 230219, Pte.
Poole, C. C., 230428, Cpl.
Powell, A., 34187, Pte.
Price, S., 18813, Pte.
Price, T. V., 230085, Sgt.
Pryke, W., 230206, Pte.

Reynolds, W. E., 33162, Pte.
Richards, J., 31869, Pte.
Richards, J., 231037, Pte.
Riley, G. H., 25872, Pte.
Roberts, A., 230387, Pte.
Roberts, E., 230078, Pte.
Roberts, P. G., 29951, Pte.
Roberts, W., 34189, Pte.
Roberts, W., 230389, Pte.
Robinson, T., 230306, Pte.
Rogers, G., 225546, Pte.
Rogers, T. R., 19311, Pte.
Round, J., 34068, Pte.
Rowlands, W. H., 203611, Pte.
Rushton, J., 11930, Pte.

Sankey, D. E., 230094, L/Cpl.
Sarginson, T. W., 34082, Pte.

APPENDIX II

TENTH BATTALION—(*continued*)

Saunders, W. H., 230051, Cpl.
Seaton, E., 31891, Pte.
Sellers, R. A., 230825, L/Cpl.
Shaw, F. O., 33739, Pte.
Smith, C., 31860, Pte.
Smith, H., 230967, Pte.
Smith, P., 8149, Pte.
Smyth, C. A., 27676, Pte.
Snape, W., 24331, Pte.
Southerton, G., 26711, Pte.
Studley, T., 230744, Pte.
Sturman, J. R., 230859, Pte.
Summers, C. J., 24010, Pte.
Suthon, J. R., 33003, Pte.

Taylor, C., 31863, Pte.
Teanby, E., 230686, Pte.
Thomas, R., 34094, Pte.
Titterton, A., 230930, Pte.
Tomlin, W., 6578, Cpl.
Tribe, H., 25287, Pte.
Trower, L. E., 231066, Pte.
Turner, J. G., 33282, Pte.
Turner, J., 16005, Pte.

Venables, J. E., 230372, Pte.
Vincent, W. J., 27647, Pte.

Wain, W., 230588, Sgt.
Wakeley, I. L., 16380, Pte.
Wale, A. J., 25905, Pte.
Walker, C. W., 230290, Pte.
Walker, F., 36701, L/Cpl.
Walker, J., 34236, Pte.
Ware, P., 34080, Pte.
Watkins, W., 230267, Pte.
Watson, T., 230846, L/Cpl.
Webb, H. W. G., 32312, Pte.
Webster, R., 32910, Pte.
Wharton, B., 226088, Pte.
Whittaker, E., 30090, Pte.
Wilde, E., 230178, Pte.
Williams, J. R., 230254, Pte.
Williams, N., 230969, Pte.
Winkle, J., 230986, Pte.
Winstanley, A., 32905, Pte.
Wood, J., 230997, Pte.
Woodruff, H., 11576, Pte.
Woodruff, R., 32523, Pte.
Wright, C., 230889, Pte.
Wycherley, J., 18307, Pte.
Wynn, E., 230469, L/Cpl.

Yapp, W. T., 230408, Pte.
Yoxall, E. L., 230681, Sgt.

DEPOT

Allen, F. W., 17625, S.Q.M.S.
Bain, W., 18993, Pte.
Blount, W., 14655, Sgt.
Collins, G. A., 13625, Sgt.
Elkington, H., 200568, Pte.
Griffiths, W., 207873, Pte.
Humphreys, O., 10019, Pte.
Kirby, J. W., 35013, Pte.
Leah, J., 13628, C.S.M.
Liggett, J., 209078, Pte.
Magson, W., 14257, Pte.

Martin, E., 4721, Pte.
McLoughlin, G., 203971, Pte.
Paskin, W., 6381, Pte.
Phillips, F., 11801, Cpl.
Rogers, F., 18457, Pte.
Rowe, C. T., 10533, Pte.
Salter, P. E., 19486, Pte.
Seymour, S., 8103, Pte.
Smith, A., 18896, Pte.
Soame, R. E. B. H., 14394, Sgt.

THE KING'S SHROPSHIRE LIGHT INFANTRY

SERVING AT THE TIME OF DEATH WITH THE
1/1ST HEREFORDS

Barnsley, H., 200161, L/Cpl.
Bright, W. G., 29630, Pte.
Bubb, G. A., 33427, Pte.

Cardwell, A., 35621, Pte.
Carrier, T. E., 28745, Pte.

Fischer, E. J., 29646, Pte.
Fox, W., 33705, Pte.

Gorrell, J. H., 25450, Pte.

Harvey, F. S., 35659, Pte.
Hotchkiss, F., 33415, Pte.
Hudson, A. C., 28879, Pte.

Jackman, A., 29635, Pte.
Jackson, T., 33426, Pte.
Jones, J., 29637, Pte.
Jones, T., 21398, Pte.

Lanyon, S., 29059, Pte.
Long, M. W., 28874, Pte.
Lunt, G. T., 33425, Pte.

Mason, C., 25995, Pte.
Mawer, E. L., 28777, Pte.
McCaig, W., 29008, Pte.

Mitchell, T., 29006, Pte.
Moore, G., 8087, Pte.
Munden, A. G., 35632, Pte.
Murray, H., 29010, Pte.
Musk, E. E., 20884, Pte.

Parkinson, J., 29016, Pte.
Philpott, C., 28791, Pte.

Quilliam, T. C., 230961, Pte.

Reed, G., 28969, Pte.
Rees, S. G., 28765, Pte.
Revell, J., 35643, Pte.

Smallridge, H., 29603, Pte.
Soper, F. H., 29611, Pte.
Southern, S. H., 28905, Pte.
Stevens, W. C., 25857, L/Cpl.
Strugnell, G. E., 29607, Pte.
Sykes, H., 33411, Pte.

Taylor, C., 8182, Pte.
Taylor, J., 35670, Pte.

Weaving, F. E., 29634, Pte.
Willis, H., 28780, Pte.

TOTALS.

Officers	258	3/4th Reserve	1
Other Ranks :	4,452	5th Battalion	667
Depot	21	6th ,,	555
1st Battalion	988	7th ,,	1,048
2nd ,,	354	8th ,,	136
3rd ,,	35	9th ,,	17
1/4th ,,	369	10th ,,	238
4th Reserve	13		
2/4th ,,	10		4,710

APPENDIX III

REWARDS

ALL RANKS

(The ranks, etc., shown are those held at the time of the award.)

V.C.
Whitfield, H., Pte., 230199

K.C.B.
Townshend, Major-General C. V. F., D.S.O.

K.C.M.G.
Dawkins, Major-General C. T., C.B., C.M.G.

C.B.
Banon, Br.-General F. L.
Bridgford, Br.-General R. J., C.M.G., D.S.O.
Dawkins, Major-General C. T., C.M.G.
Groves, Br.-General P. R. C., C.M.G., D.S.O.
Lloyd, Br.-General A. H. O., C.M.G., M.V.O.
Shipley, Br.-General C. O.
Strick, Bt.-Colonel J. A., D.S.O.

C.M.G.
Austen, Bt.-Colonel A. R.
Borrett, Br.-General O. C., D.S.O.
Bridgford, Lt.-Colonel R. J., D.S.O.
Giles, Lt.-Colonel E. D., D.S.O.
Groves, Br.-General P. R. C., D.S.O.
Hanbury, Bt.-Lt.-Colonel P. L., D.S.O.
Higginson, Lt.-Colonel C. P., D.S.O.
Lloyd, Br.-General A. H. O., M.V.O.
Meynell, Lt.-Colonel G.
Money, Br.-General N. E., D.S.O.
Reade, Major-General R. N. R., C.B.
Rogers, Br.-General H. S., D.S.O.
Spens, Major-General J., C.B.
Wood, Br.-General E. A., D.S.O.

C.V.O.
Capper, Colonel W. B.

C.B.E.
Garrett, Colonel A. N. B., T.D.

407

REWARDS—(*continued*)

D.S.O.

Atchison, Major C. E.

Howell-Evans, Lt.-Colonel H. J.

Bailey, Lt.-Colonel J. H.
Borrett, Bt.-Lt.-Colonel O. C.
Bowen, Lt.-Colonel W. A.

Jackson, Major B. A., M.C.
James, Captain E. G.

Lloyd, Captain E. G. R.

Chatterton, Lt.-Colonel G. D. L.
Collins, Captain H. S.
Corbett, Major C. U.

Luard, Major E. B.

Mansfield, Captain W. H. C.
McKimm, Captain D. S. A., M.C.

Delmé-Murray, Major G. A.
Downes, Lt.-Colonel J. W., M.C.

Murray, Major B. E.

English, Major E. R. M.
Erskine, Lt.-Colonel J. D. B.

Negus, Lt.-Colonel R. E.

Prince, Lt.-Colonel P.

Fitzgerald, Major P. F.

Rhodes, Lieut. F. W.
Robinson, Captain E. H., M.C.

Giles, Lt.-Colonel E. D.
Groves, Lt.-Colonel P. R. C.

Rogers, Major H. S.

Smithard, Lt.-Colonel R. G., M.C.

Hanbury, Captain P. L.
Hayes, Lt.-Colonel J. H.
Heywood-Lonsdale, Lt.-Colonel H. H., T.D.
Heywood - Lonsdale, Major J. P. H., T.D.
Holmes à Court, Major R. E.
Hooper, Major J. C.

Strick, Major J. A.

Thomas, Lt.-Colonel S. F.

Welch, Lt.-Colonel H. E.
Winterscale, Lt.-Colonel C. F. B.
Wood, Lt.-Colonel E. A.

BAR TO D.S.O.

Borrett, Bt.-Lt.-Colonel O. C., D.S.O.
Bowen, Lt.-Colonel W. A., D.S.O.
Money, Lt.-Colonel N. E., D.S.O.
Robinson, Captain E. H., D.S.O., M.C.
Welch, Lt.-Colonel H. E., D.S.O.
Wood, Lt.-Colonel E. A., D.S.O.

APPENDIX III

REWARDS—*(continued)*

SECOND BAR TO D.S.O.

Wood, Br.-General E. A., D.S.O.

THIRD BAR TO D.S.O.

Wood, Br.-General E. A., C.M.G., D.S.O.

O.B.E.

McMahon, Major K. E.
Meredith, Major H. C.
Middleton, Major W.
Owen, Lt.-Colonel R. C. R.,
C.M.G.

Smith, Qr.-Master and Captain
J. W.
Surtees, Captain R. L.
Tayleur, Lt.-Colonel W.
Underhill, Major O.

M.B.E.

Barker, Major E. C.
Matthews, Captain E. F.

Penberthy, Captain P. P. C.
Watson, Captain A. M.

M.C.

Addy, 2nd Lieut. J. F.
Aubrey, Captain H. A. R.

Baker, Captain W. A. N.
Banks, 2nd Lieut. R. H.
Barlow, No. 12168 C.S.M. H.
Bavin, Lieut. C.
Beadon, Captain H. D.
Beckett, 2nd Lieut. W. C.
Beer, 2nd Lieut. A. G.
Benbow-Rowe, Captain O. S.
Benson, Captain J. I.
Benson, Captain F. R.
Bettington, Captain J. B.
Blackford, Lieut. F. W. E.
Boddington, Captain M.
Bonser, No. 14396 C.S.M. A.
Bowen, Captain A. P.
Bowie, Captain D. D.
Breffit, Captain G. V.

Brooks, Lieut. N. B.
Brooks, Captain T. M.
Browne, 2nd Lieut. A. G. W.
Browne, Captain S. N.
Bruce, Captain R. W. O. J.
Bryans, Lieut. R.
Bulmer, 2nd Lieut. G. P.
Busby, No. 4953 C.S.M.
J. H.
Bush, 2nd Lieut. H.
Butt, Lieut. G. W. T.

Caesar, 2nd Lieut. J. H.
Carr, Captain G.
Carter, 2nd Lieut. F. W. A.
Clark, Lieut. W.
Clayton, 2nd Lieut. H.
Colin, 2nd Lieut. H.
Craigie, Captain R. C.
Curtis, 2nd Lieut. C. N.

REWARDS—M.C.—*(continued)*

Davies, 2nd Lieut. H. B.
Day, Captain E. C.
de Gruchy, Lieut. H. E. B.
Denyer, No. 9109 C.S.M.
  G. S. E.

Evans, No. 7449 C.S.M. J.

Faithorn, 2nd Lieut. E.
Farrant, Captain R., F.R.C.S.
Farrer, Lieut. J. O.
Fisher, 2nd Lieut. T.
Fox, Lieut. A.
Furber, No. 9406 C.S.M. G. C.

Gimes, No. 9324 C.S.M. J.
Gittins, 2nd Lieut. A.
Gleave, 2nd Lieut. J.
Graves, 2nd Lieut. H.
Green, 2nd Lieut. E. T.
Greenhough, 2nd Lieut.
  A. B. W.
Grover, Captain J. M. L.

Hall, Captain T. C. N.
Hallowes, Lieut. J. W.
Hamer, 2nd Lieut. C. M. I.
Hamersley, Major A. H. St. G.
Hands, 2nd Lieut. H. G.
Hannah, 2nd Lieut. E. M.
Harris, Lieut. H. E.
Haslewood, Captain R. J. R.
Hetherington, 2nd Lieut. A.C.
Hinmers, Captain J. R.
Hudsons, 2nd Lieut. P. J.

Jackson, Captain B. A.
Jackson, Captain R. D.
Jarvis, 2nd Lieut. J. H.
Jinks, 2nd Lieut. J. C.

Jones, 2nd Lieut. G. F.
Jones, 2nd Lieut. H. R.

Kersey, 2nd Lieut. A. O.
Kimpster, 2nd Lieut. W. A.
Kinchin-Smith, Captain A. E.

Lanyon, Lieut. T. S.
Latham, Capt. E. R.
Lawrence, Lieut. A. E.
Leech, 2nd Lieut. S. F.
Lindop, 2nd Lieut. K. J. H.
Lindsay, 2nd Lieut. A. W.
Linton, Captain H., M.V.O.
Lloyd, Captain O. R.
Lloyd, Lieut. R. L. M.
Lloyd, Captain W. L.
Lovelock, Qr.-Master and Hon.
  Lieut. J.

Mackenzie, 2nd Lieut. A. V.
Marindin, 2nd Lieut. H. E. A.
Marriott, 2nd Lieut. R. H.
Marris, 2nd Lieut. H. M.
Mason, 2nd Lieut. W. E.
McKimm, 2nd Lieut. D. S. A.
Mealing, Captain M. E.
Middleton, 2nd Lieut. J.
Milton, Lieut. W. J.
Mitchem, 2nd Lieut. F., M.M.
Moore, No. 4404 S.M. S. G.
Morris, 2nd Lieut. B. F.
Morris, 2nd Lieut. J.
Morris, Major L. H.
Moses, 2nd Lieut. R.
Moss, Lieut. F. W.
Mound, No. 8489 C.S.M. S.
Munn, Captain R. B. S.
Murphy. No. 4386 S.M. A. J.
Murphy, 2nd Lieut. T. W.

APPENDIX III

Nicholson, Captain D.

O'Connor, Captain H. M.

Parker, Captain C. E.
Parker, 2nd Lieut. M. J.
Peake, 2nd Lieut. H.
Pearson, 2nd Lieut. P. W.
Philips, Captain F. G. P.
Pitt, No. 9135 S.M. J. A.
Plowden, Captain J. C.
Poyntz, Captain R. H.
Prestage, Captain D. L.
Pritchard, 2nd Lieut. L. B.
Pugh, 2nd Lieut. C. H. W.
Ractivand, Lieut. D.
Rentoul, Captain W. W.
Retallick, 2nd Lieut. R. T.
Roberts, Lieut. R. C. L.
Robertson, 2nd Lieut. A.
Robinson, Lieut. E. H.
Rogers, 2nd Lieut. A. B.
Rogers, Captain H. M.

Sellers, Rev. W., C.F.
Shackles, 2nd Lieut. R. G.
Shaw, 2nd Lieut. J. P.
Sheldon, 2nd Lieut. B. E.
Simpson, 2nd Lieut. A. H.
Smith, 2nd Lieut. D. G.
Smith, Captain G. C.
Smith, Captain R. F.

Smith, Captain W. W.
Smithard, Captain R. G.
Sparrow, Captain B. H.
Spink, Captain E. V. T. A.
Stafford, 2nd Lieut. F. S.
Statham, 2nd Lieut. W. H.
Steer, Captain H. E.
Steward, 2nd Lieut. H.
Sully, 2nd Lieut. E.

Thompstone, Captain E. W.
Thomson, 2nd Lieut. R. G.
Thursfield, Captain A. B. M.
Torin, Captain L. H.
Tully, Captain D. G.
Turner, Captain G.
Turner, 2nd Lieut. H. K.

van Cutsem, Captain E. C. L.
Vaughan, 2nd Lieut. R. C.
Voelcker, Captain F. W.

Wace, Lieut. R. C.
Waterfield, Captain A. C.
Webb, Captain C. W. V.
Webber, Lieut. N. V.
Weston, 2nd Lieut. W. R.
Whitmore, Captain R. S.
Wiles, Lieut. O. D.
Williams, 2nd Lieut. E. T.,
    M.M.

BAR TO MILITARY CROSS

Bryans, Captain R., M.C.
Craigie, Captain R. C., M.C.
Day, Captain E. C., M.C.
Denyer, 2nd Lieut. G.S.E., M.C.
Grover, Captain J. M. L., M.C.
Hetherington, Lieut. A.C., M.C.
Jackson, Captain R. D., M.C.
Lindop, Lieut. K. J. H., M.C.

Lloyd, Captain R. L. M., M.C.
Mitchem, 2nd Lieut. F., M.C.,
    M.M.
Nicholson, Captain D., M.C.
Robinson, Captain E. H., M.C.
Rogers, Lieut. A. B., M.C.
Smith, Captain R. F., M.C.
Stafford, 2nd Lieut. F. S., M.C.

REWARDS—*(continued)*

D.C.M.

NAME.	RANK.	REGTL. NO.
Allsopp, V. P.	Pte.	20066
Badcock, W.	Sgt.	7665
Barlow, H., M.C.	C.S.M.	12168
Barrett, T.	Sgt.	9159
Bate, J. A.	Sgt.	8940
Beard, J.	C.S.M..	200039
Beddoes, W.	Sgt.	13162
Beeston, H.	Sgt.	9714
Bowen, H. A.	L.-Corpl.	8017
Bridgwater, W.	Pte.	7898
Broadhurst, P.	Pte.	18336
Bromley, J. B.	Pte.	22439
Brooks, A.	L.-Corpl.	204487
Brooks, C.	Sgt.	29211
Brough, H. W.	Pte.	230591
Brown, W. H.	Pte.	10097
Bufton, H. E.	Sgt.	17229
Burnham, J.	Sgt.	10598
Butler, J.	Sgt.	11420
Buttifant, F. J.	Pte.	12071
Carpenter, J. R.	C.S.M.	200001
Cattlin, J. W.	L.-Corpl.	20008
Cheetham, W.	Pte.	17446
Clark, J.	Sgt.	26415
Clarke, F. C.	Sgt.	10435
Clarke, G. E.	C.S.M.	9163
Clarke, J.	Pte.	8767
Cooke, R. H.	L.-Sgt.	7756
Cornes, H.	Sgt.	8183
Corney, A.	Pte.	11344
Crittenden, H. L.	L.-Corpl.	9194
Darke, B. J.	Sgt.	8206
Davies, A.	Corpl.	11671
Davies, C.	Sgt.	15922

APPENDIX III

NAME.	RANK.	REGTL. NO.
Davies, T. B.	Corpl.	230089
Derbyshire, J.	C.S.M.	7569
Dixon, M.	L.-Corpl.	14667
Dixon, W.	Sgt.	11971
Donovan, C.	Sgt.	8796
Dugmore, W. H.	Sgt.	8598
Evans, G. L.	Pte.	230277
Evans, S.	C.S.M.	7775
Farthing, J.	R.S.M.	3850
Fidler, A.	Pte.	11915
Flanagan, T.	L.-Corpl.	7793
Fletcher, T.	Sgt.	9377
Fuller, W.	L.-Corpl.	11327
Fuller, W. J.	Corpl.	236891
Gardiner, S.	Pte.	237861
Gollins, H.	Corpl.	7338
Griffiths, W.	C.S.M.	8097
Groom, J.	Corpl.	9865
Hamilton, A.	Pte.	11702
Hankey, J.	Pte.	9403
Hargreaves, H.	Pte.	18851
Harmer, O.	Sgt.	27337
Hayward, F. O., M.M.	C.S.M.	12988
Hockenhull, L.	Sgt.	7943
Hodkinson, W.	C.S.M.	6711
Holland, E. D.	Sgt.	200024
Holmes, J.	Corpl.	11940
Holmes, W. E., M.M.	Sgt.	8232
Hunt, W.	Corpl.	38462
James, G.	Pte.	17632
Johnstone, J.	Corpl.	10101
Jones, A.	Sgt.	8058
Jones, E. T.	C.S.M.	8349
Jones, H.	Sgt.	27338

REWARDS—D.C.M.—(*continued*)

NAME.	RANK.	REGTL. NO.
Jones, H. J.	Sgt.	9373
Jones, J. W.	Sgt.	6392
Kettle, H. F.	Corpl.	10420
King, T. R.	Pte.	230283
Kingstone, W. E.	Sgt.	12374
Knight, A.	C.S.M.	8233
Knight, T.	Pte.	6532
Lang, J. R.	Sgt.	8358
Langford, F., M.M.	Sgt.	7133
Langford, H.	Pte.	7857
Layton, W.	Pte.	9044
Lewis, D.	Pte.	29762
Lewis, E.	Pte.	17375
Lewis, W.	Corpl.	10963
Lloyd, B. B.	Sgt.	8198
Lloyd, F.	Sgt.	17253
Lloyd, G. W.	C.S.M.	7271
Lloyd, R. J.	Corpl.	9718
Lockley, E.	L.-Corpl.	11908
Middleton, S. H.	Sgt.	9527
Millington, G.	R.S.M.	5000
Morgan, J. R.	Sgt.	11089
Moore, W. F.	Pte.	9651
Morris, T.	L.-Corpl.	9018
Morris, W. W.	Pte.	230436
Nicolls, G.	Pte.	16443
Noble, J. L.	Sgt.	8895
Orris, R. S.	Pte.	9696
Osborne, E. R.	Sgt.	8562
Parry, R. H.	Pte.	230394
Peake, B. J.	Sgt.	14272
Pope, G. E., M.M.	Sgt.	10455
Poynton, F.	L.-Sgt.	26279

414

APPENDIX III

NAME.	RANK.	REGTL NO.
Price, J. H.	C.S.M.	10518
Price, W.	Sgt.	200923
Prior, F. G.	Pte.	17470
Purcell, J., M.M.	L.-Sgt.	10500
Purdy, T.	Sgt.	9467
Richards, F. H.	Corpl.	12954
Riches, C. W.	Sgt.	230795
Roberts, C.	Corpl.	7929
Rutter, A.	C.S.M.	230542
Scriven, J.	L.-Sgt.	15848
Sergeant, G. M.	Pte.	11851
Sheldon, G.	L.-Corpl.	13141
Simpson, H.	Sgt.	12904
Smith, J.	Corpl.	12316
Smith, T.	Pte.	205836
Smith, T. S.	Sgt.	18439
Taylor, T. H.	Pte.	230230
Thomas, R. J.	Sgt.	231042
Threadgold, J.	C.Q.M.S.	8811
Topping, P.	C.S.M.	7459
Turner, H. A.	C.S.M.	7238
Turner, T.	Corpl.	7280
Wain, F.	Pte.	204133
Whitney, W.	Sgt.	10099
Wildig, G.	Sgt.	9269
Williams, S.	Corpl.	15520
Wilson, G. H.	R.S.M.	200261

BAR TO D.C.M.

Bufton, H. E., D.C.M., M.M.	C.S.M.	17229
Carpenter, J. R., D.C.M.	C.S.M.	200001
Smith, J., D.C.M.	Sgt.	12316

REWARDS—*(continued)*

M.M.

NAME.	RANK.	REGTL. NO.
Acton, E.	Pte.	16592
Adamson, J.	L.-Corpl.	15330
Aldridge, N. J.	Pte.	19635
Allcock, A. J.	L.-Corpl.	27736
Allen, G.	L.-Corpl.	16500
Allen, J.	Pte.	25397
Andrews, E.	Pte.	12028
Ankers, E.	L.-Sgt.	26730
Arrowsmith, J. C.	Corpl.	16361
Ashley, H.	Pte.	31964
Ashton, W.	Pte.	10685
Ashworth, F. M.	Pte.	10856
Aspinall, G. R.	Pte.	18675
Atkinson, C.	Sgt.	11269
Attwell, G.	Pte.	200188
Badrock, W.	Pte.	26897
Baker, F. G.	Pte.	238889
Baker, W. H.	Sgt.	11262
Banton, G.	Pte.	7661
Barber, E.	Pte.	20025
Barrett, H. H. D.	Pte.	10788
Barrett, W. H.	L.-Corpl.	26532
Bebb, J. M.	Pte.	11570
Beckett, C.	Pte.	10040
Bell, R. J.	Pte.	26770
Benson, R.	Pte.	20001
Bevan, W.	Pte.	24723
Billinghurst, A. N.	Sgt.	28434
Billington, W. H. T.	L.-Corpl.	13003
Birchall, W. V.	Pte.	26600
Bird, T.	Pte.	34208
Bithell, J. W.	Pte.	18170
Blacklock, J.	L.-Corpl.	20060
Blower, J.	Pte.	9626
Blud, J.	Sgt.	7527
Bolton, H.	Pte.	12816

APPENDIX III

NAME.	RANK.	REGTL. NO.
Botting, A.	Pte.	14491
Bowen, J.	Pte.	23508
Bradbury, C. E.	Pte.	20053
Bradley, T.	Pte.	33012
Brammer, J.	Sgt.	12926
Bray, A. E.	Pte.	235410
Brookes, G. W.	Pte.	12340
Brooks, J.	Pte.	17216
Bromley, J. A.	Pte.	8994
Broome, A. J.	Pte.	26534
Broome, G.	Pte.	200305
Broome, T.	Pte.	16994
Brown, F.	Sgt.	13287
Bryant, E.	L.-Corpl.	14014
Bryant, G. B.	Pte.	17629
Buckley, J.	Sgt.	7116
Buckley, W.	Pte.	20056
Bufton, H. E.	Corpl.	17229
Bullock, W.	Sgt.	16024
Burgess, J. E.	Pte.	27264
Butler, J.	L.-Sgt.	11420
Butterworth, S.	Pte.	15891
Bydawell, F.	Pte.	18906
Callard, E. J.	Pte.	231011
Callister, B. R.	Sgt.	27078
Carr, H.	Pte.	6444
Carter, W. H.	Pte.	11848
Cartwright, L.	Pte.	18408
Caswell, W.	Pte.	11720
Challinor, J. C.	Pte.	16350
Chapman, E. G.	Pte.	22145
Charles, T. W.	Corpl.	27179
Chebsey, H.	Pte.	200393
Chester, G. H.	Corpl.	11552
Childs, F.	Pte.	15126
Childs, N.	Pte.	24874
Chirgwin, F.	Pte.	26741
Chorley, W. R. G.	Pte.	10820

2 E

REWARDS—M.M.—*(continued)*

NAME.	RANK.	REGTL. NO.
Church, W.	Pte.	8787
Clarke, E. F.	Pte.	9945
Clarke, F.	Sgt.	200250
Clarke, H. T.	Pte.	20933
Clay, J. H.	Pte.	26010
Clayton, F.	L.-Sgt.	200646
Clee, S. C.	Pte.	19703
Cockle, A. G. C.	Pte.	12752
Cole, W. C.	L.-Corpl.	28263
Coleman, P.	Pte.	25786
Cook, W.	L.-Sgt.	25882
Cooke, A.	L.-Corpl.	230204
Cooke, F. A.	Pte.	21349
Cooke, N.	L.-Sgt.	28441
Cooper, A. E.	Pte.	20098
Cooper, J.	Pte.	29756
Cooper, W.	Pte.	14554
Cope, H.	L.-Corpl.	26603
Corbett, W.	Pte.	15424
Cough, H. W.	Pte.	10721
Cowper, C. F.	L.-Sgt.	11376
Crawshaw, J.	Pte.	16044
Crummack, F.	L.-Corpl.	36615
Dakin, J.	Pte.	26304
Darlow, H.	L.-Corpl.	12719
Davey, R.	Corpl.	8192
Davies, A.	Pte.	111036
Davies, A. G.	Pte.	200746
Davies, E. J.	L.-Sgt.	20157
Davies, G.	L.-Corpl.	11607
Davies, G.	L.-Corpl.	12165
Davies, G. T.	Sgt.	35907
Davies, J.	Pte.	7324
Davies, J.	Pte.	26745
Davies, R.	L.-Corpl.	18166
Davies, S.	Pte.	200231
Davies, W.	L.-Corpl.	11680
Davies, W.	Pte.	11862

APPENDIX III

NAME.	RANK.	REGTL. NO.
Davies, W.	Corpl.	16332
Davies, W. J.	Pte.	29785
Davis, C. J.	Pte.	19596
Deakin, J. E.	L.-Corpl.	14978
Degnan, W.	L.-Corpl.	7391
Dix, E.	Pte.	5944
Dixon, M.	L.-Corpl.	14667
Dodson, F. P.	Pte.	200477
Doggett, J. D.	Corpl.	24571
Donald, J. D.	L.-Corpl.	15669
Donbavand, A. E.	Pte.	26364
Donnelly, L. H.	Pte.	15486
Doody, W.	Pte.	19037
Downing, H.	Corpl.	25123
Draper, R.	Pte.	20164
Dunn, F.	Pte.	11840
Durbin, F.	Sgt.	14049
Dyer, W.	L.-Corpl.	200786
Dyke, W. T.	Sgt.	9260
Eames, S. T.	Sgt.	17078
Edevane, R.	Pte.	16266
Edgar, A. J.	Pte.	36502
Edwards, G.	Corpl.	12241
Edwards, S.	L.-Corpl.	10328
Edwards, W. H.	Pte.	6945
Ellis, T.	Corpl.	19712
Emery, W.	Sgt.	200124
Evans, E.	Pte.	201490
Evans, J. H.	Pte.	16546
Evans, W.	C.S.M.	7734
Farrington, G.	Pte.	17448
Ferrington, T.	Pte.	27090
Flaherty, E.	Pte.	29820
Fletcher, C. A.	Sgt.	12891
Fletcher, H.	Pte.	200044
Foley, J.	Sgt.	7369
Forsythe, P. A.	Pte.	12795

REWARDS—M.M.—*(continued)*

NAME.	RANK.	REGTL. NO.
Fox, J.	Pte.	393811
Freeman, J.	Sgt.	200302
Furber, T.	Pte.	200585
Garmston, G.	Corpl.	16146
Garner, W. H.	Pte.	16888
Gilbank, E.	Sgt.	12282
Gilbert, D.	Pte.	26382
Gimes, J.	C.Q.M.S.	9324
Glassey, F.	Pte.	230514
Golding, J.	Pte.	5486
Gould, J. H. A.	Pte.	12499
Graves, W.	Pte.	27717
Greatwich, S.	C.Q.M.S.	13186
Green, G. H.	Pte.	11332
Green, H. W.	Corpl.	19271
Green, J.	Sgt.	18561
Greenough, R.	Pte.	6501
Griffin, H.	L.-Corpl.	19348
Griffin, W.	Corpl.	19347
Hailey, E. A.	Sgt.	10772
Hale, F.	Pte.	13075
Halford, A. E. H.	Corpl.	12112
Hallowfield, L.	Pte.	13972
Hamar, E.	Pte.	10786
Hambleton, T.	Sgt.	12179
Hamilton, J.	Pte.	12996
Hamilton, R.	Pte.	16218
Hamlett, J. A.	Pte.	11798
Hance, W. H.	Sgt.	8445
Handley, A.	Sgt.	204675
Hankins, W. J.	Pte.	26166
Harper, B.	Pte.	10250
Harris, F.	Pte.	26895
Harris, J. E.	L.-Corpl.	9873
Hassall, F.	Pte.	25268
Hawkins, A.	Pte.	26175
Hayes, T.	Pte.	6532

APPENDIX III

NAME.	RANK.	REGTL. NO.
Hayward, A.	Pte.	17981
Hayward, F.	Sgt.	12988
Heath, J. W.	Sgt.	9728
Harring, C.	Pte.	17003
Hewson, H.	Corpl.	8943
Hicks, J.	Pte.	11943
Hinchley, V. C. L.	Sgt.	16407
Hoard, C. J. A.	Pte.	17952
Hockenhull, L.	Sgt.	7943
Hodgson, T.	Pte.	32388
Hodkinson, S.	L.-Corpl.	27005
Hollis, H.	Pte.	18926
Holmes, C. J.	Pte.	17722
Holmes, W. E.	Sgt.	8232
Hopkins, J. M.	Pte.	16679
Hopwood, J.	Pte.	17488
Hordern, J.	L.-Sgt.	7311
Horn, W. H.	L.-Corpl.	26882
Hudson, V. W. A.	Sgt.	9461
Hughes, C. A.	Pte.	10969
Hughes, R. T.	Pte.	29129
Hughes, W.	Pte.	11246
Huxley, J.	L.-Corpl.	230463
Irwin, H.	Sgt.	13699
Isaac, G.	Pte.	14778
Jackson, R.	L.-Corpl.	15931
Jackson, S.	Corpl.	200343
Jackson, W. D.	Pte.	12548
James, A.	L.-Corpl.	11087
James, C.	Pte.	11064
James, F. A.	Pte.	239027
Jenkins, F.	Sgt.	6393
Jenks, E. C.	Pte.	8207
John, W. L.	Sgt.	20229
Johnson, D.	L.-Corpl.	12633
Johnson, F.	Pte.	16101
Jones, A.	L.-Corpl.	16578

REWARDS—M.M.—(continued)

NAME.	RANK.	REGTL. NO.
Jones, C. E.	L.-Corpl.	12190
Jones, D.	Corpl.	9444
Jones, F. T.	Pte.	13745
Jones, G.	Pte.	16357
Jones, G.	Pte.	21006
Jones, H.	Corpl.	230836
Jones, I.	Pte.	26555
Jones, J.	Pte.	16268
Jones, J.	Pte.	19299
Jones, J. W.	Pte.	16627
Jones, T.	Pte.	8844
Jones, T. W.	Pte.	12414
Jones, W. E.	Pte.	17839
Jordan, T.	Pte.	11780
Kearle, W.	Pte.	14121
Kenham, W.	Sgt.	14185
Kennea, A.	Sgt.	14347
Kennedy, H. J.	Sgt.	8218
Kent, W.	Corpl.	27466
King, A.	Sgt.	11495
Kirkham, W.	Pte.	6327
Kynaston, A. E.	Corpl.	10984
Kynaston, E. A.	Corpl.	12214
Lane, G.	Corpl.	11677
Langford, F.	Sgt.	7133
Lawley, J.	Pte.	11508
Layton, W.	Pte.	9044
Leah, J.	Pte.	22326
Leake, F. C.	Pte.	12424
Lees, N.	Pte.	15198
Legg, H. J. V.	Pte.	14090
Leighton, J. S.	Pte.	238893
Leighton, S.	Sgt.	12864
Lewis, E. R.	Sgt.	230559
Lewis, G.	Pte.	14036
Lewis, J. W.	L.-Corpl.	11834
Lewis, R. J.	Sgt.	13386

APPENDIX III

NAME.	RANK.	REGTL. NO.
Lewis, W.	Pte.	17469
Lewis, W. H.	Pte.	14387
Lewis, W. J.	Pte.	91272
Lloyd, J.	Pte.	10981
Lloyd, R.	Pte.	6446
Lloyd, R. H.	Pte.	11128
Longworth, W.	Pte.	17707
Lovatt, J. H.	Corpl.	24549
Lowe, J. J.	Pte.	7968
Mabbutt, A.	Pte.	10917
Maddox, J. E.	Sgt.	10773
Madeley, W.	L.-Corpl.	26586
Maiden, A. H.	Pte.	14710
Malt, V.	Corpl.	11648
Manford, W.	Pte.	14962
Marchant, C. R.	L.-Corpl.	8903
Marsh, G.	Pte.	20914
Marshall, J. T.	Pte.	16325
Marston, J.	Pte.	10143
Matthews, W.	Pte.	11942
Matton, J.	Pte.	21406
Maylor, R. G.	Sgt.	28161
McDonald, A.	Sgt.	6947
McDonald, J.	Sgt.	7960
McKenna, P.	Corpl.	9156
McKeon, J.	Pte.	6843
McMaster, W.	Corpl.	7623
Meeson, W. J.	Bugler	9764
Melia, J.	Pte.	26396
Meredith, H. J.	Pte.	12934
Millin, C. V.	L.-Corpl.	9041
Mills, W.	Pte.	20769
Minton, C.	Corpl.	24308
Mitton, A.	L.-Corpl.	20117
Moore, T.	Corpl.	7720
Moran, G.	Pte.	200443
Morgan, C. H.	Pte.	24092
Morgan, H.	Pte.	13916

REWARDS—M.M.—(continued)

NAME.	RANK.	REGTL. NO.
Morgan, R.	Pte.	14162
Morgan, W. G.	Pte.	200207
Morrell, A. A.	Pte.	8911
Morris, C. E.	Pte.	6705
Morris, H.	Pte.	12889
Morris, R.	L.-Corpl.	16075
Morris, S.	L.-Corpl.	17619
Moss, C.	Pte.	38509
Murray, A.	Pte.	9206
Nash, W.	L.-Corpl.	13597
Nicholas, W. R.	Pte.	26520
Nicholson, J. H.	Pte.	230811
Nixon, F. J.	Sgt.	28436
Nock, G. W. H.	Pte.	15821
Northwood, W.	Pte.	16334
O'Leary, J.	Sgt.	6783
Oliver, S.	Pte.	17271
Ollman, S.	Pte.	18677
Ormsby, F.	Sgt.	18361
Osborne, G. E.	Pte.	15465
Owen, F.	Pte.	12223
Owen, T. C.	Pte.	200264
Palmer, E.	Sgt.	14769
Parker, H.	Corpl.	11726
Parker, J.	Sgt.	8165
Parry, E.	Pte.	18046
Parsons, F. G.	L.-Corpl.	14863
Passey, G.	Pte.	27506
Patrick, H. A.	Sgt.	8749
Payne, H.	Pte.	13173
Peake, B. J., D.C.M.	C.S.M.	14272
Pearce, A.	Corpl.	15695
Pearce, W. H.	Sgt.	14683
Peate, E.	L.-Corpl.	10673
Phillips, C. H.	Pte.	23774
Phillips, F.	Corpl.	11801

APPENDIX III

NAME.	RANK.	REGTL. NO.
Phillips, J.	Corpl.	12355
Pilbury, W.	Pte.	16356
Piper, J. A.	Sgt.	13202
Pope, F.	Sgt.	8078
Pope, G. E.	Sgt.	10455
Pople, G.	L.-Sgt.	14022
Potts, F.	Pte.	18020
Povall, J.	Pte.	239253
Powell, A.	Pte.	7991
Preece, S. R.	Pte.	18633
Price, G.	Sgt.	11725
Price, J.	Pte.	28553
Price, V. W. J.	Pte.	33236
Probert, H.	Pte.	8170
Pryce, E.	Pte.	15163
Pryke, G.	Pte.	230331
Pugh, F. C.	Sgt.	17268
Pugh, H.	Sgt.	8062
Pugh, T.	Pte.	16566
Purcell, J.	Pte.	10500
Purslow, T. W.	L.-Corpl.	15307
Pye, F. A.	Pte.	22237
Raby, B.	C.S.M.	7069
Ratcliff, C. E.	Sgt.	26204
Rayner, C. W.	Pte.	26120
Redford, A.	Corpl.	15386
Richards, F.	L.-Corpl.	10144
Rider, W. H.	L.-Corpl.	15046
Riley, C.	Sgt.	10847
Roberts, L.	L.-Corpl.	19774
Roberts, R. F.	Pte.	13304
Roberts, S.	Sgt.	18076
Roberts, T.	Sgt.	12375
Roberts, W. J.	Pte.	13984
Robertson, E.	Corpl.	230778
Robinson, A. W. F.	Pte.	27138
Robinson, W. A.	Sgt.	12852
Robley, J.	L.-Corpl.	26886

REWARDS—M.M.—(continued)

NAME.	RANK.	REGTL. NO.
Rogers, J.	Corpl.	10677
Rowlands, H.	Corpl.	27348
Rowson, G.	Pte.	17014
Salmon, E.	Pte.	14604
Sanders, F. C.	Sgt.	8889
Sanderson, J.	Sgt.	7686
Saunders, J.	Sgt.	12015
Seddon, I.	Pte.	31397
Shaw, H.	Pte.	24990
Sheffield, W.	Pte.	13577
Simcox, W.	L.-Corpl.	5926
Sims, T.	Corpl.	14436
Simpson, C. F. W.	Corpl.	13749
Slater, H.	Pte.	201318
Smart, S. A.	Pte.	31898
Smith, A.	Pte.	19742
Smith, H. C.	Corpl.	205134
Smith, J. A.	Sgt.	11498
Smith, R. H.	L.-Corpl.	6995
Spencer, F.	Pte.	19713
Spencer, W. J.	Pte.	19627
Stephens, R. W.	Sgt.	14291
Stevenson, F.	Pte.	18183
Stevenson, R.	L.-Sgt.	16779
Tart, L.	Pte.	200203
Taylor, A. W.	L.-Corpl.	10241
Taylor, C.	Pte.	24655
Taylor, C. S.	Sgt.	10217
Taylor, P.	Pte.	24435
Tebby, H.	L.-Corpl.	26720
Teal, L.	Pte.	10252
Thelwell, J. J.	Sgt.	28445
Thomas, A.	Pte.	19833
Thomas, F.	Sgt.	8373
Thomas, H.	Pte.	12162
Thomas, T.	Pte.	13705
Thomas, T. J.	Corpl.	15663

APPENDIX III

NAME.	RANK.	REGTL. NO.
Thomas, W.	Pte.	11512
Thomas, W.	Pte.	21323
Thomas, W.	Pte.	17025
Thornton, W. T.	Corpl.	8543
Thorpe, S.	Pte.	10365
Thwaites, A.	Pte.	17186
Tomkins, T.	L.-Sgt.	11088
Tonks, S.	Corpl.	11923
Tozer, T.	Sgt.	8722
Trevor, O. W.	Pte.	11135
Turner, H.	Sgt.	10180
Twigg, T.	Pte.	31236
Urion, G.	Sgt.	11693
Vaughan, T.	Pte.	10511
Vaughan, W.	Pte.	25283
Verney, A. S.	Pte.	25944
Viney, P. C.	L.-Corpl.	27754
Wain, W.	Sgt.	230588
Walker, G.	Pte.	201034
Walker, J.	L.-Corpl.	204130
Wall, R.	C.S.M.	8853
Waller, F. W.	L.-Corpl.	27808
Walley, F.	Corpl.	33180
Walley, P.	L.-Corpl.	11249
Wallwork, S.	Sgt.	16328
Ward, G.	Pte.	17975
Ward, G. E.	Pte.	200240
Wassell, S.	Pte.	27544
Watkin, E. W.	Pte.	11409
Watkins, A. G.	Corpl.	14632
Watkins, J. H.	Corpl.	6272
Watkiss, J.	Pte.	7436
Watson, W. A.	L.-Corpl.	18327
Watts, A. H.	Pte.	25390
Wellens, H.	Pte.	6289
Wellington, J.	Sgt.	8301

REWARDS—M.M.—(continued)

NAME.	RANK.	REGTL. NO.
Wellon, W. J.	L.-Corpl.	29237
Wells, G.	Pte.:	17930
Wells, H.	Sgt.	9223
White, F. G.	L.-Corpl.	9205
White, H.	L.-Corpl.	17652
Whitney, W., D.C.M.	Sgt.	10099
Wickstead, R.	Pte.	21339
Wild, T. L.	L.-Corpl.	203767
Wilkes, W.	Pte.	13621
Wilkins, C. E.	L.-Corpl.	9211
Williams, D.	Sgt.	6572
Williams, D.	Pte.	19479
Williams, E.	C.S.M.	9440
Williams, E.	Pte.	12253
Williams, F.	Pte.	10704
Williams, J.	Pte.	10760
Williams, J. G.	C.Q.M.S.	200633
Williams, T.	Sgt.	10522
Willis, C.	Sgt.	15503
Wilson, A.	Pte.	230864
Wilson, G.	L.-Corpl.	230714
Winkle, J.	Pte.	230986
Woodend, L.	Pte.	11012
Wolley, W.	Corpl.	12482
Woosnam, E. J.	Sgt.	13535
Woosnam, S. J.	Pte.	201467
Wright, H.	Pte.	11488
Wright, S. G.	Sgt.	10810
Yomans, A. H.	L.-Corpl.	12461

BAR TO M.M.

Bowen, J., M.M.	Pte.	23508
Broome, G., M.M.	Sgt.	200305
Callard, E. J., M.M.	Sgt.	231011
*Cook, J. R., M.M.	Pte.	101565
Graves, W., M.M.	Pte.	27717

* Original award won while serving with another unit.

REWARDS—BAR TO M.M.—*(continued)*

NAME.	RANK.	REGTL. NO.
Hawkins, A., M.M.	Pte.	26175
Herring, C., M.M.	L.-Corpl.	17003
Hockenhull, L., M.M.	Sgt.	7943
Hughes, C. A., M.M.	Pte.	10969
Jenks, E. C., M.M.	Pte.	8207
Johnson, D., M.M.	L.-Corpl.	12633
Jordan, T., M.M.	Pte.	11780
Kennea, A., M.M.	L.-Sgt.	14347
Meeson, W. J., M.M.	L.-Sgt.	9764
Murray, A., M.M.	Corpl.	9206
Ormsby, F., M.M.	Sgt.	18361
Parker, J., M.M.	L.-Sgt.	8165
Pople, G., M.M.	Sgt.	14022
*Purkiss, H,. M.M.	Sgt.	29717
Richards, F., M.M.	L.-Corpl.	10144
Teal, L., M.M.	L.-Corpl.	10252
Thomas, T. J., M.M.	Corpl.	15663
Trevor, O. W., M.M.	Pte.	11135
Willis, C., M.M.	C.S.M.	15503

M.S.M.

Avery, A.	S.M.	6456
Badger, W. E.	Sgt.	13207
Baikie, S. J. C.	R.S.M.	6304
Beck, J. H.	C.Q.M.S.	12255
Brittan, S.	C.S.M.	10091
Brookbanks, G. R.	Sgt.	8087
Butt, G.	Pte.	14642
Chatten, E.	Sgt.	7816
Cole, T. H.	Sgt.	7392
Corfield, A. A.	Sgt.	239183
Crooke, C. J.	R.Q.M.S.	4531

* Original award won while serving with another unit.

REWARDS—M.S.M.—(continued)

NAME.	RANK.	REGTL. NO.
Dorrington, F. C.	Q.M.S.	200049
Edwards, F. P.	Sgt.	230046
Ellis, W. H.	Supt. Clk.	17495
Evans, E.	Sgt.	8034
Faithorn, B. W.	R.S.M.	9408
Foxal, J.	L.-Corpl.	200360
Goldthorpe, E.	C.S.M.	4507
Goodfellow, G. W.	R.Q.M.S.	160089
Gray, A.	Sgt.	8839
Gwynne, W.	Sgt.	200018
Halford, W. H.	Pte.	230498
Harris, E. C.	Pte.	8727
Heywood, C.	Sgt.	35781
Holden, C. G.	R.S.M.	14404
Hotchkiss, A.	Corpl.	13064
Hughes, W.	Q.M.S.	—
Hughes, W. A.	S.Q.M.S.	160013
Hyson, W. A.	Pte.	8566
Jackson, B. H.	Sgt.	26501
Jarvis, J.	R.Q.M.S.	14351
Johnson, P. F.	Corpl.	11475
Jones, J.	Sgt.	200678
Jones, J. E.	Q.M.S.	230037
Langbry, H.	Clr.-Sgt.	8507
Lear, T.	Sgt.	13246
Madden, T.	Clr. Sgt.	—
Manning, J.	R.Q.M.S.	10941
Marriage, A. C.	Sgt.	9166
Moger, A. E. G.	Q.M.S.˙	6520
Morgan, J.	C.Q.M.S.	13653
Mortimer, T.	Pte.	16625

APPENDIX III

REWARDS—M.S.M.—(*continued*)

NAME.	RANK.	REGTL. NO.
Poole, G. E.	C.S.M.	7946
Pritchard, W.	Sgt.	7965
Read, B.	Sgt.	7764
Reynolds, B. C.	R.Q.M.S.	13223
Roberts, E.	Sgt.	200836
Roberts, J. H.	Pte.	230287
Roberts, T.	Sgt.	13757
Roberts, T. C.	Sgt.	13878
Rotherham, J.	C.S.M.	6607
Shaw, P. T.	C.Q.M.S.	14423
Shufflebotham, C.	S.S.M.	17505
Simpson, J.	Sgt.	200086
Small, J.	C.S.M.	25846
Statham, W. H.	Sgt.	—
Thomasson, W.	Sgt.	15661
Tilley, J.	Sgt.	200093
Whitney, J. J.	S.M.	5558
Williams, A. J.	Sgt.	9498
Wright, H.	R.S.M.	5117

APPENDIX IV

FOREIGN DECORATIONS

BELGIUM

ORDRE DE LEOPOLD

Dawkins, Major-General C. T., C.B., C.M.G.
(Commandeur)
van Cutsem, Captain E. C. L., M.C. (Chevalier)

ORDRE DE LA COURONNE (officier)

Fitzgerald, Bt. Lt.-Colonel P. F., D.S.O.

CROIX DE GUERRE

Britton, No. 13312 Pte. H.
Caloe, No. 6937 C.S.M. S.
Evans, No. 12979 Pte. A. H.
Griggs, No. 8816 L.-Sgt. W. G.
Hayes, Lt.-Colonel J. H., D.S.O.
Lang, No. 8358 Sgt. J. R.
Pardoe, No. 6285 Sgt. G.
van Cutsem, Captain E. C. L., M.C.

DECORATION MILITAIRE

Clark, No. 10435 Sgt. F. C.
Mabbutt, No. 10917 Pte. A.

CHINA

ORDER OF WEN-HU (5th class)

Lowder, Captain H. G.

EGYPT

ORDER OF THE NILE (3rd class)

Lloyd, Lt.-Colonel A. H. O., C.B., C.M.G.,
M.V.O.

APPENDIX IV

FOREIGN DECORATIONS—*(continued)*

FRANCE

LEGION D'HONNEUR (officier)

Borrett, Br.-General O. C., C.M.G., D.S.O.
Hanbury, Bt. Lt.-Colonel P. L., C.M.G., D.S.O.
Rogers, Lt.-Colonel H. S., D.S.O.

LEGION D'HONNEUR (chevalier)

Groves, Br.-General P. R. C., C.B., C.M.G., D.S.O.
Strick, Bt. Lt.-Colonel J. A., D.S.O.

CROIX DE GUERRE

Bright, Captain G. W.
Brooks, Captain T. M., M.C.
Clark, Lieut. W., M.C.
Dodd, No. 16571 Sgt. C.
English, Major E. R. M., D.S.O.
Erskine, Lt.-Col. J. D. B., D.S.O.
Graves, Captain H., M.C.
Greaves, No. 26384 Pte. R. A.
Hanbury, Bt. Lt.-Colonel P. L., C.M.G., D.S.O.
Hinmers, Captain J. R.
Jackson, Lt.-Colonel B. A., M.C.
Jackson, Captain R. D., M.C.
Jones, No. 18113 Corpl. J.
Kynaston, Lieut. J. E.
Lloyd, No. 7271 C.S.M. G. W., D.C.M.
Lloyd, Captain R. L. M., M.C.
McKenna, No. 9156 Corpl. P.
Metcalf, No. 7312 Sgt. J.
Morris, No. 10617 Sgt. G.
Poole, No. 200463 Sgt. T. E.
Robertson, 2nd Lieut. A.
Stafford, 2nd Lieut. F. S.
Wood, Br.-General E. A., C.M.G., D.S.O.

2 F

433

THE KING'S SHROPSHIRE LIGHT INFANTRY

CROIX DE GUERRE AVEC PALMES

Aubrey, Lt.-Colonel H. A. R., M.C.

MÉDAILLE MILITAIRE

Davies, No. 200231 Pte. S.
Griffiths, No. 8097 C.S.M., W.
Hollowfield, No. 13972 Pte. L.
Jones, No. 10077 Pte. H.
Robinson, No. 12852 Sgt. W. A.
Skirving, No. 6597 R.S.M. J.
Thelwell, No. 28445 Sgt. J. J.

ORDRE DU MÉRITE AGRICOLE

Dawkins, Major-General Sir C. T., K.C.M.G., C.B.
Rogers, Br.-General H. S., C.M.G., D.S.O.
(chevalier)

MÉDAILLE D'HONNEUR AVEC GLAIVES (en argent)

Cornes, No. 8183 Sgt. H.

MÉDAILLE D'HONNEUR AVEC GLAIVES (en bronze)

Donald, No. 15669 Corpl. J. D.
Phillips, No. 6672 Corpl. A. J.
Seaborne, No. 12553 Corpl. A.
Stevens, No. 12885 L.-Corpl. W. T.

GREECE

ORDER OF KING GEORGE I

Lloyd, Br.-General A. H. O., C.B., C.M.G.,
M.V.O. (Grand Commander)
Reade, Major-General R. N. R., C.B., C.M.G. (Commander)

ORDER OF THE REDEEMER (4th class, officer)

Hanbury, Bt. Lt.-Colonel P. L., D.S.O.

APPENDIX IV

FOREIGN DECORATIONS—*(continued)*

GREEK MEDAL FOR MILITARY MERIT (1st class)
Reade, Major-General R. N. R., C.B., C.M.G.

GREEK MILITARY CROSS
Beasty, No. 4412 Pte. J.
Hanbury, Bt. Lt.-Colonel P. L., C.M.G., D.S.O.
Leighton, No. 12864 Sgt. S., M.M.
Murphy, Lieut. T. W., M.C.
Plowden, Lt.-Colonel J. C., M.C.
Taylor, No. 24435 Pte. P., M.M.
Turner, No. 20657 Pte. H.

ITALY

ORDER OF ST. MAURICE AND ST. LAZARUS (cavalier)
Hanbury, Lt.-Colonel P. L., D.S.O.

ORDER OF THE CROWN OF ITALY (commander)
Strick, Major-General J. A., C.B., D.S.O.

ORDER OF THE CROWN OF ITALY (officer)
Barratt, Lieut. A. W., M.B.E.
Breffit, Captain G. V., M.C.
Brunskill, Bt.-Major G. S., M.C.

SILVER MEDAL FOR MILITARY VALOUR
Thompstone, Lieut. E. W., M.C.

BRONZE MEDAL FOR MILITARY VALOUR
Bruce, Captain R. W. O. J.
Hockenhull, No. 7943 Sgt. L.
Hurds, No. 12895 Sgt. A.
Roberts, No. 13984 Pte. W. J.

CROCE DI GUERRA
Strick, Br.-General J. A., C.B., D.S.O.

FOREIGN DECORATIONS—(*continued*)

PORTUGAL

ORDER OF AVIZ

Corbett, Major C. U., D.S.O.

ROUMANIA

ORDER OF THE CROWN OF ROUMANIA (officer)

Barratt, Lieut. A. W., M.B.E.

ORDER OF THE STAR OF ROUMANIA (knight)

Barratt, Major A. W.
Denyer, Captain G. S. E.
Hamersley, Captain A. H. St. G., M.C.

RUSSIA

ORDER OF ST. ANNE (1st class, with swords)

Dawkins, Major-General C. T., C.B., C.M.G.

ORDER OF ST. VLADIMIR (4th class, with swords)

Dawkins, Major-General C. T., C.B., C.M.G.

CROSS OF THE ORDER OF ST. GEORGE (4th class)

Noble, No. 8895 Sgt. J. L.
Taylor, No. 8619 Sgt. L. H. S.
Williams, No. 6845 Corpl. D.

MEDAL OF ST. GEORGE (3rd class)

Degnam, No. 7391 Pte. W.
Evans, No. 9123 Corpl. A. A.
Venning, No. 9646 Pte. E. M.
Wellens, No. 6289 Pte. H.

MEDAL OF ST. GEORGE (4th class)

Maddox, No. 10152 L.-Corpl. G.

APPENDIX IV

FOREIGN DECORATIONS—*(continued)*

SERBIA

ORDER OF THE WHITE EAGLE (4th class, with swords)

Groves, Lt.-Colonel P. R. C.

Hanbury, Bt. Lt.-Colonel P. L., C.M.G., D.S.O.

Radcliffe, Lt.-Colonel W. S. W.

Torin, Bt.-Major L. H., M.C.

CROSS OF KARAGEORGE (1st class)

Fox, No. 8905 Pte. J.

GOLD MEDAL

Davies, No. 9556 Pte. G. H.

SILVER MEDAL

Jones, No. 8662 Pte. A.

SAMARITAN CROSS

Ketteringham, No. 44427 Pte. C. E.

UNITED STATES

DISTINGUISHED SERVICE MEDAL

Giles, Lt.-Colonel E. D., C.M.G., D.S.O.

APPENDIX V

MENTION IN DESPATCHES

Arblaster, Lieut. W., M.C.
Atchison, Lt.-Colonel C. E., D.S.O. (3)
Atkinson, Captain W. F.
Aubrey, Captain H. A. R.
Ayling, Captain A. E

Bailey, Bt. Lt.-Colonel J. H., D.S.O. (4)
Bailey, Captain W. C. F.
Banon, Br.-General F.L., C.B. (2)
Barber, Lieut. E. A.
Barker, Major E. C. (3)
Battye, Lt.-Colonel C. W., D.S.O. (3)
Beacall, Lieut. H.
Beadon, Captain H. D.
Benson, Captain F. R., M.C.
Benson, Major J. I., M.C. (3)
Bettington, Captain J. B.
Borrett, Lt.-Colonel O. C., D.S.O. (6)
Bosville, Captain J. G. B.
Bowen, Captain A. P.
Bowen, Lt.-Colonel W. A., D.S.O. (3)
Bowie, Captain D. D. (2)
Bradshaw, Lieut. P.
Breffit, Major G. V., M.C. (3)
Bridgford, Br.-General R. J., C.M.G., D.S.O. (5)
Browse, Lieut. A. C.
Bryans, Captain R., M.C. (2)
Bryant, Captain H. G., D.S.O.
Burne, Lt.-Colonel N. H. M., D.S.O.
Butt, Lieut. G. W. T. (2)

Carr, Captain G.
Casey, Captain J. (2)
Cautley, Lt.-Colonel C. H.
Chatterton, Lt.-Colonel G. D. L., D.S.O. (2)
Collins, Captain H. S.
Cooke, Captain F. A.
Corbett, Major C. U., D.S.O. (3)

APPENDIX V

MENTION IN DESPATCHES—(continued)

OFFICERS

Cosgrove, Lieut. N. R.
Crane, Captain V. H.
Crooke, Lieut. C. J.

Day, Captain E. C., M.C.
Dawkins, Major-General C. T., C.B., C.M.G. (5)
Deedes, Lieut. R.
Delmé-Murray, Lt.-Colonel G. A.
Dorrien-Smith, Captain E. P., D.S.O.
Downes, Lt.-Colonel J. W., D.S.O., M.C. (3)
Dyer, Lieut. A. C.

Edwards, Lieut. C. B.
Elder, Lieut. A. A.
English, Major E. R. M. (2)
Erskine, Lt.-Colonel J. D. B. (2)

Failes, Lieut. C. R.
Farrer, Lieut. J. O.
Fitzgerald, Bt. Lt.-Colonel P. F., D.S.O. (4)

Garrett, Colonel A. N. B., C.B.E., T.D.
Giles, Lt.-Colonel E. D., C.M.G., D.S.O. (4)
Groves, Lt.-Colonel P. R. C., D.S.O. (3)
Grugeon, Captain H.
Gubbins, Major R. R., D.S.O. (2)

Hallowes, Lieut. J. W.
Hamersley, Major A. H. St. G. (2)
Hanbury, Bt. Lt.-Colonel P. L., C.M.G., D.S.O. (7)
Harris, Captain C. D.
Haslewood, Captain R. J. R., M.C.
Hayes, Lt.-Colonel J. H. (4)
Heywood-Lonsdale, Lt.-Colonel H. H. (2)
Heywood-Lonsdale, Major J. P. H.
Higginson, Lt.-Colonel C. P., D.S.O.
Hilditch, Lieut. J. N.
Holmes à Court, Lt.-Colonel R. E., D.S.O. (3)
Hooper, Major J. C. (2)

439

MENTION IN DESPATCHES—(continued)

OFFICERS

Hopcraft, Captain J. G.
Howell-Evans, Lt.-Colonel H. J., D.S.O.
Huth, Captain P. C., D.S.O.

Jackson, Major B. A., M.C. (4)
Jackson, Lieut. J. W.
James, Captain E. G. (2)
Johns, 2nd Lieut. A. W.
Johnston, Lt.-Colonel F.

Kettlewell, Lt.-Colonel H. W. (3)
Kinchin-Smith, Captain A. E.

Lanyon, Lieut. E. C. G.
Latham, Captain J.
Leach, Captain F. J.
Lees, Major A. C. L. D.
Linton, Captain H., M.V.O.
Lloyd, Br.-General A. H. O., C. B., C.M.G., M.V.O. (5)
Lloyd, Captain E. G. R., D.S.O.
Lloyd, Lieut. R. L. M.
Lloyd, Lieut. T.
Lockett, 2nd Lieut. G. G.
Lovelock, Captain J., M.C.
Luard, Lt.-Colonel E. B., D.S.O. (3)

Macleod, Captain D. J.
Madge, Captain F. G.
Mansfield, Lt.-Colonel W. H. C., D.S.O. (2)
Marriott, Lieut. R. H.
Marshall, Captain S. R.
Matthews, Captain E. F. (2)
Maunsell, Lieut. F. H. R.
McKimm, Captain D. S. A., D.S.O., M.C.
Meredith, Major H. C. (2)
Meynell, Br.-General G., C.M.G. (4)
Middleton, Major W. (2)
Millyard, Captain G.
Money, Br.-General N. E., C.M.G., D.S.O. (3)

APPENDIX V

MENTION IN DESPATCHES—(*continued*)

OFFICERS

Moore, Lieut. E. D.
Morley, Lieut. G. H.
Murray, Bt. Lt.-Colonel B. E., D.S.O. (5)
Mylius, 2nd Lieut. J. K.

Nalder, Captain F. S.
Negus, Lt.-Colonel R. E., D.S.O. (2)
Newill, 2nd Lieut. W. M.
Norton, Captain R. C.

Oliver, 2nd Lieut. S. C.
Owen, Lt.-Colonel R. C. R., C.M.G., O.B.E.

Packman, Lieut. H. S.
Peace, Captain G. L.
Peake, 2nd Lieut. H., M.C.
Pettit, Captain H. R.
Philips, Captain F. G. P.
Plowden, Lt.-Colonel J. C., M.C. (2)
Prince, Lt.-Colonel P. (2)

Rangecroft, Major G. S.
Reade, Major-General R. N. R., C.B., C.M.G.
Reid, 2nd Lieut. S. E.
Rhodes, Lieut. F. W.
Richards, Major R. W. St. J. W.
Richmond, Lieut. G. H. (2)
Robinson, Captain E. H., D.S.O., M.C.
Rogers, Lieut. H. M.
Rogers, Br.-General H. S., D.S.O. (7)

Scott, Captain H. H.
Sheffield, 2nd Lieut. A. D.
Smith, Captain C. S.
Smith, Lt.-Colonel H. M., D.S.O.
Smith, Captain J. W. (3)
Smith, Captain W. W.
Smithard, Lt.-Colonel R. G., D.S.O., M.C.
Spens, Major-General J., C.B., C.M.G.

MENTION IN DESPATCHES—*(continued)*

OFFICERS

Steer, Captain H. E. (2)
Strick, Major-General J. A., C.B., D.S.O. (8)
Surtees, Captain R. L.
Swire, Captain D. W.

Taylor, Lieut. J. F.
Thomas, Lt.-Colonel S. F. (2)
Thursfield, Captain A. B. M.
Torin, Major L. H., M.C. (3)
Townsend, 2nd Lieut. C. V.
Townshend, Major-General C. V. F., C.B., D.S.O. (4)
Tully, 2nd Lieut. D. G.
Turner, 2nd Lieut. H. A. , D.C.M.
Turner, 2nd Lieut. H. K.

Underhill, Major O. (2)

Vassar-Smith, Captain C. M.
Vyvyan, Lieut. W. D.

Walker, Lieut. C. B. O.
Waterfield, Captain A. C.
Watson, Captain A. M.
Webb, Lieut. C. W. V.
Welch, Lt.-Colonel H. E., D.S.O. (2)
Westcott, Lieut. V. R.
Wilson, Captain C.
Wilson, Lt.-Colonel H. M.
Winterscale, Lt.-Colonel C. F. B. (3)
Wood, Br.-General E. A., C.M.G., D.S.O. (4)

WARRANT OFFICERS, N.C.O.'S AND MEN

NAME.	RANK.	REGTL. NO.
Amos, R.C.	Sgt.	6656
Baikie, S. J. C.	R.S.M.	6304 (2)
Barnwell, C.	Corpl.	200144
Berrow, E.	Corpl.	230693
Blakely, F. J.	Sgt.	230018 (2)
Blud, J.	Sgt.	7527

APPENDIX V

NAME.	RANK.	REGTL. NO.
Bond, F.	Sgt.	18550
Bradley, C.	Sgt.	7602
Brittain, S.	C.S.M.	10091
Burridge, R. J., M.M.	Corpl.	29135
Busby, J. H.	C.S.M.	4953
Butters, R. T.	Sgt.	8326
Butterworth, S.	Pte.	15891
Buttery, F. F.	Corpl.	6563
Buxton, H.	Sgt.	230900
Cartwright, J. R.	Pte.	10476
Chorley, W. R. G.	Pte.	10820
Church, W.	Pte.	8787
Clarke, C.	Pte.	11366
Cleaver, A.	Sgt.	8771
Cole, T. H.	Sgt.	7392 (2)
Coton, J. T.	Pte.	10106
Cowles, A. E.	Pte.	6061
Cowper, C. F.	L.-Sgt.	11376
Crawshaw, J.	Pte.	16044
Cummings, P. V.	Sgt.	8658
Davidson, J.	Sgt.	7567
Dean, A.	L.-Corpl.	11845
Dixon, M.	Pte.	14667
Dobinson, W.	Pte.	8834
Donald, J. D.	Corpl.	16559
Elton, H.	Sgt.	10929
Evans, H.	Pte.	11450
Farrington, H.	R.S.M.	5834
Farthing, J.	R.S.M.	3850
Ferrington, J.	R.S.M.	8881
Fletcher, T.	Sgt.	9377
Gardiner, R. C.	Sgt.	200057
Gardner, F. G.	Sgt.	9133
Gibson, G. R.	Corpl.	29106

MENTION IN DESPATCHES—(*continued*)

NAME.	RANK.	REGTL. NO.
Gough, H. W.	Pte.	10721
Gray, A.	Sgt.	8839
Greatwich, H.	Pte.	18723
Greening, L. H.	Sgt.	14836
Griffiths, J. S.	Col.-Sgt.	13906
Griggs, W. G.	Pte.	8816
Grimley, F. H.	R.Q.M.S.	10843
Halstead, J.	Sgt.	201788
Harris, E. C.	Pte.	8727
Haughton, A.	Corpl.	9378 (2)
Hayley, H.	C.S.M.	5732
Higginson, J.	Sgt.	7326
Hind, B.	Pte.	6550
Hirst, G.	Sgt.	9483
Holden, G. T.	Pte.	12188
Holmes, W. E.	Pte.	8232
Hotchkiss, E.	Sgt.	7762
Hughes, A.	Pte.	230446
Hughes, J.	Q.M.S.	13903
Hughes, R. J.	R.Q.M.S.	13012
Hurds, A.	Sgt.	12895
Hurley, D.	Pte.	8840
Hyson, W. A.	Pte.	8566
John, G. B.	Pte.	13395
Jones, A.	Pte.	8662
Jones, A. A.	Sgt.	14469
Jones, E.	C.S.M.	8394
Jones, F. W.	Corpl.	9571
Jones, J.	Pte.	16268
King, A.	L.-Corpl.	11495
Knight, A.	C.S.M.	8233
Knight, T. H.	Pte.	201305
Lang, J. R.	Sgt.	8358
Lear, T.	Sgt.	13246
Lever, R.	Sgt.	16400

444

APPENDIX V

NAME.	RANK.	REGTL. NO.
Lewis, R. J.	Corpl.	200270
Lloyd, R.	Pte.	6446
Lloyd, R.	Pte.	11128
Lloyd, T.	R.Q.M.S.	5757
Lowe, S. B.	L.-Corpl.	12335
Manning, J.	Q.M.S.	10941
Marriage, A.	Sgt.	9166
McFarlane, A. C. V.	Bandsman	9227
Meredith, C.	Bugler	9305
Meredith, W. A.	L.-Corpl.	9305
Moore, S. G.	S.M.	4404
Moran, J. D.	Sgt.	7332
Morris, G.	L.-Corpl.	10617
Morris, J.	Sgt.	5812
Morris, R.	L. Corpl.	16075
Morris, W. F.	Corpl.	7967
Mulvaney, J.	C.Q.M.S.	230135
Nicholson, H.	Corpl.	16233
Openshaw, W.	Pte.	5822
Osborne, E. R.	Sgt.	9562
Owens, D.	Pte.	15803
Palmer, E.	Sgt.	14769
Poole, G. E.	C.Q.M.S.	7946 (2)
Potts, F.	Sgt.	230644
Preedey, B.	Pte.	14954
Pugh, R.	L.-Corpl.	21444
Rippard, F.	Corpl.	8320 (2)
Roberts, T.	Sgt.	13757
Robertson, D. S.	Pte.	16308
Rogers, G.	L.-Sgt.	9805
Rogers, J. W.	Corpl.	17490
Rotherham, J.	C.S.M.	6607
Rowlands, C.	L.-Sgt.	11152
Rutter, A.	C.S.M.	230542

MENTION IN DESPATCHES—(*continued*)

NAME.	RANK.	REGTL. NO.
Silver, C. W.	Sgt.	9518
Skirving, J.	R.S.M.	6597 (2)
Smart, G.	Sgt.	14094
Smith, G. R.	L.-Corpl.	6842
Smith, W.	Pte.	24224
Speake, G.	L.-Corpl.	6258
Swannick, E. I.	Pte.	13864
Swift, L.	Pte.	9157
Taylor, H.	Pte.	34192
Taylor, P.	Pte.	24435
Threadgold, J.	C.Q.M.S.	8811
Thornton, W. T.	C.S.M.	8543
Trewin, J. H.	L.-Sgt.	230198
Turner, H.	Pte.	20657
Usher, P. E.	L.-Corpl.	230508
Veevers, T. W.	Corpl.	27123
Wallbank, H. A. C.	O.R.S.	8255
Walley, P.	L.-Corpl.	11249
West, R.	Corpl.	12830
Whitehouse, G. F.	R.Q.M.S.	12986
Williams, A. J.	Sgt.	9498
Williams, J. A.	R.S.M.	13770
Wolley, W.	Pte.	12972
Woods, W. G.	Pte.	230329
Yorke, J.	Pte.	7254

APPENDIX VI

MENTION "B" (PRESS MENTIONS)

OFFICERS

Barratt, Major A. W.
Blower, Captain B. W.
Bowen, Major A. P., M.C.
Browne, Major A. S.

Capper, Colonel W. B.
Cooke, Lt.-Colonel J. H.
Corbett, Major E. R. T.

Dickin, Lt.-Colonel T.

Farrer, Captain J. O., M.C.
Felton, Major T. D.
Forrester, Lt.-Colonel Hon. G. C. B.
Foster, Lt.-Colonel A. W.

Garsia, Captain C. J.
Gilroy, Major A. T. L.

Hill, Captain P. S.

Lees, Captain A. C. L. D.

MacMahon, Lt.-Colonel K. E.
Maunsell, Captain F. H.
Marescaux, Bt.-Major O. H. E.

Patchell, Major J.
Perkin, Captain T. D.

Radcliffe, Lt.-Colonel W. S.W.

Smith, Lt.-Colonel R. A.
Stanier, Captain B., M.P.
Stirland, Captain J.

Tindal-Carill-Worsley, Major P. E.

Watson, Captain A. M.
Westcott, Captain W. H.
Wildig, Major T.
Woodland, Major A. R. (2)

OTHER RANKS

NAME.	RANK.	REGTL. NO.
Armstrong, J. T.	Sgt.	17510
Bebbington, W.	Q.M.S.	17621
Boulton, C. E.	Corpl.	31999
Brown, F. J.	Q.M.S.	17581
Bugg, J. W.	R.S.M.	1839
Calve, S. J.	R.S.M.	6937
Davenport, W. A.	Q.M.S.	5677
Downes, T. H.	Q.M.S.	17509
Ellis, W. H.	Sup. Clk.	17495

MENTION "B" (PRESS MENTIONS)—(continued)

NAME.	RANK.	REGTL. NO.
Gardiner, W.	C.S.M.	4101
Glover, E.	Q.M.S.	17262
Greatbatch, J.	C.S.M.	25087
Hand, W. H.	Corpl.	31329
Hopwood, C. E.	Q.M.S.	31339
Jones, E.	Q.M.S.	17522
Knighley, E. J.	Sgt.	8435
Langy, H.	Col.-Sgt.	8507
Marsh, A.	Q.M.S.	17516
McLean, J.	Q.M.S.	17514
Moger, A. E. G.	Q.M.S.	6520
Murphy, A. J.	R.S.M.	4386
Shufflebotham, C.	Q.M.S.	17505
Steele, G. A.	Q.M.S.	17527
Wheeler, G. A.	Q.M.S.	17578

APPENDIX VII

AWARDS OF BREVET RANK

BREVET COLONEL

Borrett, Br.-General O. C., C.M.G., D.S.O.
Bridgford, Br.-General R. J., C.M.G., D.S.O.
Strick, Br.-General J. A., D.S.O.

BREVET LT.-COLONEL

Bailey, Lt.-Colonel J. H., D.S.O.
Battye, Lt.-Colonel C. W., D.S.O.
Borrett, Lt.-Colonel O. C., D.S.O.
Erskine, Lt.-Colonel J. D. B., D.S.O.
Fitzgerald, Lt.-Colonel P. F., D.S.O
Giles, Lt.-Colonel E. D., C.M.G., D.S.O.
Hanbury, Lt.-Colonel P. L., D.S.O.
Holmes à Court, Lt.-Colonel R. E., D.S.O.
Kettlewell, Lt.-Colonel H. W.
Marescaux, Major O. H. E.
Money, Major E. W. K.
Murray, Lt.-Colonel B. E.
Payn, Major W. A.
Rogers, Lt.-Colonel H. S., D.S.O.
Smith, Lt.-Colonel H. M., D.S.O.
Strick, Lt.-Colonel J. A.
Winterscale, Lt.-Colonel C. F. B., D.S.O.

BREVET MAJOR

Dorrien-Smith, Captain E. P., D.S.O.
Erskine, Capt. J. D. B.
Harris, Captain C. D.
Huth, Captain C. P., D.S.O.
Rogers, Captain H. S.
Torin, Major L. H., M.C.

NEXT HIGHER RATE OF PAY (under Article 241 of
Royal Warrant)
Smith, J. W., Q.M. and Hon. Lt.

2 G

LIST OF SUBSCRIBERS

Abercrombie, Mrs. George
Arbouin, Capt. G. B.
Armitage, Clifford, Esq.
Anstice, Col. Sir Arthur,
    K.C.B., V.D., T.D.
Arnott, Mrs. N.
Asbury, C. S., Esq., A.C.A.
Atherton, Samuel, Esq.
Attoe, L. R., Esq.
Aubrey, Major H. A. R.,
    O.B.E., M.C.
Anonymous, In Memory of
    2nd Lt. Thomas Paul
    Bauser

Bailey, Lt.-Col. J. H., D.S.O.
Banon, Brig.-Gen. F. L., C.B.
Barratt, Major A. W., M.B.E.,
    T.D.
Baxter, Major W.
Beadon, Mrs. E. M.
Beadon, Miss L. G.
Beckwith, Capt. J. H.
Bellasis, W. Dalglish, Esq.
Bench, G. E., Esq.
Bettington, Capt. J. B., M.C.
Bird, Capt. E.
Black, R. A., Esq.
Blore, J. L., Esq.
Booker, H. G., Esq.
Bowen, Major A. P., M.C.
Braybrooke, A. R., Esq.
Breffit, Major G. V., M.C.
Bridgeman, Right Hon. W. C.
Bridgford, Brig.-Gen. R. J.,
    C.B., C.M.G., D.S.O.
Bright, Capt. G. W.
Brownell, Major E. L. D.
Brooke, The Lady Wilhelmina
Brooke, Mrs. William
Bryans, Capt. R., M.C.
Bryant, Mrs. H. G.

Bryant, Miss M.
Buchanan, Mrs.
Buchanan, Major G. L.
Bulman, Col. P., D.S.O.
Bulmer, Mrs. Percival
Burne, S. A. H., Esq.
Button, H. S., Esq.

Caborne, W. R., Esq.
Caesar, J. H., Esq.
Campbell, Lt.-Col. J. R.
Capper, Col. W. B., C.V.O.
Carter, F. W. A., Esq., M.C.
Chambers, L. B., Esq.
Charles, Rev. J. H.
Cholmondelay, Brig.-Gen. H.
    C., C.B., C.B.E.
Cockburn, Major Sir Robert,
    Bart.
Collins, Capt. H. S., D.S.O.
Colville, H. K., Esq.
Corbett, Major E. R. T.,
    M.B.E.
Corbett, R. A., Esq.
Cotterell, Sir J. R. G., Bart.
Crane, Capt. V. H.
Croft, Major O. G. S.
Currie, Rivers G., Esq.
Curtis, Capt. C. N., M.C.

Darby, Alfred E. W., Esq.
Dawkins, The Hon. Lady
Deane, Col. R. W., C.B.E.
Deedes, Capt J.
Deedes, R., Esq.
Dickin, Col. T.
Doyle, Col. A. H. J.
Durst, Major W. H., M.C.
Dymock, R. G. V., Esq.

Eagar, Capt. F. M.
Ebden, W. S., Esq.
Egerton-Savory, A., Esq.

451

Eltome, G., Esq.
Ely, T. H., Esq.
English, Lt.-Col. E. R. M., D.S.O.
Exham, Major A. R. F., M.D., V.D.

Faithfull, A. F., Esq.
Farmer, J. H., Esq.
Farrer, Capt. J. D., M.C.
Firth, J. C., Esq.
Fitzgerald, Lt.-Col. P. F., D.S.O.
Forbes, Major J. G.
Forester, Lt.-Col. The Hon. F. H. C. Weld
Forster-Knight, G., Esq.
Foster, Lt.-Col. Arthur W.
Foster, Capt James
Fowler, Capt. R. H.
Foxall, Jas. T., Esq.
Fraser, Capt. W. J. Ian, C.B.E.

Gardiner, E. W., Esq.
Garrett, Col. A. N. B., C.B.E., T.D.
Graham, Mrs. Fergus
Green, Capt. R. L. H.
Grey, W. A., Esq.
Griffiths, W., Esq.
Grover, Capt. J. M. L.

Hall, Capt. T. C., M.C.
Hanbury, Lt.-Col. P. L., C.M.G., D.S.O.
Harlech, Col. Lord, C.B.
Haslewood, Capt. R. J. R., M.C.
Heywood-Lonsdale, Lt.-Col. H. H., D.S.O., T.D.
Heard, Major J. R.
Heber-Percy, Capt. Hugh L.

Herbert, Col. E. W., C.B.
Hetherington, Capt. A. C., M.C.
Heygate, Mrs. Mounsey
Hicks, Major J. H.
Higginson, Brig.-Gen. C. P., C.M.G., D.S.O.
Hodgson, N. H., Esq.
Holloway, W. H., Esq.
Holmes à Court, Lt.-Col. Hon. E. A.
Holmes à Court, Lt.-Col. R. E., D.S.O.
Hooper, Major J. C., D.S.O.
Hooper, R. H., Esq.
Howard-McLean, Col. J. R., V.D.
Hughes-Hallett, N. M., Esq.
Huntbach, Major G. W.
Huntbach, W. M., Esq.
Huth, Major P. C., D.S.O.

Inglis, Mrs. Rupert
Ingram, Mrs.
Ingram, Mrs. Thomas L.

James, J. C., Esq.
James, Mrs. F. R.
Jebb, Richard, Esq.
Johnston, Mrs. Charles
Johnston, Mrs. Frank
Jones, Capt. R. T.
Jones, H. G. E. E., Esq.
Jones, H. R., Esq.

Kenyon, R. Lloyd, Esq.
Kettlewell, Lt.-Col. H. W.
Knox, Lt.-Gen. Sir Charles, K.C.B.
Kynaston, W. R. O., Esq.
K.S.L.I., 1st Batt. A Company
K.S.L.I., 1st Batt. B Company

K.S.L.I., 1st Batt. C Company
K.S.L.I., 1st Batt. D Company
K.S.L.I., 1st Batt. Head-quarter Company
K.S.L.I., 1st Batt. Corporals' Club
K.S.L.I., 1st Batt. Officers' Mess
K.S.L.I., 1st Batt. Regimental Institute
K.S.L.I., 1st Batt. Sergeants' Mess
K.S.L.I., 2nd Batt. Officers' Mess
K.S.L.I., 2nd Batt. Regimental Institute
K.S.L.I., Depot
K.S.L.I., 4th Batt. B Company Territorial Club

Leather, Col. F. H., D.S.O.
Leeke, Col. Ralph
Lee-Roberts, Capt. R.
Lees, Mrs. A. D.
Lees, Major A. C. L. D.
Leighton, Major B. E. Parker
Litt, W. E., Esq.
Lloyd, Brig.-Gen. A. H. O., C.B., C.M.G., M.V.O.
Lloyd, J. B., Esq.
Longe, R. B., Esq.
Longueville, Lt.-Col. R.
Luard, Mrs. E. B., M.B.E.
Luard, Lt.-Col. R. C.

Maitland, Dr. G. P.
Mansfield, Major W. H. C., D.S.O.
Marriott, Capt. T. G.
Marsh, Capt. C. R. C., M.B.E.
Masefield, Mrs. Robert
Mason, Mrs.

Mattey, T. H., Esq.
Maunsell, Capt. F. H. R.
Maunsell, Major R. G.
Mavrogordato, Mrs. A.
McAlister, Capt. D. A., M.B.E.
McMahon, Lt.-Col. K. E.
McKimm, D. S. A., Esq., D.S.O., M.C.
Meynell, Col. G., C.M.G.
Meynell, G., Esq.
Middleton, Major W., O.B.E.
Miles, H. P., Esq.
Moger, A. E. G., Esq.
Moore, Lt.-Col. S. G.
Moseley, Major H. R.
Mounsey-Heysham, Miss
Murray, Lt.-Col. B. E., D.S.O.

Negus, Lt.-Col. R. E., D.S.O.
Norton, R. C., Esq.

Oldham, J. B., Esq.

Parker, C. E., Esq., M.C.
Parry, F. H., Esq.
Partridge, Capt. H. F.
Pateshall, Lt.-Col. H. E. P., D.S.O.
Payn, Lt.-Col. W. A.
Pendlebury, H. M., Esq.
Perkin, Capt. T. D.
Persse, Capt. R. B. L.
Philips, Major F. G. P., M.C.
Philips, Miss
Pigot, Rev. E. C.
Platt, Mrs. Ernest
Plymouth, The Earl of, P.C., G.B.E., C.B.
Powis, Col. The Earl of
Poyntz, Major R. H.
Pugh, C. W. H., Esq., M.C.
Pulley, Sir Charles, Kt.
Purcell, P., Esq.

453

Rankin, Lt.-Col. Sir Reginald, Bart.
Reade, Major-Gen. R. N. R., C.B., C.M.G.
Reade, Mrs. Raymonde
Reid-Walker, J., Esq.
Rees, V. W., Esq.
Ridgway, W. H., Esq.
Riley, John, Esq.
Roberts, R. T., Esq.
Robinson, Col. F. W.
Robinson, Miss E. Maud
Rogers, Col. H. S., C.M.G., D.S.O.
Rogers, A. B., Esq., M.C.
Rogerson, Col. W.
Rooke, Col. H. D.

Sharpe, L. W., Esq.
Shaw, H. D., Esq.
Shears, Capt. R. H.
Shrewsbury, Corporation of
Slaney, J. N., Esq.
Smith, Capt. Colin S.
Smith, G. R., Esq.
Smith, Lt.-Col. H. M., D.S.O.
Smith, Lt.-Col. R. Astley
Smith, Capt. W. W., M.C.
Smithard, Capt. R. G., D.S.O., M.C.
Southey, H. W., Esq.
Southwell, W. Lascelles, Esq.
Sparrow, Mrs. E. F.
Sparrow, Capt. J. A. G.
Speer, L. A. T., Esq.
Spens, Major-Gen. J., C.B., C.M.G.
Sprot, E. M., Esq.
Steward, Harry, Esq., M.C.
Strick, Col. J. A., C.B., D.S.O.
Surtees, Major R. L., O.B.E.
Styring, E. Lenten, Esq.

Swindell, J. A., Esq.
Symonds-Taylor, Col. R. H.

Tarr, F. C., Esq.
Tarrant, A. J. B., Esq.
Taverner, R. L., Esq.
Thomas, E. S. de V., Esq.
Thompson, d'A. P. P., Esq.
Torin, Major L. H., M.C.
Trumper, Capt. E. H. G.
Tunmer, Capt. E. J. E.
Tully, D. G., Esq., M.C.

Upton, John St. C., Esq.

Vaughan, Capt. R. C., M.C.
Voelcker, Capt. F. W., M C.

Wace, Capt. R. C., M.C.
Wakeman, Sir Offley, Bart.
Wallace, Capt. W. F. A.
Ward, C. E., Esq.
Weir, Major A. V.
Wellington Journal and Shropshire News
Whitmore, Mrs. A.
Wijk, Mrs.
Williams, Q.M.S. John Gardner M.M.
Williams-Freeman, Miss E.
Wilkinson, Mrs. Clement
Wolryche-Whitmore, Col. F. A.
Wolryche-Whitmore, Capt. G. C.
Wood, Major-Gen. Sir Elliott, K.C.B.
Wood, Miss
Wood, Capt. T.
Wood, Major W de B.

Yate, Lt.-Col. A. C.

INDEX

INDEX

INDEX

INDEX

458

INDEX

Gough, A. V., 43
Gracie, B. E., 35
Graham, S., 256, 261, 262
Gray, Mrs., 328
Gray, W., 327
Greatwich, S., 182
Greaves, R. A., 117
Green, A. T., 54, 60
Green, C. E., 228
Green, G. B., 255
Green, R. E. O. L., 167, 169, 174
Green, R. J. H., 66
Green, R. L. H., 36
Green, W. R., 47
Greene, C. H., 104, 107
Greenhough, R., 35
Grierson, W. B., 266
Griffen, H. S., 149, 153
Griffen, H., 198
Griffiths, W., 17, 20, 38
Grimley, F. H., 155
Grischotti, W., 1, 14
Groom, J., 15
Grover, J. M. L., 27, 31, 34, 35, 52, 61, 87, 88
Groves, A. W., 149, 161
Groves, P. R. C., 2, 7
Guillemont, battle of, 178

Haig, D., 25, 27, 169
Haines, A. L., 253, 255
Hair, D. C., 180
Halford, A. E. H., 188, 192
Hall, R., 214
Hall, T. C. N., 16, 23, 24, 81
Hallowes, Mrs., 330
Hallows, W. E., 290, 293, 296
Hambleton, T., 182
Hamer, C. M. I., 148, 162
Hamersley, A. H. St. G., 82, 83
Hamilton, A., 26

Hamilton, G., 18, 23, 26
Hannah, E. M., 21, 23, 26, 35, 186, 187
Hannon, T. J., 187, 197
Hares, V. C., 187, 290
Harford, A. D., 131
Hargreaves, H., 43
Harlech, Lord, 337, 339
Harper, B., 35
Harper, T. D., 63
Harris, C. D., 28, 34, 37, 140
Harris, F. H., 66
Harris, H. E., 279
Harris, J., 40
Harris-Edge, H. P., 97, 98, 104, 106
Harrop, J. A., 61
Harty, W., 120
Haseler, D. B., 42, 48, 52
Haslewood, R., 97, 99, 101, 104
Hatfield, P., 226
Hatfield-Wright, M., 51
Hawkins, E. S., 97, 101, 104, 106, 112
Hawkins, W. P., 168, 172
Hayward, F. O., 182, 188, 192
Hazard, C. P., 21, 24, 88
Hazard, D. G., 87
Hearne, T. R., 37, 40
Heathcote, Hon. Mrs., 325, 326, 328
Heathcote, R. E. M., 228, 230
Hellier, M. J., 169, 194
Helmore, E. A., 209
Henningsen, C. E., 290
Hepworth, J. H., 297
Herbert, W. S., 247, 250
Herd, W. L., 126, 134
Herdman, A. W., 1, 5
Hetherington, A. C., 221, 229, 231, 232, 239, 250, 256, 267
Hewson, H., 42

460

INDEX

INDEX

464

INDEX

INDEX

INDEX

1303570R0

Printed in Great Britain by
Amazon.co.uk, Ltd.,
Marston Gate.